MARANATHA

THE LORD IS COMING

To order, call **1-800-765-6955**.

ELLEN G. WHITE

Maranatha

THE LORD IS COMING

REVIEW AND HERALD® PUBLISHING ASSOCIATION
Since 1861 | www.reviewandherald.com

Cover design copyright © 2014 by Review and Herald® Publishing Association.
Cover design by Daniel Añez/Review and Hearald® Design Center

Printed by Pacific Press® Publishing Association.
Printed in U.S.A.
Printed in 2014

Unless otherwise noted, Bible texts in this book are from the King James Version.

Bible texts credited to A.R.V. are from *The Holy Bible*, edited by the American Revision Committee, Thomas Nelson & Sons, 1901.

Bible texts credited to Bible in Basic English are from the *Bible in Basic English*. Copyright © 1956 by E. P. Dutton & Co., Inc.

Bible texts credited to Goodspeed are from Smith and Goodspeed, *The Complete Bible: An American Translation*. Copyright 1939 by the Universty of Chicago.

Bible texts credited to Moffatt are from *The Bible: A New Translation*, by James Moffatt. Copyright by James Moffatt 1954. Used by permission of Harper & Row, Publisher, Incorporated.

Bible texts credited to N.E.B. are from *The New English Bible*, © The Delegates of the Oxford University Press and the Syndics of the Cambridge University Press 1961, 1970. Reprinted by permission.

Bible texts credited to R.S.V. are from the Revised Standard Version of the Bible. Copyright © 1946, 1952, 1971, by the Division of Christian Education of the National Council of the Churches of Christ in the U.S.A. Used by permission.

Bible texts credited to R.V. are from the Revised Version, Oxford University Press, 1911.

ISBN 978-0-8280-2801-1

December 2021

FOREWORD

"The doctrine of the second advent is the very keynote of the Sacred Scriptures," declared the author of the inspired messages selected for this devotional volume. "About His coming cluster the glories of that 'restitution of all things, which God hath spoken by the mouth of all his holy prophets since the world began.' Acts 3:21. Then the long-continued rule of evil shall be broken; 'the kingdoms of this world' will become 'the kingdoms of our Lord, and of his Christ; and he shall reign for ever and ever.' Rev. 11:15."—*The Great Controversy*, pp. 299-301.

The hearts of God's people, young and old, throb with intense longing for that day of deliverance so near at hand. With fast fulfilling prophecy confirming their faith in the imminence of our Lord's return, the White Estate Trustees commissioned this compilation of readings clustering about the general theme of eschatology, with emphasis upon the coming of our Lord. The collection would be incomplete without readings dealing with the signs that mark the approach of the coming King, the events that transpire in relationship to His second appearing, His millennial reign in glory, and insights into prophecies to be fulfilled at the close of the thousand years of silence, during which Satan is a prisoner on this earth.

Key statements on a subject so vital to Seventh-day Adventists have appeared in print in the Ellen G. White books, as well as in many articles in the journals of the church. Therein lies the explanation for the frequent reference to *The Great Controversy*, *The Desire of Ages*, *Early Writings*, the nine volumes of the *Testimonies for the Church*, the *Review and Herald*, and *The Signs of the Times*. Numerous statements from unpublished manuscripts enrich the presentation, especially in the section dealing with the national Sunday law and subsequent events.

Certain necessary deletions within the text of the materials selected have been made in order to eliminate repetition or statements less pertinent to the topic presented or to accommodate a given reading to the limits of a single page. Special care has been taken to ensure that these omissions in no way distort or alter the meaning of the original passage.

References directing the reader to the original sources appear at the close of the volume. The Scripture index includes only the verse chosen with each reading.

We believe that this devotional volume, the eleventh Spirit of Prophecy devotional book, with its accent on fulfilled and fulfilling prophecies, is timely. The material is straightforward, frank, and stirring. The message should bring an awakening of the truest kind, stirring the reader to awareness concerning the Second-Advent theme so dear to all of our hearts, and preparation for that event. It is our prayer that many will be sealed with the seal of the living God and enabled to pass through the time of trouble and meet the coming King in peace as a result of applying these readings to their lives. Maranatha—the Lord is coming!

MONTHLY TOPICS

THE FIRST COMING OF JESUS

When the fulness of the time was come, God sent forth his Son, . . . to redeem them that were under the law, that we might receive the adoption of sons. Gal. 4:4, 5.

The Saviour's coming was foretold in Eden. When Adam and Eve first heard the promise, they looked for its speedy fulfillment. They joyfully welcomed their first-born son, hoping that he might be the Deliverer. But the fulfillment of the promise tarried. Those who first received it died without the sight. From the days of Enoch the promise was repeated through patriarchs and prophets, keeping alive the hope of His appearing, and yet He came not. The prophecy of Daniel revealed the time of His advent, but not all rightly interpreted the message. Century after century passed away; the voices of the prophets ceased. The hand of the oppressor was heavy upon Israel, and many were ready to exclaim, "The days are prolonged, and every vision faileth." Ezek. 12:22.

But like the stars in the vast circuit of their appointed path, God's purposes know no haste and no delay. Through the symbols of the great darkness and the smoking furnace, God had revealed to Abraham the bondage of Israel in Egypt, and had declared that the time of their sojourning should be four hundred years. "Afterward," He said, "shall they come out with great substance." Gen. 15:14. Against that word, all the power of Pharaoh's proud empire battled in vain. On "the self-same day" appointed in the divine promise, "it came to pass, that all the hosts of the Lord went out from the land of Egypt." Ex. 12:41. So in heaven's council the hour for the coming of Christ had been determined. When the great clock of time pointed to that hour, Jesus was born in Bethlehem.

"When the fulness of the time was come, God sent forth his Son." Providence had directed the movements of nations, and the tide of human impulse and influence, until the world was ripe for the coming of the Deliverer. . . .

Then Jesus came to restore in man the image of his Maker. None but Christ can fashion anew the character that has been ruined by sin. He came to expel the demons that had controlled the will. He came to lift us up from the dust, to reshape the marred character after the pattern of His divine character, and to make it beautiful with His own glory.[1]

9

THE LESSON OF BETHLEHEM

Christ was once offered to bear the sins of many; and unto them that look for him shall he appear the second time without sin unto salvation. Heb. 9:28.

At the time of Christ's first advent the priests and scribes of the Holy City, to whom were entrusted the oracles of God, might have discerned the signs of the times and proclaimed the coming of the Promised One. The prophecy of Micah designated His birthplace; Daniel specified the time of His advent. God committed these prophecies to the Jewish leaders; they were without excuse if they did not know and declare to the people that the Messiah's coming was at hand. Their ignorance was the result of sinful neglect. . . .

All the people should have been watching and waiting that they might be among the first to welcome the world's Redeemer. But, lo, at Bethlehem two weary travelers from the hills of Nazareth traverse the whole length of the narrow street to the eastern extremity of the town, vainly seeking a place of rest and shelter for the night. No doors are open to receive them. In a wretched hovel prepared for cattle, they at last find refuge, and there the Saviour of the world is born. . . .

There is no evidence that Christ is expected, and no preparation for the Prince of life. In amazement the celestial messenger is about to return to heaven with the shameful tidings, when he discovers a group of shepherds who are watching their flocks by night, and as they gaze into the starry heavens, are contemplating the prophecy of a Messiah to come to earth, and longing for the advent of the world's Redeemer. Here is a company that is prepared to receive the heavenly message. And suddenly the angel of the Lord appears, declaring the good tidings of great joy. . . .

Oh, what a lesson is this wonderful story of Bethlehem! How it rebukes our unbelief, our pride and self-sufficiency. How it warns us to beware, lest by our criminal indifference we also fail to discern the signs of the times, and therefore know not the day of our visitation.[2]

WHEN JESUS WAS BORN—

When Jesus was born in Bethlehem . . . there came wise men from the east to Jerusalem, saying, Where is he that is born King of the Jews? Matt. 2:1, 2.

The King of glory stooped low to take humanity; and angels, who had witnessed His splendor in the heavenly courts, as He was worshiped by all the heavenly hosts, were disappointed to find their divine Commander in a position of so great humiliation.

The Jews had separated themselves so far from God by their wicked works, that angels could not communicate to them the tidings of the advent of the infant Redeemer. God chooses the wise men of the East to do His will. . . .

These wise men had seen the heavens illuminated with light, which enshrouded the heavenly host who heralded the advent of Christ to the humble shepherds. . . .

This light was a distant cluster of flaming angels, which appeared like a luminous star. The unusual appearance of the large bright star, which they had never seen before, hanging as a sign in the heavens, attracted their attention. . . . The wise men directed their course where the star seemed to lead them. And as they drew nigh to the city of Jerusalem, the star was enshrouded in darkness, and no longer guided them. They reasoned that the Jews could not be ignorant of the great event of the advent of the Messiah, and they made inquiries in the vicinity of Jerusalem.

The wise men are surprised to see no unusual interest upon the subject of the coming of the Messiah. . . . They marvel that the Jews are not interested and joyful in prospect of this great event of the advent of Christ.

The churches of our time are seeking worldly aggrandizement, and are as unwilling to see the light of the prophecies, and receive the evidences of their fulfillment which show that Christ is soon to come, as were the Jews in reference to His first appearing. They were looking for the temporal and triumphant reign of Messiah in Jerusalem. Professed Christians of our time are expecting the temporal prosperity of the church, in the conversion of the world, and the enjoyment of the temporal millennium.[3]

THE HOPE OF THE SECOND COMING

He which testifieth these things saith, Surely I come quickly. Amen. Even so, come, Lord Jesus. Rev. 22:20.

The [second] coming of the Lord has been in all ages the hope of His true followers. The Saviour's parting promise upon Olivet, that He would come again, lighted up the future for His disciples, filling their hearts with joy and hope that sorrow could not quench nor trials dim. Amid suffering and persecution, "the appearing of the great God and our Saviour Jesus Christ" was the "blessed hope." When the Thessalonian Christians were filled with grief as they buried their loved ones, who had hoped to live to witness the coming of the Lord, Paul, their teacher, pointed them to the resurrection, to take place at the Saviour's advent. Then the dead in Christ should rise, and together with the living be caught up to meet the Lord in the air. "And so," he said, "shall we ever be with the Lord. Wherefore comfort one another with these words." 1 Thess. 4:16-18. . . .

From the dungeon, the stake, the scaffold, where saints and martyrs witnessed for the truth, comes down the centuries the utterance of their faith and hope. Being "assured of His personal resurrection, and consequently of their own at His coming, for this cause," says one of these Christians, "they despised death, and were found to be above it."—Daniel T. Taylor, *The Reign of Christ on Earth: or, The Voice of the Church in All Ages*, p. 33. They were willing to go down to the grave, that they might "rise free." They looked for the "Lord to come from heaven in the clouds with the glory of His Father," "bringing to the just the times of the kingdom." The Waldenses cherished the same faith. Wycliffe looked forward to the Redeemer's appearing as the hope of the church.[4]

On rocky Patmos the beloved disciple hears the promise, "Surely I come quickly," and his longing response voices the prayer of the church in all her pilgrimage, "Even so, come, Lord Jesus." Rev. 22:20.[5]

THE KEYNOTE OF SCRIPTURE

I know that my Redeemer liveth, and that he shall stand at the latter day upon the earth. Job 19:25.

One of the most solemn and yet most glorious truths revealed in the Bible is that of Christ's second coming, to complete the great work of redemption. To God's pilgrim people, so long left to sojourn in "the region and shadow of death," a precious, joy-inspiring hope is given in the promise of His appearing, who is "the resurrection and the life," to "bring home again His banished." The doctrine of the second advent is the very key-note of the Sacred Scriptures. From the day when the first pair turned their sorrowing steps from Eden, the children of faith have waited the coming of the Promised One to break the destroyer's power and bring them again to the lost Paradise. . . . Enoch, only the seventh in descent from them that dwelt in Eden, he who for three centuries on earth walked with his God, was permitted to behold from afar the coming of the Deliverer. "Behold," he declared, "the Lord cometh with ten thousands of his saints, to execute judgment upon all." The patriarch Job in the night of his affliction exclaimed with unshaken trust: "I know that my redeemer liveth, and that he shall stand at the latter day upon the earth: . . . in my flesh shall I see God: whom I shall see for myself, and mine eyes shall behold, and not another." [6]

May the God of all grace so enlighten your understanding that you may discern eternal things, that by the light of truth your own errors, which are many, may be discovered to you just as they are, that you may make the necessary effort to put them away, and in the place of this evil, bitter fruit may bring forth fruit which is precious unto eternal life.

Humble your poor, proud, self-righteous heart before God; get low, very low, all broken in your sinfulness at His feet. Devote yourself to the work of preparation. Rest not until you can truly say: My Redeemer liveth, and, because He lives, I shall live also.

If you lose heaven, you lose everything; if you gain heaven, you gain everything. Do not make a mistake in this matter, I implore you. Eternal interests are here involved. [7]

FAITH OF THE REFORMERS

The last enemy that shall be destroyed is death. 1 Cor. 15:26.

Luther declared: "I persuade myself verily, that the day of judgment will not be absent full three hundred years. God will not, cannot, suffer this wicked world much longer." "The great day is drawing near in which the kingdom of abominations shall be overthrown."—Daniel T. Taylor, *The Reign of Christ on Earth: or, The Voice of the Church in All Ages,* p. 33.

"This aged world is not far from its end," said Melanchthon. Calvin bids Christians "not to hesitate, ardently desiring the day of Christ's coming as of all events most auspicious;" and declares that "the whole family of the faithful will keep in view that day." "We must hunger after Christ, we must seek, contemplate," he says, "till the dawning of that great day, when our Lord will fully manifest the glory of His kingdom."—*Ibid.,* pages 158, 134.

"Has not the Lord Jesus carried up our flesh into heaven?" said Knox, the Scotch Reformer, "and shall He not return? We know that He shall return, and that with expedition." Ridley and Latimer, who laid down their lives for the truth, looked in faith for the Lord's coming. Ridley wrote: "The world without doubt—this I do believe, and therefore I say it—draws to an end. Let us with John, the servant of God, cry in our hearts unto our Saviour Christ, Come, Lord Jesus, come." —*Ibid.,* pages 151, 145.

"The thoughts of the coming of the Lord," said Baxter, "are most sweet and joyful to me."—Richard Baxter, *Works,* vol. 17, p. 555. "It is the work of faith and the character of His saints to love His appearing and to look for that blessed hope." "If death be the last enemy to be destroyed at the resurrection, we may learn how earnestly believers should long and pray for the second coming of Christ, when this full and final conquest shall be made."—*Ibid.,* vol. 17, p. 500. "This is the day that all believers should long, and hope, and wait for, as being the accomplishment of all the work of their redemption, and all the desires and endeavors of their souls." "Hasten, O Lord, this blessed day!"—*Ibid.,* vol. 17, pp. 182, 183. Such was the hope of the apostolic church, of the "church in the wilderness," and of the Reformers.[8]

THE KEY TO HISTORY

Watchman, what of the night? The watchman said, The morning cometh, and also the night: if ye will enquire, enquire ye: return, come. Isa. 21:11 (last part), 12.

An understanding of the hope of Christ's second coming is the key that unlocks all the history that follows, and explains all the future lessons.[9]

The voice of the true watchman needs now to be heard all along the line, "The morning cometh, and also the night." The trumpet must give a certain sound, for we are in the great day of the Lord's preparation.

The truths of prophecy are bound up together, and as we study them, they form a beautiful cluster of practical Christian truth. All the discourses that we give are plainly to reveal that we are waiting, working, and praying for the coming of the Son of God. His coming is our hope. This hope is to be bound up with all our words and works, with all our associations and relationships. . . .

The second coming of the Son of man is to be the wonderful theme kept before the people. Here is a subject that should not be left out of our discourses. Eternal realities must be kept before the mind's eye, and the attractions of the world will appear as they are, altogether profitless as vanity. What are we to do with the world's vanities, its praises, its riches, its honors, or its enjoyments?

We are pilgrims and strangers who are waiting, hoping, and praying for that blessed hope, the glorious appearing of our Lord and Saviour Jesus Christ. If we believe this and bring it into our practical life, what vigorous action would this faith and hope inspire; what fervent love one for another; what careful holy living for the glory of God; and in our respect for the recompense of the reward, what distinct lines of demarcation would be evidenced between us and the world. . . .

The truth that Christ is coming should be kept before every mind.[10]

PARALLEL DISAPPOINTMENTS

Behold, we count them happy which endure. Ye have heard of the patience of Job, and have seen the end of the Lord; that the Lord is very pitiful, and of tender mercy. James 5:11.

Not infrequently the minds of the people, and even of God's servants, are so blinded by human opinions, the traditions and false teaching of men, that they are able only partially to grasp the great things which He has revealed in His word. Thus it was with the disciples of Christ, even when the Saviour was with them in person. Their minds had become imbued with the popular conception of the Messiah as a temporal prince, who was to exalt Israel to the throne of the universal empire, and they could not understand the meaning of His words foretelling His sufferings and death. . . .

From their very birth their hearts had been set upon the anticipated glory of an earthly empire, and this blinded their understanding. . . .

The experience of the disciples who preached the "gospel of the kingdom" at the first advent of Christ, had its counterpart in the experience of those who proclaimed the message of His second advent. . . .

Like the first disciples, William Miller and his associates did not, themselves, fully comprehend the import of the message which they bore. Errors that had been long established in the church prevented them from arriving at a correct interpretation of an important point in the prophecy. Therefore, though they proclaimed the message which God had committed to them to be given to the world, yet through a misapprehension of its meaning they suffered disappointment. . . .

With these believers, as with the first disciples, that which in the hour of trial seemed dark to their understanding would afterward be made plain. When they should see the "end of the Lord" they would know that, notwithstanding the trial resulting from their errors, His purposes of love toward them had been steadily fulfilling. They would learn by a blessed experience that He is "very pitiful, and of tender mercy;" that all His paths "are mercy and truth unto such as keep his covenant and his testimonies." [11]

HUMBLE MEN PROCLAIM THE MESSAGE

We have also a more sure word of prophecy; whereunto ye do well that ye take heed, as unto a light that shineth in a dark place, until the day dawn, and the day star arise in your hearts. 2 Peter 1:19.

This message [Rev. 14:6, 7] is declared to be a part of "the everlasting gospel." The work of preaching the gospel has not been committed to angels, but has been entrusted to men. Holy angels have been employed in directing this work, they have in charge the great movements for the salvation of men; but the actual proclamation of the gospel is performed by the servants' of Christ upon the earth.

Faithful men, who were obedient to the promptings of God's Spirit and the teachings of His word, were to proclaim this warning to the world. They were those who had taken heed to the "sure word of prophecy," the "light that shineth in a dark place, until the day dawn, and the day star arise." 2 Peter 1:19. They had been seeking the knowledge of God more than all hid treasures, counting it "better than the merchandise of silver, and the gain thereof than fine gold." Proverbs 3:14. And the Lord revealed to them the great things of the kingdom. "The secret of the Lord is with them that fear him; and he will show them his covenant." Psalm 25:14.

It was not the scholarly theologians who had an understanding of this truth, and engaged in its proclamation. Had these been faithful watchmen, diligently and prayerfully searching the Scriptures, they would have known the time of night; the prophecies would have opened to them the events about to take place. But they did not occupy this position, and the message was given by humbler men. Said Jesus: "Walk while ye have the light, lest darkness come upon you." John 12:35. Those who turn away from the light which God has given, or who neglect to seek it when it is within their reach, are left in darkness. But the Saviour declares: "He that followeth me shall not walk in darkness, but shall have the light of life." John 8:12. Whoever is with singleness of purpose seeking to do God's will, earnestly heeding the light already given, will receive greater light; to that soul some star of heavenly radiance will be sent to guide him into all truth.[12]

THE TRUTH WILL TRIUMPH

The angel . . . sware by him that liveth for ever . . . that there should be time no longer. Rev. 10:5, 6.

The message of Revelation 14, proclaiming that the hour of God's judgment is come, is given in the time of the end; and the angel of Revelation 10 is represented as having one foot on the sea and one foot on the land, showing that the message will be carried to distant lands, the ocean will be crossed, and the islands of the sea will hear the proclamation of the last message of warning. . . .

"And the angel which I saw stand upon the sea and upon the earth lifted up his hand to heaven, and sware by him that liveth for ever and ever, who created heaven, and the things that therein are, and the earth, and the things that therein are, and the sea, and the things which are therein, that there should be time no longer" (Rev. 10:5, 6). This message announces the end of the prophetic periods. The disappointment of those who expected to see our Lord in 1844 was indeed bitter to those who had so ardently looked for His appearing. It was in the Lord's order that this disappointment should come. . . .

Not one cloud has fallen upon the church that God has not prepared for; not one opposing force has risen to counterwork the work of God but He has foreseen. All has taken place as He has predicted through His prophets. He has not left His church in darkness, forsaken, but has traced in prophetic declarations what would occur, and through His providence, acting in its appointed place in the world's history, He has brought about that which His Holy Spirit inspired the prophets to foretell. All His purposes will be fulfilled and established. His law is linked with His throne, and satanic agencies combined with human agencies cannot destroy it. Truth is inspired and guarded by God; it will live, and will succeed, although it may appear at times to be overshadowed. The gospel of Christ is the law exemplified in character. The deceptions practiced against it, every device for vindicating falsehood, every error forged by satanic agencies, will eventually be eternally broken, and the triumph of truth will be like the appearing of the sun at noonday. The Sun of Righteousness shall shine forth with healing in His wings, and the whole earth shall be filled with His glory.[13]

HASTENING OUR LORD'S RETURN

He will finish the work, and cut it short in righteousness: because a short work will the Lord make upon the earth. Rom. 9:28.

In the prophecy of Jerusalem's destruction Christ said, "Because iniquity shall abound, the love of many shall wax cold. But he that shall endure unto the end, the same shall be saved. And this gospel of the kingdom shall be preached in all the world for a witness unto all nations; and then shall the end come." This prophecy will again be fulfilled. The abounding iniquity of that day finds its counterpart in this generation. So with the prediction in regard to the preaching of the gospel. Before the fall of Jerusalem, Paul, writing by the Holy Spirit, declared that the gospel was preached to "every creature which is under heaven." Col. 1:23. So now, before the coming of the Son of man, the everlasting gospel is to be preached "to every nation, and kindred, and tongue, and people." Rev. 14:6, 14. God "hath appointed a day, in the which he will judge the world." Acts 17:31. Christ tells us when that day shall be ushered in. He does not say that all the world will be converted, but that "this gospel of the kingdom shall be preached in all the world for a witness unto all nations; and then shall the end come." By giving the gospel to the world it is in our power to hasten our Lord's return. We are not only to look for but to hasten the coming of the day of God. 2 Peter 3:12, margin. Had the church of Christ done her appointed work as the Lord ordained, the whole world would before this have been warned, and the Lord Jesus would have come to our earth in power and great glory.[14]

It is the unbelief, the worldliness, unconsecration, and strife among the Lord's professed people that have kept us in this world of sin and sorrow so many years. . . .

We may have to remain here in this world because of insubordination many more years, as did the children of Israel; but for Christ's sake, His people should not add sin to sin by charging God with the consequence of their own wrong course of action.[15]

LAST WARNINGS OF THE THIRD ANGEL

After these things I saw another angel come down from heaven, having great power; and the earth was lightened with his glory. Rev. 18:1.

The angel who unites in the proclamation of the third angel's message is to lighten the whole earth with his glory. A work of world-wide extent and unwonted power is here foretold. The advent movement of 1840-44 was a glorious manifestation of the power of God; the first angel's message was carried to every missionary station in the world, and in some countries there was the greatest religious interest which has been witnessed in any land since the Reformation of the sixteenth century; but these are to be exceeded by the mighty movement under the last warning of the third angel. . . .

The great work of the gospel is not to close with less manifestation of the power of God than marked its opening. The prophecies which were fulfilled in the outpouring of the former rain at the opening of the gospel are again to be fulfilled in the latter rain at its close. . . .

Servants of God, with their faces lighted up and shining with holy consecration, will hasten from place to place to proclaim the message from heaven. By thousands of voices, all over the earth, the warning will be given. Miracles will be wrought, the sick will be healed, and signs and wonders will follow the believers. Satan also works with lying wonders, even bringing down fire from heaven in the sight of men. Revelation 13:13. Thus the inhabitants of the earth will be brought to take their stand. . . .

The publications distributed by missionary workers have exerted their influence, yet many whose minds were impressed have been prevented from fully comprehending the truth or from yielding obedience. Now the rays of light penetrate everywhere, the truth is seen in its clearness, and the honest children of God sever the bands which have held them. Family connections, church relations, are powerless to stay them now. Truth is more precious than all besides. Notwithstanding the agencies combined against the truth, a large number take their stand upon the Lord's side.[16]

HE SHALL REIGN FOREVER

The seventh angel sounded; and there were great voices in heaven, saying, The kingdoms of this world are become the kingdoms of our Lord, and of his Christ; and he shall reign for ever and ever. Rev. 11:15.

The coming of Christ to usher in the reign of righteousness has inspired the most sublime . . . utterances of the sacred writers. . . . The psalmist sang of the power and majesty of Israel's King: . . . "Let the heavens rejoice, and let the earth be glad . . . before the Lord: for he cometh, for he cometh to judge the earth: he shall judge the world with righteousness, and the people with his truth." Psalm 96:11-13.

Said the prophet Isaiah: . . . "He will swallow up death in victory; and the Lord God will wipe away tears from off all faces; and the' rebuke of his people shall he take away from off all the earth; for the Lord hath spoken it. . . ." Isaiah 25:8. . . .

When the Saviour was about to be separated from His disciples, He comforted them in their sorrow with the assurance that He would come again: "Let not your heart be troubled. . . . In my Father's house are many mansions. . . . I go to prepare a place for you. And if I go and prepare a place for you, I will come again, and receive you unto myself." John 14:1-3. . . .

The angels who lingered upon Olivet after Christ's ascension repeated to the disciples the promise of His return: "This *same* Jesus, which is taken up from you into heaven, shall *so* come in like manner as ye have seen him go into heaven." Acts 1:11. And the apostle Paul, speaking by the Spirit of Inspiration, testified: "The Lord *himself* shall descend from heaven with a shout, with the voice of the archangel, and with the trump of God." 1 Thessalonians 4:16. Says the prophet of Patmos: "Behold, he cometh with clouds; and every eye shall see him." Revelation 1:7.

About His coming cluster the glories of that "restitution of all things, which God hath spoken by the mouth of all his holy prophets since the world began." Acts 3:21. Then the long-continued rule of evil shall be broken; "the kingdoms of this world" will become "the kingdoms of our Lord, and of his Christ; and he shall reign for ever and ever." Revelation 11:15.[17.]

THE ELIJAH PROPHECY

Behold, I will send you Elijah the prophet before the coming of the great and dreadful day of the Lord: And he shall turn the heart of the fathers to the children, and the heart of the children to their fathers, lest I come and smite the earth with a curse. Mal. 4:5, 6.

Those who are to prepare the way for the second coming of Christ are represented by faithful Elijah, as John came in the spirit of Elijah to prepare the way for Christ's first advent.[18]

The work of John the Baptist, and the work of those who in the last days go forth in the spirit and power of Elijah to arouse the people from their apathy, are in many respects the same. His work is a type of the work that must be done in this age. Christ is to come the second time to judge the world in righteousness.[19]

John separated himself from friends and from the luxuries of life. The simplicity of his dress, a garment woven of camel's hair, was a standing rebuke to the extravagance and display of the Jewish priests, and of the people generally. His diet, purely vegetable, of locusts and wild honey, was a rebuke to the indulgence of appetite and the gluttony that everywhere prevailed. . . . The great subject of reform is to be agitated, and the public mind is to be stirred. Temperance in all things is to be connected with the message, to turn the people of God from their idolatry, their gluttony, and their extravagance in dress and other things.

The self-denial, humility, and temperance required of the righteous, whom God especially leads and blesses, is to be presented to the people in contrast to the extravagant, health-destroying habits of those who live in this degenerate age. God has shown that health reform is as closely connected with the third angel's message as the hand is with the body.[20]

As John the Baptist . . . called their attention to the Ten Commandments, so we are to give, with no uncertain sound, the message: "Fear God, and give glory to him; for the hour of his judgment is come." With the earnestness that characterized Elijah the prophet and John the Baptist, we are to strive to prepare the way for Christ's second advent.[21]

UPLIFT JESUS AS THE CENTER

I am the root and the offspring of David, and the bright and morning star. Rev. 22:16.

The perils of the last days are upon us, and in our work we are to warn the people of the danger they are in. Let not the solemn scenes which prophecy has revealed be left untouched. If our people were half awake, if they realized the nearness of the events portrayed in the Revelation, a reformation would be wrought in our churches, and many more would believe the message. We have no time to lose. . . . Advance new principles, and crowd in the clear-cut truth. It will be as a sword cutting both ways. But be not too ready to take a controversial attitude. There will be times when we must stand still and see the salvation of God. Let Daniel speak, let the Revelation speak, and tell what is truth. But whatever phase of the subject is presented, uplift Jesus as the center of all hope, "the root and the offspring of David, and the bright and morning star."

We do not go deep enough in our search for truth. Every soul who believes present truth will be brought where he will be required to give a reason of the hope that is in him. The people of God will be called upon to stand before kings, princes, rulers, and great men of the earth, and they must know that they do know what is truth. They must be converted men and women. God can teach you more in one moment by His Holy Spirit than you could learn from the great men of the earth. The universe is looking upon the controversy that is going on upon the earth. At an infinite cost, God has provided for every man an opportunity to know that which will make him wise unto salvation. How eagerly do angels look to see who will avail himself of this opportunity! When a message is presented to God's people, they should not rise up in opposition to it; they should go to the Bible, comparing it with the law and the testimony, and if it does not bear this test, it is not true. God wants our minds to expand. He desires to put His grace upon us. We may have a feast of good things every day, for God can open the whole treasure of heaven to us.[22]

THE FIELD IS THE WORLD

Go ye therefore, and teach all nations, baptizing them in the name of the Father, and of the Son, and of the Holy Ghost. Matt. 28:19.

While in California in the year 1874, I was given an impressive dream. . . .

I dreamed that several of the brethren in California were in council, considering the best plan for labor during the coming season. . . .

A young man whom I had frequently seen in my dreams, came into the council. He listened with deep interest to the words that were spoken, and then, speaking with deliberation and authoritative confidence, said:

"The cities and villages constitute a part of the Lord's vineyard. They must hear the messages of warning. The enemy of truth is making desperate efforts to turn the people from the truth of God to falsehood. . . . You are to sow beside all waters.

"It may be that you will not at once see the result of your labor, but this should not discourage you. Take Christ as your example. He had many hearers, but few followers." . . .

The messenger continued: "You are entertaining too limited ideas of the work for this time. You are trying to plan the work so that you can embrace it in your arms. You must take broader views. Your light must not be put under a bushel or under a bed, but on a candlestick, that it may give light to all that are in the house. Your house is the world. . . .

"Many countries are waiting for the advanced light the Lord has for them; and your faith is limited, it is very small. Your conception of the work needs to be greatly enlarged. . . . Go forward. God will work with great power if you will walk in all humility of mind before Him. It is not faith to talk of impossibilities. Nothing is impossible with God. The light of the binding claims of the law of God is to test . . . the world." . . .

Time is short; and all who believe this message, should feel a solemn obligation resting upon them to be disinterested workers, exerting their influence on the right side, and never by word or action be found arrayed against those who are seeking to advance the interests of God's cause. . . . The light God has given us isn't worth much to the world unless it can be seen by being presented before them.[23]

GOD'S JUDGMENTS IN THE LAND

Men's hearts failing them for fear, and for looking after those things which are coming on the earth. Luke 21:26.

O that God's people had a sense of the impending destruction of thousands of cities, now almost given to idolatry! . . .

Not long ago a very impressive scene passed before me. I saw an immense ball of fire falling among some beautiful mansions, causing their instant destruction. I heard someone say, "We knew that the judgments of God were coming upon the earth, but we did not know that they would come so soon." Others said, "You knew? Why then did you not tell us? We did not know." On every side I heard such words spoken. . . .

Soon grievous troubles will arise among the nations—trouble that will not cease until Jesus comes. As never before we need to press together, serving Him who has prepared His throne in the heavens and whose kingdom ruleth over all. God has not forsaken His people, and our strength lies in not forsaking Him.

The judgments of God are in the land. The wars and rumors of wars, the destruction by fire and flood, say clearly that the time of trouble, which is to increase until the end, is very near at hand. We have no time to lose. The world is stirred with the spirit of war. The prophecies of the eleventh of Daniel have almost reached their final fulfillment. . . .

Last Friday morning, just before I awoke, a very impressive scene was presented before me. I seemed to awake from sleep but was not in my home. From the windows I could behold a terrible conflagration. Great balls of fire were falling upon houses, and from these balls fiery arrows were flying in every direction. It was impossible to check the fires that were kindled, and many places were being destroyed. The terror of the people was indescribable.[24]

Strictly will the cities of the nations be dealt with, and yet they will not be visited in the extreme of God's indignation, because some souls will yet break away from the delusions of the enemy, and will repent and be converted, while the mass will be treasuring up wrath against the day of wrath.[25]

A BETTER AND NOBLER WAY

Wash you, make you clean; put away the evil of your doings from before mine eyes; cease to do evil; learn to do well. Isa. 1:16, 17.

Ignorance, pleasure loving, and sinful habits, corrupting soul, body, and spirit, make the world full of moral leprosy; a deadly moral malaria is destroying thousands and tens of thousands.[26]

Many are sunken in sin. Many are in distress. They are pressed with suffering, want, unbelief, despondency. Disease of every type afflicts them, both in body and in soul. They long to find a solace for their troubles, and Satan tempts them to seek it in lusts and pleasures that lead to ruin and death. He is offering them the apples of Sodom, that will turn to ashes upon their lips.[27]

A terrible picture of the condition of the world has been presented before me. Immorality abounds everywhere. Licentiousness is the special sin of this age. Never did vice lift its deformed head with such boldness as now. . . . The iniquity which abounds is not merely confined to the unbeliever and the scoffer. Would that this were the case, but it is not. Many men and women who profess the religion of Christ are guilty. Even some who profess to be looking for His appearing are no more prepared for that event than Satan himself. They are not cleansing themselves from all pollution. They have so long served their lust that it is natural for their thoughts to be impure and their imaginations corrupt. It is as impossible to cause their minds to dwell upon pure and holy things as it would be to turn the course of Niagara and send its waters pouring up the falls. . . . Every Christian will have to learn to restrain his passions and be controlled by principle. . . .

If lasciviousness, pollution, adultery, crime, and murder are the order of the day among those who know not the truth, and who refuse to be controlled by the principles of God's word, how important that the class professing to be followers of Christ, closely allied to God and angels, should show them a better and nobler way! How important that by their chastity and virtue they stand in marked contrast to that class who are controlled by brute passions! [28]

WHEN THE LOUD CRY SOUNDS

And that, knowing the time, that now it is high time to awake out of sleep: for now is our salvation nearer than when we believed. Rom. 13:11.

The end is near, stealing upon us stealthily, imperceptibly, like the noiseless approach of a thief in the night. May the Lord grant that we shall no longer sleep as do others, but that we shall watch and be sober. The truth is soon to triumph gloriously, and all who now choose to be laborers together with God, will triumph with it. The time is short; the night soon cometh when no man can work. . . .

The time is coming when there will be as many converted in a day as there were on the day of Pentecost, after the disciples had received the Holy Spirit. . . .

Many have let the gospel invitation go unheeded; they have been tested and tried; but mountainous obstacles have seemed to loom up before their faces, blocking their onward march. Through faith, perseverance, and courage, many will surmount these obstructions and walk out into the glorious light.

Almost unconsciously barriers have been erected in the strait and narrow way; stones of stumbling have been placed in the path; these will be rolled away. The safeguards which false shepherds have thrown around their flocks will become as nought; thousands will step out into the light, and work to spread the light. Heavenly intelligences will combine with the human agencies. Thus encouraged, the church will indeed arise and shine, throwing all her sanctified energies into the contest; thus the design of God is accomplished; the lost pearls are recovered. . . .

During the loud cry, the church, aided by the providential interpositions of her exalted Lord, will diffuse the knowledge of salvation so abundantly that light will be communicated to every city and town. The earth will be filled with the knowledge of salvation. So abundantly will the renewing Spirit of God have crowned with success the intensely active agencies, that the light of present truth will be seen flashing everywhere.[29]

27

THE FAITHFUL ONES WILL NOT FAIL

Here is the patience of the saints: here are they that keep the commandments of God, and the faith of Jesus. Rev. 14:12.

We have need now for more than human wisdom in reading and searching the Scriptures; and if we come to God's Word with humble hearts, He will raise up a standard for us against the lawless element.

It is difficult to hold fast the beginning of our confidence firm unto the end; and the difficulty increases when there are hidden influences constantly at work to bring in another spirit, a counterworking element, on Satan's side of the question. In the absence of persecution, there have drifted into our ranks some who appear sound, and their Christianity unquestionable, but who, if persecution should arise, would go out from us. In the crisis, they would see force in specious reasoning that has had an influence on their minds. Satan has prepared various snares to meet varied minds. When the law of God is made void the church will be sifted by fiery trials, and a larger proportion than we now anticipate, will give heed to seducing spirits and doctrines of devils. Instead of being strengthened when brought into strait places, many prove that they are not living branches of the True Vine. . . .

But when the world makes void the law of God, what will be the effect upon the truly obedient and righteous? Will they be carried away by the strong current of evil? Because so many rank themselves under the banner of the prince of darkness, will God's commandment-keeping people swerve from their allegiance? Never! Not one who is abiding in Christ will fail or fall. His followers will bow in obedience to a higher authority than that of any earthly potentate. While the contempt placed upon God's commandments leads many to suppress the truth and show less reverence for it, the faithful ones will with greater earnestness hold aloft its distinguishing truths. We are not left to our own direction. . . . We should consult His Word with humble hearts, ask His counsel, and give up our will to His. We can do nothing without God.[30]

28

LABOR TO WIN EVEN ONE SOUL

What man of you, having an hundred sheep, if he lose one of them, doth not leave the ninety and nine in the wilderness, and go after that which is lost, until he find it? Luke 15:4.

For the conversion of one soul we should tax our resources to the utmost. One soul won to Christ will flash heaven's light all around him, penetrating the moral darkness and saving other souls.

If Christ left the ninety and nine, that He might seek and save the one lost sheep, can we be justified in doing less? Is not a neglect to work even as Christ worked, to sacrifice as He sacrificed, a betrayal of sacred trusts, an insult to God?

Sound an alarm throughout the length and breadth of the earth. Tell the people that the day of the Lord is near and hasteth greatly. Let none be left unwarned. We might have been in the place of the poor souls that are in error. We might have been placed among barbarians. According to the truth we have received above others, we are debtors to impart the same to them.

We have no time to lose. The end is near. The passage from place to place to spread the truth will soon be hedged with dangers on the right hand and on the left. Everything will be placed to obstruct the way of the Lord's messengers, so that they will not be able to do that which it is possible for them to do now. We must look our work fairly in the face and advance as fast as possible in aggressive warfare. From the light given me of God I know that the powers of darkness are working with intense energy from beneath, and with stealthy tread Satan is advancing to take those who are now asleep, as a wolf taking his prey. We have warnings now which we may give, a work now which we may do; but soon it will be more difficult than we can imagine. God help us to keep in the channel of light, to work with our eyes fastened on Jesus our Leader, and patiently, perseveringly press on to gain the victory.[31]

In our life here, earthly, sin-restricted though it is, the greatest joy and the highest education are in service. And in the future state, untrammeled by the limitations of sinful humanity, it is in service that our greatest joy and our highest education will be found.[32]

29

STUDY DANIEL
AND THE REVELATION

Blessed is he that readeth, and they that hear the words of this prophecy, and keep those things which are written therein: for the time is at hand. Rev. 1:3.

A message that will arouse the churches is to be proclaimed. Every effort is to be made to give the light, not only to our people, but to the world. I have been instructed that the prophecies of Daniel and the Revelation should be printed in small books, with the necessary explanations, and should be sent all over the world. Our own people need to have the light placed before them in clearer lines.[33]

Those who eat the flesh and drink the blood of the Son of God will bring from the books of Daniel and Revelation truth that is inspired by the Holy Spirit. They will start into action forces that cannot be repressed. The lips of children will be opened to proclaim the mysteries that have been hidden from the minds of men. . . .

Many of the prophecies are about to be fulfilled in quick succession. Every element of power is about to be set to work. Past history will be repeated; old controversies will arouse to new life, and peril will beset God's people on every side. Intensity is taking hold of the human family. It is permeating everything upon the earth. . . .

Study Revelation in connection with Daniel, for history will be repeated. . . . We, with all our religious advantages, ought to know far more today than we do know.

Angels desire to look into the truths that are revealed to the people who with contrite hearts are searching the word of God and praying for greater lengths and breadths and depths and heights of the knowledge which He alone can give.

As we near the close of this world's history, the prophecies relating to the last days especially demand our study. The last book of the New Testament Scriptures is full of truth that we need to understand. Satan has blinded the minds of many so that they have been glad of any excuse for not making the Revelation their study. But Christ through His servant John has here declared what shall be in the last days; and He says, "Blessed is he that readeth, and they that hear the words of this prophecy, and keep those things which are written therein."[34]

INTOLERANCE AND PERSECUTION

If they have persecuted me, they will also persecute you; if they have kept my saying, they will keep your's also. John 15:20.

Persecution in its varied forms is the development of a principle which will exist as long as Satan exists and Christianity has vital power. No man can serve God without enlisting against himself the opposition of the hosts of darkness. Evil angels will assail him, alarmed that his influence is taking the prey from their hands. Evil men, rebuked by his example, will unite with them in seeking to separate him from God by alluring temptations. When these do not succeed, then a compelling power is employed to force the conscience.

But so long as Jesus remains man's intercessor in the sanctuary above, the restraining influence of the Holy Spirit is felt by rulers and people. It still controls to some extent the laws of the land. Were it not for these laws, the condition of the world would be much worse than it now is. While many of our rulers are active agents of Satan, God also has His agents among the leading men of the nation. The enemy moves upon his servants to propose measures that would greatly impede the work of God; but statesmen who fear the Lord are influenced by holy angels to oppose such propositions with unanswerable arguments. Thus a few men will hold in check a powerful current of evil. The opposition of the enemies of truth will be restrained that the third angel's message may do its work. When the final warning shall be given, it will arrest the attention of these leading men through whom the Lord is now working, and some of them will accept it, and will stand with the people of God through the time of trouble. . . .

"Be glad then, ye children of Zion, and rejoice in the Lord your God. . . ." Joel 2:23. "In the last days, saith God, I will pour out of my Spirit upon all flesh." "And it shall come to pass, that whosoever shall call on the name of the Lord shall be saved." Acts 2:17, 21.

The great work of the gospel is not to close with less manifestation of the power of God than marked its opening.[35]

THE CHURCH WILL NOT FALL

Upon this rock I will build my church; and the gates of hell shall not prevail against it. Matt. 16:18.

Those who keep the commandments of God and the faith of Jesus will feel the ire of the dragon and his hosts. Satan numbers the world as his subjects, he has gained control of the apostate churches; but here is a little company that are resisting his supremacy. If he could blot them from the earth, his triumph would be complete. As he influenced the heathen nations to destroy Israel, so in the near future he will stir up the wicked powers of earth to destroy the people of God. . . . Their only hope is in the mercy of God; their only defense will be prayer.

The trying experiences that came to God's people in the days of Esther were not peculiar to that age alone. The revelator, looking down the ages to the close of time, has declared, "The dragon was wroth with the woman, and went to make war with the remnant of her seed, which keep the commandments of God, and have the testimony of Jesus Christ." Rev. 12:17. Some who today are living on the earth will see these words fulfilled.

The wrath of Satan increases as his time grows short, and his work of deceit and destruction will reach its culmination in the time of trouble.[36]

Satan will work his miracles to deceive; he will set up his power as supreme. The church may appear as about to fall, but it does not fall. It remains, while the sinners in Zion will be sifted out—the chaff separated from the precious wheat. This is a terrible ordeal, but nevertheless it must take place. None but those who have been overcoming by the blood of the Lamb and the word of their testimony will be found with the loyal and true, without spot or stain of sin, without guile in their mouths.[37]

God declares that even a mother may forget her child, "yet will I not forget thee." . . . God thinks of His children with the tenderest solicitude and keeps a book of remembrance before Him, that He may never forget the children of His care.[38]

THE COUNTERFEIT REVIVAL

This know also, that in the last days perilous times shall come. For men shall be lovers of their own selves, covetous, boasters, proud, blasphemers, disobedient to parents, unthankful, unholy, . . . having a form of godliness, but denying the power thereof: from such turn away. 2 Tim. 3:1, 2, 5.

Before the final visitation of God's judgments upon the earth there will be among the people of the Lord such a revival of primitive godliness as has not been witnessed since apostolic times. The Spirit and power of God will be poured out upon His children. At that time many will separate themselves from those churches in which the love of this world has supplanted love for God and His word. Many, both of ministers and people, will gladly accept those great truths which God has caused to be proclaimed at this time to prepare a people for the Lord's second coming. The enemy of souls desires to hinder this work; and before the time for such a movement shall come, he will endeavor to prevent it by introducing a counterfeit. In those churches which he can bring under his deceptive power he will make it appear that God's special blessing is poured out; there will be manifest what is thought to be great religious interest. Multitudes will exult that God is working marvelously for them, when the work is that of another spirit. Under a religious guise, Satan will seek to extend his influence over the Christian world.

In many of the revivals which have occurred during the last half century, the same influences have been at work, to a greater or less degree, that will be manifest in the more extensive movements of the future. There is an emotional excitement, a mingling of the true with the false, that is well adapted to mislead. Yet none need be deceived. In the light of God's word it is not difficult to determine the nature of these movements. Wherever men neglect the testimony of the Bible, turning away from those plain, soul-testing truths which require self-denial and renunciation of the world, there we may be sure that God's blessing is not bestowed. And by the rule which Christ Himself has given, "Ye shall know them by their fruits" (Matthew 7:16), it is evident that these movements are not the work of the Spirit of God.[39]

PRESUMPTUOUS, CARELESS DELAY

Behold, I come as a thief. Blessed is he that watcheth, and keepeth his garments, lest he walk naked, and they see his shame. Rev. 16:15.

The evil servant says in his heart, "My lord delayeth his coming." He does not say that Christ will not come. He does not scoff at the idea of His second coming. But in his heart and by his actions and words he declares that the Lord's coming is delayed. He banishes from the mind of others the conviction that the Lord is coming quickly. His influence leads men to presumptuous, careless delay. . . . He mingles with the world. . . . It is a fearful assimilation. With the world he is taken in the snare. . . .

"If therefore thou shalt not watch, I will come on thee as a thief, and thou shalt not know what hour I will come upon thee." Rev. 3:3. The advent of Christ will surprise the false teachers. They are saying, "Peace and safety." Like the priests and teachers before the fall of Jerusalem, they look for the church to enjoy earthly prosperity and glory. The signs of the times they interpret as foreshadowing this. But what saith the word of Inspiration? "Sudden destruction cometh upon them." 1 Thess. 5:3. Upon all who dwell on the face of the whole earth, upon all who make this world their home, the day of God will come as a snare. . . .

The world, full of rioting, full of godless pleasure, is asleep, asleep in carnal security. Men are putting afar off the coming of the Lord. They laugh at warnings. The proud boast is made, "All things continue as they were from the beginning." "To morrow shall be as this day, and much more abundant." 2 Peter 3:4; Isa. 56:12. We will go deeper into pleasure loving. But Christ says, "Behold, I come as a thief." Rev. 16:15. At the very time when the world is asking in scorn, "Where is the promise of his coming?" the signs are fulfilling. While they cry, "Peace and safety," sudden destruction is coming. When the scorner, the rejecter of truth, has become presumptuous; when the routine of work in the various money-making lines is carried on without regard to principle; when the student is eagerly seeking knowledge of everything but his Bible, Christ comes as a thief.[40]

A HEAVEN TO WIN

Watch ye therefore, and pray always. Luke 21:36.

The days in which we live are solemn and important. The Spirit of God is gradually but surely being withdrawn from the earth. . . .

The condition of things in the world shows that troublous times are right upon us. The daily papers are full of indications of a terrible conflict in the near future. Bold robberies are of frequent occurrence. Strikes are common. Thefts and murders are committed on every hand. Men possessed of demons are taking the lives of men, women, and little children. Men have become infatuated with vice, and every species of evil prevails.[41]

Everything in the world is in agitation. The signs of the times are ominous. Coming events cast their shadows before. The Spirit of God is withdrawing from the earth, and calamity follows calamity by sea and by land. There are tempests, earthquakes, fires, floods, murders of every grade. . . . Rapidly are men ranging themselves under the banner they have chosen. Restlessly are they waiting and watching the movements of their leaders. There are those who are waiting and watching and working for our Lord's appearing. Another class are falling into line under the generalship of the first great apostate. Few believe with heart and soul that we have a hell to shun and a heaven to win.

The crisis is stealing gradually upon us. The sun shines in the heavens, passing over its usual round. . . . Men are still eating and drinking, planting and building, marrying, and giving in marriage. Merchants are still buying and selling. Men are jostling one against another, contending for the highest place. Pleasure lovers are still crowding to theaters, horse races, gambling hells. The highest excitement prevails, yet probation's hour is fast closing, and every case is about to be eternally decided. . . .

Solemnly there come to us down through the centuries the warning words of our Lord from the Mount of Olives: "Take heed to yourselves, lest at any time your hearts be overcharged with surfeiting, and drunkenness, and cares of this life, and so that day come upon you unawares." [42]

BLESSINGS UPON THE WATCHFUL ONES

Blessed are those servants, whom the lord when he cometh shall find watching: verily I say unto you, that he shall gird himself, and make them to sit down to meat, and will come forth and serve them. Luke 12:37.

God has always given men warning of coming judgments. Those who had faith in His message for their time, and who acted out their faith, in obedience to His commandments, escaped the judgments that fell upon the disobedient and unbelieving. The word came to Noah, "Come thou and all thy house into the ark; for thee have I seen righteous before me." Noah obeyed and was saved. The message came to Lot, "Up, get you out of this place; for the Lord will destroy this city." Gen. 7:1; 19:14. Lot placed himself under the guardianship of the heavenly messengers, and was saved. So Christ's disciples were given warning of the destruction of Jerusalem. Those who watched for the sign of the coming ruin, and fled from the city, escaped the destruction. So now we are given warning of Christ's second coming and of the destruction to fall upon the world. Those who heed the warning will be saved.

Because we know not the exact time of His coming, we are commanded to watch. "Blessed are those servants, whom the lord when he cometh shall find watching." Luke 12:37. Those who watch for the Lord's coming are not waiting in idle expectancy. The expectation of Christ's coming is to make men fear the Lord, and fear His judgments upon transgression. It is to awaken them to the great sin of rejecting His offers of mercy. Those who are watching for the Lord are purifying their souls by obedience to the truth. With vigilant watching they combine earnest working. Because they know that the Lord is at the door, their zeal is quickened to co-operate with the divine intelligences in working for the salvation of souls. These are the faithful and wise servants who give to the Lord's household "their portion of meat in due season." Luke 12:42. They are declaring the truth that is now specially applicable. As Enoch, Noah, Abraham, and Moses each declared the truth for his time, so will Christ's servants now give the special warning for their generation.[43]

TROUBLES ON ALL SIDES

Seek ye the Lord, all ye meek of the earth, which have wrought his judgment; seek righteousness, seek meekness: it may be ye shall be hid in the day of the Lord's anger. Zeph. 2:3.

There is no sadder spectacle than that of those who have been purchased by the blood of Christ . . . turning to jest the messages graciously sent to them in the gospel, denying the divinity of Christ, and trusting to their own finite reasoning, and to arguments that have no foundation. When tested with affliction, when brought face to face with death, all these fallacies they have cherished will be melted away like frost before the sun.

How terrible it is to stand by the coffin of one who has rejected the appeals of divine mercy! How terrible to say: Here is a life lost! Here is one who might have reached the highest standard, and gained immortal life, but he surrendered his life to Satan, became ensnared by the vain philosophies of men, and was a plaything of the evil one! The Christian's hope is an anchor to the soul, both sure and steadfast, and entereth into that which is within the veil, whither Christ the forerunner is for us entered. We have an individual work to do to prepare for the great events that are before us.

The youth should seek God more earnestly. The tempest is coming, and we must get ready for its fury by having repentance toward God and faith toward our Lord Jesus Christ. The Lord will arise to shake terribly the earth. We shall see troubles on all sides. Thousands of ships will be hurled into the depths of the sea. Navies will go down, and human lives will be sacrificed by millions. Fires will break out unexpectedly, and no human effort will be able to quench them. The palaces of earth will be swept away in the fury of the flames. Disasters by rail will become more and more frequent; confusion, collision, and death without a moment's warning will occur on the great lines of travel. The end is near, probation is closing. Oh, let us seek God while He may be found, call upon Him while He is near! The prophet says: "Seek ye the Lord, all ye meek of the earth, which have wrought his judgment; seek righteousness, seek meekness: it may be ye shall be hid in the day of the Lord's anger." [44]

INTERCESSORY PRAYERS FOR SOULS

Again I say unto you, That if two of you shall agree on earth as touching any thing that they shall ask, it shall be done for them of my Father which is in heaven. Matt. 18:19.

I remember in Battle Creek when there were those who felt the burden for the unconverted, and those who were in darkness and saw no light; then prayer meetings were appointed that they might make the strength of God their strength. In every case the heavenly intelligences worked with these efforts, and souls were saved.[45]

If there is a large number in the church, let the members be formed into small companies, to work not only for the church members, but for unbelievers. If in one place there are only two or three who know the truth, let them form themselves into a band of workers. Let them keep their bond of union unbroken, pressing together in love and unity, encouraging one another to advance, each gaining courage and strength from the assistance of the others. Let them reveal Christlike forbearance and patience, speaking no hasty words, using the talent of speech to build one another up in the most holy faith. Let them labor in Christlike love for those outside the fold. . . . As they work and pray in Christ's name, their numbers will increase.[46]

There is home missionary work that is to be done, and we hear the plea, So long as there is so much sin and such need of labor in our own country, why manifest such zeal for foreign countries? I answer, Our field is the world. . . . The Saviour directed His disciples to begin their work in Jerusalem, and then pass on through Judea and Samaria, and unto the uttermost part of the earth. Only a small proportion of the people accepted the doctrine; but the messengers bore the message rapidly from place to place, passing from country to country, lifting the standard of the gospel in all the near and far-off places of the earth. But there was a preparatory work. The Saviour's promise was, "But ye shall receive power, after that the Holy Ghost is come upon you: and ye shall be witnesses unto me." Those who will not follow their own will and desires, but seek counsel of the Lord, will not be dull scholars for the Lord will teach them.[47]

TO WEEP OR TO REJOICE?

The harvest is past, the summer is ended, and we are not saved. Jer. 8:20.

I appeal to the members of our churches not to disregard the fulfilling of the signs of the times, which say so plainly that the end is near. O, how many who have not cared for the salvation of their souls will soon make the bitter lamentation, "The harvest is past, the summer is ended, and we are not saved!"

O, that we would remember that it is court week with us, and that our cases are pending! Now is the time to watch and pray, to put away all self-indulgence, all pride, all selfishness. The precious moments that are now by many worse than wasted should be spent in meditation and prayer. Many of those who profess to be keeping the commandments of God are following inclination instead of duty. As they are now, they are unworthy of eternal life. To these careless, indifferent ones, I would say, Your vain thoughts, your unkind words, your selfish acts, are recorded in the book of heaven. The angels that were present at Belshazzar's idolatrous revelry stand beside you as you dishonor your Redeemer. Sadly they turn away, grieved that you should thus crucify Him afresh, and put Him to open shame. . . .

On Christ's coronation day He will not acknowledge as His any who bear spot or wrinkle or any such thing. But to His faithful ones He will give crowns of immortal glory. Those who would not that He should reign over them will see Him surrounded by the army of the redeemed, each of whom bears the sign, THE LORD OUR RIGHTEOUSNESS. They will see the head once crowned with thorns crowned with a diadem of glory.

In that day the redeemed will shine forth in the glory of the Father and His Son. The angels of heaven, touching their golden harps, will welcome the King, and those who are the trophies of His victory—those who have been washed and made white in the blood of the Lamb. A song of triumph will peal forth, filling all heaven. Christ has conquered. He enters the heavenly courts accompanied by His redeemed ones, the witnesses that His mission of suffering and self-sacrifice has not been in vain.[48]

CLIMACTIC MOMENT

Who may abide the day of his coming? and who shall stand when he appeareth? for he is like a refiner's fire, and like fullers' soap. Mal. 3:2.

The people of Israel, because of their sinfulness, were forbidden to approach the mount when God was about to descend upon it to proclaim His law, lest they should be consumed by the burning glory of His presence. If such manifestations of His power marked the place chosen for the proclamation of God's law, how terrible must be His tribunal when He comes for the execution of these sacred statutes. How will those who have trampled upon His authority endure His glory in the great day of final retribution? . . .

When the divine Presence was manifested upon Sinai, the glory of the Lord was like devouring fire. . . . But when Christ shall come in glory with His holy angels the whole earth shall be ablaze with the terrible light of His presence. . . .

Never since man was created had there been witnessed such a manifestation of divine power as when the law was proclaimed from Sinai. . . . Amid the most terrific convulsions of nature the voice of God, like a trumpet, was heard from the cloud. The mountain was shaken from base to summit, and the hosts of Israel, pale and trembling with terror, lay upon their faces upon the earth. He whose voice then shook the earth has declared, "Yet once more I shake not the earth only, but also heaven." . . .

When Moses came from the divine Presence in the mount, where he had received the tables of the testimony, guilty Israel could not endure the light that glorified his countenance. How much less can transgressors look upon the Son of God when He shall appear in the glory of His Father, surrounded by all the heavenly host, to execute judgment upon the transgressors of His law and the rejecters of His atonement. . . .

But amid the tempest of divine judgment the children of God will have no cause for fear. "The Lord will be the hope of his people, and the strength of the children of Israel." The day that brings terror and destruction to the transgressors of God's law, will bring to the obedient, "joy unspeakable, and full of glory." [1]

A HIGH STANDARD

And ye shall be holy unto me: for I the Lord am holy, and have severed you from other people, that ye should be mine. Lev. 20:26.

I also saw many do not realize what they must be in order to live in the sight of the Lord without a high priest in the sanctuary through the time of trouble. Those who receive the seal of the living God and are protected in the time of trouble must reflect the image of Jesus fully.

I saw that many were neglecting the preparation so needful and were looking to the time of "refreshing" and the "latter rain" to fit them to stand in the day of the Lord and to live in His sight. Oh, how many I saw in the time of trouble without a shelter! They had neglected the needful preparation; therefore they could not receive the refreshing that all must have to fit them to live in the sight of a holy God. Those who . . . fail to purify their souls in obeying the whole truth . . . will come up to the time of the falling of the plagues, and then see that they needed to be hewed and squared for the building. But there will be . . . no Mediator to plead their cause before the Father. Before this time the awfully solemn declaration has gone forth, "He that is unjust, let him be unjust still: and he which is filthy, let him be filthy still: and he that is righteous, let him be righteous still: and he that is holy, let him be holy still."

I saw that none could share the "refreshing" unless they obtain the victory over every besetment, over pride, selfishness, love of the world, and over every wrong word and action. We should, therefore, be drawing nearer and nearer to the Lord and be earnestly seeking that preparation necessary to enable us to stand in the battle in the day of the Lord. Let all remember that God is holy and that none but holy beings can ever dwell in His presence.[2]

We are today to watch that we offend not in word or deed. . . . We must today seek God and be determined that we will not rest satisfied without His presence. We should watch and work and pray as though this were the last day that would be granted us. How intensely earnest, then, would be our life. How closely would we follow Jesus in all our words and deeds.[3]

WEIGHING TIME

The Lord is a God of knowledge, and by him actions are weighed. 1 Sam. 2:3.

I have seen an angel standing with scales in his hands weighing the thoughts and interest of the people of God, especially the young. In one scale were the thoughts and interest tending heavenward; in the other were the thoughts and interest tending to earth. And in this scale were thrown all the reading of storybooks, thoughts of dress and show, vanity, pride, et cetera. Oh, what a solemn moment! the angels of God standing with scales, weighing the thoughts of His professed children—those who claim to be dead to the world and alive to God. The scale filled with thoughts of earth, vanity, and pride quickly went down, notwithstanding weight after weight rolled from the scale. The one with the thoughts and interest tending to heaven went quickly up as the other went down, and oh, how light it was! I can relate this as I saw it; but never can I give the solemn and vivid impression stamped upon my mind, as I saw the angel with the scales weighing the thoughts and interest of the people of God. Said the angel: "Can such enter heaven? No, no, never. Tell them the hope they now possess is vain, and unless they speedily repent, and obtain salvation, they must perish." . . .

I saw that many measure themselves among themselves, and compare their lives with the lives of others. This should not be. No one but Christ is given us as an example. He is our true Pattern, and each should strive to excel in imitating Him. . . .

I saw that some hardly know as yet what self-denial or sacrifice is, or what it is to suffer for the truth's sake. But none will enter heaven without making a sacrifice. A spirit of self-denial and sacrifice should be cherished. Some have not sacrificed themselves, their own bodies, on the altar of God. They indulge in hasty, fitful temper, gratify their appetites, and attend to their own self-interest, regardless of the cause of God. Those who are willing to make any sacrifice for eternal life, will have it; and it will be worth suffering for, worth crucifying self for, and sacrificing every idol for. The far more exceeding and eternal weight of glory swallows up everything and eclipses every earthly pleasure.[4]

WILL YOU STAND THE TEST?

Thou shalt remember all the way which the Lord thy God led thee these forty years in the wilderness, to humble thee, and to prove thee, to know what was in thine heart, whether thou wouldest keep his commandments, or no. Deut. 8:2.

God will prove His people. . . . If the message [the 1844 proclamation] had been of as short duration as many of us supposed, there would have been no time for them to develop character. Many moved from feeling, not from principle and faith, and this solemn, fearful message stirred them. It wrought upon their feelings, and excited their fears, but did not accomplish the work which God designed that it should. . . .

God leads His people on, step by step. He brings them up to different points calculated to manifest what is in the heart. Some endure at one point, but fall off at the next. At every advanced point the heart is tested and tried a little closer. If the professed people of God find their hearts opposed to this straight work, it should convince them that they have a work to do to overcome. . . . Some are willing to receive one point; but when God brings them to another testing point, they shrink from it and stand back, because they find that it strikes directly at some cherished idol. Here they have opportunity to see what is in their hearts that shuts out Jesus. They prize something higher than the truth, and their hearts are not prepared to receive Jesus. Individuals are tested and proved a length of time to see if they will sacrifice their idols. . . . Those who come up to every point, and stand every test, and overcome, be the price what it may, have heeded the counsel of the True Witness, and they will receive the latter rain, and thus be fitted for translation.

God proves His people in this world. . . . Here, in this world, in these last days, persons will show what power affects their hearts and controls their actions. If it is the power of divine truth, it will lead to good works. It will elevate the receiver, and make him noblehearted and generous, like his divine Lord. . . .

Young and old, God is now testing you. You are deciding your own eternal destiny.[5]

AN INFALLIBLE GUIDE

Be ye doers of the word, and not hearers only, deceiving your own selves. James 1:22.

God calls upon those who know His will to be doers of His word. Weakness, halfheartedness, and indecision provoke the assaults of Satan; and those who permit these traits to grow will be borne helplessly down by the surging waves of temptation. Everyone who professes the name of Christ is required to grow up to the full stature of Christ, the Christian's living head.

We all need a guide through the many strait places in life as much as the sailor needs a pilot over the sandy bar or up the rocky river, and where is this guide to be found? We point you . . . to the Bible. Inspired of God, written by holy men, it points out with great clearness and precision the duties of both old and young. It elevates the mind, softens the heart, and imparts gladness and holy joy to the spirit. The Bible presents a perfect standard of character; it is an infallible guide under all circumstances, even to the end of the journey of life. Take it as the man of your counsel, the rule of your daily life. . . .

In the Scriptures thousands of gems of truth lie hidden from the surface seeker. The mine of truth is never exhausted. The more you search the Scriptures with humble hearts, the greater will be your interest, and the more you will feel like exclaiming with Paul: "O the depth of the riches both of the wisdom and knowledge of God! how unsearchable are his judgments, and his ways past finding out!"

Every day you should learn something new from the Scriptures. Search them as for hid treasures, for they contain the words of eternal life. Pray for wisdom and understanding to comprehend these holy writings. If you would do this you would find new glories in the word of God; you would feel that you had received new and precious light on subjects connected with the truth, and the Scriptures would be constantly receiving a new value in your estimation. . . .

Be diligent in the use of every means of grace, that you may be transformed in character and may grow up to the full stature of men and women in Christ Jesus.[6]

44

READY TO ANSWER

Sanctify the Lord God in your hearts: and be ready always to give an answer to every man that asketh you a reason of the hope that is in you with meekness and fear. 1 Peter 3:15.

I have been shown that many who profess to have a knowledge of present truth know not what they believe. They do not understand the evidences of their faith. They have no just appreciation of the work for the present time. When the time of trial shall come, there are men now preaching to others who will find, upon examining the positions they hold, that there are many things for which they can give no satisfactory reason. Until thus tested they know not their great ignorance. And there are many in the church who take it for granted that they understand what they believe; but, until controversy arises, they do not know their own weakness. When separated from those of like faith and compelled to stand singly and alone to explain their belief, they will be surprised to see how confused are their ideas of what they had accepted as truth. . . .

God will arouse His people; if other means fail, heresies will come in among them, which will sift them, separating the chaff from the wheat. The Lord calls upon all who believe His word to awake out of sleep. Precious light has come, appropriate for this time. . . . Believers are not to rest in suppositions and ill-defined ideas of what constitutes truth. Their faith must be firmly founded upon the word of God so that when the testing time shall come and they are brought before councils to answer for their faith they may be able to give a reason for the hope that is in them, with meekness and fear.[7]

The servants of Christ are to prepare no set speech to present when brought to trial for their faith. Their preparation is to be made day by day, in treasuring up in their hearts the precious truths of God's word, in feeding upon the teaching of Christ, and through prayer strengthening their faith; then, when brought into trial, the Holy Spirit will bring to their remembrance the very truths that will reach the hearts of those who shall come to hear.

God will flash the knowledge obtained by diligent searching of the Scriptures, into their memory at the very time when it is needed.[8]

THE FEAST THAT SATISFIES

Blessed are they which do hunger and thirst after righteousness: for they shall be filled. Matt. 5:6.

Let those men and women who are satisfied with their dwarfed, crippled condition in divine things be suddenly transported to heaven and for an instant witness the high, the holy state of perfection that ever abides there—every soul filled with love; every countenance beaming with joy; . . . could such persons, I ask, mingle with the heavenly throng, participate in their songs, and endure the pure, exalted, transporting glory that emanates from God and the Lamb? Oh, no! . . .

Those who have trained the mind to delight in spiritual exercises are the ones who can be translated and not be overwhelmed with the purity and transcendent glory of heaven. You may have a good knowledge of the arts, you may have an acquaintance with the sciences, you may excel in music and in penmanship, your manners may please your associates, but what have these things to do with a preparation for heaven? What have they to do to prepare you to stand before the tribunal of God?

Be not deceived. God is not mocked. Nothing but holiness will prepare you for heaven. It is sincere, experimental piety alone that can give you a pure, elevated character and enable you to enter into the presence of God, who dwelleth in light unapproachable. The heavenly character must be acquired on earth, or it can never be acquired at all.[9]

Desires for goodness and true holiness are right so far as they go; but if you stop here, they will avail nothing. Good purposes are right, but will prove of no avail unless resolutely carried out. Many will be lost while hoping and desiring to be Christians; but they made no earnest effort, therefore they will be weighed in the balances and found wanting. The will must be exercised in the right direction. I *will* be a wholehearted Christian. I *will* know the length and breadth, the height and depth, of perfect love.

Listen to the words of Jesus: "Blessed are they which do hunger and thirst after righteousness: for they shall be filled." Ample provisions are made by Christ to satisfy the soul that hungers and thirsts for righteousness.[10]

MORAL INDEPENDENCE

Wherefore come out from among them, and be ye separate, saith the Lord, and touch not the unclean thing; and I will receive you, and will be a Father unto you, and ye shall be my sons and daughters, saith the Lord Almighty. 2 Cor. 6:17, 18.

Many today have veils upon their faces. These veils are sympathy with the customs and practices of the world, which hide from them the glory of the Lord. God desires us to keep our eyes fixed upon Him, that we may lose sight of the things of this world.

As the truth is brought into practical life, the standard is to be elevated higher and higher to meet the requirements of the Bible. This will necessitate opposition to the fashions, customs, practices, and maxims of the world. Worldly influences, like the waves of the sea, beat against the followers of Christ to sweep them away from the true principles of His meekness and grace; but we are to stand as firm as a rock to principle. It will require moral courage to do this, and those whose souls are not riveted to the eternal Rock will be swept away by the worldly current. We can stand firm only as our life is hid with Christ in God. Moral independence is wholly in place when opposing the world. By conforming entirely to the will of God, we shall be placed upon vantage ground, and shall see the necessity of decided separation from the customs and practices of the world. We are not to elevate our standard just a little above the world's standard, but we are to make the distinction decidedly apparent.
. . .

It is no easy matter to gain the priceless treasure of eternal life. No one can do this and drift with the current of the world. He must come out from the world and be separate and touch not the unclean. No one can act like a worldling without being carried down by the current of the world. No one will make any upward progress without persevering effort. He who would overcome must hold fast to Christ. He must not look back, but keep the eye ever upward, gaining one grace after another. Individual vigilance is the price of safety. . . .

The end of all things is at hand. There is need now of men armed and equipped to battle for God.[11]

ANY IDOLS HERE?

Little children, keep yourselves from idols. 1 John 5:21.

Every true child of God will be sifted as wheat, and in the sifting process every cherished pleasure which diverts the mind from God must be sacrificed. In many families the mantel shelves, stands, and tables are filled with ornaments and pictures. . . . Thus the thoughts, which should be upon God and heavenly interests, are brought down to common things. Is not this a species of idolatry? Should not the money thus spent have been used to bless humanity, to relieve the suffering, to clothe the naked, and to feed the hungry? Should it not be placed in the Lord's treasury to advance His cause and build up His kingdom in the earth?

This matter is of great importance, and it is urged upon you to save you from the sin of idolatry. Blessing would come to your souls if you would obey the word spoken by the Holy One of Israel, "Thou shalt have no other gods before me." Many are creating unnecessary cares and anxieties for themselves by devoting time and thought to the unnecessary ornaments with which their houses are filled. The power of God is needed to arouse them from this devotion; for to all intents and purposes it is idolatry.

He who searches the heart, desires to win His people from every species of idolatry. Let the Word of God, the blessed book of life, occupy the tables now filled with useless ornaments. Spend your money in buying books that will be the means of enlightening the mind in regard to present truth. . . . Grasp the Word of the Lord as the treasure of infinite wisdom and love; this is the Guidebook that points out the path to heaven. . . .

O that you would search the Scriptures with prayerful hearts, and a spirit of surrender to God! O that you would search your hearts as with a lighted candle, and discover and break the finest thread that binds you to worldly habits, which divert the mind from God! Plead with God to show you every practice that draws your thoughts and affections from Him. God has given His holy law to man as His measure of character. By this law you may see and overcome every defect in your character. You may sever yourself from every idol, and link yourself to the throne of God by the golden chain of grace and truth.[12]

SEARCH YOUR OWN HEART

Examine yourselves, to see whether you are holding to your faith. Test yourselves. Do you not realize that Jesus Christ is in you?—unless indeed you fail to meet the test! 2 Cor. 13:5, R.S.V.

Nothing is more treacherous than the deceitfulness of sin. It is the god of this world that deludes, and blinds, and leads to destruction. Satan does not enter with his array of temptations at once. He disguises these temptations with a semblance of good. . . . Beguiled souls take one step, then are prepared for the next. . . . Oh, how Satan watches to see his bait taken so readily, and to see souls walking in the very path he has prepared! . . .

There is a necessity for close self-examination, and to closely investigate in the light of God's word, Am I sound, or am I rotten, at heart? Am I renewed in Christ, or am I still carnal at heart, with an outside, new dress put on? Rein yourself up to the tribunal of God, and see as in the light of God if there is any secret sin, any iniquity, any idol you have not sacrificed. Pray . . . as you have never prayed before, that you may not be deluded by Satan's devices; that you may not be given up to a heedless, careless, and vain spirit. . . .

One of the sins that constitute one of the signs of the last days, is that professed Christians are lovers of pleasure more than lovers of God. Deal truly with your own souls. Search carefully. How few, after a faithful examination, can look up to Heaven and say, " . . . I am not a lover of pleasure more than a lover of God." How few can say, "I am dead to the world, . . . and when He who is my life shall appear, then shall I also appear with Him in glory."

The love and grace of God! Oh precious grace! more valuable than fine gold. It elevates and ennobles the spirit beyond all other principles. It sets the heart and affections upon Heaven. While those around us may be engaged in worldly vanity, pleasure-seeking, and folly, the conversation is in heaven, whence we look for the Saviour; the soul is reaching out after God for pardon and peace, for righteousness and true holiness. Converse with God and contemplation of things above transform the soul into the likeness of Christ.[13]

SEARCHING QUESTIONS

Who shall ascend into the hill of the Lord? or who shall stand in his holy place? He that hath clean hands, and a pure heart; who hath not lifted up his soul unto vanity, nor sworn deceitfully. Ps. 24:3, 4.

A soul united with Christ . . . will war against all transgression and every approach of sin. He becomes every day more like a bright and shining light, and more victorious. He goes on from strength to strength, not from weakness to weakness.

Let no one deceive his own soul in this matter. If you harbor pride, self-esteem, a love for the supremacy, vainglory, unholy ambition, murmuring, discontent, bitterness, evil-speaking, lying, deception, slandering, you have not Christ abiding in your heart. . . . You must have a Christian character that will stand. . . .

There must be thorough conversions among those who claim to believe the truth, or they will fall in the day of trial. God's people must reach a high standard. They must be a holy nation, a peculiar people, a chosen generation—zealous of good works. Christ has not died for you that you may possess the passions, tastes, and habits of men of the world. . . .

No man enters the portals of glory but he who sets his heart thitherward. Then let the questions come home, Do you mind earthly things? Are your thoughts pure? Are you breathing the atmosphere of heaven? Do you carry with you the miasma of pollution? . . . Are you earnest and devoted, serving God with purity and in the beauty of holiness? Ask sincerely, Am I a child of God, or am I not? . . .

We need a thorough reformation in all our churches. The converting power of God must come into the church. . . . Put not off the day of preparation. Slumber not in a state of unpreparedness, having no oil in your vessels with your lamps. . . . Let not the question remain in perilous uncertainty. Ask yourselves earnestly, Am I among the saved, or the unsaved? Shall I stand, or shall I not stand? He only that hath clean hands and a pure heart shall stand in that day.[14]

It is the privilege of every son of God to be a true Christian moment by moment; then he has all heaven enlisted on his side.[15]

DARE YOU BE DIFFERENT?

Ye are a chosen generation, a royal priesthood, an holy nation, a peculiar people; that ye should shew forth the praises of him who hath called you out of darkness into his marvellous light. 1 Peter 2:9.

The warning that the Son of man is soon to come in the clouds of heaven has become to many a familiar tale. They have left the waiting, watching position. The selfish, worldly spirit manifested in the life reveals the sentiment of the heart, "My lord delayeth his coming." . . .

The same spirit of selfishness, of conformity to the practices of the world, exists in our day as in Noah's. Many who profess to be children of God follow their worldly pursuits with an intensity that gives the lie to their profession. They will be planting and building, buying and selling, eating and drinking, marrying and giving in marriage, up to the last moment of their probation. This is the condition of a large number of our own people. . . .

My soul is burdened as I see the great want of spirituality among us. The fashions and customs of the world, pride, love of amusement, love of display, extravagance in dress, in houses, in lands—these are robbing the treasury of God, turning to the gratification of self the means which should be used to send forth the light of truth to the world. . . .

The children of the light and of the day are not to gather about them the shades of night and darkness which encompass the workers of iniquity. On the contrary, they are to stand faithfully at their post of duty as light bearers, gathering light from God to shed upon those in darkness. The Lord requires His people to maintain their integrity, touching not—that is, imitating not—the practices of the ungodly.

Christians will be in this world "an holy nation, a peculiar people," showing forth the praises of Him who hath called them "out of darkness into his marvellous light." This light is not to grow dim, but to shine brighter and brighter unto the perfect day. . . . The thrilling truth that has been sounding in our ears for many years, "The Lord is at hand; be ye also ready," is no less the truth today than when we first heard the message.[16]

51

UPROOT EVERY SEED OF DOUBT

Cast not away therefore your confidence, which hath great recompence of reward. For ye have need of patience, that, after ye have done the will of God, ye might receive the promise. . . . We are not of them who draw back unto perdition; but of them that believe to the saving of the soul. Heb. 10:35-39.

I saw that we are now in the shaking time. Satan is working with all his power to wrest souls from the hand of Christ and cause them to trample underfoot the Son of God. . . .

Character is being developed. Angels of God are weighing moral worth. God is testing and proving His people. These words were presented to me by the angel: "Take heed, brethren, lest there be in any of you an evil heart of unbelief, in departing from the living God. But exhort one another daily, while it is called To day; lest any of you be hardened through the deceitfulness of sin. For we are made partakers of Christ, if we hold the *beginning of our confidence stedfast unto the end.*"

God is displeased that any of His people who have known the power of His grace should talk their doubts, and by thus doing make themselves a channel for Satan to transmit his suggestions to other minds. A seed of unbelief and evil sown is not readily rooted up. Satan nourishes it every hour, and it flourishes and becomes strong. A good seed sown needs to be nourished, watered, and tenderly cared for; because every poisonous influence is thrown about it to hinder its growth and cause it to die. Satan's efforts are more powerful now than ever before, for he knows that his time to deceive is short. . . .

God's people will be sifted, even as corn is sifted in a sieve, until all the chaff is separated from the pure kernels of grain. We are to look to Christ for an example and imitate the humble pattern. . . .

I was shown the saints' reward, the immortal inheritance. Then I was shown how much God's people had endured for the truth's sake, and that they would count heaven cheap enough. They reckoned that the sufferings of this present time were not worthy to be compared with the glory which should be revealed in them. The people of God in these last days will be tried. But soon their last trial will come, and then they will receive the gift of eternal life.[17]

SPIRITUAL GIANT OR DWARF?

Having therefore these promises, dearly beloved, let us cleanse ourselves from all filthiness of the flesh and spirit, perfecting holiness in the fear of God. 2 Cor. 7:1.

The Lord reproves and corrects the people who profess to keep His law. He points out their sins and lays open their iniquity because He wishes to separate all sin and wickedness from them, that they may perfect holiness in His fear and be prepared to die in the Lord or to be translated to heaven. . . .

God will accept nothing but purity and holiness; one spot, one wrinkle, one defect in the character, will forever debar them from heaven, with all its glories and treasures.[18]

Most professed Christians have no sense of the spiritual strength they might obtain were they as ambitious, zealous, and persevering to gain a knowledge of divine things as they are to obtain the paltry, perishable things of this life. The masses professing to be Christians have been satisfied to be spiritual dwarfs. They have no disposition to make it their object to seek first the kingdom of God and His righteousness; hence godliness is a hidden mystery to them, they cannot understand it. They know not Christ by experimental knowledge.[19]

Ample provisions have been made for all who sincerely, earnestly, and thoughtfully set about the work of perfecting holiness in the fear of God. Strength, grace, and glory have been provided through Christ, to be brought by ministering angels to the heirs of salvation. None are so low, so corrupt and vile, that they cannot find in Jesus, who died for them, strength, purity, and righteousness, if they will put away their sins, cease their course of iniquity, and turn with full purpose of heart to the living God. He is waiting to strip them of their garments, stained and polluted by sin, and to put upon them the white, bright robes of righteousness; and He bids them live and not die. In Him they may flourish. Their branches will not wither nor be fruitless. If they abide in Him, they can draw sap and nourishment from Him, be imbued with His Spirit, walk even as He walked, overcome as He overcame, and be exalted to His own right hand.[20]

WISE OR FOOLISH?

Then shall the kingdom of heaven be likened unto ten virgins, which took their lamps, and went forth to meet the bridegroom. And five of them were wise, and five were foolish. Matt. 25:1, 2.

We are not to rest in the idea that because we are church-members we are saved, while we give no evidence that we are conformed to the image of Christ, while we cling to our old habits, and weave our fabric with the threads of worldly ideas and customs. . . .

The ten virgins are watching in the evening of this earth's history. All claim to be Christians. All have a call, a name, a lamp, and all claim to be doing God's service. All apparently watch for His appearing. But five are wanting. Five will be found surprised, dismayed, outside the banquet hall.[21]

We are represented either by the wise or by the foolish virgins. There are many who will not remain at the feet of Jesus, and learn of Him. They have not a knowledge of His ways; they are not prepared for His coming. They have made a pretense of waiting for their Lord. They have not watched and prayed with that faith which works by love and purifies the soul. They have lived a life of carelessness. They have heard and assented to the truth, but they have never brought it into their practical life. The oil of grace is not feeding their lamps, and they are not prepared to enter into the marriage supper of the Lamb.[22]

Be not like the foolish virgins, who take for granted that the promises of God are theirs, while they do not follow the injunctions of Christ. Christ teaches us that profession is nothing. "If any man will come after me," He says, "let him deny himself, and take up his cross daily, and follow me.". . .

When we stand the test of God in the refining, purifying process; when the furnace fire consumes the dross, and the true gold of a purified character appears, we may still say, with Paul, "Not as though I had already attained, either were already perfect: but I follow after. . . . This one thing I do, forgetting those things which are behind, and reaching forth unto those things which are before, I press toward the mark for the prize of the high calling of God in Christ Jesus." [23]

NOW—ALWAYS NOW

Watch therefore, for ye know neither the day nor the hour wherein the Son of man cometh. Matt. 25:13.

The coming of Christ will be as it were at midnight, when all are sleeping. It will be well for every one to have his accounts all straightened up before sunset. All his works should be right, all his dealings just, between himself and his fellow-men. All dishonesty, all sinful practices should be put far away. The oil of grace should be in our vessels with our lamps. . . . Sad indeed will be the condition of the soul who has had a form of godliness but has denied the power thereof; who has called Christ, Lord, Lord, and yet who has not His image and superscription. . . .

God graciously grants a day of probation, a time of test and trial. He gives the invitation: "Seek ye the Lord while he may be found, call ye upon him while he is near.". . .

To-day the voice of mercy is calling, and Jesus is drawing men by the cords of His love; but the day will come when Jesus will put on the garments of vengeance. . . . The wickedness of the world is increasing every day, and when a certain line is reached, the register will be closed, and the account settled. There will be no more a sacrifice for sin. The Lord cometh. Long has mercy extended a hand of love, of patience and forbearance, toward a guilty world. The invitation has been given, "Let him take hold of my strength. . . ." But men have presumed upon His mercy and refused His grace.

Why has the Lord so long delayed His coming? The whole host of heaven is waiting to fulfil the last work for this lost world, and yet the work waits. It is because the few who profess to have the oil of grace in their vessels with their lamps, have not become burning and shining lights in the world. It is because missionaries are few. . . .

Every week counts one week less, every day one day nearer to the appointed time of the judgment. Alas that so many have only a spasmodic religion—a religion dependent upon feeling and governed by emotion. "He that endureth to the end shall be saved." Then see that you have the oil of grace in your hearts. The possession of this will make every difference with you in the judgment.[24]

THE LAST WATCH

Watch ye therefore: for ye know not when the master of the house cometh, at even, or at midnight, or at the cockcrowing, or in the morning: lest coming suddenly he find you sleeping. Mark 13:35, 36.

A company was presented before me. . . . Their eyes were directed heavenward, and the words of their Master were upon their lips: "What I say unto you I say unto all, Watch.". . . The Lord intimates a delay before the morning finally dawns. But He would not have them give way to weariness, nor relax their earnest watchfulness, because the morning does not open upon them as soon as they expected. . . .

I saw that it was impossible to have the affections and interests engrossed in worldly cares, to be increasing earthly possessions, and yet be in a waiting, watching position, as our Saviour has commanded. Said the angel: "They can secure but one world. In order to acquire the heavenly treasure, they must sacrifice the earthly. They cannot have both worlds.". . .

I saw that watch after watch was in the past. Because of this, should there be a lack of vigilance? Oh, no! There is the greater necessity of unceasing watchfulness, for now the moments are fewer than before the passing of the first watch. . . . If we watched with unabated vigilance then, how much more need of double watchfulness in the second watch. The passing of the second watch has brought us to the third, and now it is inexcusable to abate our watchfulness. The third watch calls for threefold earnestness. To become impatient now would be to lose all our earnest, persevering watching heretofore. The long night of gloom is trying; but the morning is deferred in mercy, because if the Master should come, so many would be found unready. God's unwillingness to have His people perish has been the reason for so long delay. . . .

The difference between those who love the world and those who love Christ is so plain as to be unmistakable. While worldlings are all earnestness and ambition to secure earthly treasure, God's people are not conformed to the world, but show by their earnest, watching, waiting position that they are transformed; that their home is not in this world, but that they are seeking a better country, even a heavenly.[25]

ONLY ONE SAFE COURSE

Watch and pray, that ye enter not into temptation. Matt. 26:41.

What shall I say to arouse the remnant people of God? . . . I warn all who profess the name of Christ to closely examine themselves and make full and thorough confession of all their wrongs, that they may go beforehand to judgment, and that the recording angel may write pardon opposite their names. My brother, my sister, if these precious moments of mercy are not improved, you will be left without excuse. If you make no special effort to arouse, if you will not manifest zeal in repenting, these golden moments will soon pass, and you will be weighed in the balance and found wanting.[26]

In the warning to "watch and pray," Jesus has indicated the only safe course. There is need of watchfulness. Our own hearts are deceitful; we are compassed with the weaknesses and frailties of humanity, and Satan is intent to destroy. We may be off our guard, but our adversary is never idle. Knowing his tireless vigilance, let us not sleep, as do others, but "watch and be sober." The spirit and influence of the world must be met, but they must not be allowed to take possession of the mind and heart.[27]

Closely examine your own heart as in the light of eternity. Hide nothing from your examination. Search, oh! search, as for your life, and condemn yourself, pass judgment upon yourself, and then by faith claim the cleansing blood of Christ to remove the stains from your Christian character. Do not flatter or excuse yourself. Deal truly with your own soul. And then as you view yourself a sinner, fall, all broken, at the foot of the cross. Jesus will receive you, all polluted as you are, and will wash you in His blood, and cleanse you from all pollution, and make you fit for the society of heavenly angels, in a pure, harmonious heaven. There is no jar, no discord, there. All is health, happiness, and joy.[28]

This world is a training school for the higher school, this life a preparation for the life to come. Here we are to be prepared for entrance into the heavenly courts. Here we are to receive and believe and practice the truth until we are made ready for a home with the saints in light.[29]

THE FAITH THAT WORKS

The end of all things is at hand: be ye therefore sober, and watch unto prayer. 1 Peter 4:7.

Do you believe that the end of all things is at hand, that the scenes of this earth's history are fast closing? If so, show your faith by your works. A man will show all the faith he has. Some think they have a good degree of faith, when if they have any, it is dead, for it is not sustained by works. "Faith, if it hath not works, is dead, being alone." Few have that genuine faith which works by love and purifies the soul. But all who are accounted worthy of everlasting life must obtain a moral fitness for the same. "Beloved, now are we the sons of God, and it doth not yet appear what we shall be: but we know that, when he shall appear, we shall be like him; for we shall see him as he is. And every man that hath this hope in him purifieth himself, even as he is pure." This is the work before you. . . .

You must experience a death to self, and must live unto God. "If ye then be risen with Christ, seek those things which are above, where Christ sitteth on the right hand of God." Self is not to be consulted. Pride, self-love, selfishness, avarice, covetousness, love of the world, hatred, suspicion, jealousy, evil surmisings, must all be subdued and sacrificed forever. When Christ shall appear, it will not be to correct these evils and then give a moral fitness for His coming. This preparation must all be made before He comes. It should be a subject of thought, of study, and earnest inquiry, What shall we do to be saved? What shall be our conduct that we may show ourselves approved of God?

When tempted to murmur, censure, and indulge in fretfulness, wounding those around you, and in so doing wounding your own soul, oh! let the deep, earnest, anxious inquiry come from your soul, Shall I stand without fault before the throne of God? Only the faultless will be there. None will be translated to heaven while their hearts are filled with the rubbish of earth. Every defect in the moral character must first be remedied, every stain removed by the cleansing blood of Christ, and all the unlovely, unlovable traits of character overcome.[30]

BEWARE OF SATAN'S AGENTS

Now the Spirit speaketh expressly, that in the latter times some shall depart from the faith, giving heed to seducing spirits, and doctrines of devils. 1 Tim. 4:1.

After the passing of the time in 1844, we had fanaticism of every kind to meet. . . . The experience of the past will be repeated. In the future Satan's superstitions will assume new forms. Errors will be presented in a pleasing and flattering manner. False theories, clothed with garments of light, will be presented to God's people. Thus Satan will try to deceive, if possible, the very elect. Most seducing influences will be exerted; minds will be hypnotized.

Corruptions of every type, similar to those existing among the antediluvians, will be brought in to take minds captive. The exaltation of nature as God, the unrestrained license of the human will, the counsel of the ungodly—these Satan uses as his agencies to bring about certain ends. He will employ the power of mind over mind to carry out his designs. The most sorrowful thought of all is that under his deceptive influence men will have a form of godliness, without having a real connection with God. Like Adam and Eve, who ate the fruit from the tree of the knowledge of good and evil, many are even now feeding upon the deceptive morsels of error.

Satanic agencies are clothing false theories in an attractive garb, even as Satan in the Garden of Eden concealed his identity from our first parents by speaking through the serpent. These agencies are instilling into human minds that which in reality is deadly error. The hypnotic influence of Satan will rest upon those who turn from the plain word of God to pleasing fables.

It is those who have had the most light that Satan most assiduously seeks to ensnare. He knows that if he can deceive them, they will, under his control, clothe sin with garments of righteousness, and lead many astray.

I say to all: Be on your guard; for as an angel of light Satan is walking in every assembly of Christian workers, and in every church, trying to win the members to his side. I am bidden to give to the people of God the warning: "Be not deceived; God is not mocked." Gal. 6:7.[31]

TEMPTATIONS IN DISGUISE

I know this, that after my departing shall grievous wolves enter in among you, not sparing the flock. Also of your own selves shall men arise, speaking perverse things, to draw away disciples after them. Acts 20:29, 30.

God has not passed His people by and chosen one solitary man here and another there as the only ones worthy to be entrusted with His truth. He does not give one man new light contrary to the established faith of the body. In every reform men have arisen making this claim. . . .

One accepts some new and original idea which does not seem to conflict with the truth. He . . . dwells upon it until it seems to him to be clothed with beauty and importance, for Satan has power to give this false appearance. At last it becomes the all-absorbing theme, the one great point around which everything centers; and the truth is uprooted from the heart. . . .

I warn you to beware of these side issues, whose tendency is to divert the mind from the truth. Error is never harmless. It never sanctifies, but always brings confusion and dissension. . . .

There are a thousand temptations in disguise prepared for those who have the light of truth; and the only safety for any of us is in receiving no new doctrine, no new interpretation of the Scriptures, without first submitting it to brethren of experience. Lay it before them in a humble, teachable spirit, with earnest prayer; and if they see no light in it, yield to their judgment. . . .

Satan is constantly at work; but few have any idea of his activity and subtlety. The people of God must be prepared to withstand the wily foe. It is this resistance that Satan dreads. He knows better than we do the limit of his power and how easily he can be overcome if we resist and face him. Through divine strength the weakest saint is more than a match for him and all his angels, and if brought to the test he would be able to prove his superior power. Therefore Satan's step is noiseless, his movements stealthy, and his batteries masked. He does not venture to show himself openly, lest he arouse the Christian's dormant energies and send him to God in prayer.[32]

WHY CHRIST DELAYS HIS COMING

But this I do say, brothers. The appointed time has grown very short. 1 Cor. 7:29, Goodspeed.

The angels of God in their messages to men represent time as very short. Thus it has always been presented to me. It is true that time has continued longer than we expected in the early days of this message. Our Saviour did not appear as soon as we hoped. But has the word of the Lord failed? Never! It should be remembered that the promises and threatenings of God are alike conditional.

God had committed to His people a work to be accomplished on earth. The third angel's message was to be given, the minds of believers were to be directed to the heavenly sanctuary, where Christ had entered to make atonement for His people. The Sabbath reform was to be carried forward. The breach in the law of God must be made up. The message must be proclaimed with a loud voice, that all the inhabitants of earth might receive the warning. The people of God must purify their souls through obedience to the truth, and be prepared to stand without fault before Him at His coming.

Had Adventists, after the great disappointment in 1844, held fast their faith, and followed on unitedly in the opening providence of God, receiving the message of the third angel and in the power of the Holy Spirit proclaiming it to the world, . . . the Lord would have wrought mightily with their efforts, the work would have been completed, and Christ would have come ere this to receive His people to their reward.

But in the period of doubt and uncertainty that followed the disappointment, many of the advent believers yielded their faith. . . . Thus the work was hindered, and the world was left in darkness. . . .

For forty years did unbelief, murmuring, and rebellion shut out ancient Israel from the land of Canaan. The same sins have delayed the entrance of modern Israel into the heavenly Canaan. In neither case were the promises of God at fault. It is the unbelief, the worldliness, unconsecration, and strife among the Lord's professed people that have kept us in this world of sin and sorrow so many years.[33]

A GOAL TO REACH

The very God of peace sanctify you wholly; and I pray God your whole spirit and soul and body be preserved blameless unto the coming of our Lord Jesus Christ. 1 Thess. 5:23.

When Paul wrote, "And the very God of peace sanctify you wholly," he did not exhort his brethren to aim at a standard which it was impossible for them to reach; he did not pray that they might have blessings which it was not the will of God to give. He knew that all who would be fitted to meet Christ in peace, must possess a pure and holy character.[34]

If Seventh-day Adventists practiced what they profess to believe, if they were sincere health reformers, they would indeed be a spectacle to the world, to angels, and to men. And they would show a far greater zeal for the salvation of those who are ignorant of the truth.

Greater reforms should be seen among the people who claim to be looking for the soon appearing of Christ. Health reform is to do among our people a work which it has not yet done. There are those who ought to be awake to the danger of meat-eating, who are still eating the flesh of animals, thus endangering the physical, mental, and spiritual health. Many who are now only half converted on the question of meat-eating will go from God's people, to walk no more with them.[35]

The controlling power of appetite will prove the ruin of thousands, when, if they had conquered on this point, they would have had moral power to gain the victory over every other temptation of Satan. But those who are slaves to appetite will fail in perfecting Christian character. The continual transgression of man for six thousand years has brought sickness, pain, and death as its fruits. And as we near the close of time, Satan's temptation to indulge appetite will be more powerful and more difficult to overcome.[36]

Again and again I have been shown that God is trying to lead us back, step by step, to His original design—that man should subsist upon the natural products of the earth. Among those who are waiting for the coming of the Lord, meat-eating will eventually be done away; flesh will cease to form a part of their diet. We should ever keep this end in view, and endeavor to work steadily toward it.[37]

NO TIME TO DO THE DEVIL'S WORK

Seeing then that all these things shall be dissolved, what manner of persons ought ye to be in all holy conversation and godliness, looking for and hasting unto the coming of the day of God. 2 Peter 3:11, 12.

It is essential that all shall know what atmosphere surrounds their own souls, whether they are in co-partnership with the enemy of righteousness, and unconsciously doing his work, or whether they are yoked up with Christ, doing His work.. . . .

Satan would be pleased to have anyone and everyone become his allies in the work of weakening the confidence of brother in brother, and sowing discord among those who profess to believe the truth. Satan can accomplish his purpose most successfully through professed friends of Christ who are not walking and working in Christ's lines. . . .

This is the day of the Lord's preparation. We have no time now to talk unbelief or . . . to do the devil's work. Let everyone beware of unsettling the faith of others by sowing seeds of envy, jealousy, disunion; for God hears the words, and He judges, not by assertions which are yea and nay, but by the fruit of one's course of action. . . .

As yet the four winds are held until the servants of God shall be sealed in their foreheads. Then the powers of earth will marshal their forces for the last great battle. How carefully we should improve the little remaining period of our probation! How earnestly we should examine ourselves! . . .

It is discipline of spirit, cleanness of heart and thought that is needed. This is of more value than brilliant talent, tact, or knowledge. An ordinary mind, trained to obey a "Thus saith the Lord," is better qualified for God's work than are those who have capabilities, but do not employ them rightly. . . . Men may take pride of their knowledge of worldly things; but if they have not a knowledge of the true God, of Christ, the Way, the Truth, and the Life, they are deplorably ignorant, and their knowledge will perish with them. Secular knowledge is power; but the knowledge of the Word, which has a transforming influence upon the human mind, is imperishable.[38]

SATAN'S LAST CAMPAIGN

Little children, it is the last time: and as ye have heard that antichrist shall come, even now are there many antichrists; whereby we know that it is the last time. 1 John 2:18.

The enemy is preparing for his last campaign against the church. He has so concealed himself from view that many can hardly believe that he exists, much less can they be convinced of his amazing activity and power. . . .

Man is Satan's captive and is naturally inclined to follow his suggestions and do his bidding. He has in himself no power to oppose effectual resistance to evil. It is only as Christ abides in him by living faith . . . that man may venture to face so terrible a foe. Every other means of defense is utterly vain. It is only through Christ that Satan's power is limited. This is a momentous truth that all should understand. Satan is busy every moment, going to and fro, walking up and down in the earth, seeking whom he may devour. But the earnest prayer of faith will baffle his strongest efforts. . . .

Satan hopes to involve the remnant people of God in the general ruin that is coming upon the earth. As the coming of Christ draws nigh, he will be more determined and decisive in his efforts to overthrow them. Men and women will arise professing to have some new light or some new revelation whose tendency is to unsettle faith in the old landmarks. Their doctrines will not bear the test of God's word, yet souls will be deceived. False reports will be circulated, and some will be taken in this snare. . . . We cannot be too watchful against every form of error, for Satan is constantly seeking to draw men from the truth. . . .

Some men have no firmness of character. They are like a ball of putty and can be pressed into any conceivable shape. . . . This weakness, indecision, and inefficiency must be overcome. There is an indomitableness about true Christian character which cannot be molded or subdued by adverse circumstances. Men must have moral backbone, an integrity which cannot be flattered, bribed, or terrified. . . .

God has set bounds that Satan cannot pass. Our most holy faith is this barrier; and if we build ourselves up in the faith, we shall be safe in the keeping of the Mighty One.[39]

THROUGH HEAVEN'S GATES

By faith Enoch was translated that he should not see death; . . . for before his translation he had this testimony, that he pleased God. Heb. 11:5.

We are living in an evil age. . . . Because iniquity abounds, the love of many waxes cold. Enoch walked with God three hundred years. Now the shortness of time seems to be urged as a motive to seek righteousness. Should it be necessary that the terrors of the day of God be held before us in order to compel us to right action? Enoch's case is before us. Hundreds of years he walked with God. He lived in a corrupt age, when moral pollution was teeming all around him; yet he trained his mind to devotion, to love purity. His conversation was upon heavenly things. He educated his mind to run in this channel, and he bore the impress of the divine. . . .

Enoch had temptations as well as we. He was surrounded with society no more friendly to righteousness than is that which surrounds us. The atmosphere he breathed was tainted with sin and corruption, the same as ours; yet he lived a life of holiness. He was unsullied with the prevailing sins of the age in which he lived. So may we remain pure and uncorrupted. He was a representative of the saints who live amid the perils and corruptions of the last days. For his faithful obedience to God he was translated. So, also, the faithful, who are alive and remain, will be translated.[40]

"Blessed are the pure in heart: for they shall see God." For three hundred years Enoch had been seeking purity of heart, that he might be in harmony with heaven. For three centuries he had walked with God. Day by day he had longed for a closer union; nearer and nearer had grown the communion, until God took him to Himself. He had stood at the threshold of the eternal world, only a step between him and the land of the blest; and now the portals opened, the walk with God, so long pursued on earth, continued, and he passed through the gates of the holy city, the first from among men to enter there. . . .

To such communion God is calling us. As was Enoch's must be their holiness of character who shall be redeemed from among men at the Lord's second coming.[41]

THE VISION IS SURE

The vision is yet for an appointed time, but at the end it shall speak, and not lie: though it tarry, wait for it; because it will surely come, it will not tarry. Hab. 2:3.

The faith that strengthened Habakkuk and all the holy and the just in those days of deep trial was the same faith that sustains God's people today. In the darkest hours, under circumstances the most forbidding, the Christian believer may keep his soul stayed upon the source of all light and power. Day by day, through faith in God, his hope and courage may be renewed. . . . In the service of God there need be no despondency, no wavering, no fear. The Lord will more than fulfill the highest expectations of those who put their trust in Him. He will give them the wisdom their varied necessities demand.

Of the abundant provision made for every tempted soul, the apostle Paul bears eloquent testimony. To him was given the divine assurance, "My grace is sufficient for thee: for my strength is made perfect in weakness." In gratitude and confidence the tried servant of God responded: "Most gladly therefore will I rather glory in my infirmities, that the power of Christ may rest upon me. Therefore I take pleasure in infirmities, in reproaches, in necessities, in persecutions, in distresses for Christ's sake: for when I am weak, then am I strong." 2 Cor. 12:9, 10.

We must cherish and cultivate the faith of which prophets and apostles have testified—the faith that lays hold on the promises of God and waits for deliverance in His appointed time and way. The sure word of prophecy will meet its final fulfillment in the glorious advent of our Lord and Saviour Jesus Christ, as King of kings and Lord of lords. The time of waiting may seem long, the soul may be oppressed by discouraging circumstances, many in whom confidence has been placed may fall by the way; but with the prophet who endeavored to encourage Judah in a time of unparalleled apostasy, let us confidently declare, "The Lord is in his holy temple: let all the earth keep silence before him."

Let us ever hold in remembrance the cheering message, "The vision is yet for an appointed time, but at the end it shall speak, and not lie: though it tarry, wait for it; because it will surely come, it will not tarry. . . . The just shall live by his faith." [42]

A SAFE REFUGE

Behold, the Lord cometh out of his place to punish the inhabitants of the earth for their iniquity: the earth also shall disclose her blood, and shall no more cover her slain. Isa. 26:21.

There is coming rapidly and surely an almost universal guilt upon the inhabitants of the cities, because of the steady increase of determined wickedness. The corruption that prevails, is beyond the power of the human pen to describe. Every day brings fresh revelations of strife, bribery, and fraud; every day brings its heart-sickening record of violence and lawlessness, of indifference to human suffering, of brutal, fiendish destruction of human life. . . .

Our God is a God of mercy. With long-sufferance and tender compassion He deals with the transgressors of His law. . . . The Lord bears long with men, and with cities, mercifully giving warnings to save them from divine wrath; but a time will come when pleadings for mercy will no longer be heard. . . .

The conditions prevailing in society, and especially in the great cities of the nations, proclaim in thunder tones that the hour of God's judgment is come and that the end of all things earthly is at hand. We are standing on the threshold of the crisis of the ages. In quick succession the judgments of God will follow one another—fire, and flood, and earthquake, with war and bloodshed. . . .

The storm of God's wrath is gathering; and those only will stand who respond to the invitations of mercy, . . . and become sanctified through obedience to the laws of the divine Ruler. The righteous alone will be hid with Christ in God till the desolation be overpast. Let the language of the soul be:

"Other refuge have I none;
Hangs my helpless soul on Thee;
Leave, Oh leave me not alone!
Still support and comfort me.

"Hide me, O my Saviour, hide,
Till the storm of life is past;
Safe into the haven guide;
Oh, receive my soul at last!" [43]

A CRISIS AHEAD

Alas for the day! for the day of the Lord is at hand, and as a destruction from the Almighty shall it come. Joel 1:15.

The prophecies which the great I AM has given in His word, uniting link after link in the chain of events, from eternity in the past to eternity in the future, tell us where we are today in the procession of the ages, and what may be expected in the time to come. All that prophecy has foretold as coming to pass, until the present time, has been traced on the pages of history, and we may be assured that all which is yet to come will be fulfilled in its order.

Today the signs of the times declare that we are standing on the threshold of great and solemn events. Everything in our world is in agitation. Before our eyes is fulfilling the Saviour's prophecy of the events to precede His coming: "Ye shall hear of wars and rumors of wars. . . . Nation shall rise against nation, and kingdom against kingdom: and there shall be famines, and pestilences, and earthquakes, in divers places."

The present is a time of overwhelming interest to all living. Rulers and statesmen, men who occupy positions of trust and authority, thinking men and women of all classes, have their attention fixed upon the events taking place about us. They are watching the relations that exist among the nations. They observe the intensity that is taking possession of every earthly element, and they recognize that something great and decisive is about to take place—that the world is on the verge of a stupendous crisis.

The Bible, and the Bible only, gives a correct view of these things. Here are revealed the great final scenes in the history of our world, . . . the sound of their approach causing the earth to tremble and men's hearts to fail them for fear.[1]

Today men and nations are being tested by the plummet in the hand of Him who makes no mistake. All are by their own choice deciding their destiny, and God is overruling all for the accomplishment of His purposes.[2]

Christians should be preparing for what is soon to break upon the world as an overwhelming surprise, and this preparation they should make by diligently studying the word of God and striving to conform their lives to its precepts.[3]

HEALING FOR SIN-SICK SOULS

The whole head is sick, and the whole heart faint. From the sole of the foot even unto the head there is no soundness in it; but wounds, and bruises, and putrifying sores: they have not been closed, neither bound up, neither mollified with ointment. Isa. 1:5, 6.

There is a remedy for the sin-sick soul. That remedy is in Jesus. Precious Saviour! His grace is sufficient for the weakest; and the strongest must also have His grace or perish.

I saw how this grace could be obtained. Go to your closet, and there alone plead with God: "Create in me a clean heart, O God; and renew a right spirit within me." Be in earnest, be sincere. . . . Jacoblike, wrestle in prayer. Agonize. . . . You must make an effort. . . .

Seek the Lord with all your heart. Come with zeal, and when you sincerely feel that without the help of God you perish, when you pant after Him as the hart panteth after the water brooks, then will the Lord strengthen you speedily. Then will your peace pass all understanding. If you expect salvation, you must pray. Take time. Be not hurried and careless in your prayers. Beg of God to work in you a thorough reformation, that the fruits of His Spirit may dwell in you, and you shine as lights in the world. Be not a hindrance or curse to the cause of God; you can be a help, a blessing. Does Satan tell you that you cannot enjoy salvation full and free? Believe him not.

I saw that it is the privilege of every Christian to enjoy the deep movings of the Spirit of God. A sweet, heavenly peace will pervade the mind, and you will love to meditate upon God and heaven. You will feast upon the glorious promises of His word. . . .

If professed Christians love Jesus better than the world, they will love to speak of Him, their best Friend, in whom their highest affections are centered. He came to their aid when they felt their lost and perishing condition. When weary and heavyladen with sin, they turned unto Him. He removed their burden of guilt and sin, . . . and turned the whole current of their affections. The things they once loved, they now hate; and the things they hated, they now love.

Has this great change taken place in you? [4]

A NEW LIFE

Truly, truly, I say to you, unless one is born of water and the Spirit, he cannot enter the kingdom of God. . . . You must be born anew. John 3:5-7, R.S.V.

He who is trying to reach heaven by his own works in keeping the law is attempting an impossibility. There is no safety for one who has merely a legal religion, a form of godliness. The Christian's life is not a modification or improvement of the old, but a transformation of nature. There is a death to self and sin, and a new life altogether. This change can be brought about only by the effectual working of the Holy Spirit. . . .

A person may not be able to tell the exact time or place, or to trace all the circumstances in the process of conversion; but this does not prove him to be unconverted. By an agency as unseen as the wind, Christ is constantly working upon the heart. Little by little, perhaps unconsciously to the receiver, impressions are made that tend to draw the soul to Christ. . . . Suddenly, as the Spirit comes with more direct appeal, the soul gladly surrenders itself to Jesus. By many this is called sudden conversion; but it is the result of long wooing by the Spirit of God,—a patient, protracted process.

While the wind is itself invisible, it produces effects that are seen and felt. So the work of the Spirit upon the soul will reveal itself in every act of him who has felt its saving power. When the Spirit of God takes possession of the heart, it transforms the life. Sinful thoughts are put away, evil deeds are renounced; love, humility, and peace take the place of anger, envy, and strife. Joy takes the place of sadness, and the countenance reflects the light of heaven. No one sees the hand that lifts the burden, or beholds the light descend from the courts above. The blessing comes when by faith the soul surrenders itself to God. Then that power which no human eye can see creates a new being in the image of God.

It is impossible for finite minds to comprehend the work of redemption. Its mystery exceeds human knowledge; yet he who passes from death to life realizes that it is a divine reality. The beginning of redemption we may know here through a personal experience. Its results reach through the eternal ages.[5]

LIFE'S TOP PRIORITY

Seek ye first the kingdom of God, and his righteousness; and all these things shall be added unto you. Matt. 6:33.

This is the first great object—the kingdom of heaven, the righteousness of Christ. Other objects to be attained should be secondary to these.

Satan will present the path of holiness as difficult while the paths of worldly pleasure are strewed with flowers. In false and flattering colors will the tempter array the world with its pleasures before you. Vanity is one of the strongest traits of our depraved natures, and he knows that he can appeal to it successfully. He will flatter you through his agents. You may receive praise which will gratify your vanity and foster in you pride and self-esteem, and you may think that with such advantages and attractions it really is a great pity for you to come out from the world and be separate, and become a Christian. . . . But consider that the pleasures of earth will have an end, and that which you sow you must also reap. Are personal attractions, ability, or talents too valuable to devote to God, the Author of your being, He who watches over you every moment? Are your qualifications too precious to devote to God?

The young urge that they need something to enliven and divert the mind. I saw that there is pleasure in industry, a satisfaction in pursuing a life of usefulness. Some still urge that they must have something . . . to which the mind can turn for relief and refreshment amid cares and wearing labor. The Christian's hope is just what is needed. Religion will prove to the believer a comforter, a sure guide to the Fountain of true happiness. The young should study the word of God and give themselves to meditation and prayer, and they will find that their spare moments cannot be better employed.

Young friends, you should take time to prove your own selves, whether you are in the love of God. Be diligent to make your calling and election sure.[6]

Seek first the kingdom of God and His righteousness. Make this first and last. Seek most earnestly to know Him whom to know aright is life eternal. Christ and His righteousness is the salvation of the soul.[7]

HEAVEN'S FLAWLESS PEARL

The kingdom of heaven is like unto a merchant man, seeking goodly pearls: who, when he had found one pearl of great price, went and sold all that he had, and bought it. Matt. 13: 45, 46.

Christ Himself is the pearl of great price. . . . The righteousness of Christ, as a pure, white pearl, has no defect, no stain. No work of man can improve the great and precious gift of God. It is without a flaw. In Christ are "hid all the treasures of wisdom and knowledge." Col. 2:3. He is "made unto us wisdom, and righteousness, and sanctification, and redemption." 1 Cor. 1:30. All that can satisfy the needs and longings of the human soul, for this world and for the world to come, is found in Christ. Our Redeemer is the pearl so precious that in comparison all things else may be accounted loss. . . .

In the parable the pearl is not represented as a gift. The merchantman bought it at the price of all that he had. Many question the meaning of this, since Christ is represented in the Scriptures as a gift. He is a gift, but only to those who give themselves, soul, body, and spirit, to Him without reserve. We are to give ourselves to Christ, to live a life of willing obedience to all His requirements. All that we are, all the talents and capabilities we possess, are the Lord's, to be consecrated to His service. When we thus give ourselves wholly to Him, Christ, with all the treasures of heaven, gives Himself to us. We obtain the pearl of great price. . . .

In the market of which divine mercy has the management, the precious pearl is represented as being bought without money and without price. In this market all may obtain the goods of heaven. The treasury of the jewels of truth is open to all. . . . The Saviour's voice earnestly and lovingly invites us: "I counsel thee to buy of Me gold tried in the fire, that thou mayest be rich." . . . The poorest are as well able as the richest to purchase salvation; for no amount of worldly wealth can secure it. It is obtained by willing obedience, by giving ourselves to Christ as His own purchased possession. . . .

We cannot earn salvation, but we are to seek for it with as much interest and perseverance as though we would abandon everything in the world for it.[8]

CHRIST THE ONLY SAVIOUR

Who hath delivered us from the power of darkness, and hath translated us into the kingdom of his dear Son: in whom we have redemption through his blood. Col. 1:13, 14.

No matter who you are or what your life has been, you can be saved only in God's appointed way. You must repent; you must fall helpless on the Rock, Christ Jesus. You must feel your need of a physician and of the only remedy for sin, the blood of Christ. This remedy can be secured only by repentance toward God and faith toward our Lord Jesus Christ. . . . The blood of Christ will avail for none but those who feel their need of its cleansing power.

What surpassing love and condescension, that when we had no claim upon divine mercy, Christ was willing to undertake our redemption! But our great Physician requires of every soul unquestioning submission. We are never to prescribe for our own case. Christ must have the entire management of will and action. . . .

We may flatter ourselves . . . that our moral character has been correct and we need not humble ourselves before God like the common sinner. But we must be content to enter into life in the very same way as the chief of sinners. We must renounce our own righteousness and plead for the righteousness of Christ to be imputed to us. We must depend wholly upon Christ for our strength. Self must die. We must acknowledge that all we have is from the exceeding riches of divine grace. Let this be the language of our hearts: "Not unto us, O Lord, not unto us, but unto thy name give glory, for thy mercy, and for thy truth's sake."

Genuine faith is followed by love, and love by obedience. All the powers and passions of the converted man are brought under the control of Christ. His Spirit is a renewing power, transforming to the divine image all who will receive it. . . .

"Whosoever is born of God doth not commit sin." He feels that he is the purchase of the blood of Christ and bound by the most solemn vows to glorify God in his body and in his spirit, which are God's. The love of sin and the love of self are subdued in him. He daily asks: "What shall I render unto the Lord for all his benefits toward me?" "Lord, what wilt thou have me to do?" [9]

TASTE FOR YOURSELF

O taste and see that the Lord is good: blessed is the man that trusteth in him. Ps. 34:8.

How shall we know for ourselves God's goodness and His love? The psalmist tells us—not, hear and know, read and know, or believe and know; but—"*Taste* and see that the Lord is good." Instead of relying upon the word of another, taste for yourself.

Experience is knowledge derived from experiment. Experimental religion is what is needed now. . . . Some—yes, a large number—have a theoretical knowledge of religious truth, but have never felt the renewing power of divine grace upon their own hearts. . . . They believe in the wrath of God, but put forth no earnest efforts to escape it. They believe in heaven, but make no sacrifice to obtain it. . . . They know a remedy for sin, but do not use it. They know the right, but have no relish for it. All their knowledge will but increase their condemnation. They have never tasted and learned by experience that the Lord is good.

To become a disciple of Christ is to deny self and follow Jesus through evil as well as good report. . . . Every darling indulgence that hinders our religious life must be cut off. . . . Will we put forth efforts and make sacrifices proportionate to the worth of the object to be attained?

Every association we form, however limited, exerts some influence upon us. The extent to which we yield to that influence will be determined by the degree of intimacy, the constancy of the intercourse, and our love and veneration for the one with whom we associate. Thus by acquaintance and association with Christ we may become like Him, the one faultless Example.

Communion with Christ—how unspeakably precious! Such communion it is our privilege to enjoy if we will seek it, if we will make any sacrifice to secure it.[10]

So everyone may be able, through his own experience, to "set his seal to this, that God is true." John 3:33, A.R.V. . . . He can testify: "I needed help, and I found it in Jesus. Every want was supplied, the hunger of my soul was satisfied. . . . I believe in Jesus because He is to me a divine Saviour. I believe the Bible because I have found it to be the voice of God to my soul."[11]

CITIZENS OF HEAVEN

Now therefore ye are no more strangers and foreigners, but fellow-citizens with the saints, and of the household of God. Eph. 2:19.

Jesus says: "Behold, I come quickly." We should keep these words ever in mind, and act as though we do indeed believe that the coming of the Lord is nigh, and that we are pilgrims and strangers upon the earth.[12]

Every means of grace should be diligently improved that the love of God may abound in the soul more and more, "that ye may approve things that are excellent; that ye may be sincere and without offense till the day of Christ; being filled with the fruits of righteousness." Your Christian life must take on vigorous and stalwart forms. You can attain to the high standard set before you in the Scriptures, and you must if you would be children of God. You cannot stand still; you must either advance or retrograde. . . .

Will you have a stinted Christian growth, or will you make healthy progress in the divine life? Where there is spiritual health there is growth. The child of God grows up to the full stature of a man or woman in Christ. There is no limit to his improvement. . . .

Some who ought to be strong and established in Christ are as babes in understanding and experimental knowledge of the workings of the Spirit of God. After years of experience they are able to comprehend only the first principles of that grand system of faith and doctrine that constitutes the Christian religion. They do not comprehend that perfection of character which will receive the commendation: "Well done.". . .

We have great victories to gain, and a heaven to lose if we do not gain them. The carnal heart must be crucified; for its tendency is to moral corruption, and the end thereof is death. . . . Pray that the mighty energies of the Holy Spirit . . . may fall like an electric shock on the palsy-stricken soul, causing every nerve to thrill with new life, restoring the whole man from his dead, earthly, sensual state to spiritual soundness. You will thus become partakers of the divine nature, . . . and in your souls will be reflected the image of Him by whose stripes you are healed.[13]

A FULLER KNOWLEDGE OF GOD

This is life eternal, that they might know thee the only true God, and Jesus Christ, whom thou hast sent. John 17:3.

Only by knowing God here can we prepare to meet Him at His coming. . . . But many of those who profess to believe in Christ do not know God. They have only a surface religion. They do not love God; they do not study His character; therefore they do not know how to trust, how to look and live. They do not know what restful love is, or what it means to walk by faith. . . . They fail of understanding that it is their duty to receive, in order that they may enrich others.

The world by wisdom knows not God. Many have talked eloquently about Him, but their reasoning brings men no nearer to Him, because they themselves are not in vital connection with Him. Professing themselves to be wise, they become fools. Their knowledge of God is imperfect.[14]

We cannot by searching find out God, but He has revealed Himself in His Son, who is the brightness of the Father's glory and the express image of His person. If we desire a knowledge of God we must be Christlike. . . . Living a pure life through faith in Christ as a personal Saviour will bring to the believer a clearer, higher conception of God.[15]

Christ is a perfect revelation of God. "No man hath seen God at any time," He says; "the only begotten Son, which is in the bosom of the Father, he hath declared him." Only by knowing Christ can we know God. And as we behold Him, we shall be changed into His image, prepared to meet Him at His coming. . . .

Now is the time to prepare for the coming of our Lord. Readiness to meet Him cannot be attained in a moment's time. Preparatory to that solemn scene there must be vigilant waiting and watching, combined with earnest work. So God's children glorify Him. Amid the busy scenes of life their voices will be heard speaking words of encouragement, hope, and faith. All they have and are is consecrated to the Master's service. Thus they prepare to meet their Lord; and when He comes, they will say, with joy, "This is our God; we have waited for him, and he will save us. . . . We will be glad and rejoice in his salvation."[16]

THE HIGHEST KIND OF MEDITATION

Behold, what manner of love the Father hath bestowed upon us, that we should be called the sons of God. 1 John 3:1.

What love, what matchless love, that, sinners and aliens as we are, we may be brought back to God and adopted into His family! We may address Him by the endearing name, "Our Father." . . .

All the paternal love which has come down from generation to generation through the channel of human hearts, all the springs of tenderness which have opened in the souls of men, are but as a tiny rill to the boundless ocean when compared with the infinite, exhaustless love of God. Tongue cannot utter it; pen cannot portray it. You may meditate upon it every day of your life; you may search the Scriptures diligently in order to understand it; you may summon every power and capability that God has given you, in the endeavor to comprehend the love and compassion of the heavenly Father; and yet there is an infinity beyond. You may study that love for ages; yet you can never fully comprehend the length and the breadth, the depth and the height, of the love of God in giving His Son to die for the world. Eternity itself can never fully reveal it. Yet as we study the Bible and meditate upon the life of Christ and the plan of redemption, these great themes will open to our understanding more and more.[17]

Christ came to reveal God to the world as a God of love, full of mercy, tenderness, and compassion.[18]

It would be well to spend a thoughtful hour each day reviewing the life of Christ from the manger to Calvary. We should take it point by point and let the imagination vividly grasp each scene, especially the closing ones of His earthly life. By thus contemplating His teachings and sufferings, and the infinite sacrifice made by Him for the redemption of the race, we may strengthen our faith, quicken our love, and become more deeply imbued with the spirit which sustained our Saviour. If we would be saved at last we must all learn the lesson of penitence and faith at the foot of the cross. . . . Everything noble and generous in man will respond to the contemplation of Christ upon the cross.[19]

WHITE RAIMENT REQUIRED

When the king came in to see the guests, he saw there a man which had not on a wedding garment: and he saith unto him, Friend, how camest thou in hither not having a wedding garment? Matt. 22:11, 12.

By the wedding garment in the parable is represented the pure, spotless character which Christ's true followers will possess. To the church it is given "that she should be arrayed in fine linen, clean and white," "not having spot, or wrinkle, or any such thing." Rev. 19:8; Eph 5:27. The fine linen, says the Scripture, "is the righteousness of saints." Rev. 19:8. It is the righteousness of Christ, His own unblemished character, that through faith is imparted to all who receive Him as their personal Saviour.

The white robe of innocence was worn by our first parents when they were placed by God in holy Eden.... But when sin entered, they severed their connection with God, and the light that had encircled them departed.... Nothing can man devise to supply the place of his lost robe of innocence.... Only the covering which Christ Himself has provided can make us meet to appear in God's presence. This covering, the robe of His own righteousness, Christ will put upon every repenting, believing soul.... This robe, woven in the loom of heaven, has in it not one thread of human devising. Christ in His humanity wrought out a perfect character, and this character He offers to impart to us. "All our righteousnesses are as filthy rags." Isa. 64:6. Everything that we of ourselves can do is defiled by sin. But the Son of God "was manifested to take away our sins; and in him is no sin." 1 John3:5....

By His perfect obedience He has made it possible for every human being to obey God's commandments. When we submit ourselves to Christ, the heart is united with His heart, the will is merged in His will, the mind becomes one with His mind, the thoughts are brought into captivity to Him; we live His life. This is what it means to be clothed with the garment of His righteousness. Then as the Lord looks upon us He sees, not the fig-leaf garment, not the nakedness and deformity of sin, but His own robe of righteousness, which is perfect obedience to the law of Jehovah.[20]

JOY IN OBEDIENCE

I have longed for thy salvation, O Lord; and thy law is my delight. Ps. 119:174.

The true Christian will never complain that the yoke of Christ is galling to the neck. He accounts the service of Jesus as the truest freedom. The law of God is his delight. Instead of seeking to bring down the divine commands, to accord with his deficiencies, he is constantly striving to rise to the level of their perfection.

Such an experience must be ours if we would be prepared to stand in the day of God. Now, while probation lingers, while mercy's voice is still heard, is the time for us to put away our sins. . . .

God has made ample provision that we may stand perfect in His grace, wanting in nothing, waiting for the appearing of our Lord. Are you ready? Have you the wedding garment on? That garment will never cover deceit, impurity, corruption, or hypocrisy. The eye of God is upon you. . . . We may conceal our sins from the eyes of men, but we can hide nothing from our Maker.

God spared not His own Son, but delivered Him to death for our offenses and raised Him again for our justification. Through Christ we may present our petitions at the throne of Grace. Through Him, unworthy as we are, we may obtain all spiritual blessings. Do we come to Him, that we may have life?[21]

The will of God is expressed in the precepts of His holy law, and the principles of this law are the principles of heaven. The angels of heaven attain unto no higher knowledge than to know the will of God, and to do His will is the highest service that can engage their powers.

But in heaven, service is not rendered in the spirit of legality. When Satan rebelled against the law of Jehovah, the thought that there was a law came to the angels almost as an awakening to something unthought of. In their ministry the angels are not as servants, but as sons. . . . Obedience is to them no drudgery. Love for God makes their service a joy. So in every soul wherein Christ, the hope of glory, dwells, His words are re-echoed, "I delight to do thy will, O my God: yea, thy law is within my heart."[22]

SHAPING UP IN GOD'S WORKSHOP

Do you not know that your body is a temple of the Holy Spirit within you, which you have from God? You are not your own; you were bought with a price. So glorify God in your body. 1 Cor. 6:19, 20, R.S.V.

We are not our own. We have been purchased with a dear price, even the sufferings and death of the Son of God. If we could understand this, and fully realize it, we would feel a great responsibility resting upon us to keep ourselves in the very best condition of health, that we might render to God perfect service. . . .

We believe without a doubt that Christ is soon coming. . . . We have no doubt, neither have we had a doubt for years, that the doctrines we hold today are present truth, and that we are nearing the judgment. We are preparing to meet Him who, escorted by a retinue of holy angels, is to appear in the clouds of heaven to give the faithful and the just the finishing touch of immortality. When He comes He is not to cleanse us of our sins, to remove from us the defects in our characters, or to cure us of the infirmities of our tempers and dispositions. If wrought for us at all, this work will all be accomplished before that time.

When the Lord comes, those who are holy will be holy still. Those who have preserved their bodies and spirits in holiness, in sanctification and honor, will then receive the finishing touch of immortality. But those who are unjust, unsanctified, and filthy will remain so forever. No work will then be done for them to remove their defects and give them holy characters. . . . This is all to be done in these hours of probation. It is *now* that this work is to be accomplished for us. . . .

We are now in God's workshop. Many of us are rough stones from the quarry. But as we lay hold upon the truth of God, its influence affects us. It elevates us and removes from us every imperfection and sin, of whatever nature. Thus we are prepared to see the King in His beauty and finally to unite with the pure and heavenly angels in the kingdom of glory. It is here that this work is to be accomplished for us, here that our bodies and spirits are to be fitted for immortality.[23]

PHYSICAL HEALTH AND NOBLE THINKING

Dearly beloved, I beseech you as strangers and pilgrims, abstain from fleshly lusts, which war against the soul. 1 Peter 2:11.

Many regard this text as a warning against licentiousness only; but it has a broader meaning. It forbids every injurious gratification of appetite or passion. Every perverted appetite becomes a warring lust. Appetite was given us for a good purpose, not to become the minister of death by being perverted, and thus degenerating into "lusts, which war against the soul." Peter's admonition is a most direct and forcible warning against the use of all stimulants and narcotics. These indulgences may well be classed among the lusts that exert a pernicious influence upon moral character.[24]

Let none who profess godliness regard with indifference the health of the body, and flatter themselves that intemperance is no sin and will not affect their spirituality. A close sympathy exists between the physical and the moral nature. The standard of virtue is elevated or degraded by the physical habits. Excessive eating of the best of food will produce a morbid condition of the moral feelings. And if the food is not the most healthful, the effects will be still more injurious. Any habit which does not promote healthful action in the human system degrades the higher and nobler faculties. . . . Indulgence of appetite strengthens the animal propensities, giving them the ascendancy over the mental and spiritual powers.[25]

The strength of the temptation to indulge appetite can be measured only by the inexpressible anguish of our Redeemer in that long fast in the wilderness. He knew that the indulgence of perverted appetite would so deaden man's perceptions that sacred things could not be discerned. . . . If the power of indulged appetite was so strong upon the race, that, in order to break its hold, the divine Son of God, in man's behalf, had to endure a fast of nearly six weeks, what a work is before the Christian! Yet, however great the struggle, he may overcome. By the help of that divine power which withstood the fiercest temptations that Satan could invent, he, too, may be entirely successful in his warfare with evil, and at last may wear the victor's crown in the kingdom of God.[26]

81

THE SOWING AND REAPING OF LIFE

Flee also youthful lusts: but follow after righteousness, faith, charity, peace, with them that call on the Lord out of a pure heart. 2 Tim. 2:22.

A little time spent in sowing your wild oats, dear young friends, will produce a crop that will embitter your whole life; an hour of thoughtlessness, once yielding to temptation, may turn the whole current of your life in the wrong direction. You can have but one youth; make that useful. When once you have passed over the ground you can never return to rectify your mistakes. . . .

Satan . . . transforms himself into an angel of light and comes to the youth with his specious temptations and succeeds in winning them, step by step, from the path of duty. He is described as an accuser, a deceiver, a liar, a tormentor, and a murderer. . . . It is Satan's act to tempt you, but your own act to yield. It is not in the power of all the host of Satan to force the tempted to transgress. There is no excuse for sin.[27]

Temptation is not sin. Jesus was holy and pure; yet He was tempted in all points as we are, but with a strength and power that man will never be called upon to endure. In His successful resistance He has left us a bright example, that we should follow in His steps. If we are self-confident or self-righteous we shall be left to fall under the power of temptation; but if we look to Jesus and trust in Him we call to our aid a power that has conquered the foe on the field of battle, and with every temptation He will make a way of escape. When Satan comes in like a flood, we must meet his temptations with the sword of the Spirit, and Jesus will be our helper and will lift up for us a standard against him.[28]

One wrong trait of character, one sinful desire cherished, will eventually neutralize all the power of the gospel. . . . The pains of duty and the pleasures of sin are the cords with which Satan binds men in his snares. Those who would rather die than perform a wrong act are the only ones who will be found faithful.[29]

The youth may have principles so firm that the most powerful temptations of Satan will not draw them away from their allegiance.[30]

THE CHARACTER HEAVEN APPROVES

Let no man despise thy youth; but be thou an example of the believers, in word, in conversation, in charity, in spirit, in faith, in purity. 1 Tim. 4:12.

Jesus, the Majesty of heaven, has left an example for the youth. He toiled in the workshop at Nazareth for His daily bread. He was subject to His parents, and sought not to control His own time or to follow His own will. By a life of easy indulgence a youth can never attain to real excellence as a man or as a Christian. God does not promise us ease, honor, or wealth in His service; but He assures us that all needed blessings will be ours, "with persecutions," and in the world to come "life everlasting." Nothing less than entire consecration to His service will Christ accept. This is the lesson which every one of us must learn. . . .

We have marked illustrations of the sustaining power of firm, religious principle. . . . The gaping lions' den could not keep Daniel from his daily prayers, nor could the fiery furnace induce Shadrach and his companions to fall down before the idol which Nebuchadnezzar set up. Young men who have firm principles will eschew pleasure, defy pain, and brave even the lions' den and the heated fiery furnace rather than be found untrue to God. Mark the character of Joseph. Virtue was severely tested, but its triumph was complete. At every point the noble youth endured the test. The same lofty, unbending principle appeared at every trial. The Lord was with him, and His word was law.[31]

Those who study the Bible, counsel with God, and rely upon Christ will be enabled to act wisely at all times and under all circumstances. Good principles will be illustrated in actual life. Only let the truth for this time be cordially received and become the basis of character, and it will produce steadfastness of purpose, which the allurements of pleasure, the fickleness of custom, the contempt of the world-loving, and the heart's own clamors for self-indulgence are powerless to influence. Conscience must be first enlightened, the will must be brought into subjection. The love of truth and righteousness must reign in the soul, and a character will appear which heaven can approve.[32]

CLIMBING PETER'S LADDER

Beside this, giving all diligence, add to your faith virtue; and to virtue knowledge; and to knowledge temperance; and to temperance patience; and to patience godliness; and to godliness brotherly kindness; and to brotherly kindness charity. 2 Peter 1:5-7.

Point the youth to Peter's ladder of eight rounds, and place their feet, not on the highest round, but on the lowest, and with earnest solicitation urge them to climb to the very top.

Christ . . . is the ladder. The base is planted firmly on the earth in His humanity; the topmost round reaches to the throne of God in His divinity. The humanity of Christ embraces fallen humanity, while His divinity lays hold upon the throne of God. We are saved by climbing round after round of the ladder, looking to Christ, clinging to Christ, mounting step by step to the height of Christ, so that He is made unto us wisdom and righteousness and sanctification and redemption. Faith, virtue, knowledge, temperance, patience, godliness, brotherly kindness, and charity are the rounds of this ladder. All these graces are to be manifested in the Christian character; and "if ye do these things, ye shall never fall: for so an entrance shall be ministered unto·you abundantly into the everlasting kingdom of our Lord and Saviour Jesus Christ." [33]

You are not to think that you must wait until you have perfected one grace before cultivating another. No; they are to grow up together . . . ; every day that you live, you can be perfecting the blessed attributes fully revealed in the character of Christ. . . .[34]

Do not become overwhelmed with the great amount of work you must do in your lifetime, for you are not required to do it all at once. Let every power of your being go to each day's work, improve each precious opportunity, appreciate the helps that God gives you, and make advancement up the ladder of progress step by step. Remember that you are to live but one day at a time, that God has given you one day, and heavenly records will show how you have valued its privileges and opportunities. May you so improve every day given you of God, that at last you may hear the Master say, "Well done, thou good and faithful servant." [35]

THE BREATH OF THE SOUL

Pray without ceasing. 1 Thess. 5:17.

Prayer is the breath of the soul, the channel of all blessings. As . . . the repentant soul offers its prayer, God sees its struggles, watches its conflicts, and marks its sincerity. He has His finger upon its pulse, and He takes note of every throb. Not a feeling thrills it, not an emotion agitates it, not a sorrow shades it, not a sin stains it, not a thought or purpose moves it, of which He is not cognizant. That soul was purchased at an infinite cost, and is loved with a devotion that is unalterable.

Prayer to the Great Physician for the healing of the soul brings the blessing of God. Prayer unites us one to another and to God. Prayer brings Jesus to our side, and gives new strength and fresh grace to the fainting, perplexed soul. . . .

Christ our Saviour was tempted in all points like as we are, yet He was without sin. He took human nature, being made in fashion as a man, and his necessities were the necessities of a man. He had bodily wants to be supplied, bodily weariness to be relieved. It was by prayer to His Father that He was braced for duty and for trial. Day by day He followed His round of duty, seeking to save souls. . . . And He spent whole nights in prayer in behalf of the tempted ones. . . .

The night seasons of prayer which the Saviour spent in the mountain or in the desert were essential to prepare Him for the trials He must meet in the days to follow. He felt the need of the refreshing and invigorating of soul and body, that He might meet the temptations of Satan; and those who are striving to live His life will feel this same need. . . .

He says to us, "If any man will come after me, let him deny himself, and take up his cross daily, and follow me." Christ alone can make us capable of responding when He says, "Take my yoke upon you, and learn of me; for I am meek and lowly in heart." This means that every day self must be denied. Christ can give us the noble resolve, the will to suffer, and to fight the battles of the Lord with persevering energy. The weakest, aided by divine grace, may have strength to be more than conqueror.[36]

THE SECRET OF PROGRESS

Trust in him at all times; ye people, pour out your heart before him: God is a refuge for us. Ps. 62:8.

We must be much in prayer if we would make progress in the divine life. When the message of truth was first proclaimed, how much we prayed. How often was the voice of intercession heard in the chamber, in the barn, in the orchard, or the grove. Frequently we spent hours in earnest prayer, two or three together claiming the promise; often the sound of weeping was heard and then the voice of thanksgiving and the song of praise. Now the day of God is nearer than when we first believed, and we should be more earnest, more zealous, and fervent than in those early days. Our perils are greater now than then.[37]

It was in hours of solitary prayer that Jesus in His earth-life received wisdom and power. Let the youth follow His example in finding at dawn and twilight a quiet season for communion with their Father in heaven. And throughout the day let them lift up their hearts to God. At every step of our way He says, "I the Lord thy God will hold thy right hand; . . . fear not; I will help thee." Isa. 41:13. Could our children learn this lesson in the morning of their years, what freshness and power, what joy and sweetness, would be brought into their lives![38]

Let your heart break for the longing it has for God, for the living God. The life of Christ has shown what humanity can do by being partaker of the divine nature. All that Christ received from God we too may have. Then ask and receive. With the persevering faith of Jacob, with the unyielding persistence of Elijah, claim for yourself all that God has promised.

Let the glorious conceptions of God possess your mind. Let your life be knit by hidden links to the life of Jesus. He who commanded the light to shine out of darkness is willing to shine in your heart, to give the light of the knowledge of the glory of God in the face of Jesus Christ. The Holy Spirit will take the things of God and show them unto you. . . . Christ will lead you to the threshold of the Infinite. You may behold the glory beyond the veil, and reveal to men the sufficiency of Him who ever liveth to make intercession for us.[39]

UNWAVERING FAITH

Let him ask in faith, nothing wavering. For he that wavereth is like a wave of the sea driven with the wind and tossed. James 1:6.

Prayer and faith are closely allied, and they need to be studied together. In the prayer of faith there is a divine science; it is a science that everyone who would make his life-work a success must understand. Christ says, "What things soever ye desire, when ye pray, believe that ye receive them, and ye shall have them." Mark 11:24. He makes it plain that our asking must be according to God's will; we must ask for the things that He has promised, and whatever we receive must be used in doing His will. The conditions met, the promise is unequivocal.

For the pardon of sin, for the Holy Spirit, for a Christlike temper, for wisdom and strength to do His work, for any gift He has promised, we may ask; then we are to believe that we receive, and return thanks to God that we have received. We need look for no outward evidence of the blessing. The gift is in the promise, and we may go about our work assured that what God has promised He is able to perform, and that the gift, which we already possess, will be realized when we need it most.

To live thus by the word of God means the surrender to Him of the whole life. There will be felt a continual sense of need and dependence, a drawing out of the heart after God. Prayer is a necessity; for it is the life of the soul. Family prayer, public prayer, have their place; but it is secret communion with God that sustains the soul life. . . .

An intensity such as never before was seen is taking possession of the world. In amusement, in money-making, in the contest for power, in the very struggle for existence, there is a terrible force that engrosses body and mind and soul. In the midst of this maddening rush, God is speaking. He bids us come apart and commune with Him. "Be still, and know that I am God." . . .

Not a pause for a moment in His presence, but personal contact with Christ, to sit down in companionship with Him—this is our need.[40]

PURE IN HEART AND LIFE

Blessed are the pure in heart: for they shall see God. Matt. 5:8.

Into the city of God there will enter nothing that defiles. All who are to be dwellers there will here have become pure in heart. In one who is learning of Jesus, there will be manifest a growing distaste for careless manners, unseemly language, and coarse thought. When Christ abides in the heart, there will be purity and refinement of thought and manner.

But the words of Jesus . . . have a deeper meaning—not merely pure in the sense in which the world understands purity, free from that which is sensual, pure from lust, but true in the hidden purposes and motives of the soul, free from pride and self-seeking, humble, unselfish, childlike.

Only like can appreciate like. Unless you accept in your own life the principle of self-sacrificing love, which is the principle of His character, you cannot know God. . . .

When Christ shall come in His glory, the wicked cannot endure to behold Him. The light of His presence, which is life to those who love Him, is death to the ungodly. . . . When He shall appear, they will pray to be hidden from the face of Him who died to redeem them.

But to hearts that have become purified through the indwelling of the Holy Spirit, all is changed. These can know God. Moses was hid in the cleft of the rock when the glory of the Lord was revealed to him; and it is when we are hid in Christ that we behold the love of God. . . .

By faith we behold Him here and now. In our daily experience we discern His goodness and compassion in the manifestation of His providence. We recognize Him in the character of His Son. . . . The pure in heart see God in a new and endearing relation, as their Redeemer; and while they discern the purity and loveliness of His character, they long to reflect His image. They see Him as a Father longing to embrace a repenting son, and their hearts are filled with joy unspeakable and full of glory. . . .

The pure in heart live as in the visible presence of God during the time He apportions them in this world. And they will also see Him face to face in the future, immortal state, as did Adam when he walked and talked with God in Eden.[41]

BIBLE SANCTIFICATION DEFINED

Sanctify them through thy truth: thy word is truth. John 17:17.

Those who are sanctified through the truth are living recommendations of its power, and representatives of their risen Lord. The religion of Christ will refine the taste, sanctify the judgment, elevate, purify, and ennoble the soul, making the Christian more and more fit for the society of the heavenly angels.[42]

"And for their sakes I sanctify myself, that they also might be sanctified through the truth." John 17:19. "Seeing ye have purified your souls in obeying the truth through the Spirit unto unfeigned love of the brethren, see that ye love one another with a pure heart fervently." 1 Peter 1:22. "Having therefore these promises, dearly beloved, let us cleanse ourselves from all filthiness of the flesh and spirit, perfecting holiness in the fear of God." 2 Cor. 7:1. . . .

Here is Bible sanctification. It is not merely a show or outside work. It is sanctification received through the channel of truth. It is truth received in the heart, and practically carried out in the life.

There is no Bible sanctification for those who cast a part of the truth behind them. There is light enough given in the word of God, so that none need err. . . . Jesus, considered as a man, was perfect, yet He grew in grace. "And Jesus increased in wisdom and stature, and in favour with God and man." Luke 2: 52. Even the most perfect Christian may increase continually in the knowledge and love of God. . . .

Sanctification is not the work of a moment, an hour, or a day. It is a continual growth in grace. . . . Satan lives, and is active, and every day we need to cry earnestly to God for help and strength to resist him. As long as Satan reigns we shall have self to subdue, besetments to overcome, and there is no stopping place, there is no point to which we can come and say we have fully attained. . . .

The Christian life is constantly an onward march. Jesus sits as a refiner and purifier of His people; and when His image is perfectly reflected in them, they are perfect and holy, and prepared for translation.[43]

BE ALERT FOR SATAN'S DEVICES

Be sober, be vigilant; because your adversary the devil, as a roaring lion, walketh about, seeking whom he may devour: whom resist stedfast in the faith. 1 Peter 5:8, 9.

Let every soul be on the alert. The adversary is on your track. Be vigilant, watching diligently lest some carefully concealed and masterly snare shall take you unawares. Let the careless and indifferent beware lest the day of the Lord come upon them as a thief in the night. Many will wander from the path of humility, and, casting aside the yoke of Christ, will walk in strange paths. Blinded and bewildered, they will leave the narrow path that leads to the city of God. . . .

He who overcomes must watch; for, with worldly entanglements, error, and superstition, Satan strives to win Christ's followers from Him. It is not enough that we avoid glaring dangers and perilous, inconsistent moves. We are to keep close to the side of Christ, walking in the path of self-denial and sacrifice. We are in an enemy's country. He who was cast out of heaven has come down with great power. With every conceivable artifice and device he is seeking to take souls captive. Unless we are constantly on guard we shall fall an easy prey to his unnumbered deceptions.[44]

Everything is now clothed with a solemnity that all who believe the truth for this time should realize. They should act in reference to the day of God. The judgments of God are about to fall upon the world, and we need to be preparing for that great day.

Our time is precious. We have but few, very few days of probation in which to make ready for the future, immortal life. We have no time to spend in haphazard movements. We should fear to skim the surface of the word of God.[45]

If your whole interest is in the truth and the preparatory work for this time you will be sanctified through the truth and receive a fitness for immortality. . . . The thorough work of preparation must go on with all who profess the truth, until we stand before the throne of God without fault, without a spot, or wrinkle, or any such thing. God will cleanse you if you will submit to the purifying process.[46]

PROOF AGAINST EVERY TEMPTATION

Yield yourselves unto God, . . . and your members as instruments of righteousness unto God. For sin shall not have dominion over you. Rom. 6:13, 14.

There is but one power that can break the hold of evil from the hearts of men, and that is the power of God in Jesus Christ. . . . His grace alone can enable us to resist and subdue the tendencies of our fallen nature.[47]

The infinite value of the sacrifice required for our redemption reveals the fact that sin is a tremendous evil. Through sin the whole human organism is deranged, the mind is perverted, the imagination corrupted. Sin has degraded the faculties of the soul. Temptations from without find an answering chord within the heart, and the feet turn imperceptibly toward evil. As the sacrifice in our behalf was complete, so our restoration from the defilement of sin is to be complete. There is no act of wickedness that the law will excuse; there is no unrighteousness that will escape its condemnation. The life of Christ was a perfect fulfillment of every precept of the law. He said; "I have kept my Father's commandments." John 15:10. His life is our standard of obedience and service.[48]

Today Satan presents the same temptations that he presented to Christ, offering us the kingdoms of the world in return for our allegiance. But upon him who looks to Jesus as the author and finisher of his faith, Satan's temptations have no power. He cannot cause to sin the one who will accept by faith the virtues of Him who was tempted in all points as we are, yet without sin.[49]

The expulsion of sin is the act of the soul itself. True, we have no power to free ourselves from Satan's control; but when we desire to be set free from sin, and in our great need cry out for a power out of and above ourselves, the powers of the soul are imbued with the divine energy of the Holy Spirit, and they obey the dictates of the will in fulfilling the will of God.[50]

God will have a people zealous of good works, standing firm amid the pollutions of this degenerate age. There will be a people who hold so fast to the divine strength that they will be proof against every temptation.[51]

WHY PROBATION LINGERS

The Lord is not slack concerning his promise, as some men count slackness; but is longsuffering to us-ward, not willing that any should perish, but that all should come to repentance. 2 Peter 3:9.

I was shown our danger, as a people, of becoming assimilated to the world rather than to the image of Christ. We are now upon the very borders of the eternal world, but it is the purpose of the adversary of souls to lead us to put far off the close of time. Satan will in every conceivable manner assail those who profess to be the commandment-keeping people of God and to be waiting for the second appearing of our Saviour in the clouds of heaven with power and great glory. He will lead as many as possible to put off the evil day and become in spirit like the world, imitating its customs. I felt alarmed as I saw that the spirit of the world was controlling the hearts and minds of many who make a high profession of the truth. . . .

In consideration of the shortness of time we as a people should watch and pray, and in no case allow ourselves to be diverted from the solemn work of preparation for the great event before us. Because the time is apparently extended, many have become careless and indifferent in regard to their words and actions. They do not realize their danger and do not see and understand the mercy of our God in lengthening their probation, that they may have time to form characters for the future, immortal life. Every moment is of the highest value. Time is granted them, not to be employed in studying their own ease and becoming dwellers on the earth, but to be used in the work of overcoming every defect in their own characters and in helping others, by example and personal effort, to see the beauty of holiness. God has a people upon the earth who in faith and holy hope are tracing down the roll of fast-fulfilling prophecy and are seeking to purify their souls by obeying the truth, that they may not be found without the wedding garment when Christ shall appear. . . .

The signs foretold in prophecy are fast fulfilling around us. This should arouse every true follower of Christ to zealous action.[52]

YOUR CASE COMING UP!

Fear God, and give glory to him; for the hour of his judgment is come. Rev. 14:7.

In 1844 our great High Priest entered the most holy place of the heavenly sanctuary, to begin the work of the investigative judgment.[53]

As the books of record are opened in the judgment, the lives of all who have believed on Jesus come in review before God. Beginning with those who first lived upon the earth, our Advocate presents the cases of each successive generation, and closes with the living. Every name is mentioned, every case closely investigated. Names are accepted, names rejected. When any have sins remaining upon the books of record, unrepented of and unforgiven, their names will be blotted out of the book of life. . . .

We are now living in the great day of atonement. In the typical service, while the high priest was making the atonement for Israel, all were required to afflict their souls by repentance of sin and humiliation before the Lord, lest they be cut off from among the people. In like manner, all who would have their names retained in the book of life, should now, in the few remaining days of their probation, afflict their souls before God by sorrow for sin and true repentance. There must be deep, faithful searching of heart. . . . There is earnest warfare before all who would subdue the evil tendencies that strive for the mastery. The work of preparation is an individual work. We are not saved in groups. The purity and devotion of one will not offset the want of these qualities in another. . . . Every one must be tested, and found without spot or wrinkle or any such thing.[54]

All who have truly repented of sin, and by faith claimed the blood of Christ as their atoning sacrifice, have had pardon entered against their names in the books of heaven; as they have become partakers of the righteousness of Christ, and their characters are found to be in harmony with the law of God, their sins will be blotted out, and they themselves will be accounted worthy of eternal life. The Lord declares, . . . "I, even I, am he that blotteth out thy transgressions for mine own sake, and will not remember thy sins." Isa. 43:25.[55]

A STANDARD YOU CAN TRUST

Put on the whole armour of God, that ye may be able to stand against the wiles of the devil. Eph. 6:11.

At every revival of God's work, the prince of evil is aroused to more intense activity; he is now putting forth his utmost efforts for a final struggle against Christ and His followers. The last great delusion is soon to open before us. Antichrist is to perform his marvelous works in our sight. So closely will the counterfeit resemble the true, that it will be impossible to distinguish between them except by the Holy Scriptures. By their testimony every statement and every miracle must be tested. . . .

None but those who have fortified the mind with the truths of the Bible will stand through the last great conflict. To every soul will come the searching test: Shall I obey God rather than men? The decisive hour is even now at hand. Are our feet planted on the rock of God's immutable word? Are we prepared to stand firm in defense of the commandments of God and the faith of Jesus? . . .

It is the first and highest duty of every rational being to learn from the Scriptures what is truth, and then to walk in the light, and encourage others to follow his example. We should day by day study the Bible diligently, weighing every thought, and comparing scripture with scripture. With divine help we are to form our opinions for ourselves as we are to answer for ourselves before God. . . .

Jesus promised His disciples: "The Comforter, which is the Holy Ghost, whom the Father will send in my name, he shall teach you all things, and bring all things to your remembrance, whatsoever I have said unto you." John 14:26. But the teachings of Christ must previously have been stored in the mind, in order for the Spirit of God to bring them to our remembrance in the time of peril. . . .

When the testing time shall come, those who have made God's word their rule of life will be revealed. . . . Let persecution be kindled, and the halfhearted and hypocritical will waver and yield the faith; but the true Christian will stand firm as a rock, his faith stronger, his hope brighter, than in days of prosperity.[56]

THE SCRIPTURES OUR SAFEGUARD

Are they not all ministering spirits, sent forth to minister for them who shall be heirs of salvation? Heb. 1:14.

So long as the people of God preserve their fidelity to Him, so long as they cling by living faith to Jesus, they are under the protection of heavenly angels, and Satan will not be permitted to exercise his hellish arts upon them to their destruction. But those who separate themselves from Christ by sin are in great peril. . . .

Satan is now more earnestly engaged in playing the game of life for souls than at any previous time; and unless we are constantly on our guard, he will establish in our hearts, pride, love of self, love of the world, and many other evil traits. He will also use every possible device to unsettle our faith in God and in the truths of His Word. If we have not a deep experience in the things of God, if we have not a thorough knowledge of His Word, we shall be beguiled to our ruin by the errors and sophistries of the enemy. False doctrines will sap the foundations of many, because they have not learned to discern truth from error. Our only safeguard against the wiles of Satan is to study the Scriptures diligently, to have an intelligent understanding of the reasons of our faith, and faithfully to perform every known duty. The indulgence of one known sin will cause weakness and darkness, and subject us to fierce temptation. . . .

Are we opening the door of the heart to Jesus, and closing every means of entrance to Satan? Are we daily obtaining clearer light, and greater strength, that we may stand in Christ's righteousness? Are we emptying our hearts of all selfishness, and cleansing them, preparatory to receiving the latter rain from heaven? . . .

The work of overcoming is a great work. Shall we take hold of it with energy and perseverance? Unless we do, our "filthy garments" will not be taken from us. We need never expect that these will be torn from us violently; we must first show a desire to rid ourselves of them. We must seek to separate sin from us, relying upon the merits of the blood of Christ; and then in the day of affliction, when the enemy presses us, we shall walk among the angels.[57]

GOD'S PLEDGE OF SECURITY

The Lord knoweth how to deliver the godly out of temptations, and to reserve the unjust unto the day of judgment to be punished. 2 Peter 2:9.

In the time of trial before us God's pledge of security will be placed upon those who have kept the word of His patience. . . . The pillar of cloud which speaks wrath and terror to the transgressor of God's law is light and mercy and deliverance to those who have kept His commandments. The arm strong to smite the rebellious will be strong to deliver the loyal. Every faithful one will surely be gathered. . . .

What part will you act in the closing scenes of this world's history? . . . Do you realize the grand work of preparation that is going on in heaven and on earth? . . . Let none now tamper with sin, the source of every misery in our world. . . . Let not the destiny of your soul hang upon an uncertainty. Know that you are fully on the Lord's side. Let the inquiry go forth from sincere hearts and trembling lips, "Who shall be able to stand?" Have you, in these last precious hours of probation, been putting the very best material into your character building? Have you been purifying your souls from every stain? Have you followed the light? Have you works corresponding to your profession of faith?

Is the softening, subduing influence of the grace of God working upon you? . . . Are you letting your light shine to illumine the nations that are perishing in their sins? Do you realize that you are to stand in defense of God's commandments before those who are treading them underfoot?

It is possible to be a partial, formal believer, and yet be found wanting and lose eternal life. It is possible to practice some of the Bible injunctions and be regarded as a Christian, and yet perish because you lack qualifications essential to Christian character. . . . While mercy lingers, while the Saviour is making intercession, let us make thorough work for eternity.[58]

The great crisis is just before us. To meet its trials and temptations, and to perform its duties, will require persevering faith. But we may triumph gloriously; not one watching, praying, believing soul will be ensnared by the enemy.[59]

A DEEP AND LIVING EXPERIENCE

How shall we escape if we neglect such a great salvation? It was declared at first by the Lord, and it was attested to us by those who heard him. Heb. 2:3, R.S.V.

I saw that we should not put off the coming of the Lord. Said the angel: "Prepare, prepare, for what is coming upon the earth. Let your works correspond with your faith." I saw that the mind must be stayed upon God, and that our influence should tell for God and His truth. We cannot honor the Lord when we are careless and indifferent. . . . We must be in earnest to secure our own soul's salvation, and to save others. All importance should be attached to this, and everything besides should come in secondary.

I saw the beauty of heaven. I heard the angels sing their rapturous songs, ascribing praise, honor, and glory to Jesus. I could then realize something of the wondrous love of the Son of God. He left all the glory, all the honor which He had in heaven, and was so interested for our salvation that He patiently and meekly bore every indignity and slight which man could heap upon Him. He was wounded, smitten, and bruised; He was stretched on Calvary's cross and suffered the most agonizing death to save us from death, that we might be washed in His blood and be raised up to live with Him in the mansions He is preparing for us, to enjoy the light and glory of heaven, to hear the angels sing, and to sing with them.

I saw that all heaven is interested in our salvation; and shall we be indifferent? Shall we be careless, as though it were a small matter whether we are saved or lost? Shall we slight the sacrifice that has been made for us? . . .

A Book has been given us to guide our feet through the perils of this dark world to heaven. It tells us how we can escape the wrath of God, and also tells of the sufferings of Christ for us, the great sacrifice that has been made that we might be saved and enjoy the presence of God forever.[60]

A form of godliness will not save any. All must have a deep and living experience. This alone will save them in the time of trouble. Then their work will be tried of what sort it is; and if it is gold, silver, and precious stones, they will be hid in the secret of the Lord's pavilion.[61]

"GET READY, GET READY, GET READY"

Prepare to meet thy God, O Israel. Amos 4:12.

Suppose that today Christ should appear in the clouds of heaven, who . . . would be ready to meet Him? Suppose we should be translated into the kingdom of heaven just as we are. Would we be prepared to unite with the saints of God, to live in harmony with the royal family, the children of the heavenly King? What preparation have you made for the judgment? Have you made your peace with God? Are you laboring together with God? Are you seeking to help those around you, those in your home, those in your neighborhood, those with whom you come in contact that are not keeping the commandments of God? . . . Are we getting ready to meet the King? . . .

If it were possible for us to be admitted into heaven as we are, how many of us would be able to look upon God? How many of us have on the wedding-garment? How many of us are without spot or wrinkle or any such thing? How many of us are worthy to receive the crown of life? . . . Position does not make the man. It is Christ formed within that makes a man worthy of receiving the crown of life, that fadeth not away.[62]

I was pointed to the remnant on the earth. The angel said to them, "Will ye shun the seven last plagues? . . . If so, ye must die that ye may live. Get ready, get ready, get ready. Ye must have a greater preparation than ye now have. . . . Sacrifice all to God. Lay all upon His altar—self, property, and all, a living sacrifice. It will take all to enter glory." [63]

Christ is coming with power and great glory. He is coming with His own glory and with the glory of the Father. . . . While the wicked flee from His presence, Christ's followers will rejoice. . . . To His faithful followers Christ has been a daily companion and familiar friend. They have lived in close contact, in constant communion with God. Upon them the glory of the Lord has risen. . . . Now they rejoice in the undimmed rays of the brightness and glory of the King in His majesty. They are prepared for the communion of heaven; for they have heaven in their hearts.[64]

If you are right with God today, you are ready if Christ should come today.[65]

GREATEST WORK IN THE WORLD

Go ye into all the world, and preach the gospel to every creature. Mark 16:15.

"Go ye into all the world, and preach the gospel to every creature," is Christ's command to His followers. Not that all are called to be ministers or missionaries in the ordinary sense of the term; but all may be workers with Him in giving the "glad tidings" to their fellow men. To all, great or small, learned or ignorant, old or young, the command is given.[1]

Upon every one who knows the truth for this time rests the responsibility of making it known to others. The servants of Christ are in a large measure responsible for the well-being and the salvation of the world. They are to be co-laborers with God in the work of winning souls to Christ.[2]

The theme that attracts the heart of the sinner is Christ, and Him crucified. On the cross of Calvary, Jesus stands revealed to the world in unparalleled love. Present Him thus to the hungering multitudes, and the light of His love will win men from darkness to light, from transgression to obedience and true holiness. Beholding Jesus upon the cross of Calvary arouses the conscience to the heinous character of sin as nothing else can do.[3]

Will not our church members keep their eyes fixed on a crucified and risen Saviour, in whom their hopes of eternal life are centered? This is our message, our argument, our doctrine, our warning to the impenitent, our encouragement for the sorrowing, the hope for every believer. If we can awaken an interest in men's minds that will cause them to fix their eyes on Christ, we may step aside, and ask them only to continue to fix their eyes upon the Lamb of God. . . . He whose eyes are fixed on Jesus will leave all. He will die to selfishness. He will believe in all the Word of God, which is so gloriously and wonderfully exalted in Christ.[4]

It is the privilege of every Christian, not only to look for, but to hasten the coming of our Lord Jesus Christ. Were all who profess His name bearing fruit to His glory, how quickly the whole world would be sown with the seed of the gospel. Quickly the last harvest would be ripened, and Christ would come to gather the precious grain.[5]

THE MESSAGE OF THE CROSS

God forbid that I should glory, save in the cross of our Lord Jesus Christ, by whom the world is crucified unto me, and I unto the world. Gal. 6:14.

God has given me a message for His people. . . . You have been bought with a price, and all that you have and are is to be used to the glory of God and for the good of your fellow men. Christ died on the cross to save the world from perishing in sin. He asks your co-operation in this work. You are to be His helping hand. With earnest, unwearying effort you are to seek to save the lost. . . .

The transforming power of Christ's grace molds the one who gives himself to God's service. . . . No longer can he be indifferent to the souls perishing around him. . . . He realizes that every part of his being belongs to Christ, who has redeemed him from the slavery of sin; that every moment of his future has been bought with the precious lifeblood of God's only-begotten Son.

Have you so deep an appreciation of the sacrifice made on Calvary that you are willing to make every other interest subordinate to the work of saving souls? The same intensity of desire to save sinners that marked the life of the Saviour marks the life of His true follower. The Christian has no desire to live for self. He delights to consecrate all that he has and is to the Master's service. He is moved by an inexpressible desire to win souls to Christ. . . .

How can I best glorify Him whose I am by creation and by redemption? This is to be the question that we are to ask ourselves. With anxious solicitude the one who is truly converted seeks to rescue those who are still in Satan's power. . . .

We have now only a little time in which to prepare for eternity. . . . People need the truth, and by earnest, faithful effort it is to be communicated to them. Souls are to be sought for, prayed for, labored for. . . .

Upon us rests the weighty responsibility of warning the world of its coming doom. . . . God calls upon His church to arise and clothe herself with power. Immortal crowns are to be won; the kingdom of heaven is to be gained; the world, perishing in ignorance, is to be enlightened.[6]

MOTIVATED BY LOVE

And this commandment we have from him, That he who loveth God love his brother also. 1 John 4:21.

Love is the basis of godliness. Whatever the profession, no man has pure love to God unless he has unselfish love for his brother. . . . When self is merged in Christ, love springs forth spontaneously. The completeness of Christian character is attained when the impulse to help and bless others springs constantly from within—when the sunshine of heaven fills the heart and is revealed in the countenance. . . .

Connected with Christ, we are connected with our fellow men by the golden links of the chain of love. Then the pity and compassion of Christ will be manifest in our life. We shall not wait to have the needy and unfortunate brought to us. We shall not need to be entreated to feel for the woes of others. It will be as natural for us to minister to the needy and suffering as it was for Christ to go about doing good. . . .

The glory of heaven is in lifting up the fallen, comforting the distressed. . . . No distinction on account of nationality, race, or caste is recognized by God. . . . All men are of one family by creation, and all are one through redemption. Christ came to demolish every wall of partition, to throw open every compartment of the temple, that every soul may have free access to God. His love is so broad, so deep, so full, that it penetrates everywhere. It lifts out of Satan's circle the poor souls who have been deluded by his deceptions. It places them within reach of the throne of God, the throne encircled by the rainbow of promise. . . .

Christ is seeking to uplift all who will be lifted to companionship with Himself, that we may be one with Him as He is one with the Father. He permits us to come in contact with suffering and calamity in order to call us out of our selfishness; He seeks to develop in us the attributes of His character—compassion, tenderness, and love. . . .

"If thou wilt keep my charge," the Lord declares, "I will give thee places to walk among these that stand by"—even among the angels that surround His throne. (Zech. 3:7.) By cooperating with heavenly beings in their work on earth, we are preparing for their companionship in heaven.[7]

THE PLACE TO BEGIN WITNESSING

That our sons may be as plants grown up in their youth; that our daughters may be as corner stones, polished after the similitude of a palace. Ps. 144:12.

Our work for Christ is to begin with the family in the home. . . . There is no missionary field more important than this.[8]

Happy are the parents whose lives are a true reflection of the divine, so that the promises and commands of God awaken in the child gratitude and reverence; the parents whose tenderness and justice and long-suffering interpret to the child the love and justice and long-suffering of God; and who, by teaching the child to love and trust and obey them, are teaching him to love and trust and obey his Father in heaven. Parents who impart to a child such a gift have endowed him with a treasure more precious than the wealth of all the ages—a treasure as enduring as eternity.[9]

God wants every child of tender age to be His child, to be adopted into His family. Young though they may be, the youth may be members of the household of faith and have a most precious experience. They may have hearts that are tender and ready to receive impressions that will be lasting. They may have their hearts drawn out in confidence and love for Jesus, and live for the Saviour. Christ will make them little missionaries. The whole current of their thought may be changed, so that sin will not appear a thing to be enjoyed, but to be shunned and hated.[10]

By precept and example parents are to teach their children to labor for the unconverted. The children should be so educated that they will sympathize with the aged and afflicted and will seek to alleviate the sufferings of the poor and distressed. . . . From their earliest years self-denial and sacrifice for the good of others and the advancement of Christ's cause should be inculcated, that they may be laborers together with God. . . .

God designs that the families of earth shall be a symbol of the family in heaven. Christian homes, established and conducted in accordance with God's plan, are among His most effective agencies for the formation of Christian character and for the advancement of His work.[11]

A WORLD IN NEED

We wait for light, but behold obscurity; for brightness, but we walk in darkness. Isa. 59:9.

There are many who are reading the Scriptures who cannot understand their true import. All over the world men and women are looking wistfully to heaven. Prayers and tears and inquiries go up from souls longing for light, for grace, for the Holy Spirit. Many are on the verge of the kingdom, waiting only to be gathered in.[12]

Everywhere there are hearts crying out for something which they have not. They long for a power that will give them mastery over sin, a power that will deliver them from the bondage of evil, a power that will give health and life and peace. Many who once knew the power of God's word have dwelt where there is no recognition of God, and they long for the divine presence.

The world needs today what it needed nineteen hundred years ago—a revelation of Christ. A great work of reform is demanded, and it is only through the grace of Christ that the work of restoration, physical, mental, and spiritual, can be accomplished.

Christ's method alone will give true success in reaching the people. The Saviour mingled with men as one who desired their good. He showed His sympathy for them, ministered to their needs, and won their confidence. Then He bade them, "Follow me."

There is need of coming close to the people by personal effort. . . . We are to weep with those that weep, and rejoice with those that rejoice. Accompanied by the power of persuasion, the power of prayer, the power of the love of God, this work will not, cannot, be without fruit.[13]

Heavenly intelligences are waiting to cooperate with human instrumentalities, that they may reveal to the world what human beings may become, and what, through union with the Divine, may be accomplished for the saving of souls that are ready to perish. There is no limit to the usefulness of one who, putting self aside, makes room for the working of the Holy Spirit upon his heart and lives a life wholly consecrated to God.[14]

TEACHING FROM HOUSE TO HOUSE

I kept back nothing that was profitable unto you, but have shewed you, and have taught you publickly, and from house to house. Acts 20:20.

Among the members of our churches there should be more house-to-house labor in giving Bible readings and distributing literature. . . . As we sow beside all waters we shall realize that "he which soweth bountifully shall reap also bountifully."

Christ's example must be followed by those who claim to be His children. Relieve the physical necessities of your fellow men, and their gratitude will break down the barriers and enable you to reach their hearts. . . . Women as well as men can engage in the work. . . . They can do in families a work that men cannot do, a work that reaches the inner life. They can come close to the hearts of those whom men cannot reach. Their work is needed. Discreet and humble women can do a good work in explaining the truth to the people in their homes. The word of God thus explained will do its leavening work, and . . . whole families will be converted. . . .

In the home circle, at your neighbor's fireside, at the bedside of the sick, in a quiet way you may read the Scriptures and speak a word for Jesus and the truth. Precious seed may thus be sown that will spring up and bring forth fruit. . . .

There is missionary work to be done in many unpromising places. The missionary spirit needs to take hold of our souls, inspiring us to reach classes for whom we had not planned to labor and in ways and places that we had no idea of working. The Lord has His plan for the sowing of the gospel seed. In sowing according to His will, we shall so multiply the seed that His word may reach thousands who have never heard the truth.[15]

Thousands upon thousands, and ten thousand times ten thousand angels are waiting to co-operate with members of our churches in communicating the light that God has generously given, that a people may be prepared for the coming of Christ.[16]

Our sisters, the youth, the middle-aged, and those of advanced years, may act a part in the closing work for this time; and in doing this as they have opportunity, they will obtain an experience of the highest value to themselves. In forgetfulness of self, they will grow in grace.[17]

ONE-TO-ONE WITNESSING

For God so loved the world, that he gave his only begotten Son, that whosoever believeth in him should not perish, but have everlasting life. John 3:16.

Why are not all who claim to love God seeking to enlighten their neighbors and their associates, that they may not longer neglect this great salvation? Christ gave Himself to a shameful, agonizing death, showing His great travail of soul to save the perishing. Oh, Christ is able, Christ is willing, Christ is longing, to save all who will come unto Him!

Talk to souls in peril and get them to behold Jesus upon the cross, dying to make it possible for Him to pardon. Talk to the sinner with your own heart overflowing with the tender, pitying love of Christ. Let there be deep earnestness; but not a harsh, loud note should be heard from the one who is trying to win the soul to look and live.

First have your own soul consecrated to God. As you look upon our Intercessor in heaven, let your heart be broken. Then, softened and subdued, you can address repenting sinners as one who realizes the power of redeeming love. Pray with these souls, by faith bringing them to the foot of the cross; carry their minds up with your mind, and fix the eye of faith where you look, upon Jesus the Sin Bearer. Get them to look away from their poor, sinful selves to the Saviour, and the victory is won. They behold for themselves the Lamb of God that taketh away the sin of the world. They see the Way, the Truth, the Life. The Sun of Righteousness sheds its bright beams into the heart. The strong tide of redeeming love pours into the parched and thirsty soul, and the sinner is saved to Jesus Christ.

Christ crucified—talk it, pray it, sing it, and it will break and win hearts. This is the power and wisdom of God to gather souls for Christ. Formal, set phrases, the presentation of merely argumentative subjects, is productive of little good. The melting love of God in the hearts of the workers will be recognized by those for whom they labor. Souls are thirsting for the waters of life. Do not be empty cisterns. If you reveal the love of Christ to them, you may lead the hungering, thirsting ones to Jesus, and He will give them the bread of life and the water of salvation.[18]

SOUND AN ALARM!

Blow ye the trumpet in Zion, and sound an alarm in my holy mountain: let all the inhabitants of the land tremble: for the day of the Lord cometh, for it is nigh at hand. Joel 2:1.

The things that concern our eternal welfare are now to absorb our attention. We cannot afford to give heavenly things the second place. . . . The judgments of God are in the land. They speak in solemn warning, saying, "Be ye also ready: for in such an hour as ye think not the Son of man cometh."

There are many, many in our churches who know little of the real meaning of the truth for this time. I appeal to them not to disregard the fulfilling of the signs of the times, which say so plainly that the end is near. O how many who have not sought their soul's salvation will soon make the bitter lamentation, "The harvest is past, the summer is ended, and my soul is not saved"!

We are living in the closing scenes of this earth's history. Prophecy is rapidly fulfilling. The hours of probation are fast passing. We have no time—not a moment—to lose. Let us not be found sleeping on guard. Let no one say in his heart or by his works, "My lord delayeth his coming." Let the message of Christ's soon return sound forth in earnest words of warning. Let us persuade men and women everywhere to repent, and flee from the wrath to come. Let us arouse them to immediate preparation; for we little know what is before us. Let ministers and lay members go forth into the ripening fields. . . .

The Lord is soon to come, and we must be prepared to meet Him in peace. Let us be determined to do all in our power to impart light to those around us. We are not to be sad, but cheerful, and we are to keep the Lord Jesus ever before us. . . . We must be ready and waiting for His appearing. O how glorious it will be to see Him, and be welcomed as His redeemed ones! Long have we waited, but our faith is not to become weak. If we can but see the King in His beauty, we shall be forever and forever blessed. I feel as if I must cry aloud, "Homeward bound." We are nearing the time when Christ will come with power and great glory, to take His ransomed ones to their eternal home.[19]

GOD'S SPECIAL MESSAGE FOR TODAY

The night is far spent, the day is at hand: let us therefore cast off the works of darkness, and let us put on the armour of light. Rom. 13:12.

In a time like this, we should have but one object in view— the employing of every means that God has provided by which the truth may be planted in the hearts of men. . . . It is the duty of every Christian to strive to the utmost of his ability to spread abroad the knowledge of the truth.[20]

God has waited long, and He is waiting still, to have the beings that are His by both creation and redemption, listen to His voice, and obey Him as loving, submissive children, whose desire is to be near His side, and to have the light of His countenance shining upon them. We are to bear the third angel's message to the world, warning men against the worship of the beast and his image, and directing them to take their places in the ranks of those who "keep the commandments of God, and the faith of Jesus." God has not revealed to us the time when this message will close, or when probation will have an end. . . . It is our duty to watch and work and wait, to labor every moment for the souls of men that are ready to perish. . . .

Now, just now, is the time for us to be watching, working, and waiting. . . . The end of all things is at hand. . . . The Spirit of the Lord is working to take the truth of the inspired word and stamp it upon the soul so that the professed followers of Christ will have a holy, sacred joy that they will be able to impart to others. . . .

There is need of a deeper, stronger, more constraining testimony on the power of the truth as seen in the practical godliness of those who profess to believe it.[21]

We are to have the truth planted in the heart, and teach it to others as it is in Jesus. The world is in a very solemn period; for souls are deciding what will be their eternal destiny. Satan and his angels are continually plotting to make void the law of God, and thus to enslave the souls of men in the toils of sin. The darkness which is covering the earth is deepening, but those who walk humbly with God have nothing to fear.[22]

A TIME FOR DECISION!

Choose you this day whom ye will serve. Joshua 24:15.

Today the world is mad: an insanity is upon men and women, and is hurrying them on to eternal ruin. Every species of indulgence prevails, and men have become so infatuated with vice that they will not listen to warnings or appeals.

The Lord says to the people of the earth, "Choose you this day whom ye will serve." All are now deciding their eternal destiny. Men need to be aroused to realize the solemnity of the time, the nearness of the day when human probation shall be ended. God gives no man a message that it will be five years or ten years or twenty years before this earth's history shall close. He would not give any living being an excuse for delaying the preparation for His appearing. He would have no one say, as did the unfaithful servant, "My lord delayeth his coming;" for this leads to reckless neglect of the opportunities and privileges given to prepare us for that great day. Everyone who claims to be a servant of God is called to do His service as if each day might be the last. . . .

Talk of the speedy appearing of the Son of man in the clouds of heaven with power and great glory. Put not off that day. . . .

Here is the great burden to be carried by each one. Are my sins forgiven? Has Christ, the burden-bearer, taken away my guilt? Have I a clean heart, purified by the righteousness of Jesus Christ? Woe be to any soul who is not seeking a refuge in Christ. Woe be to all who shall in any way divert the mind from the work, and cause any soul to be less vigilant now. . . .

The great work from which the mind should not be diverted is the consideration of our personal standing in the sight of God. Are our feet on the Rock of Ages? Are we hiding ourselves in the only Refuge? The storm is coming, relentless in its fury. Are we prepared to meet it? Are we one with Christ as He is one with the Father? Are we heirs of God and joint heirs with Christ? . . .

The character of Christ is to be our character. We are to be transformed by the renewing of our hearts. Here is our only safety. Nothing can separate a living Christian from God.[23]

LIVING TO SAVE OTHERS

If any man will come after me, let him deny himself, and take up his cross daily, and follow me. Luke 9:23.

The sin which is indulged to the greatest extent, and which separates us from God and produces so many contagious spiritual disorders, is selfishness. There can be no returning to the Lord except by self-denial. Of ourselves we can do nothing; but, through God strengthening us, we can live to do good to others, and in this way shun the evil of selfishness. We need not go to heathen lands to manifest our desire to devote all to God in a useful, unselfish life. We should do this in the home circle, in the church, among those with whom we associate and with whom we do business. Right in the common walks of life is where self is to be denied and kept in subordination.

Paul could say: "I die daily." It is the daily dying to self in the little transactions of life that makes us overcomers. We should forget self in the desire to do good to others. With many there is a decided lack of love for others. Instead of faithfully performing their duty, they seek rather their own pleasure.

God positively enjoins upon all His followers a duty to bless others with their influence and means, and to seek that wisdom of Him which will enable them to do all in their power to elevate the thoughts and affections of those who come within their influence. In doing for others, a sweet satisfaction will be experienced, an inward peace which will be a sufficient reward. When actuated by a high and noble desire to do others good, they will find true happiness in a faithful discharge of life's manifold duties. This will bring more than an earthly reward; for every faithful, unselfish performance of duty is noticed by the angels and shines in the life record.

In heaven none will think of self, nor seek their own pleasure; but all, from pure, genuine love, will seek the happiness of the heavenly beings around them. If we wish to enjoy heavenly society in the earth made new, we must be governed by heavenly principles here.[24]

The greatest work that can be done in our world is to glorify God by living the character of Christ.[25]

PATHWAY TO LIFE

Enter ye in at the strait gate: for wide is the gate, and broad is the way, that leadeth to destruction, and many there be which go in thereat: because strait is the gate, and narrow is the way, which leadeth unto life, and few there be that find it. Matt. 7:13, 14.

Christ calls upon us to enter the narrow pathway, where every step means a denial of self. He calls upon us to stand upon the platform of eternal truth, and contend, yes, contend earnestly, for the faith once delivered to the saints. . . .

As we near the time when principalities and powers and spiritual wickedness in high places will be fully brought into the warfare against the truth, when Satan's deceptive power will be so great that, if it were possible, he would deceive the very elect, our discernment must be sharpened by divine enlightenment, that we may not be ignorant of Satan's devices. . . . By giving us the cooperation of the holy angels, God has made it possible for our work to be . . . a glorious success. But success will seldom result from scattered effort. The united influence of all the members of the church is required.

The church today needs men who, like Enoch, walk with God, revealing Christ to the world. Church-members need to reach a higher standard. Heavenly messengers are waiting to communicate with those who have sunk self out of sight, whose lives are a fulfilling of the words, "I live; yet not I, but Christ liveth in me: and the life which I now live in the flesh I live by the faith of the Son of God, who loved me, and gave himself for me." Of such men and women must the church be composed before her light can shine forth to the world in clear, distinct rays. Our views of the Sun of Righteousness are clouded by self-seeking. Christ is crucified afresh by many who through self-indulgence allow Satan to gain control over them. . . .

It is God's purpose that all shall be tested and tried, that He may see whether they are loyal or disloyal to the laws that govern the kingdom of heaven. To the last, God permits Satan to reveal himself as a liar, an accuser, and a murderer. Thus the final triumph of His people is made more marked, more glorious, more full and complete.[26]

IN PARTNERSHIP WITH CHRIST

I am the vine, ye are the branches: He that abideth in me, and I in him, the same bringeth forth much fruit: for without me ye can do nothing. John 15:5.

The end is near! God calls upon the church to set in order the things that remain. Workers together with God, you are empowered by the Lord to take others with you into the kingdom. You are to be God's living agents, channels of light to the world, and round about you are angels of heaven with their commission from Christ to sustain, strengthen, and uphold you in working for the salvation of souls. . . .

Stand out separate and distinct from the world—in the world, but not of it, reflecting the bright beams of the Sun of Righteousness, being pure, holy, and undefiled, and in faith carrying light into all the highways and byways of the earth.

Let the churches awake before it is everlastingly too late. Let every member take up his individual work and vindicate the name of the Lord by which he is called. Let sound faith and earnest piety take the place of slothfulness and unbelief. When faith lays hold upon Christ, the truth will bring delight to the soul, and the services of religion will not be dull and uninteresting. . . . Daily you will have a rich experience as you practice the Christianity you profess. Sinners will be converted. . . .

Oh, that all may arouse and manifest to the world that theirs is a living faith, that a vital issue is before the world, that Jesus will soon come. Let men see that we believe that we are on the borders of the eternal world.

The upbuilding of the kingdom of God is retarded or urged forward according to the unfaithfulness or fidelity of human agencies. The work is hindered by the failure of the human to cooperate with the divine. Men may pray, "Thy kingdom come. Thy will be done in earth, as it is in heaven"; but if they fail of acting out this prayer in their lives, their petitions will be fruitless. But though you may be weak, erring, and sinful, the Lord holds out to you the offer of partnership with Himself. He invites you to come under divine instruction. Uniting with Christ, you may work the works of God. "Without me," Christ said, "ye can do nothing." [27]

REPRESENTATIVES OF THE SAVIOUR

Maintain good conduct among the Gentiles, so that in case they speak against you as wrongdoers, they may see your good deeds and glorify God on the day of visitation. 1 Peter 2:12, R.S.V.

God expects those who bear the name of Christ to represent Him. . . . They are to be a sanctified, purified, holy people, communicating light to all with whom they come in contact. . . .

The followers of Christ are to be separate from the world in principles and interests, but they are not to isolate themselves from the world. The Saviour mingled constantly with men, not to encourage them in anything that was not in accordance with God's will, but to uplift and ennoble them. "I sanctify myself," He declared, "that they also might be sanctified." John 17:19. So the Christian is to abide among men, that the savor of divine love may be as salt to preserve the world from corruption. . . .

The power of a higher, purer, nobler life is our great need. The world is watching to see what fruit is borne by professed Christians. . . . Impressions favorable or unfavorable to Bible religion are constantly being made on the minds of all with whom we have to do.

And God and the angels are watching. God desires His people to show by their lives the advantage of Christianity over worldliness, to show that they are working on a high, holy plane. He longs to see them showing that the truth they have received has made them children of the heavenly King. He longs to make them channels through which He can pour His boundless love and mercy.

Christ is waiting with longing desire for the manifestation of Himself in His church. When the character of the Saviour shall be perfectly reproduced in His people, then He will come to claim His own. It is the privilege of every Christian, not only to look for, but to hasten, the coming of our Lord. Were all who profess His name bearing fruit to His glory, how quickly the whole world would be sown with the seed of the gospel! Quickly the last great harvest would be ripened, and Christ would come.[28]

A CHARACTER THE WORLD WILL RECOGNIZE

That ye may be blameless and harmless, the sons of God, without rebuke, in the midst of a crooked and perverse nation, among whom ye shine as lights in the world. Phil. 2:15.

It is God's purpose to manifest through His people the principles of His kingdom. That in life and character they may reveal these principles, He desires to separate them from the customs, habits, and practices of the world. . . . By beholding the goodness, the mercy, the justice, and the love of God revealed in His church, the world is to have a representation of His character. And when the law of God is thus exemplified in the life, even the world will recognize the superiority of those who love and fear and serve God above every other people in the world.

Seventh-day Adventists, above all people, should be patterns of piety, holy in heart and in conversation. To them have been entrusted the most solemn truths ever committed to mortals. Every endowment of grace and power and efficiency has been liberally provided. They look for the near return of Christ in the clouds of heaven. For them to give to the world the impression that their faith is not a dominating power in their lives is greatly to dishonor God.

Because of the increasing power of Satan's temptations, the times in which we live are full of peril for the children of God, and we need to learn constantly of the Great Teacher, that we may take every step in surety and righteousness. Wonderful scenes are opening before us; and at this time a living testimony is to be borne in the lives of God's professed people, so that the world may see that in this age, when evil reigns on every side, there is yet a people who are laying aside their will and are seeking to do God's will—a people in whose hearts and lives God's law is written. . . .

Their thoughts are to be pure, their words noble and uplifting. The religion of Christ is to be interwoven with all that they do and say. They are to be a sanctified, purified, holy people, communicating light to all with whom they come in contact. It is His purpose that by exemplifying the truth in their lives, they shall be a praise in the earth. The grace of Christ is sufficient to bring this about.[29]

THE TESTIMONY THE WORLD NEEDS

You yourselves are our letter of recommendation, written on your hearts, to be known and read by all men. 2 Cor. 3:2, R.S.V.

Transformation of character is to be the testimony to the world of the indwelling love of Christ. The Lord expects His people to show that the redeeming power of grace can work upon the faulty character and cause it to develop in symmetry and abundant fruitfulness.

But in order for us to fulfill God's purpose, there is a preparatory work to be done. The Lord bids us empty our hearts of the selfishness which is the root of alienation. He longs to pour upon us His Holy Spirit in rich measure, and He bids us clear the way by self-renunciation. When self is surrendered to God, our eyes will be opened to see the stumbling stones which our un-Christlikeness has placed in the way of others. All these God bids us remove. He says: "Confess your faults one to another, and pray one for another, that ye may be healed." James 5:16. Then we may have the assurance that David had when, after confession of his sin, he prayed: "Restore unto me the joy of thy salvation; and uphold me with thy free spirit. Then will I teach transgressors thy ways; and sinners shall be converted unto thee." Psalm 51:12, 13.

When the grace of God reigns within, the soul will be surrounded with an atmosphere of faith and courage and Christlike love, an atmosphere invigorating to the spiritual life of all who inhale it. . . . Everyone who is a partaker of Christ's pardoning love, everyone who has been enlightened by the Spirit of God and converted to the truth, will feel that for these precious blessings he owes a debt to every soul with whom he comes in contact. Those who are humble in heart the Lord will use to reach souls whom the ordained ministers cannot approach. They will be moved to speak words which reveal the saving grace of Christ.

And in blessing others they will themselves be blessed. God gives us opportunity to impart grace, that He may refill us with increased grace. Hope and faith will strengthen as the agent for God works with the talents and facilities that God has provided. He will have a divine agency to work with him.[30]

WHEN GOD MAKES UP DEFICIENCIES

We then, as workers together with him, beseech you also that ye receive not the grace of God in vain. 2 Cor. 6:1.

We are to be partners in the work of God throughout the world; wherever there are souls to be saved, we are to lend our help, that many sons and daughters may be brought to God. The end is near, and for this reason we are to make the most of every entrusted ability and every agency that shall offer help to the work. . . .

How the angels must feel as they see the end approaching, and see so many of those entrusted with the last message of mercy huddling together, attending meetings for the sake of benefit to their own souls, and feeling dissatisfied if there is not much preaching, while they have little burden and are doing little for the salvation of others. All who are indeed united to Christ by living faith will be partakers of the divine nature. They will be constantly receiving from Him spiritual life, and they cannot be silent.

Life always shows itself in action. If the heart is living, it will send the lifeblood to every part of the body. Those whose hearts are filled with spiritual life will not need to be urged to reveal it. The divine life will flow forth from them in rich currents of grace. As they pray, as they speak, and as they labor, God is glorified. . . .

It is not the most brilliant or the most talented whose work produces the greatest and most lasting results. Who are the most efficient laborers? Those who will respond to the invitation: "Take my yoke upon you, and learn of me; for I am meek and lowly in heart."

If men to whom God has entrusted talents of intellect refuse to use these gifts to His glory, after test and trial He will leave them to their own imaginings and will take men who do not appear to be so richly endowed, who have not large self-confidence, and He will make the weak strong because they trust in God to do for them those things which they cannot do for themselves. God will accept the wholehearted service, and will Himself make up the deficiencies.[31]

Angels are listening to hear what kind of report you are bearing to the world about your heavenly Master.[32]

115

PREACHING WITH POWER

In those days came John the Baptist, preaching in the wilderness of Judea, "Repent, for the kingdom of heaven is at hand." Matt. 3:1, 2, R.S.V.

John the Baptist in his desert life was taught of God. He studied the revelations of God in nature. Under the guiding of the Divine Spirit, he studied the scrolls of the prophets. By day and by night, Christ was his study, his meditation, until mind and heart and soul were filled with the glorious vision.

He looked upon the King in His beauty, and self was lost sight of. He beheld the majesty of holiness and knew himself to be inefficient and unworthy. It was God's message that he was to declare. It was in God's power and His righteousness that he was to stand. He was ready to go forth as Heaven's messenger, unawed by the human, because he had looked upon the Divine. He could stand fearless in the presence of earthly monarchs because with trembling he had bowed before the King of kings.

With no elaborate arguments or finespun theories did John declare his message. Startling and stern, yet full of hope, his voice was heard from the wilderness: "Repent ye: for the kingdom of heaven is at hand." Matthew 3:2. With a new, strange power it moved the people. The whole nation was stirred. Multitudes flocked to the wilderness. . . .

In this age, just prior to the second coming of Christ in the clouds of heaven, such a work as that of John is to be done. God calls for men who will prepare a people to stand in the great day of the Lord. . . . As a people who believe in Christ's soon appearing, we have a message to bear—"Prepare to meet thy God." Amos 4:12. Our message must be as direct as was the message of John. He rebuked kings for their iniquity. Notwithstanding that his life was imperiled, he did not hesitate to declare God's word. And our work in this age must be done as faithfully.

In order to give such a message as John gave, we must have a spiritual experience like his. The same work must be wrought in us. We must behold God, and in beholding Him lose sight of self.[33]

"BEHOLD THE LAMB OF GOD"

Behold the Lamb of God, which taketh away the sin of the world. John 1:29.

John had by nature the faults and weaknesses common to humanity; but the touch of divine love had transformed him. When, after Christ's ministry began, the disciples of John came to him with the complaint that all men were following the new Teacher, John showed how clearly he understood his relation to the Messiah, and how gladly he welcomed the One for whom he had prepared the way.

"A man can receive nothing," he said, "except it be given him from heaven. Ye yourselves bear me witness, that I said, I am not the Christ, but that I am sent before him. . . . This my joy therefore is fulfilled. He must increase, but I must decrease." John 3:27-30.

Looking in faith to the Redeemer, John had risen to the height of self-abnegation. He sought not to attract men to himself, but to lift their thoughts higher and still higher, until they should rest upon the Lamb of God. He himself had been only a voice, a cry in the wilderness. Now with joy he accepted silence and obscurity, that the eyes of all might be turned to the Light of life.

Those who are true to their calling as messengers for God will not seek honor for themselves. Love for self will be swallowed up in love for Christ. They will recognize that it is their work to proclaim, as did John the Baptist: "Behold the Lamb of God, which taketh away the sin of the world." John 1:29. They will lift up Jesus, and with Him humanity will be lifted up. . . .

The soul of the prophet, emptied of self, was filled with the light of the Divine. . . . He bore witness to the Saviour's glory. . . . In this glory of Christ, all His followers are to share. . . . We can receive of heaven's light only as we are willing to be emptied of self. We can discern the character of God, and accept Christ by faith, only as we consent to the bringing into captivity of every thought to the obedience of Christ. To all who do this, the Holy Spirit is given without measure. In Christ "dwelleth all the fulness of the Godhead bodily. And ye are complete in him." Col. 2:9, 10.[34]

GOD'S CALL TO REFORM

He shall go before him in the spirit and power of Elias, to turn the hearts of the fathers to the children, and the disobedient to the wisdom of the just; to make ready a people prepared for the Lord. Luke 1:17.

John the Baptist went forth in the spirit and power of Elijah to prepare the way of the Lord and to turn the people to the wisdom of the just. He was a representative of those living in these last days to whom God has entrusted sacred truths to present before the people to prepare the way for the second appearing of Christ. . . .

Those who are to prepare the way for the second coming of Christ are represented by faithful Elijah, as John came in the spirit of Elijah to prepare the way for Christ's first advent. The great subject of reform is to be agitated, and the public mind is to be stirred. Temperance in all things is to be connected with the message, to turn the people of God from their idolatry, their gluttony, and their extravagance in dress and other things.

The self-denial, humility, and temperance required of the righteous, whom God especially leads and blesses, is to be presented to the people in contrast to the extravagant, health-destroying habits of those who live in this degenerate age. God has shown that health reform is as closely connected with the third angel's message as the hand is with the body. There is nowhere to be found so great a cause of physical and moral degeneracy as a neglect of this important subject. Those who indulge appetite and passion, and close their eyes to the light for fear they will see sinful indulgences which they are unwilling to forsake, are guilty before God. . . .

Providence has been leading the people of God out from the extravagant habits of the world, away from the indulgence of appetite and passion, to take their stand upon the platform of self-denial and temperance in all things. The people whom God is leading will be peculiar. They will not be like the world. But if they follow the leadings of God they will accomplish His purposes, and will yield their will to His will. Christ will dwell in the heart. . . . Your body, says the apostle, is the temple of the Holy Ghost.[35]

PROMOTE HEALTHFUL LIVING

I beseech you therefore, brethren, by the mercies of God, that ye present your bodies a living sacrifice, holy, acceptable unto God, which is your reasonable service. Rom. 12:1.

It is impossible for a man to present his body a living sacrifice, holy, acceptable to God, while continuing to indulge habits that are depriving him of physical, mental, and moral vigor. Again the apostle says, "Be not conformed to this world: but be ye transformed by the renewing of your mind, that ye may prove what is that good, and acceptable, and perfect, will of God." Rom. 12:2.[36]

We are in a world that is opposed to righteousness or purity of character, and especially to growth in grace. Wherever we look, we see defilement and corruption, deformity and sin. How opposed is all this to the work that must be accomplished in us just previous to receiving the gift of immortality! God's elect must stand untainted amid the corruptions teeming around them in these last days. Their bodies must be made holy, their spirits pure. If this work is to be accomplished, it must be undertaken at once, earnestly and understandingly. The Spirit of God should have perfect control, influencing every action.

The health reform is one branch of the great work which is to fit a people for the coming of the Lord. . . . Men and women cannot violate natural law by indulging depraved appetites and lustful passions, without violating the law of God. Therefore He has permitted the light of health reform to shine upon us, that we may realize the sinfulness of breaking the laws which He has established in our very being. . . .

To make natural law plain, and to urge obedience to it, is a work that accompanies the third angel's message. . . . He [God] designs that the subject shall be agitated, and the public mind deeply stirred to investigate it; for it is impossible for men and women, while under the power of sinful, health-destroying, brain-enervating habits, to appreciate sacred truth. . . .

He who cherishes the light which God has given him upon health reform, has an important aid in the work of becoming sanctified through the truth, and fitted for immortality.[37]

VIRTUE OF SELF-FORGETFULNESS

I am crucified with Christ: nevertheless I live; yet not I, but Christ liveth in me: and the life which I now live in the flesh I live by the faith of the Son of God, who loved me, and gave himself for me. Gal. 2:20.

By faith Paul appropriated the grace of Christ, and this grace supplied the necessities of his soul. By faith he received the heavenly gift, and imparted it to souls longing for light. This is the experience we need. . . . Pray for this faith. Strive for it. Believe that God will give it to you.

There is a great work to be done in our world. This is no dreamland. Before us are living realities. On every hand are to be seen the manifestations of Satan's power. Let us co-operate with Him who works to restore and uplift. And let us not forget that he who works for Christ must recruit his strength at the source of all strength. . . . Christians need power of thought, firmness of will, and knowledge that comes from the study of God's Word. They cannot afford to fill their minds with trifles. Every day they must be renewed in spiritual power.

Learn of Him who has said, "I am meek and lowly in heart." Learning of Him, you will find rest. Day by day you will gain an experience in the things of God, day by day realize the greatness of His salvation and the glory of a union with Him. Constantly you will learn better how to live Christlike, and constantly you will grow more like the Saviour.

If we will die to self, if we will enlarge our idea of what Christ can be to us and what we can be to Him, if we will unite with one another in the bonds of Christian fellowship, God will work through us with mighty power. Then we shall be sanctified through the truth. We shall indeed be chosen by God and controlled by His Spirit. Every day of life will be precious to us, because we shall see in it an opportunity to use our entrusted gifts for the blessing of others.[38]

We must forget self in loving service for others. . . . We may not remember some act of kindness which we do, . . . but eternity will bring out in all its brightness every act done for the salvation of souls, every word spoken for the comfort of God's children; and these deeds done for Christ's sake will be a part of our joy through all eternity.[39]

THE YOUTH, GOD'S INSTRUMENTS

It is good for a man that he bear the yoke in his youth. Lam. 3:27.

God calls young men in the vigor and strength of their youth to share with Him self-denial, sacrifice, and suffering. If they accept the call, He will make them His instruments to save souls for whom He died. But He would have them count the cost and enter upon their work with a full knowledge of the conditions upon which they serve a crucified Redeemer. . . .

Our first work should be to bring our own hearts into harmony with God, and then we are prepared to labor for others. In former days there was great searching of heart among our earnest workers. They counseled together and united in humble, fervent prayer for divine guidance. . . . Christ's coming is nearer than when we believed. Every passing day leaves us one less to proclaim the message of warning to the world. Would that there were today more earnest intercession with God, greater humility, greater purity, and greater faith.[40]

We have a grand work to do for the Master, to open the word of God to those who are in the darkness of error. Young friends, act as though you had a sacred charge. You should be Bible students, ever ready to give to every man that asketh you a reason of the hope that is in you. By your true Christian dignity give evidence that you know you have a truth that it is for the interest of the people to hear. If this truth is inwrought in the soul, it will manifest itself in the countenance and demeanor, in a calm, noble self-possession and peace which the Christian alone can possess. Those who have genuine humility, and whose minds have been expanded by the truths unfolded in the gospel, will have an influence that will be felt. They will make an impression upon minds and hearts.[41]

I have no higher wish than to see our youth imbued with the spirit of pure religion which will lead them to take up the cross and follow Jesus. Go forth, young disciples of Christ, controlled by principle, clad in the robes of purity and righteousness. Your Saviour will guide you into the position best suited to your talents and where you can be most useful. In the path of duty you may be sure of receiving grace sufficient for your day.[42]

A WORK FOR ALL AGES

I write to you, fathers, because you know him who is from the beginning. I write to you, young men, because you are strong, and the word of God abides in you, and you have overcome the evil one. 1 John 2:14, R.S.V.

There are many lines in which the youth can find opportunity for helpful effort. . . . In this closing work of the gospel there is a vast field to be occupied; and, more than ever before, the work is to enlist helpers from the common people. Both the youth and those older in years will be called from the field, from the vineyard, and from the workshop, and sent forth by the Master to give His message. Many of these may have had little opportunity for education, but Christ sees in them qualifications that will enable them to fulfill His purpose. If they put their hearts into the work and continue to be learners, He will fit them to labor for Him. . . .

However large, however small, your talents, remember that what you have is yours only in trust. Thus God is testing you, giving you an opportunity to prove yourself true. To Him you are indebted for all your capabilities. To Him belong your powers of body, mind, and soul, and for Him these powers are to be used. Your time, your influence, your capabilities, your skill—all must be accounted for to Him who gives all.[43]

The youth who finds joy and happiness in reading the word of God and in the hour of prayer is constantly refreshed by drafts from the Fountain of life. He will attain a height of moral excellence and a breadth of thought of which others cannot conceive. . . . Those who thus connect their souls with God are acknowledged by Him as His sons and daughters. They are constantly reaching higher and still higher, obtaining clearer views of God and of eternity, until the Lord makes them channels of light and wisdom to the world.[44]

With such an army of workers as our youth, rightly trained, might furnish, how soon the message of a crucified, risen, and soon-coming Saviour might be carried to the whole world! How soon might the end come—the end of suffering and sorrow and sin! [45]

WHY SO MANY IDLERS?

You shall be my witnesses in Jerusalem and in all Judea and Samaria and to the end of the earth. Acts 1:8, R.S.V.

In the trust given to the first disciples, believers in every age have shared. Everyone who has received the gospel has been given sacred truth to impart to the world. God's faithful people have always been aggressive missionaries, consecrating their resources to the honor of His name, and wisely using their talents in His service. . . .

The members of God's church are to be zealous of good works, separating from worldly ambition, and walking in the footsteps of Him who went about doing good. With hearts filled with sympathy and compassion, they are to minister to those in need of help, bringing to sinners a knowledge of the Saviour's love. Such work calls for laborious effort, but it brings a rich reward. Those who engage in it with sincerity of purpose will see souls won to the Saviour. . . .

"The Spirit and the bride say, Come. And let him that heareth say, Come." Rev. 22:17. The charge to give this invitation includes the entire church. Everyone who has heard the invitation is to echo the message from hill and valley, saying, "Come.". . .

Hundreds, yea, thousands, who have heard the message of salvation, are still idlers in the market place, when they might be engaged in some line of active service. To these Christ is saying, "Why stand ye here all the day idle?" and He adds, "Go ye also into the vineyard." Matt. 20:6, 7. Why is it that many more do not respond to the call? Is it because they think themselves excused in that they do not stand in the pulpit? Let them understand that there is a large work to be done outside the pulpit by thousands of consecrated lay members.

Long has God waited for the spirit of service to take possession of the whole church so that everyone shall be working for Him according to his ability. When the members of the church of God do their appointed work in the needy fields at home and abroad, in fulfillment of the gospel commission, the whole world will soon be warned, and the Lord Jesus will return to this earth with power and great glory. "This gospel of the kingdom shall be preached in all the world for a witness unto all nations; and then shall the end come." Matt. 24:14.[46]

ALL OUR TREASURES FOR GOD

Freely ye have received, freely give. Matt. 10:8.

All that men receive of God's bounty still belongs to God. Whatever He has bestowed in the valuable and beautiful things of earth is placed in our hands to test us, to sound the depths of our love for Him and our appreciation of His favors. Whether it be the treasures of wealth or of intellect, they are to be laid, a willing offering, at the feet of Jesus.[47]

In commissioning His disciples to go "into all the world, and preach the gospel to every creature," Christ assigned to men the work of extending the knowledge of His grace. But while some go forth to preach, He calls upon others . . . for offerings with which to support His cause in the earth.[48]

Not all can make large offerings, not all can do great works, magnificent deeds; but all can practice self-denial, all can reveal the unselfishness of the Saviour. Some can bring large gifts to the Lord's treasury; others can bring only mites; but every gift brought in sincerity is accepted by the Lord.[49]

Many would be surprised to see how much could be saved for the cause of God by acts of self-denial. The small sums saved by deeds of sacrifice will do more for the upbuilding of the cause of God than larger gifts will accomplish that have not called for denial of self.[50]

The spirit of liberality is the spirit of heaven. Christ's self-sacrificing love is revealed upon the cross. That man might be saved, He gave all that He had and then gave Himself. The cross of Christ appeals to the benevolence of every follower of the blessed Saviour. The principle there illustrated is to give, give. . . . The principle of worldlings is to get, get. . . .

The light of the gospel shining from the cross of Christ rebukes selfishness. . . . Many of God's people are in danger of being ensnared by worldliness and covetousness. They should understand that it is His mercy that multiplies the demands for their means. . . . He thus makes man the medium through which to distribute His blessings on earth. God planned the system of beneficence in order that man might become like his Creator, benevolent and unselfish in character, and finally be a partaker with Christ of the eternal, glorious reward.[51]

A TWOFOLD LIFE

Our fellowship is with the Father, and with his Son Jesus Christ. 1 John 1:3.

Nothing is more needed in our work than the practical results of communion with God. We should show by our daily lives that we have peace and rest in the Saviour. His peace in the heart will shine forth in the countenance. . . . Communion with God will ennoble the character and the life. Men will take knowledge of us, as of the first disciples, that we have been with Jesus. This will impart to the worker a power that nothing else can give. Of this power he must not allow himself to be deprived. We must live a twofold life—a life of thought and action, of silent prayer and earnest work.[52]

All who are under the training of God need the quiet hour for communion with their own hearts, with nature, and with God. . . . We must individually hear Him speaking to the heart. When every other voice is hushed, and in quietness we wait before Him, the silence of the soul makes more distinct the voice of God. He bids us, "Be still, and know that I am God." Ps. 46:10. This is the effectual preparation for all labor for God. Amidst the hurrying throng, and the strain of life's intense activities, he who is thus refreshed will be surrounded with an atmosphere of light and peace. He will receive a new endowment of both physical and mental strength. His life will breathe out a fragrance, and will reveal a divine power that will reach men's hearts.[53]

Many, even in their seasons of devotion, fail of receiving the blessing of real communion with God. They are in too great haste. With hurried steps they press through the circle of Christ's loving presence, pausing perhaps a moment within the sacred precincts, but not waiting for counsel. They have no time to remain with the divine Teacher. With their burdens they return to their work.

These workers can never attain the highest success until they learn the secret of strength. They must give themselves time to think, to pray, to wait upon God for a renewal of physical, mental, and spiritual power. They need the uplifting influence of His Spirit. Receiving this, they will be quickened by fresh life.[54]

MISTAKEN ZEAL

For I bear them record that they have a zeal of God, but not according to knowledge. Rom. 10:2.

There is a noisy zeal, without aim or purpose, which is not according to knowledge, which is blind in its operations and destructive in its results. This is not Christian zeal. Christian zeal is controlled by principle and is not spasmodic. It is earnest, deep, and strong, engaging the whole soul and arousing to exercise the moral sensibilities.

The salvation of souls and the interests of the kingdom of God are matters of the highest importance. What object is there that calls for greater earnestness than the salvation of souls and the glory of God? There are considerations here which cannot be lightly regarded. They are as weighty as eternity. Eternal destinies are at stake. Men and women are deciding for weal or woe. Christian zeal will not exhaust itself in talk, but will feel and act with vigor and efficiency. Yet Christian zeal will not act for the sake of being seen. Humility will characterize every effort and be seen in every work. Christian zeal will lead to earnest prayer and humiliation, and to faithfulness in home duties. In the family circle will be seen the gentleness and love, benevolence and compassion, which are ever the fruits of Christian zeal. . . .

Oh, how few feel the worth of souls! How few are willing to sacrifice to bring souls to the knowledge of Christ! There is much talking, much professed love for perishing souls; but talk is cheap stuff. It is earnest Christian zeal that is wanted—a zeal that will be manifested by doing something. All must now work for themselves, and when they have Jesus in their hearts they will confess Him to others. No more could a soul who possesses Christ be hindered from confessing Him than could the waters of Niagara be stopped from flowing over the falls.[55]

Eternal life should engage the deepest interest of every Christian. To be a co-worker with Christ and the heavenly angels in the great plan of salvation! What work can bear any comparison with this! From every soul saved there comes to God a revenue of glory to be reflected upon the one saved and also upon the one instrumental in his salvation.[56]

A SURE FOUNDATION

Nevertheless the foundation of God standeth sure, having this seal, The Lord knoweth them that are his. And, Let every one that nameth the name of Christ depart from iniquity. 2 Tim. 2:19.

The Lord will have a people as true as steel, and with faith as firm as the granite rock. They are to be His witnesses in the world, His instrumentalities to do a special, a glorious work in the day of His preparation. . . .

Ministers who have preached the truth with all zeal and earnestness may apostatize and join the ranks of our enemies, but does this turn the truth of God into a lie? "Nevertheless," says the apostle, "the foundation of God standeth sure." The faith and feelings of men may change; but the truth of God, never. . . .

It is as certain that we have the truth as that God lives; and Satan, with all his arts and hellish power, cannot change the truth of God into a lie. While the great adversary will try his utmost to make of none effect the word of God, truth must go forth as a lamp that burneth.

The Lord has singled us out and made us subjects of His marvelous mercy. Shall we be charmed with the pratings of the apostate? Shall we choose to take our stand with Satan and his host? Shall we join with the transgressors of God's law? Rather let it be our prayer: "Lord, put enmity between me and the serpent." If we are not at enmity with his works of darkness, his powerful folds encircle us, and his sting is ready at any moment to be driven to our hearts. We should count him a deadly foe. We should oppose him in the name of Christ. Our work is still onward. . . . Let all who name the name of Christ clothe themselves with the armor of righteousness. . . .

The time has come when we must know for ourselves why we believe as we do. . . . Let us lay up for ourselves a good foundation against the time to come, that we may lay hold on eternal life. We must labor, not in our own strength, but in the strength of our risen Lord. What will we do and dare for Jesus? [57]

HEAVEN IS WAITING FOR YOU

As my Father hath sent me, even so send I you. John 20:21.

Of the apostles it is written, "They went forth, and preached every where, the Lord working with them, and confirming the word with signs following." Mark 16:20. As Christ sent forth His disciples, so today He sends forth the members of His church. The same power that the apostles had is for them. If they will make God their strength, He will work with them, and they shall not labor in vain. Let them realize that the work in which they are engaged is one upon which the Lord has placed His signet. God said to Jeremiah, "Say not, I am a child: for thou shalt go to all that I shall send thee, and whatsoever I command thee thou shalt speak. Be not afraid of their faces: for I am with thee to deliver thee." Then the Lord put forth His hand and touched His servant's mouth, saying, "Behold, I have put my words in thy mouth." Jer. 1:7-9. And He bids us go forth to speak the words He gives us, feeling His holy touch upon our lips.

Christ has given to the church a sacred charge. Every member should be a channel through which God can communicate to the world the treasures of His grace, the unsearchable riches of Christ. There is nothing that the Saviour desires so much as agents who will represent to the world His Spirit and His character. There is nothing that the world needs so much as the manifestation through humanity of the Saviour's love. All heaven is waiting for men and women through whom God can reveal the power of Christianity.

The church is God's agency for the proclamation of truth, empowered by Him to do a special work; and if she is loyal to Him, obedient to all His commandments, there will dwell within her the excellency of divine grace. If she will be true to her allegiance, if she will honor the Lord God of Israel, there is no power that can stand against her.

Zeal for God and His cause moved the disciples to bear witness to the gospel with mighty power. Should not a like zeal fire our hearts with a determination to tell the story of redeeming love, of Christ and Him crucified? It is the privilege of every Christian, not only to look for, but to hasten the coming of the Saviour.[58]

GOD WILL GUIDE HIS PEOPLE

When thou passest through the waters, I will be with thee; and through the rivers, they shall not overflow thee: when thou walkest through the fire, thou shalt not be burned; neither shall the flame kindle upon thee. Isa. 43:2.

God has a church upon the earth, who are His chosen people, who keep His commandments. He is leading, not stray offshoots, not one here and one there, but a people.

There is no need to doubt, to be fearful that the work will not succeed. God is at the head of the work, and He will set everything in order. If matters need adjusting at the head of the work, God will attend to that, and work to right every wrong. Let us have faith that God is going to carry the noble ship which bears the people of God safely into port.

When I voyaged from Portland, Maine, to Boston, many years ago, a storm came upon us, and the great waves dashed us to and fro. The chandeliers fell, and the trunks were rolled from side to side, like balls. The passengers were frightened, and many were screaming, waiting in expectation of death.

After a while the pilot came on board. The captain stood near the pilot as he took the wheel, and expressed fear about the course in which the ship was directed. "Will you take the wheel?" asked the pilot. The captain was not ready to do that, for he knew that he lacked experience. Then some of the passengers grew uneasy, and said they feared the pilot would dash them upon the rocks. "Will you take the wheel?" asked the pilot; but they knew that they could not manage the wheel.

When you think that the work is in danger, pray, "Lord, stand at the wheel. Carry us through the perplexity. Bring us safely into port." Have we not reason to believe that the Lord will bring us through triumphantly? . . .

You cannot with your finite minds understand the working of all the providences of God. Let God take care of His own work.[1]

SATAN REDOUBLES HIS EFFORTS

The angel of the Lord encampeth round about them that fear him, and delivereth them. Ps. 34:7.

The power and malice of Satan and his host might justly alarm us were it not that we may find shelter and deliverance in the superior power of our Redeemer. We carefully secure our houses with bolts and locks to protect our property and our lives from evil men; but we seldom think of the evil angels who are constantly seeking access to us, and against whose attacks we have, in our own strength, no method of defense. If permitted, they can distract our minds, disorder and torment our bodies, destroy our possessions and our lives. Their only delight is in misery and destruction. Fearful is the condition of those who resist the divine claims and yield to Satan's temptations, until God gives them up to the control of evil spirits. But those who follow Christ are ever safe under His watchcare. Angels that excel in strength are sent from heaven to protect them. The wicked one cannot break through the guard which God has stationed about His people.

The great controversy between Christ and Satan, that has been carried forward for nearly six thousand years, is soon to close; and the wicked one redoubles his efforts to defeat the work of Christ in man's behalf and to fasten souls in his snares. To hold the people in darkness and impenitence till the Saviour's mediation is ended, and there is no longer a sacrifice for sin, is the object which he seeks to accomplish.

When there is no special effort made to resist his power, when indifference prevails in the church and the world, Satan is not concerned; for he is in no danger of losing those whom he is leading captive at his will. But when the attention is called to eternal things, and souls are inquiring, "What must I do to be saved?" he is on the ground, seeking to match his power against the power of Christ. . . . He is in attendance when men assemble for the worship of God. Though hidden from sight, he is working with all diligence to control the minds of the worshipers.[2]

MOMENTOUS STRUGGLE BEFORE US

We ought to obey God rather than men. Acts 5:29.

A great crisis awaits the people of God. A crisis awaits the world. The most momentous struggle of all the ages is just before us. . . . The question of enforcing Sunday observance has become one of national interest and importance. We well know what the result of this movement will be. But are we ready for the issue? Have we faithfully discharged the duty which God has committed to us of giving the people warning of the danger before them? . . .

There are many who have never understood the claims of the Bible Sabbath and the false foundation upon which the Sunday institution rests. Any movement in favor of religious legislation is really an act of concession to the papacy, which for so many ages has steadily warred against liberty of conscience. Sunday observance owes its existence as a so-called Christian institution to "the mystery of iniquity"; and its enforcement will be a virtual recognition of the principles which are the very cornerstone of Romanism. When our nation shall so abjure the principles of its government as to enact a Sunday law, Protestantism will in this act join hands with popery; it will be nothing else than giving life to the tyranny which has long been eagerly watching its opportunity to spring again into active despotism. . . .

If popery or its principles shall again be legislated into power, the fires of persecution will be rekindled against those who will not sacrifice conscience and the truth in deference to popular errors. This evil is on the point of realization.

When God has given us light showing the dangers before us, how can we stand clear in His sight if we neglect to put forth every effort in our power to bring it before the people? Can we be content to leave them to meet this momentous issue unwarned? . . .

When the laws of earthly rulers are brought into opposition to the laws of the Supreme Ruler of the universe, then those who are God's loyal subjects will be true to Him.[3]

WRESTING THE SCRIPTURES

They that are unlearned and unstable wrest . . . the . . . scriptures, unto their own destruction. 2 Peter 3:16.

The position that it is of no consequence what men believe is one of Satan's most successful deceptions. He knows that the truth, received in the love of it, sanctifies the soul of the receiver; therefore he is constantly seeking to substitute false theories, fables, another gospel. . . .

The vague and fanciful interpretations of Scripture, and the many conflicting theories concerning religious faith, that are found in the Christian world are the work of our great adversary to confuse minds so that they shall not discern the truth. And the discord and division which exist among the churches of Christendom are in a great measure due to the prevailing custom of wresting the Scriptures to support a favorite theory. Instead of carefully studying God's word with humility of heart to obtain a knowledge of His will, many seek only to discover something odd or original.

In order to sustain erroneous doctrines or unchristian practices, some will seize upon passages of Scripture separated from the context, perhaps quoting half of a single verse as proving their point, when the remaining portion would show the meaning to be quite the opposite. With the cunning of the serpent they entrench themselves behind disconnected utterances construed to suit their carnal desires. Thus do many willfully pervert the word of God. Others, who have an active imagination, seize upon the figures and symbols of Holy Writ, interpret them to suit their fancy, with little regard to the testimony of Scripture as its own interpreter, and then they present their vagaries as the teachings of the Bible.

Whenever the study of the Scriptures is entered upon without a prayerful, humble, teachable spirit, the plainest and simplest as well as the most difficult passages will be wrested from their true meaning. . . . The Word of God is plain to all who study it with a prayerful heart. Every truly honest soul will come to the light of truth. "Light is sown for the righteous." Psalm 97:11. And no church can advance in holiness unless its members are earnestly seeking for truth as for hid treasure.[4]

FALSE THEORIES ABOUT GOD

Because that, when they knew God, they glorified him not as God, neither were thankful; but became vain in their imaginations, and their foolish heart was darkened. Rom. 1:21.

The theory that God is an essence pervading all nature, is one of Satan's most subtle devices. It misrepresents God, and is a dishonor to His greatness and majesty.

Pantheistic theories are not sustained by the Word of God. The light of His truth shows that these theories are soul-destroying agencies. Darkness is their element, sensuality their sphere. They gratify the natural heart, and give license to inclination. Separation from God is the result of accepting them. . . .

There is but one power that can break the hold of evil from the hearts of men, and that is the power of God in Jesus Christ. Only through the blood of the Crucified One is there cleansing from sin. His grace alone can enable us to resist and subdue the tendencies of our fallen nature. This power the spiritualistic theories concerning God make of no effect. If God is an essence pervading all nature, then He dwells in all men; and in order to attain holiness, man has only to develop the power that is within him.

These theories, followed to their logical conclusion, sweep away the whole Christian economy. They do away with the necessity for the atonement, and make man his own savior. These theories regarding God make His Word of no effect, and those who accept them are in great danger of being led finally to look upon the whole Bible as a fiction. They may regard virtue as better than vice; but God being removed from His position of sovereignty, they place their dependence upon human power, which, without God, is worthless. The unaided human will has no real power to resist and overcome evil. The defenses of the soul are broken down. Man has no barrier against sin. When once the restraints of God's Word and His Spirit are rejected, we know not to what depths one may sink.

Those who continue to hold these spiritualistic theories will surely spoil their Christian experience, sever their connection with God, and lose eternal life.[5]

THE PERILS OF FALSE SCIENCE

O Timothy, keep that which is committed to thy trust, avoiding profane and vain babblings, and oppositions of science falsely so called. 1 Tim. 6:20.

In New Hampshire there were those who were active in disseminating false ideas in regard to God. Light was given me that these men were making the truth of no effect by their ideas, some of which led to free-lovism. I was shown that these men were seducing souls by presenting speculative theories regarding God. . . .

Among other views, they held that those once sanctified could not sin, and this they were presenting as gospel food. Their false theories, with their burden of deceptive influence, were working great harm to themselves and to others. They were gaining a spiritualistic power over those who could not see the evil of these beautifully clothed theories. Great evils had already resulted. The doctrine that all were holy had led to the belief that the affections of the sanctified were never in danger of leading astray. The result of this belief was the fulfillment of the evil desires of hearts which, though professedly sanctified, were far from purity of thought and practice.

This is only one of the instances in which I was called upon to rebuke those who were presenting the doctrine of an impersonal god diffused through nature, and the doctrine of holy flesh.

In the future, truth will be counterfeited by the precepts of men. Deceptive theories will be presented as safe doctrines. False science is one of the agencies that Satan used in the heavenly courts, and it is used by him today. . . .

I beseech those who are laboring for God not to accept the spurious for the genuine. We have a whole Bible full of the most precious truth. We have no need for supposition or false excitement. In the golden censer of truth, as presented in Christ's teachings, we have that which will convict and convert souls. Present in the simplicity of Christ the truths that He came to this world to proclaim, and the power of your message will make itself felt. Do not present theories or tests that have no foundation in the Bible.[6]

A MASTERPIECE OF SATAN'S DECEPTIONS

The secret things belong unto the Lord our God: but those things which are revealed belong unto us and to our children for ever, that we may do all the words of this law. Deut. 29:29.

Human knowledge of both material and spiritual things is partial and imperfect; therefore many are unable to harmonize their views of science with Scripture statements. Many accept mere theories and speculations as scientific facts, and they think that God's word is to be tested by the teachings of "science falsely so called." 1 Timothy 6:20. The Creator and His works are beyond their comprehension; and because they cannot explain these by natural laws, Bible history is regarded as unreliable. Those who doubt the reliability of the records of the Old and New Testaments too often go a step further and doubt the existence of God and attribute infinite power to nature. Having let go their anchor, they are left to beat about upon the rocks of infidelity.

Thus many err from the faith and are seduced by the devil. . . . Human philosophy has attempted to search out and explain mysteries which will never be revealed through the eternal ages. If men would but search and understand what God has made known of Himself and His purposes, they would obtain such a view of the glory, majesty, and power of Jehovah that they would realize their own littleness and would be content with that which has been revealed. . . .

It is a masterpiece of Satan's deceptions to keep the minds of men searching and conjecturing in regard to that which God has not made known and which He does not intend that we shall understand. It was thus that Lucifer lost his place in heaven. He became dissatisfied because all the secrets of God's purposes were not confided to him, and he entirely disregarded that which was revealed concerning his own work in the lofty position assigned him. By arousing the same discontent in the angels under his command, he caused their fall. Now he seeks to imbue the minds of men with the same spirit and to lead them also to disregard the direct commands of God.[7]

THE TIMES AND SEASONS

He said unto them, It is not for you to know the times or the seasons, which the Father hath put in his own power. Acts 1:7.

The times and seasons God has put in His own power. And why has not God given us this knowledge?—Because we would not make a right use of it if He did. A condition of things would result from this knowledge among our people that would greatly retard the work of God in preparing a people to stand in the great day that is to come. . . . Jesus has told His disciples to "watch," but not for definite time. His followers are to be in the position of those who are listening for the orders of their Captain; they are to watch, wait, pray, and work, as they approach the time for the coming of the Lord; but no one will be able to predict just when that time will come; for "of that day and hour knoweth no man." You will not be able to say that He will come in one, two, or five years, neither are you to put off His coming by stating that it may not be for ten or twenty years. . . . We are not to know the definite time either for the outpouring of the Holy Spirit or for the coming of Christ.[8]

I was pointed to some who are in the great error of believing that it is their duty to go to Old Jerusalem,* and think they have a work to do there before the Lord comes. Such a view is calculated to take the mind and interest from the present work of the Lord, under the message of the third angel; for those who think that they are yet to go to Jerusalem will have their minds there, and their means will be withheld from the cause of present truth to get themselves and others there. I saw that such a mission would accomplish no real good, that it would take a long while to make a very few of the Jews believe even in the first advent of Christ, much more to believe in His second advent.[9]

---

* Written in the early 1850's when "the age-to-come" advocates taught that Old Jerusalem would be built up as a center of Christian witness fulfilling certain prophecies of the O.T.

"AS IT WAS IN THE DAYS OF NOE"

As it was in the days of Noe, so shall it be also in the days of the Son of man. Luke 17:26.

I was shown that a terrible condition of things exists in our world. The angel of mercy is folding her wings, ready to depart. . . . The law of God is made void. We see and hear of confusion and perplexity, want and famine, earthquakes and floods; terrible outrages will be committed by men; passion, not reason, bears sway. The wrath of God is upon the inhabitants of the world, who are fast becoming as corrupt as were the inhabitants of Sodom and Gomorrah. Already fire and flood are destroying thousands of lives and the property that has been selfishly accumulated by the oppression of the poor. The Lord is soon to cut short His work and put an end to sin. Oh, that the scenes which have come before me of the iniquities practiced in these last days, might make a deep impression on the minds of God's professing people.

As it was in the days of Noah, so shall it be when the Son of man shall be revealed. The Lord is removing His restrictions from the earth, and soon there will be death and destruction, increasing crime, and cruel, evil working against the rich who have exalted themselves against the poor. Those who are without God's protection will find no safety in any place or position. Human agents are being trained and are using their inventive power to put in operation the most powerful machinery to wound and to kill. . . .

My brethren and sisters . . . , I make my appeal to you. . . . The lives of many are too delicate and dainty. . . . They think themselves Christians, but they do not know what practical Christian life signifies. What does it mean to be a Christian? It means to be Christlike. . . . Co-operate with God by working in harmony with Him. Expel from the soul-temple everything that assumes the form of an idol. Now is God's time, and His time is your time. Fight the good fight of faith, refusing to think or to talk unbelief. The world is to hear the last warning message.[10]

A GREAT TERROR SOON TO COME

We are put on view to the world, and to angels, and to men. 1 Cor. 4:9, Bible in Basic English.

The world is a theater; the actors, its inhabitants, are preparing to act their part in the last great drama. With the great masses of mankind there is no unity, except as men confederate to accomplish their selfish purposes. God is looking on. His purposes in regard to His rebellious subjects will be fulfilled. The world has not been given into the hands of men, though God is permitting the elements of confusion and disorder to bear sway for a season. A power from beneath is working to bring about the last great scenes in the drama—Satan coming as Christ, and working with all deceivableness of unrighteousness in those who are binding themselves together in secret societies. Those who are yielding to the passion for confederation are working out the plans of the enemy. The cause will be followed by the effect.

Transgression has almost reached its limit. Confusion fills the world, and a great terror is soon to come upon human beings. The end is very near. We who know the truth should be preparing for what is soon to break upon the world as an overwhelming surprise. . . .

Are we as a people asleep? Oh, if the young men and young women in our institutions who are now unready for the Lord's appearing, unfitted to become members of the Lord's family, could only discern the signs of the times, what a change would be seen in them! The Lord Jesus is calling for self-denying workers to follow in His footsteps, to walk and work for Him, to lift the cross, and to follow where He leads the way.

Many are readily satisfied with offering the Lord trifling acts of service. Their Christianity is feeble. Christ gave Himself for sinners. With what anxiety for the salvation of souls we should be filled as we see human beings perishing in sin! These souls have been bought at an infinite price. The death of the Son of God on Calvary's cross is the measure of their value. Day by day they are deciding whether they will have eternal life or eternal death.[11]

YOUTH AND THE DRUG SYNDROME

Rejoice, O young man, in thy youth; and let thy heart cheer thee in the days of thy youth, and walk in the ways of thine heart, and in the sight of thine eyes: but know thou, that for all these things God will bring thee into judgment. Eccl. 11:9.

Satan was the first rebel in the universe, and ever since his expulsion from heaven he has been seeking to make every member of the human family an apostate from God, even as he is himself. He laid his plans to ruin man, and through the unlawful indulgence of appetite, led him to transgress the commandments of God. He tempted Adam and Eve to partake of the forbidden fruit, and so accomplished their fall, and their expulsion from Eden. How many say, "If I had been in Adam's place, I would never have transgressed on so simple a test." But you who make this boast have a grand opportunity of showing your strength of purpose, your fidelity to principle under trial. . . . Does God see no sin in your life? . . .

On every side, Satan seeks to entice the youth into the path of perdition; and if he can once get their feet set in the way, he hurries them on in their downward course, leading them from one dissipation to another, until his victims lose their tenderness of conscience, and have no more the fear of God before their eyes. They exercise less and less self-restraint. They become addicted to the use of wine and alcohol, tobacco and opium, and go from one stage of debasement to another. They are slaves to appetite. Counsel which they once respected, they learn to despise. They put on swaggering airs, and boast of liberty when they are the servants of corruption. They mean by liberty that they are slaves to selfishness, debased appetite, and licentiousness. . . .

Satan is determined to have the human race as his subjects, but Christ has paid an infinite price that man may be redeemed from the enemy, and that the moral image of God may be restored to the fallen race. . . . Fallen men may through Christ find access to the Father, may have grace to enable them to be overcomers through the merits of a crucified and risen Saviour.[12]

EXTERNAL PARADE
OF HEATHEN POWER

The time will come when they will not endure sound doctrine; but after their own lusts shall they heap to themselves teachers, having itching ears. 2 Tim. 4:3.

Rapidly are men ranging themselves under the banner they have chosen, restlessly waiting and watching the movements of their leaders. There are those who are watching and waiting and working for our Lord's appearing; while the other party are rapidly falling into line under the generalship of the first great apostate. They look for a God in humanity, and Satan personifies the one they seek. Multitudes will be so deluded through their rejection of truth, that they will accept the counterfeit. Humanity is hailed as God.[13]

As we near the close of time, there will be greater and still greater external parade of heathen power; heathen deities will manifest their signal power, and will exhibit themselves before the cities of the world; and this delineation has already begun to be fulfilled. By a variety of images the Lord Jesus represented to John the wicked character and seductive influence of those who have been distinguished for their persecution of God's people. All need wisdom carefully to search out the mystery of iniquity that figures so largely in the winding up of this earth's history. . . . In the very time in which we live, the Lord has called His people and has given them a message to bear. He has called them to expose the wickedness of the man of sin who has made the Sunday law a distinctive power, who has thought to change times and laws, and to oppress the people of God who stand firmly to honor Him by keeping the only true Sabbath, the Sabbath of creation. . . .

The perils of the last days are upon us, and in our work we are to warn the people of the danger they are in. Let not the solemn scenes which prophecy has revealed be left untouched. If our people were half awake, if they realized the nearness of the events portrayed in the Revelation, a reformation would be wrought in our churches, and many more would believe the message. We have no time to lose; God calls upon us to watch for souls as they that must give an account.[14]

TURMOIL IN THE CITIES

Evil men and seducers shall wax worse and worse, deceiving, and being deceived. 2 Tim. 3:13.

It was not God's purpose that His people should be crowded into cities, huddled together in terraces and tenements. In the beginning He placed our first parents in a garden amidst the beautiful sights and attractive sounds of nature, and these sights and sounds He desires men to rejoice in today.[15]

Light has been given me that the cities will be filled with confusion, violence, and crime, and that these things will increase till the end of this earth's history.[16]

It is time for our people to take their families from the cities into more retired localities, else many of the youth, and many also of those older in years, will be ensnared and taken by the enemy.[17]

"Out of the cities; out of the cities!"—this is the message the Lord has been giving me.[18]

The turmoil and confusion that fill these cities, the conditions brought about by the labor unions and the strikes, would prove a great hindrance to our work. Men are seeking to bring those engaged in the different trades under bondage to certain unions. This is not God's planning, but the planning of a power that we should in no wise acknowledge. God's word is fulfilling; the wicked are binding themselves up in bundles ready to be burned.

We are now to use all our entrusted capabilities in giving the last warning message to the world. In this work we are to preserve our individuality. We are not to unite with secret societies or with trade-unions. We are to stand free in God, looking constantly to Christ.[19]

The ungodly cities of our world are to be swept away by the besom of destruction. In the calamities that are now befalling immense buildings and large portions of cities God is showing us what will come upon the whole earth. He has told us: "Now learn a parable of the fig tree; When his branch is yet tender, and putteth forth leaves, ye know that summer is nigh: so likewise ye, when ye shall see all these things, know that it [the coming of the Son of man] is near, even at the doors." Matthew 24:32, 33.[20]

141

PREJUDICE ON THE INCREASE

Marvel not, my brethren, if the world hate you. We know that we have passed from death unto life, because we love the brethren. He that loveth not his brother abideth in death. 1 John 3:13, 14.

He who is closely connected with Christ is lifted above the prejudice of color or caste. His faith takes hold of eternal realities. The divine Author of truth is to be uplifted. Our hearts are to be filled with the faith that works by love and purifies the soul. The work of the good Samaritan is the example that we are to follow.[21]

It will be impossible to adjust all matters regarding the color question in accordance with the Lord's order until those who believe the truth are so closely united with Christ that they are one with Him. Both the white and the colored members of our churches need to be converted. There are some of both classes who are unreasonable, and when the color question is agitated, they manifest unsanctified, unconverted traits of character. Quarrelsome elements are easily aroused in those who, because they have never learned to wear the yoke of Christ, are opinionated and obstinate. In such, self clamors with an unsanctified determination for the supremacy.[22]

As time advances, and race prejudices increase, it will become almost impossible, in many places, for white workers to labor for the colored people. Sometimes the white people who are not in sympathy with our work will unite with colored people to oppose it, claiming that our teaching is an effort to break up churches and bring in trouble over the Sabbath question. White ministers and colored ministers will make false statements, arousing in the minds of the people such a feeling of antagonism that they will be ready to destroy and to kill.

The powers of hell are working with all their ingenuity to prevent the proclamation of the last message of mercy among the colored people. Satan is working to make it most difficult for the gospel minister and teacher to ignore the prejudice that exists between the white and the colored people.

Let us follow the course of wisdom. Let us do nothing that will unnecessarily arouse opposition—nothing that will hinder the proclamation of the gospel message.[23]

THE LUST FOR NAKEDNESS

Whosoever looketh on a woman to lust after her hath committed adultery with her already in his heart. Matt. 5:28.

Many of the young are eager for books. They read everything they can obtain. Exciting love stories and impure pictures have a corrupting influence. Novels are eagerly perused by many, and, as the result, their imagination becomes defiled. In the cars, photographs of females in a state of nudity are frequently circulated for sale. These disgusting pictures are . . . hung upon the walls of those who deal in engravings. This is an age when corruption is teeming everywhere. The lust of the eye and corrupt passions are aroused by beholding and by reading. The heart is corrupted through the imagination. The mind takes pleasure in contemplating scenes which awaken the lower and baser passions. These vile images, seen through defiled imagination, corrupt the morals and prepare the deluded, infatuated beings to give loose rein to lustful passions. Then follow sins and crimes which drag beings formed in the image of God down to a level with the beasts, sinking them at last in perdition. Avoid reading and seeing things which will suggest impure thoughts. Cultivate the moral and intellectual powers. Let not these noble powers become enfeebled and perverted by much reading of even storybooks. . . .

It is impossible for the youth to possess a healthy tone of mind and correct religious principles unless they enjoy the perusal of the word of God. This book contains the most interesting history, points out the way of salvation through Christ, and is their guide to a higher and better life. They would all pronounce it the most interesting book they ever perused, if their imagination had not become perverted by exciting stories of a fictitious character. You who are looking for your Lord to come the second time to change your mortal bodies, and to fashion them like unto His most glorious body, must come up upon a higher plane of action. You must work from a higher standpoint than you have hitherto done, or you will not be of that number who will receive the finishing touch of immortality.[24]

THE CRIERS OF PEACE

Come ye, say they, I will fetch wine, and we will fill ourselves with strong drink; and to morrow shall be as this day, and much more abundant. Isa. 56:12.

The evil servant says in his heart, "My lord delayeth his coming." He does not say that Christ will not come. He does not scoff at the idea of His second coming. But in his heart and by his actions and words he declares that the Lord's coming is delayed. He banishes from the minds of others the conviction that the Lord is coming quickly. His influence leads men to presumptuous, careless delay. They are confirmed in their worldliness and stupor. Earthly passions, corrupt thoughts, take possession of the mind. The evil servant eats and drinks with the drunken, unites with the world in pleasure seeking. He smites his fellow servants, accusing and condemning those who are faithful to their Master. . . .

The advent of Christ will surprise the false teachers. They are saying, "Peace and safety." Like the priests and teachers before the fall of Jerusalem, they look for the church to enjoy earthly prosperity and glory. The signs of the times they interpret as foreshadowing this. But what saith the Word of Inspiration? "Sudden destruction cometh upon them." . . .

Men are putting afar off the coming of the Lord. They laugh at warnings. The proud boast is made, "All things continue as they were from the beginning." "To morrow shall be as this day and much more abundant." 2 Peter 3:4; Isa. 56:12. We will go deeper into pleasure loving. But Christ says, "Behold, I come as a thief." Rev. 16:15. At the very time when the world is asking in scorn, "Where is the promise of his coming?" the signs are fulfilling. While they cry, "Peace and safety," sudden destruction is coming. When the scorner, the rejecter of truth, has become presumptuous; when the routine of work in the various money-making lines is carried on without regard to principle; when the student is eagerly seeking knowledge of everything but his Bible, Christ comes as a thief.[25]

SIGHTS AND SOUNDS AND CRIMINALITY

I will set no wicked thing before mine eyes: I hate the work of them that turn aside; it shall not cleave to me. A froward heart shall depart from me: I will not know a wicked person. Ps. 101:3, 4.

There is reason for deep solicitude on your part for your children, who have temptations to encounter at every advance step. It is impossible for them to avoid contact with evil associates. . . . They will see sights, hear sounds, and be subjected to influences which are demoralizing and which, unless they are thoroughly guarded, will imperceptibly but surely corrupt the heart and deform the character. . . .

Some fathers and mothers are so indifferent, so careless, that they think it makes no difference whether their children attend a church school or a public school. "We are in the world," they say, "and we cannot get out of it." But, parents, we can get a good way out of the world, if we choose to do so. We can avoid seeing many of the evils that are multiplying so fast in these last days. . . .

To the active minds of children and youth the scenes pictured in imaginary revelations of the future are realities. As revolutions are predicted and all manner of proceedings described that break down the barriers of law and self-restraint, many catch the spirit of these representations. They are led to the commission of crimes even worse, if possible, than these sensational writers depict. Through such influences as these society is becoming demoralized. The seeds of lawlessness are sown broadcast. None need marvel that a harvest of crime is the result. . . .

Say firmly: "I will not spend precious moments in reading that which will be of no profit to me, and which only unfits me to be of service to others. I will devote my time and my thoughts to acquiring a fitness for God's service. I will close my eyes to frivolous and sinful things. My ears are the Lord's, and I will not listen to the subtle reasoning of the enemy. My voice shall not in any way be subject to a will that is not under the influence of the Spirit of God. My body is the temple of the Holy Spirit, and every power of my being shall be consecrated to worthy pursuits." [26]

SPIRITISM AND REVOLUTION

He answering said, Thou shalt love the Lord thy God with all thy heart, . . . and thy neighbour as thyself. Luke 10:27.

As the youth go out into the world to encounter its allurements to sin—the passion for money getting, for amusement and indulgence, for display, luxury, and extravagance, the overreaching, fraud, robbery, and ruin—what are the teachings there to be met?

Spiritualism asserts that men are unfallen demigods; that "each mind will judge itself"; that "true knowledge places men above all law"; that "all sins committed are innocent"; for "whatever is, is right," and "God doth not condemn." The basest of human beings it represents as in heaven, and highly exalted there. Thus it declares to all men, "It matters not what you do; live as you please, heaven is your home." Multitudes are thus led to believe that desire is the highest law, that license is liberty, and that man is accountable only to himself.

With such teaching given at the very outset of life, when impulse is strongest, and the demand for self-restraint and purity is most urgent, where are the safeguards of virtue? what is to prevent the world from becoming a second Sodom?

At the same time anarchy is seeking to sweep away all law, not only divine, but human. The centralizing of wealth and power; the vast combinations for the enriching of the few at the expense of the many; the combinations of the poorer classes for the defense of their interests and claims; . . . the world-wide dissemination of the same teachings that led to the French Revolution—all are tending to involve the whole world in a struggle similar to that which convulsed France.

Such are the influences to be met by the youth of today. To stand amidst such upheavals they are now to lay the foundations of character.

In every generation and in every land the true foundation and pattern for character building have been the same. The divine law, "Thou shalt love the Lord thy God with all thy heart, . . . and thy neighbour as thyself" (Luke 10:27), the great principle made manifest in the character and life of our Saviour, is the only secure foundation and the only sure guide.[27]

BEWARE OF MAN-MADE TESTS

Beware . . . of evil workers. . . . For we are the circumcision, which worship God in the spirit, and rejoice in Christ Jesus, and have no confidence in the flesh. Phil. 3:2, 3.

There are those who need in their hearts the touch of the divine Spirit. Then the message for this time will be their burden. They will not search for human tests, for something new and strange. The Sabbath of the fourth commandment is the test for this time.[28]

The commandment of God that has been almost universally made void, is the testing truth for this time. . . . The time is coming when all those who worship God will be distinguished by this sign. They will be known as the servants of God, by this mark of their allegiance to Heaven. But all man-made tests will divert the mind from the great and important doctrines that constitute the present truth.

It is the desire and plan of Satan to bring in among us those who will go to great extremes—people of narrow minds, who are critical and sharp, and very tenacious in holding their own conceptions of what the truth means. They will be exacting, and will seek to enforce rigorous duties, and go to great lengths in matters of minor importance, while they neglect the weightier matters of the law—judgment and mercy and the love of God. Through the work of a few of this class of persons, the whole body of Sabbathkeepers will be designated as bigoted . . . and fanatical. . . .

God has a special work for the men of experience to do. They are to guard the cause of God. They are to see that the work of God is not committed to men who feel it their privilege to move out on their own independent judgment, to preach whatever they please, and to be responsible to no one for their instructions or work. Let this spirit of self-sufficiency once rule in our midst, and there will be no harmony of action, no unity of spirit, no safety for the work, and no healthful growth in the cause. . . . Christ prayed that His followers might be one as He and the Father were one. Those who desire to see this prayer answered, should seek to discourage the slightest tendency to division, and try to keep the spirit of unity and love among brethren.[29]

HEALING CAN BE FROM THE DEVIL

Be sober, be vigilant; because your adversary the devil, as a roaring lion, walketh about, seeking whom he may devour. 1 Peter 5:8.

The fallacies of Satan are now being multiplied, and those who swerve from the path of truth will lose their bearings. Having nothing to which to anchor, they will drift from one delusion to another, blown about by the winds of strange doctrines. Satan has come down with great power. Many will be deceived by his miracles.[30]

I am instructed to say that in the future great watchfulness will be needed. There is to be among God's people no spiritual stupidity. Evil spirits are actively engaged in seeking to control the minds of human beings. Men are binding up in bundles, ready to be consumed by the fires of the last days. Those who discard Christ and His righteousness will accept the sophistry that is flooding the world. Christians are to be sober and vigilant, steadfastly resisting their adversary the devil, who is going about as a roaring lion, seeking whom he may devour. Men under the influence of evil spirits will work miracles. . . .

We need not be deceived. Wonderful scenes, with which Satan will be closely connected, will soon take place. God's Word declares that Satan will work miracles. He will make people sick, and then will suddenly remove from them his satanic power. They will then be regarded as healed. These works of apparent healing will bring Seventh-day Adventists to the test. . . .

If those through whom cures are performed, are disposed, on account of these manifestations, to excuse their neglect of the law of God, and continue in disobedience, though they have power to any and every extent, it does not follow that they have the great power of God. On the contrary, it is the miracle-working power of the great deceiver. He is a transgressor of the moral law, and employs every device that he can master to blind men to its true character. We are warned that in the last days he will work with signs and lying wonders. And he will continue these wonders until the close of probation, that 'he may point to them as evidence that he is an angel of light and not of darkness.[31]

THE VIOLENT EARTH

I beheld when he had opened the sixth seal, and, lo, there was a great earthquake. Rev. 6:12.

Prophecy not only foretells the manner and object of Christ's coming, but presents tokens by which men are to know when it is near. . . . The revelator thus describes the first of the signs to precede the second advent: "There was a great earthquake; and the sun became black as sackcloth of hair, and the moon became as blood."

These signs were witnessed before the opening of the nineteenth century. In fulfilment of this prophecy there occurred, in the year 1755, the most terrible earthquake that has ever been recorded. Though commonly known as the earthquake of Lisbon, it extended to the greater part of Europe, Africa, and America. It was felt in Greenland, in the West Indies, in the island of Madeira, in Norway and Sweden, Great Britain and Ireland. It pervaded an extent of not less than four million square miles. In Africa the shock was almost as severe as in Europe. A great part of Algiers was destroyed; and a short distance from Morocco, a village containing eight or ten thousand inhabitants was swallowed up. A vast wave swept over the coast of Spain and Africa, engulfing cities, and causing great destruction.

It was in Spain and Portugal that the shock manifested its extreme violence. At Cadiz the inflowing wave was said to be sixty feet high. Mountains, "some of the largest in Portugal, were impetuously shaken, as it were, from their very foundations." . . .—Sir Charles Lyell, *Principles of Geology,* p. 495. . . . "The earthquake happened on a holy day, when the churches and convents were full of people, very few of whom escaped."— *Encyclopedia Americana,* art. "Lisbon," note (ed. 1831). . . . It has been estimated that ninety thousand persons lost their lives on that fatal day.[32]

How frequently we hear of earthquakes and tornadoes, of destruction by fire and flood, with great loss of life and property! Apparently these calamities are capricious outbreaks of disorganized, unregulated forces of nature, wholly beyond the control of man; but in them all, God's purpose may be read. They are among the agencies by which He seeks to arouse men and women to a sense of their danger.[33]

SIGNS IN THE HEAVENS

The sun shall be turned into darkness, and the moon into blood, before the great and the terrible day of the Lord come. Joel 2:31.

In the Saviour's conversation with His disciples upon Olivet, after describing the long period of trial for the church—the 1260 years of papal persecution, concerning which He had promised that the tribulation should be shortened—He thus mentioned certain events to precede His coming, and fixed the time when the first of these should be witnessed: "In those days, after that tribulation, the sun shall be darkened, and the moon shall not give her light." The 1260 days, or years, terminated in 1798. A quarter of a century earlier, persecution had almost wholly ceased. Following this persecution, according to the words of Christ, the sun was to be darkened. On the 19th of May, 1780, this prophecy was fulfilled.

"Almost if not altogether alone, as the most mysterious and as yet unexplained phenomenon of its kind, . . . stands the dark day of May 19, 1780—a most unaccountable darkening of the whole visible heavens and atmosphere in New England."— R. M. Devens, *Our First Century*, p. 89. . . .

The intense darkness of the day was succeeded, an hour or two before evening, by a partially clear sky, and the sun appeared, though it was still obscured by the black, heavy mist. "After sundown, the clouds came again overhead, and it grew dark very fast." "Nor was the darkness of the night less uncommon and terrifying than that of the day; notwithstanding there was almost a full moon, no object was discernible but by the help of some artificial light. . . ."—Isaiah Thomas, *Massachusetts Spy; or, American Oracle of Liberty*, vol. 10, No. 472 (May 25, 1780). . . .

The description of this event, as given by eyewitnesses, is but an echo of the words of the Lord, recorded by the prophet Joel, twenty-five hundred years previous to their fulfilment: "The sun shall be turned into darkness, and the moon into blood, before the great and the terrible day of the Lord come."

Christ had bidden His people watch for the signs of His advent, and rejoice as they should behold the tokens of their coming King.[34]

THE STARS OF HEAVEN FALL

The stars shall fall from heaven, and the powers of the heavens shall be shaken. Matt. 24:29.

In 1833, . . . the last of the signs appeared which were promised by the Saviour as tokens of His second advent. Said Jesus, "The stars shall fall from heaven." And John in the Revelation declared, as he beheld in vision the scenes that should herald the day of God, "The stars of heaven fell unto the earth, even as a fig tree casteth her untimely figs, when she is shaken of a mighty wind." This prophecy received a striking and impressive fulfilment in the great meteoric shower of November 13, 1833. That was the most extensive and wonderful display of falling stars which has ever been recorded; "the whole firmament, over all the United States, being then, for hours, in fiery commotion! No celestial phenomenon has ever occurred in this country, since its first settlement, which was viewed with such intense admiration by one class in the community, or with so much dread and alarm by another." "Its sublimity and awful beauty still linger in many minds. . . . Never did rain fall much thicker than the meteors fell toward the earth; east, west, north, and south, it was the same. In a word, the whole heavens seemed in motion. . . . The display, as described in Professor Silliman's Journal, was seen all over North America. . . . From two o'clock until broad daylight, . . . an incessant play of dazzlingly brilliant luminosities was kept up in the whole heavens."—R. M. Devens, *American Progress; or, The Great Events of the Greatest Century,* ch. 28, pars. 1-5. . . .

Thus was displayed the last of those signs of His coming, concerning which Jesus bade His disciples, "When ye shall see all these things, *know* that it is near, even at the doors." After these signs, John beheld, as the great event next impending, the heavens departing as a scroll, while the earth quaked, mountains and islands removed out of their places, and the wicked in terror sought to flee from the presence of the Son of man.[35]

But the day and the hour of His coming Christ has not revealed. . . . The exact time of the second coming of the Son of man is God's mystery.[36]

OTTOMAN EMPIRE IN PROPHECY

Loose the four angels which are bound in the great river Euphrates. And the four angels were loosed, which were prepared for an hour, and a day, and a month, and a year, for to slay the third part of men. Rev. 9:14, 15.

The history of nations that one after another have occupied their allotted time and place, unconsciously witnessing to the truth of which they themselves knew not the meaning, speaks to us. To every nation and to every individual of today God has assigned a place in His great plan. Today men and nations are being measured by the plummet in the hand of Him who makes no mistake. All are by their own choice deciding their destiny, and God is overruling all for the accomplishment of His purposes. . . .

All that prophecy has foretold as coming to pass, until the present time, has been traced on the pages of history, and we may be assured that all which is yet to come will be fulfilled in its order.[37]

In the year 1840, another remarkable fulfilment of prophecy excited widespread interest. Two years before, Josiah Litch, one of the leading ministers preaching the second advent, published an exposition of Revelation 9, predicting the fall of the Ottoman empire. According to his calculations, this power was to be overthrown "in A.D. 1840, sometime in the month of August;" and only a few days previous to its accomplishment he wrote: "Allowing the first period, 150 years, to have been exactly fulfilled before Deacozes ascended the throne by permission of the Turks, and that the 391 years, fifteen days, commenced at the close of the first period, it will end on the 11th of August, 1840, when the Ottoman power in Constantinople may be expected to be broken. And this, I believe, will be found to be the case."—Josiah Litch, in *Signs of the Times, and Expositor of Prophecy,* Aug. 1, 1840.

At the very time specified, Turkey, through her ambassadors, accepted the protection of the allied powers of Europe, and thus placed herself under the control of Christian nations. The event exactly fulfilled the prediction. . . . A wonderful impetus was given to the advent movement.[38]

LOW STATE OF MORALS

Fornication, and all uncleanness, or covetousness, let it not be once named among you, as becometh saints. Eph. 5:3.

There is an alarming commonness in conversation at the present day, which shows a low state of thoughts and morals. True dignity of character is very rare. True modesty and reserve are seldom seen. There are but few who are pure and undefiled. . . .

Polluted thoughts harbored become habit, and the soul is scarred and defiled. Once do a wrong action and a blot is made which nothing can heal but the blood of Christ; and if the habit is not turned from with firm determination, the soul is corrupted and the streams flowing from this defiling fountain corrupt others.

There are men and women who invite temptation; they place themselves in positions where they will be tempted, where they cannot but be tempted, when they place themselves in society that is objectionable. The best way to keep safe from sin is to move with due consideration at all times and under all circumstances, never to move or act from impulse. Move with the fear of God ever before you and you will be sure to act right.[39]

The moral dangers to which all, both old and young, are exposed are daily increasing. Moral derangement, which we call depravity, finds ample room to work, and an influence is exerted by men, women, and youth professing to be Christians that is low, sensual, devilish. . . .

Those who have learned the truth and do not have works corresponding with their profession of faith are subject to Satan's temptations. They encounter danger at every step they advance. They are brought into contact with evil, they see sights, they hear sounds, that will awaken their unsubdued passions; they are subjected to influences that lead them to choose the evil rather than the good, because they are not sound at heart. . . .

There is no training we need so much now as the preparing of young men and women to have moral rectitude and to cleanse their souls of every spot and stain of moral defilement.[40]

FANATICISM AND TONGUES SPEAKING

The spirits of the prophets are subject to the prophets. For God is not the author of confusion, but of peace, as in all churches of the saints. 1 Cor. 14:32, 33.

A spirit of fanaticism has ruled a certain class of Sabbath-keepers.... They have sipped but lightly at the fountain of truth and are unacquainted with the spirit of the message of the third angel. Nothing can be done for this class until their fanatical views are corrected. . . .

Some of these persons have exercises which they call gifts and say that the Lord has placed them in the church. They have an unmeaning gibberish which they call the unknown tongue, which is unknown not only by man but by the Lord and all heaven. Such gifts are manufactured by men and women, aided by the great deceiver. Fanaticism, false excitement, false talking in tongues, and noisy exercises have been considered gifts which God has placed in the church. Some have been deceived here. The fruits of all this have not been good. . . .

There are many restless spirits who will not submit to discipline, system, and order. They think that their liberties would be abridged were they to lay aside their own judgment and submit to the judgment of those of experience. The work of God will not progress unless there is a disposition to submit to order and expel the reckless, disorderly spirit of fanaticism from their meetings. Impressions and feelings are no sure evidence that a person is led by the Lord. Satan will, if he is unsuspected, give feelings and impressions. These are not safe guides. All should thoroughly acquaint themselves with the evidences of our faith, and the great study should be how they can adorn their profession and bear fruit to the glory of God. . . . A trifling, joking, reckless spirit should be rebuked. It is no evidence of the grace of God upon the heart for persons to talk and pray with talent in meeting, and then give up to a rough, careless manner of talking and acting when out of meeting. . . .

The truth of God will never degrade, but will elevate the receiver, refine his taste, sanctify his judgment, and perfect him for the company of the pure and holy angels in the kingdom of God.[41]

PROVE ALL THINGS

Beware of false prophets, which come to you in sheep's clothing, but inwardly they are ravening wolves. Matt. 7:15.

In the work in which my husband and I were called by the providence of God to act a part, even from its very beginning in 1843 and 1844, we have had the Lord to devise and plan for us, and He has worked out His plans through His living agents. False paths have been so often pointed out to us, and the true and safe paths so clearly defined in all the enterprises connected with the work given us to do, that I can say of a truth I am not ignorant of Satan's devices, nor of the ways and works of God. We have had to tax every power of mind, relying upon wisdom from God to guide us in our investigations, as we have had to review the different theories brought to our attention, weighing their merits and defects in the light shining from the Word of God and the things God has revealed to me through His Word and the testimonies, in order that we might not be deceived nor deceive others. We surrendered our will and way to God, and most earnestly supplicated His aid; and we never sought in vain. Many years of painful experience in connection with the work of God have made me acquainted with all kinds of false movements. Many times I have been sent to different places with the message, "I have a work for you to do in that place; I will be with you." When the occasion came, the Lord gave me a message for those who were having false dreams and visions, and in the strength of Christ I bore my testimony at the Lord's bidding. . . .

During the past forty-five years, I have had to meet persons claiming to have from God messages of reproof to others. This phase of religious fanaticism has sprung up again and again since 1844. Satan has worked in many ways to establish error. Some things spoken in these visions came to pass; but many things—in regard to the time of Christ's coming, the end of probation, and the events to take place—proved utterly false. . . .

"Take heed therefore how ye hear" (Luke 8:18), is an admonition of Christ. . . . Examine closely, "prove all things" (1 Thess. 5:21). . . . This is the counsel of God; shall we heed it? [42]

COUNTERFEITS!

To the law and to the testimony: if they speak not according to this word, it is because there is no light in them. Isa. 8:20.

The people of God are directed to the Scriptures as their safeguard against the influence of false teachers and the delusive power of spirits of darkness. Satan employs every possible device to prevent men from obtaining a knowledge of the Bible; for its plain utterances reveal his deceptions. At every revival of God's work the prince of evil is aroused to more intense activity; he is now putting forth his utmost efforts for a final struggle against Christ and His followers. The last great delusion is soon to open before us. Antichrist is to perform his marvelous works in our sight. So closely will the counterfeit resemble the true that it will be impossible to distinguish between them except by the Holy Scriptures. By their testimony every statement and every miracle must be tested. . . .

The man who makes the working of miracles the test of his faith will find that Satan can, through a species of deceptions, perform wonders that will appear to be genuine miracles.

Satan is a cunning worker, and he will bring in subtle fallacies to darken and confuse the mind and root out the doctrines of salvation. Those who do not accept the Word of God just as it reads, will be snared in his trap.

Evil angels are upon our track every moment. . . . They assume new ground and work marvels and miracles in our sight. . . .

Some will be tempted to receive these wonders as from God. The sick will be healed before us. Miracles will be performed in our sight. Are we prepared for the trial which awaits us when the lying wonders of Satan shall be more fully exhibited? Will not many souls be ensnared and taken? By departing from the plain precepts and commandments of God, and giving heed to fables, the minds of many are preparing to receive these lying wonders. We must all now seek to arm ourselves for the contest in which we must soon engage. Faith in God's word, prayerfully studied and practically applied, will be our shield from Satan's power and will bring us off conquerors through the blood of Christ.[43]

WATCH OUT FOR THE DIVIDERS!

It is impossible but that offences will come: but woe unto him, through whom they come! Luke 17:1.

God is bringing out a people and preparing them to stand as one, united, to speak the same things, and carry out the prayer of Christ for his disciples. . . . "That they all may be one; as thou, Father, art in me, and I in thee, that they also may be one in us. . . ."

There are little companies continually arising who believe that God is only with the very few, the very scattered, and their influence is to tear down and scatter that which God's servants build up. . . . The people who are putting forth every effort in accordance with God's word to be one, who are established in the message of the third angel, they look upon with suspicion, for the reason that they are extending their labor, and are gathering souls into the truth. They look upon them as being worldly, because they have influence in the world. . . .

One man arises, claiming to be led of God, who advocates the heresy of the non-resurrection of the wicked. . . . Another cherishes erroneous views in regard to the future age. . . . They all want full religious liberty, and each one goes independent of the others, and yet claims that God is especially at work among them. . . . These people are not sane; they are carried away with a false excitement, and we know that they do not have the truth. . . . Would to God they would be reformed or give up the Sabbath. They would not then stand in the way of unbelievers. . . .

God is angry with those who pursue a course to make the world hate them. If a Christian is hated because of his good works, and for following Christ, he will have a reward. But if he is hated because he does not take a course to be loved, hated because of his uncultivated manners, and because he makes the truth a matter of quarrel with his neighbors, and because he has taken a course to make the Sabbath as annoying as possible to them, he is a stumbling-block to sinners, a reproach to the sacred truth, and unless he repents it were better for him that a millstone were hung about his neck, and he cast into the sea.[44]

THE RESULTS OF FALSE VISIONS

Every tree that bringeth not forth good fruit is hewn down, and cast into the fire. Wherefore by their fruits ye shall know them. Matt. 7:19, 20.

Several now living [1890] are skeptics, have no belief in the gifts of the church, no faith in the truth, no religion at all. Such, I have been shown, is the sure result of spurious visions. . . .

Satan is . . . constantly pressing in the spurious—to lead away from the truth.

The very last deception of Satan will be to make of none effect the testimony of the Spirit of God. "Where there is no vision, the people perish" (Prov. 29:18). Satan will work ingeniously, in different ways and through different agencies, to unsettle the confidence of God's remnant people in the true testimony. He will bring in spurious visions to mislead, and will mingle the false with the true, and so disgust people that they will regard everything that bears the name of visions as a species of fanaticism; but honest souls, by contrasting false and true, will be enabled to distinguish between them. . . .

There is nothing more detrimental to the soul's interest, its purity, its true and holy conceptions of God, and of sacred and eternal things, than constantly giving heed to and exalting that which is not from God. It poisons the heart, and degrades the understanding. Pure truth can be traced to its divine Source, by its elevating, refining, sanctifying influence upon the character of the receiver. The Author of all truth prayed to His Father, "Neither pray I for these alone, but for them also which shall believe on me through their word; that they all may be one; as thou, Father, art in me, and I in thee, that they also may be one in us: that the world may believe that thou hast sent me" (John 17:20, 21).

Things will be constantly arising to cause disunion, to draw away from the truth. This questioning, criticizing, denouncing, passing judgment on others, is not an evidence of the grace of Christ in the heart. It does not produce unity. Such work has been carried on in the past by persons claiming to have wonderful light, when they were deep in sin.[45]

MOVING INTO LINE

The humble shall see this, and be glad: and your heart shall live that seek God. Ps. 69:32.

It is your privilege to be glad in the Lord, and to rejoice in the knowledge of His sustaining grace. Let His love take possession of mind and heart. Guard against becoming overwearied, careworn, depressed. Bear an uplifting testimony. Turn your eyes away from that which is dark and discouraging, and behold Jesus, our great Leader, under whose watchful supervision the cause of present truth, to which we are giving our lives and our all, is destined to triumph gloriously. . . .

Oh, let it be seen . . . that Jesus is abiding in the heart, sustaining, strengthening, comforting. It is your privilege to be endowed, from day to day, with a rich measure of His Holy Spirit, and to have broadened views of the importance and scope of the message we are proclaiming to the world. The Lord is willing to reveal to you wondrous things out of His law. Wait before Him with humility of heart. Pray most earnestly for an understanding of the times in which we live, for a fuller conception of His purpose, and for increased efficiency in soulsaving. . . .

It will be well for us to consider what is soon to come upon the earth. This is no time for trifling or self-seeking. If the times in which we are living fail to impress our minds seriously, what can reach us? . . .

Men of clear understanding are needed now. God calls upon those who are willing to be controlled by the Holy Spirit to lead out in a work of thorough reformation. I see a crisis before us, and the Lord calls for His laborers to come into line. Every soul should now stand in a position of deeper, truer consecration to God than during the years that have passed. . . .

I have been deeply impressed by scenes that have recently passed before me in the night season. There seemed to be a great movement—a work of revival—going forward in many places. Our people were moving into line, responding to God's call. . . . Shall we not heed His voice? Shall we not trim our lamps, and act like men who look for their Lord to come? The time is one that calls for light bearing, for action.[46]

COMING EVENTS CLEARLY REVEALED

The Lord God does nothing without giving to his servants the prophets knowledge of his plans. Amos 3:7, N.E.B.

The events' connected with the close of probation and the work of preparation for the time of trouble, are clearly presented. But multitudes have no more understanding of these important truths than if they had never been revealed. Satan watches to catch away every impression that would make them wise unto salvation, and the time of trouble will find them unready.[1]

As we near the close of this world's history, the prophecies relating to the last days especially demand our study. The last book of the New Testament scriptures is full of truth that we need to understand.[2]

The solemn messages that have been given in their order in the Revelation are to occupy the first place in the minds of God's people. . . .

Precious time is rapidly passing, and there is danger that many will be robbed of the time which should be given to the proclamation of the messages that God has sent to a fallen world. Satan is pleased to see the diversion of minds that should be engaged in a study of the truths which have to do with eternal realities.

The testimony of Christ, a testimony of the most solemn character, is to be borne to the world. All through the book of Revelation there are the most precious, elevating promises, and there are also warnings of the most fearfully solemn import. Will not those who profess to have a knowledge of the truth read the testimony given to John by Christ? Here is no guesswork, no scientific deception. Here are the truths that concern our present and future welfare. What is the chaff to the wheat?[3]

Only those who have been diligent students of the Scriptures and who have received the love of the truth will be shielded from the powerful delusion that takes the world captive. By the Bible testimony these will detect the deceiver in his disguise. To all the testing time will come. By the sifting of temptation the genuine Christian will be revealed. Are the people of God now so firmly established upon His word that they would not yield to the evidence of their senses? Would they, in such a crisis, cling to the Bible and the Bible only?[4]

PREPARATION FOR WHAT LIES AHEAD

Seek ye the Lord, all ye meek of the earth, which have wrought his judgment; seek righteousness, seek meekness: it may be ye shall be hid in the day of the Lord's anger. Zeph. 2:3.

Transgression has almost reached its limit. Confusion fills the world, and a great terror is soon to come upon human beings. The end is very near. God's people should be preparing for what is to break upon the world as an overwhelming surprise.[5]

The "time of trouble, such as never was," is soon to open upon us; and we shall need an experience which we do not now possess and which many are too indolent to obtain. It is often the case that trouble is greater in anticipation than in reality; but this is not true of the crisis before us. The most vivid presentation cannot reach the magnitude of the ordeal. In that time of trial, every soul must stand for himself before God. "Though Noah, Daniel, and Job" were in the land, "as I live, saith the Lord God, they shall deliver neither son nor daughter; they shall but deliver their own souls by their righteousness." Ezekiel 14:20.[6]

The last great conflict between truth and error is but the final struggle of the long-standing controversy concerning the law of God. Upon this battle we are now entering—a battle between the laws of men and the precepts of Jehovah, between the religion of the Bible and the religion of fable and tradition.[7]

We should study the great waymarks that point out the times in which we are living. . . . We should now pray most earnestly that we may be prepared for the struggles of the great day of God's preparation.[8]

Those who place themselves under God's control, to be led and guided by Him, will catch the steady tread of the events ordained by Him to take place. Inspired with the Spirit of Him who gave His life for the life of the world, they will no longer stand still in impotency, pointing to what they cannot do. Putting on the armor of heaven, they will go forth to the warfare, willing to do and dare for God, knowing that His omnipotence will supply their need.[9]

SATAN'S GROUNDWORK FOR THE FINAL CONFLICT

He shall speak words against the Most High, and shall wear out the saints of the Most High; and he shall think to change the times and the law; and they shall be given into his hand until a time and times and half a time. Dan. 7:25, R.V.

During the Christian dispensation, the great enemy of man's happiness has made the Sabbath of the fourth commandment an object of special attack. Satan says, "I will work at cross purposes with God. I will empower my followers to set aside God's memorial, the seventh-day Sabbath. Thus I will show the world that the day sanctified and blessed by God has been changed. That day shall not live in the minds of the people. I will obliterate the memory of it. I will place in its stead a day that does not bear the credentials of God, a day that cannot be a sign between God and His people. I will lead those who accept this day to place upon it the sanctity that God placed upon the seventh day.

"Through my vicegerent, I will exalt myself. The first day will be extolled, and the Protestant world will receive this spurious sabbath as genuine. Through the nonobservance of the Sabbath that God instituted, I will bring His law into contempt. The words, 'A sign between me and you throughout your generations,' I will make to serve on the side of my sabbath.

"Thus the world will become mine. I will be the ruler of the earth, the prince of the world. I will so control the minds under my power that God's Sabbath shall be a special object of contempt. A sign? I will make the observance of the seventh day a sign of disloyalty to the authorities of earth. Human laws will be made so stringent that men and women will not dare to observe the seventh-day Sabbath. For fear of wanting food and clothing, they will join with the world in transgressing God's law. The earth will be wholly under my dominion." [10]

The Sabbath will be the great test of loyalty, for it is the point of truth especially controverted. When the final test shall be brought to bear upon men, then the line of distinction will be drawn between those who serve God and those who serve Him not. [11]

THE DEVIL'S STRATEGY AGAINST SABBATHKEEPERS

Shall the throne of iniquity have fellowship with thee, which frameth mischief by a law? They gather themselves together against the soul of the righteous, and condemn the innocent blood. Ps. 94:20, 21.

As the people of God approach the perils of the last days, Satan holds earnest consultation with his angels as to the most successful plan of overthrowing their faith. . . .

Says the great deceiver: ". . . The Sabbath is the great question which is to decide the destiny of souls. We must exalt the sabbath of our creating. We have caused it to be accepted by both worldlings and church members; now the church must be led to unite with the world in its support. We must work by signs and wonders to blind their eyes to the truth, and lead them to lay aside reason and the fear of God and follow custom and tradition.

"I will influence popular ministers to turn the attention of their hearers from the commandments of God. . . .

"But our principal concern is to silence this sect of Sabbathkeepers. We must excite popular indignation against them. We will enlist great men and worldly-wise men upon our side, and induce those in authority to carry out our purposes. Then the sabbath which I have set up shall be enforced by laws the most severe and exacting. Those who disregard them shall be driven out from the cities and villages, and made to suffer hunger and privation. When once we have the power, we will show what we can do with those who will not swerve from their allegiance to God. . . . Now that we are bringing the Protestant churches and the world into harmony with this right arm of our strength, we will finally have a law to exterminate all who will not submit to our authority. When death shall be made the penalty of violating our sabbath, then many who are now ranked with commandment keepers will come over to our side.

"But before proceeding to these extreme measures, we must . . . ensnare those who honor the true Sabbath. We can separate many from Christ by worldliness, lust, and pride. They may think themselves safe because they believe the truth, but indulgence of appetite or the lower passions, which will confuse judgment and destroy discrimination, will cause their fall."[12]

THE IMAGE TO THE BEAST SET UP

[He] deceiveth them that dwell on the earth by the means of those miracles which he had power to do in the sight of the beast; saying to them that dwell on the earth, that they should make an image to the beast. Rev. 13:14.

The image of the beast will be formed before probation closes; for it is to be the great test for the people of God, by which their eternal destiny will be decided. . . .

In Revelation 13 this subject is plainly presented: "I beheld another beast coming up out of the earth; and he had two horns like a lamb, and he spake as a dragon. And he exerciseth all the power of the first beast before him, and causeth the earth and them which dwell therein to worship the first beast, whose deadly wound was healed." Then the miracle-working power is revealed: "And deceiveth them that dwell on the earth by the means of those miracles which he had power to do in the sight of the beast; saying to them that dwell on the earth, that they should make an image to the beast, which had the wound by a sword, and did live. And he had power to give life unto the image of the beast, that the image of the beast should both speak, and cause that as many as would not worship the image of the beast should be killed. And he causeth all, both small and great, rich and poor, free and bond, to receive a mark in their right hand, or in their foreheads: And that no man might buy or sell, save he that had the mark, or the name of the beast, or the number of his name."

This is the test that the people of God must have before they are sealed. All who prove their loyalty to God by observing His law, and refusing to accept a spurious sabbath, will rank under the banner of the Lord God Jehovah, and will receive the seal of the living God. Those who yield the truth of heavenly origin, and accept the Sunday sabbath, will receive the mark of the beast. . . .[13]

While John was shown the last great struggles of the church with earthly powers, he was also permitted to behold the final victory and deliverance of the faithful. . . . Looking beyond the smoke and din of the battle, he beheld a company upon Mount Zion with the Lamb, having, instead of the mark of the beast, the "Father's name written in their foreheads."[14]

APOSTASY PREPARES THE WAY

Let no man deceive you by any means: for that day shall not come, except there come a falling away first, and that man of sin be revealed, the son of perdition. 2 Thess. 2:3.

When the early church became corrupted by departing from the simplicity of the gospel and accepting heathen rites and customs, she lost the Spirit and power of God; and in order to control the consciences of the people, she sought the support of the secular power. The result was the papacy, a church that controlled the power of the state and employed it to further her own ends, especially for the punishment of "heresy." . . .

Whenever the church has obtained secular power, she has employed it to punish dissent from her doctrines. Protestant churches that have followed in the steps of Rome by forming alliance with worldly powers have manifested a similar desire to restrict liberty of conscience. An example of this is given in the long-continued persecution of dissenters by the Church of England. During the sixteenth and seventeenth centuries, thousands of nonconformist ministers were forced to flee from their churches, and many, both of pastors and people, were subjected to fine, imprisonment, torture, and martyrdom.

It was apostasy that led the early church to seek the aid of the civil government, and this prepared the way for the development of the papacy—the beast. Said Paul: "There" shall "come a falling away . . . , and that man of sin be revealed." 2 Thessalonians 2:3. So apostasy in the church will prepare the way for the image to the beast.[15]

Satan will work with all power and "with all deceivableness of unrighteousness." 2 Thessalonians 2:9, 10. His working is plainly revealed by the rapidly increasing darkness, the multitudinous errors, heresies, and delusions of these last days. Not only is Satan leading the world captive, but his deceptions are leavening the professed churches of our Lord Jesus Christ. The great apostasy will develop into darkness deep as midnight. To God's people it will be a night of trial, a night of weeping, a night of persecution for the truth's sake. But out of that night of darkness God's light will shine.[16]

SPIRITUALISM'S ROLE IN DECEPTION

Beloved, believe not every spirit, but try the spirits whether they are of God: because many false prophets are gone out into the world. 1 John 4:1.

Many will be ensnared through the belief that spiritualism is a merely human imposture; when brought face to face with manifestations which they cannot but regard as supernatural, they will be deceived, and will be led to accept them as the great power of God.[17]

As the teachings of spiritualism are accepted by the churches, the restraint imposed upon the carnal heart is removed, and the profession of religion will become a cloak to conceal the basest iniquity. A belief in spiritual manifestations opens the door to seducing spirits and doctrines of devils, and thus the influence of evil angels will be felt in the churches.[18]

The popular ministry cannot successfully resist spiritualism. They have nothing wherewith to shield their flocks from its baleful influence. Much of the sad result of spiritualism will rest upon ministers of this age; for they have trampled the truth under their feet, and in its stead have preferred fables.[19]

Satan has long been preparing for his final effort to deceive the world. The foundation of his work was laid by the assurance given to Eve in Eden: "Ye shall not surely die." "In the day ye eat thereof, then your eyes shall be opened, and ye shall be as gods, knowing good and evil." Genesis 3:4, 5. Little by little he has prepared the way for his masterpiece of deception in the development of spiritualism. He has not yet reached the full accomplishment of his designs; but it will be reached in the last remnant of time. Says the prophet: "I saw three unclean spirits like frogs. . . . They are the spirits of devils, working miracles, which go forth unto the kings of the earth and of the whole world, to gather them to the battle of that great day of God Almighty." Revelation 16:13, 14. Except those who are kept by the power of God, through faith in His word, the whole world will be swept into the ranks of this delusion. The people are fast being lulled to a fatal security, to be awakened only by the outpouring of the wrath of God.[20]

THE SPIRITS
AND THE SUNDAY LAW ISSUE

To the law and to the testimony: if they speak not according to this word, it is because there is no light in them. Isa. 8:20.

The miracle-working power manifested through spiritualism will exert its influence against those who choose to obey God rather than men. Communications from the spirits will declare that God has sent them to convince the rejecters of Sunday of their error, affirming that the laws of the land should be obeyed as the law of God. They will lament the great wickedness in the world and second the testimony of religious teachers that the degraded state of morals is caused by the desecration of Sunday. Great will be the indignation excited against all who refuse to accept their testimony.[21]

Those who oppose the teachings of spiritualism are assailing, not men alone, but Satan and his angels. They have entered upon a contest against principalities and powers and wicked spirits in high places. Satan will not yield one inch of ground except as he is driven back by the power of heavenly messengers. The people of God should be able to meet him, as did our Saviour, with the words: "It is written." Satan can quote Scripture now as in the days of Christ, and he will pervert its teachings to sustain his delusions. Those who would stand in this time of peril must understand for themselves the testimony of the Scriptures.

Many will be confronted by the spirits of devils personating beloved relatives or friends and declaring the most dangerous heresies. These visitants will appeal to our tenderest sympathies and will work miracles to sustain their pretensions. We must be prepared to withstand them with the Bible truth that the dead know not anything and that they who thus appear are the spirits of devils.[22]

Satanic agencies in human form will take part in this last great conflict to oppose the building up of the kingdom of God. And heavenly angels in human guise will be on the field of action. The two opposing parties will continue to exist till the closing up of the last great chapter in this world's history.[23]

THE FALSE REVIVAL

Then shall that Wicked be revealed, whom the Lord shall consume with the spirit of his mouth, and shall destroy with the brightness of his coming: even him, whose coming is after the working of Satan with all power and signs and lying wonders. 2 Thess. 2:8, 9.

Paul, in his second letter to the Thessalonians, points to the special working of Satan in spiritualism as an event to take place immediately before the second advent of Christ. Speaking of Christ's second coming, he declares that it is "after the working of Satan with all power and signs and lying wonders." 2 Thessalonians 2:9.[24]

Before the final visitation of God's judgments upon the earth there will be among the people of the Lord such a revival of primitive godliness as has not been witnessed since apostolic times. The Spirit and power of God will be poured out upon His children. At that time many will separate themselves from those churches in which the love of this world has supplanted love for God and His word. Many, both of ministers and people, will gladly accept those great truths which God has caused to be proclaimed at this time to prepare a people for the Lord's second coming. The enemy of souls desires to hinder this work; and before the time for such a movement shall come, he will endeavor to prevent it by introducing a counterfeit. In those churches which he can bring under his deceptive power he will make it appear that God's special blessing is poured out; there will be manifest what is thought to be great religious interest. Multitudes will exult that God is working marvelously for them, when the work is that of another spirit. Under a religious guise, Satan will seek to extend his influence over the Christian world.[25]

Young men and women will be lifted up, and will regard themselves as wonderfully favored, called to do some great thing. There will be conversions many, after a peculiar order, but they will not bear the divine signature. Immorality will come in, and extravagance, and many will make shipwreck of faith.[26]

HOW THE IMAGE TO THE BEAST EVOLVES

He exerciseth all the power of the first beast before him, and causeth the earth and them which dwell therein to worship the first beast, whose deadly wound was healed. Rev. 13:12.

In order for the United States to form an image of the beast, the religious power must so control the civil government that the authority of the state will also be employed by the church to accomplish her own ends. . . .

The "image to the beast" represents that form of apostate Protestantism which will be developed when the Protestant churches shall seek the aid of the civil power for the enforcement of their dogmas. . . .

When Sunday observance shall be enforced by law, and the world shall be enlightened concerning the obligation of the true Sabbath, then whoever shall transgress the command of God, to obey a precept which has no higher authority than that of Rome, will thereby honor popery above God. He is paying homage to Rome and to the power which enforces the institution ordained by Rome. He is worshiping the beast and his image. As men then reject the institution which God has declared to be the sign of His authority, and honor in its stead that which Rome has chosen as the token of her supremacy, they will thereby accept the sign of allegiance to Rome—"the mark of the beast." And it is not until the issue is thus plainly set before the people, and they are brought to choose between the commandments of God and the commandments of men, that those who continue in transgression will receive "the mark of the beast.". . .

In the issue of the contest all Christendom will be divided into two great classes—those who keep the commandments of God and the faith of Jesus, and those who worship the beast and his image and receive his mark. Although church and state will unite their power to compel "all, both small and great, rich and poor, free and bond" (Revelation 13:16), to receive "the mark of the beast," yet the people of God will not receive it. The prophet of Patmos beholds "them that had gotten the victory over the beast, and over his image, and over his mark, and over the number of his name, stand on the sea of glass, having the harps of God" and singing the song of Moses and the Lamb. Revelation 15:2, 3.[27]

THE SABBATH PROCLAIMED MORE FULLY

I saw another angel fly in the midst of heaven, having the everlasting gospel to preach unto them that dwell on the earth, and to every nation, and kindred, and tongue, and people, saying with a loud voice, Fear God, and give glory to him; for the hour of his judgment is come: and worship him that made heaven, and earth, and the sea, and the fountains of waters. Rev. 14:6, 7.

At the commencement of the time of trouble, we were filled with the Holy Ghost as we went forth and proclaimed the Sabbath more fully.[28]

"The commencement of that time of trouble," here mentioned, does not refer to the time when the plagues shall begin to be poured out, but to a short period just before they are poured out, while Christ is in the sanctuary. At that time, while the work of salvation is closing, trouble will be coming on the earth, and the nations will be angry, yet held in check so as not to prevent the work of the third angel. At that time the "latter rain," or refreshing from the presence of the Lord, will come, to give power to the loud voice of the third angel, and prepare the saints to stand in the period when the seven last plagues shall be poured out.[29]

[The angel of Revelation 14] presents a message that is to be proclaimed to the world just before Christ comes in the clouds of heaven. . . . Just prior to this time, then, the attention of the people is to be called to the down-trodden law of God, which is contained in the ark of the testament. . . .

They see that instead of observing the seventh day, the day that God sanctified, and commanded to be observed as the Sabbath, they are keeping the first day of the week. But they honestly desire to do God's will, and they begin to search the Scriptures to find the reason for the change. Failing to find any scriptural authority for the custom, the question arises, Shall we accept a truth that has become unpopular, and obey the commandments of God, or shall we continue with the world, and obey the commandments of men? With open Bibles they weep, and pray, and compare scripture with scripture, until, convinced of the truth, they conscientiously take their stand as keepers of the commandments of God.[30]

SECOND ANGEL'S MESSAGE
TO BE REPEATED

There followed another angel, saying, Babylon is fallen, is fallen, that great city, because she made all nations drink of the wine of the wrath of her fornication. Rev. 14:8.

The second angel's message of Revelation 14 was first preached in the summer of 1844, and it then had a more direct application to the churches of the United States, where the warning of the judgment had been most widely proclaimed and most generally rejected, and where the declension in the churches had been most rapid. But the message of the second angel did not reach its complete fulfillment in 1844. The churches then experienced a moral fall, in consequence of their refusal of the light of the advent message; but that fall was not complete. As they have continued to reject the special truths for this time they have fallen lower and lower. Not yet, however, can it be said that "Babylon is fallen, . . . because she made *all nations* drink of the wine of the wrath of her fornication." She has not yet made all nations do this.[31]

God still has a people in Babylon; and before the visitation of His judgments these faithful ones must be called out, that they partake not of her sins and "receive not of her plagues."[32]

This is the same message that was given by the second angel. Babylon is fallen, "because she made all nations drink of the wine of the wrath of her fornication." What is that wine?—her false doctrines. She has given to the world a false sabbath instead of the Sabbath of the fourth commandment, and has repeated the falsehood that Satan first told to Eve in Eden—the natural immortality of the soul. Many kindred errors she has spread far and wide, "teaching for doctrines the commandments of men.". . .

In the last work for the warning of the world, two distinct calls are made to the churches. The second angel's message is, "Babylon is fallen, is fallen, that great city, because she made all nations drink of the wine of the wrath of her fornication." And in the loud cry of the third angel's message a voice is heard from heaven saying, "Come out of her, my people, that ye be not partakers of her sins, and that ye receive not of her plagues. For her sins have reached unto heaven, and God hath remembered her iniquities."[33]

SABBATH vs SUNDAY ISSUE JOINS

The third angel followed them, saying with a loud voice, If any man worship the beast and his image, and receive his mark in his forehead, or in his hand, the same shall drink of the wine of the wrath of God. Rev. 14:9, 10.

Heretofore those who presented the truths of the third angel's message have often been regarded as mere alarmists. Their predictions that religious intolerance would gain control in the United States, that church and state would unite to persecute those who keep the commandments of God, have been pronounced groundless and absurd. . . . But as the question of enforcing Sunday observance is widely agitated, the event so long doubted and disbelieved is seen to be approaching, and the third message will produce an effect which it could not have had before. . . .

Men of faith and prayer will be constrained to go forth with holy zeal, declaring the words which God gives them. The sins of Babylon will be laid open. The fearful results of enforcing the observances of the church by civil authority, the inroads of spiritualism, the stealthy but rapid progress of the papal power —all will be unmasked. By these solemn warnings the people will be stirred. . . . As the people go to their former teachers with the eager inquiry, Are these things so? the ministers present fables, prophesy smooth things, to soothe their fears and quiet the awakened conscience. But since many refuse to be satisfied with the mere authority of men and demand a plain "Thus saith the Lord," the popular ministry, like the Pharisees of old, filled with anger as their authority is questioned, will denounce the message as of Satan and stir up the sin-loving multitudes to revile and persecute those who proclaim it.

As the controversy extends into new fields and the minds of the people are called to God's downtrodden law, Satan is astir. The power attending the message will only madden those who oppose it. The clergy will put forth almost superhuman efforts to shut away the light lest it should shine upon their flocks. By every means at their command they will endeavor to suppress the discussion of these vital questions. The church appeals to the strong arm of civil power, and, in this work, papists and Protestants unite.[34]

SYMBOLISM OF THE THREE ANGELS' MESSAGES

Behold, I will send you Elijah the prophet before the coming of the great and dreadful day of the Lord. Mal. 4:5.

To prepare a people to stand in the day of God, a great work of reform was to be accomplished [by the Advent Movement]. God saw that many of His professed people were not building for eternity, and in His mercy He was about to send a message of warning to arouse them from their stupor and lead them to make ready for the coming of the Lord.

This warning is brought to view in Revelation 14. Here is a threefold message represented as proclaimed by heavenly beings and immediately followed by the coming of the Son of man to reap "the harvest of the earth." [35]

The angels are represented as flying in the midst of heaven, proclaiming to the world a message of warning, and having a direct bearing upon the people living in the last days of this earth's history. No one hears the voice of these angels, for they are a symbol to represent the people of God who are working in harmony with the universe of heaven. [36]

The three angels' messages are to be combined, giving their threefold light to the world. In the Revelation, John says, "I saw another angel come down from heaven, having great power; and the earth was lightened with his glory.". . . This represents the giving of the last and threefold message of warning to the world. [37]

Revelation 18 points to the time when, as the result of rejecting the threefold warning of Revelation 14:6-12, the church will have fully reached the condition foretold by the second angel, and the people of God still in Babylon will be called upon to separate from her communion. This message is the last that will ever be given to the world; and it will accomplish its work. When those that "believed not the truth, but had pleasure in unrighteousness" (2 Thessalonians 2:12), shall be left to receive strong delusion and to believe a lie, then the light of truth will shine upon all whose hearts are open to receive it, and all the children of the Lord that remain in Babylon will heed the call: "Come out of her, my people" (Revelation 18:4). [38]

ARMED CONFLICT IN THE LAST DAYS

Thus saith the Lord of hosts, Behold, evil shall go forth from nation to nation, and a great whirlwind shall be raised up from the coasts of the earth. Jer. 25:32.

Soon grievous troubles will arise among the nations—trouble that will not cease until Jesus comes. As never before we need to press together, serving Him who has prepared His throne in the heavens and whose kingdom ruleth over all. God has not forsaken His people, and our strength lies in not forsaking Him.

The judgments of God are in the land. The wars and rumors of wars, the destruction by fire and flood, say clearly that the time of trouble, which is to increase until the end, is very near at hand. We have no time to lose. The world is stirred with the spirit of war. The prophecies of the eleventh of Daniel have almost reached their final fulfillment.[39]

Soon strife among the nations will break out with an intensity that we do not now anticipate. The present is a time of overwhelming interest to all living. Rulers and statesmen, men who occupy positions of trust and authority, thinking men and women of all classes, have their attention fixed upon the events taking place about us. They are watching the strained, restless relations that exist among the nations. They observe the intensity that is taking possession of every earthly element, and they realize that something great and decisive is about to take place, that the world is on the verge of a stupendous crisis.

A moment of respite has been graciously given us of God. Every power lent us of Heaven is now to be used in working for those perishing in ignorance. There must be no delay. The truth must be proclaimed in the dark places of the earth. . . . A great work is to be done, and to those who know the truth for this time, this work has been entrusted.[40]

In the last scenes of this earth's history, war will rage. There will be pestilence, plague, and famine. The waters of the deep will overflow their boundaries. Property and life will be destroyed by fire and flood. We should be preparing for the mansions that Christ has gone to prepare for them that love Him. There is a rest from earth's conflict.[41]

TROUBLOUS TIMES RIGHT UPON US

After these things I saw four angels standing on the four corners of the earth, holding the four winds of the earth, that the wind should not blow on the earth, nor on the sea, nor on any tree. Rev. 7:1.

Four mighty angels are still holding the four winds of the earth. Terrible destruction is forbidden to come in full. The . . . winds will be the stirring up of the nations to one deadly combat, while the angels hold the four winds, forbidding the terrible power of Satan to be exercised in its fury until the servants of God are sealed in their foreheads.[42]

The signs of the times give evidence that the judgments of heaven are being poured out, that the day of the Lord is at hand. The daily papers are full of indications of an intense conflict in the future. Bold robberies are of frequent occurrence. Strikes are common. Thefts and murders are committed on every hand. Men possessed by demons are taking the lives of men, women, and little children. All these things testify that the Lord's coming is near.

The restraining Spirit of God is even now being withdrawn from the world. Hurricanes, storms, tempests, disasters by sea and by land, follow one another in quick succession. The signs thickening around us, telling of the near approach of the Son of God, are attributed to any other than the true cause. . . .

The time is right upon us when there will be sorrow in the world that no human balm can heal. Even before the last great destruction comes upon the world, the flattering monuments of man's greatness will be crumbled in the dust. God's retributive judgments will fall on those who in the face of great light have continued in sin. Costly buildings, supposed to be fireproof, are erected. But as Sodom perished in the flames of God's vengeance, so will these proud structures become ashes. I have seen vessels which cost immense sums of money wrestling with the mighty ocean, seeking to breast the angry billows. But with all their treasures of gold and silver, and with all their human freight, they sank into a watery grave. . . . But amid the tumult of excitement, with confusion in every place, there is a work to be done for God in the world.[43]

CALAMITIES BLAMED ON GOD'S PEOPLE

Woe to the inhabiters of the earth and of the sea! for the devil is come down unto you, having great wrath, because he knoweth that he hath but a short time. Rev. 12:12.

As men depart further and further from God, Satan is permitted to have power over the children of disobedience. He hurls destruction among men. There is calamity by land and sea. Property and life are destroyed by fire and flood. Satan resolves to charge this upon those who refuse to bow to the idol which he has set up. His agents point to Seventh-day Adventists as the cause of the trouble. "These people stand out in defiance of law," they say. "They desecrate Sunday. Were they compelled to obey the law for Sunday observance, there would be a cessation of these terrible judgments."[44]

Calamities will come—calamities most awful, most unexpected; and these destructions will follow one after another. If there will be a heeding of the warnings that God has given, and if churches will repent, returning to their allegiance, then other cities may be spared for a time. But if men who have been deceived continue in the same way in which they have been walking, disregarding the law of God and presenting falsehoods before the people, God allows them to suffer calamity, that their senses may be awakened.[45]

The judgments will be according to the wickedness of the people and the light of truth that they have had. If they have had the truth, according to that light will be the punishment.[46]

Satan puts his interpretation upon events, and they [leading men] think, as he would have them, that the calamities which fill the land are a result of Sunday-breaking. Thinking to appease the wrath of God, these influential men make laws enforcing Sunday observance. They think that by exalting this false rest-day higher, and still higher, compelling obedience to the Sunday law, the spurious sabbath, they are doing God service. Those who honor God by observing the true Sabbath are looked upon as disloyal to God, when it is really those who thus regard them who are themselves disloyal, because they are trampling under foot the Sabbath originated in Eden.[47]

WISDOM NEEDED BY SABBATHKEEPERS

Behold, I send you forth as sheep in the midst of wolves: be ye therefore wise as serpents, and harmless as doves. Matt. 10:16.

When the practices of the people do not come in conflict with the law of God, you may conform to them. If the workers fail to do this, they will not only hinder their own work, but they will place stumbling blocks in the way of those for whom they labor, and hinder them from accepting the truth. On Sunday there is the very best opportunity for those who are missionaries to hold Sunday schools, and come to the people in the simplest manner possible, telling them of the love of Jesus for sinners, and educating them in the Scriptures. . . .

At present Sunday-keeping is not the test. The time will come when men will not only forbid Sunday work, but they will try to force men to labor on the Sabbath, and to subscribe to Sunday observance or forfeit their freedom and their lives. But the time for this has not yet come, for the truth must be presented more fully before the people as a witness. . . .

The light that I have is that God's servants should go quietly to work, preaching the grand, precious truths of the Bible—Christ and Him crucified, His love and infinite sacrifice—showing that the reason why Christ died is because the law of God is immutable, unchangeable, eternal. The Sabbath must be taught in a decided manner, but be cautious how you deal with the idol Sunday. A word to the wise is sufficient. . . .

Refraining from work on Sunday is not receiving the mark of the beast; and where this will advance the interests of the work, it should be done. We should not go out of our way to work on Sunday. . . .

When those who hear and see the light on the Sabbath take their stand upon the truth to keep God's holy day, difficulties will arise; for efforts will be brought to bear against them to compel men and women to transgress the law of God. Here they must stand firm, that they will not violate the law of God; and if the opposition and persecution are determinedly kept up, let them heed the words of Christ: "When they persecute you in this city, flee ye into another." [48]

SUNDAY MISSIONARY WORK

Preach the word, be urgent in season and out of season, convince, rebuke, and exhort, be unfailing in patience and in teaching. 2 Tim. 4:2, R.S.V.

To defy the Sunday laws will but strengthen in their persecution the religious zealots who are seeking to enforce them. Give them no occasion to call you lawbreakers. If they are left to rein up men who fear neither God nor man, the reining up will soon lose its novelty for them, and they will see that it is not consistent nor convenient for them to be strict in regard to the observance of Sunday. Keep right on with your missionary work, with your Bibles in your hands, and the enemy will see that he has worsted his own cause. One does not receive the mark of the beast because he shows that he realizes the wisdom of keeping the peace by refraining from work that gives offense, doing at the same time a work of the highest importance.

When we devote Sunday to missionary work, the whip will be taken out of the hands of the arbitrary zealots who would be well pleased to humiliate Seventh-day Adventists. . . .

Sunday can be used for carrying forward various lines of work that will accomplish much for the Lord. On this day open-air meetings and cottage meetings can be held. House-to-house work can be done. Those who write can devote this day to writing their articles. Whenever it is possible, let religious services be held on Sunday. Make these meetings intensely interesting. Sing genuine revival hymns, and speak with power and assurance of the Saviour's love. Speak on temperance and on true religious experience. You will thus learn much about how to work, and will reach many souls. . . .

The law for the observance of the first day of the week is the production of an apostate Christendom. Sunday is a child of the Papacy, exalted by the Christian world above the sacred day of God's rest. In no case are God's people to pay it homage. But I wish them to understand that they are not doing God's will by braving opposition when He wishes them to avoid it.[49]

Wonderful scenes are opening before us; and at this time a living testimony is to be borne in the lives of God's professed people, so that the world may see that in this age, when evil reigns on every side, there is yet a people who are laying aside their will and are seeking to do God's will—a people in whose hearts and lives God's law is written.[50]

GOD'S LAW MADE VOID IN AMERICA

It is time for thee, Lord, to work: for they have made void thy law. Ps. 119:126.

A time is coming when the law of God is, in a special sense, to be made void in our land [the United States]. The rulers of our nation will, by legislative enactments, enforce the Sunday law, and thus God's people will be brought into great peril. When our nation, in its legislative councils, shall enact laws to bind the consciences of men in regard to their religious privileges, enforcing Sunday observance, and bringing oppressive power to bear against those who keep the seventh-day Sabbath, the law of God will, to all intents and purposes, be made void in our land.[51]

When the land which the Lord provided as an asylum for His people, that they might worship Him according to the dictates of their own consciences, the land over which for long years the shield of Omnipotence has been spread, the land which God has favored by making it the depository of the pure religion of Christ—when that land shall, through its legislators, abjure the principles of Protestantism, and give countenance to Romish apostasy in tampering with God's law—it is then that the final work of the man of sin will be revealed. Protestants will throw their whole influence and strength on the side of the Papacy; by a national act enforcing the false sabbath, they will give life and vigor to the corrupt faith of Rome, reviving her tyranny and oppression of conscience. Then it will be time for God to work in mighty power for the vindication of His truth.

The prophet says: "I saw another angel come down from heaven, having great power; and the earth was lightened with his glory. And he cried mightily with a strong voice, saying, Babylon the great is fallen, is fallen. . . . And I heard another voice from heaven, saying, Come out of her, my people, that ye be not partakers of her sins, and that ye receive not of her plagues. For her sins have reached unto heaven, and God hath remembered her iniquities." When do her sins reach unto heaven? When the law of God is finally made void by legislation. Then the extremity of God's people is His opportunity to show who is the governor of heaven and earth. As a Satanic power is stirring up the elements from beneath, God will send light and power to His people, that the message of truth may be proclaimed to all the world.[52]

THE SIGN TO LEAVE LARGE CITIES

When ye therefore shall see the abomination of desolation, spoken of by Daniel the prophet, stand in the holy place, (whoso readeth, let him understand:) then let them which be in Judaea flee into the mountains. Matt. 24:15, 16.

The time is not far distant, when, like the early disciples, we shall be forced to seek a refuge in desolate and solitary places. As the siege of Jerusalem by the Roman armies was the signal for flight to the Judean Christians, so the assumption of power on the part of our nation [the United States] in the decree enforcing the papal sabbath will be a warning to us. It will then be time to leave the large cities, preparatory to leaving the smaller ones for retired homes in secluded places among the mountains.[53]

For years I have been given special light that we are not to center our work in the cities. The turmoil and confusion that fill these cities, the conditions brought about by the labor unions and the strikes, would prove a great hindrance to our work. Men are seeking to bring those engaged in the different trades under bondage to certain unions. This is not God's planning, but the planning of a power that we should in no wise acknowledge. God's Word is fulfilling; the wicked are binding themselves up in bundles ready to be burned.[54]

The trades unions and confederacies of the world are a snare. Keep out of them, and away from them, brethren. Have nothing to do with them. Because of these unions and confederacies, it will soon be very difficult for our institutions to carry on their work in the cities. . . . Educate our people to get out of the cities into the country, where they can obtain a small piece of land, and make a home for themselves and their children. . . .

Erelong there will be such strife and confusion in the cities, that those who wish to leave them will not be able.[55]

We are not to locate ourselves where we will be forced into close relations with those who do not honor God. . . . A crisis is soon to come in regard to the observance of Sunday. . . .

The Sunday party is strengthening itself in its false claims, and this will mean oppression to those who determine to keep the Sabbath of the Lord. . . .

If in the providence of God we can secure places away from the cities, the Lord would have us do this. There are troublous times before us.[56]

FOOD AND LANDS IN THE LAST DAYS

Take therefore no thought for the morrow: for the morrow shall take thought for the things of itself. Sufficient unto the day is the evil thereof. Matt. 6:34.

The Lord has shown me in vision, repeatedly, that it is contrary to the Bible to make any provision for our temporal wants in the time of trouble. I saw that if the saints have food laid up by them, or in the fields, in the time of trouble when sword, famine, and pestilence are in the land, it will be taken from them by violent hands, and strangers would reap their fields. Then will be the time for us to trust wholly in God, and He will sustain us. I saw that our bread and water would be sure at that time, and we'should not lack, or suffer hunger. The Lord has shown me that some of His children would fear when they see the price of food rising, and they would buy food and lay it by for the time of trouble. Then in a time of need, I saw them go to their food and look at it, and it had bred worms, and was full of living creatures, and not fit for use.[57]

Houses and lands will be of no use to the saints in the time of trouble, for they will then have to flee before infuriated mobs, and at that time their possessions cannot be disposed of to advance the cause of present truth. . . .

I saw that if any held on to their property and did not inquire of the Lord as to their duty, He would not make duty known, and they would be permitted to keep their property, and in the time of trouble it would come up before them like a mountain to crush them, and they would try to dispose of it, but would not be able. . . . But if they desired to be taught, He would teach them, in a time of need, when to sell and how much to sell.[58]

In the last great conflict of the controversy with Satan those who are loyal to God will see every earthly support cut off. Because they refuse to break His law in obedience to earthly powers, they will be forbidden to buy or sell. It will finally be decreed that they shall be put to death. . . . But to the obedient is given the promise, "He shall dwell on high: his place of defence shall be the munitions of rocks: bread shall be given him; his waters shall be sure." Isa. 33:16. By this promise the children of God will live.[59]

LABOR UNIONS AND TRUSTS

Be patient therefore, brethren, unto the coming of the Lord. Behold, the husbandman waiteth for the precious fruit of the earth, and hath long patience for it, until he receive the early and latter rain. James 5:7.

The trades unions will be one of the agencies that will bring upon this earth a time of trouble such as has not been since the world began.[60]

In all our great cities there will be a binding up in bundles by the confederacies and unions formed. Men will rule other men and demand much of them. The lives of those who refuse to unite with these unions, will be in peril.[61]

The work of the people of God is to prepare for the events of the future, which will soon come upon them with blinding force. In the world gigantic monopolies will be formed. Men will bind themselves together in unions that will wrap them in the folds of the enemy. A few men will combine to grasp all the means to be obtained in certain lines of business. Trades unions will be formed, and those who refuse to join these unions will be marked men. . . .

These unions are one of the signs of the last days. Men are binding up in bundles ready to be burned. They may be church members, but while they belong to these unions, they cannot possibly keep the commandments of God; for to belong to these unions means to disregard the entire Decalogue.

"Thou shalt love the Lord thy God with all thy heart, and with all thy soul, and with all thy strength, and with all thy mind; and thy neighbour as thyself." . . . How can men obey these words, and form combinations that rob the poorer classes of the advantages which justly belong to them, preventing them from buying or selling, except under certain conditions?[62]

Those who claim to be the children of God are in no case to bind up with the labor unions that are formed or that shall be formed. This the Lord forbids. Cannot those who study the prophecies see and understand what is before us?[63]

Important issues must soon be met, and we wish to be hid in the cleft of the rock, that we may see Jesus, and be quickened by His Holy Spirit. We have no time to lose, not a moment.[64]

FORBIDDEN TO BUY OR SELL

And that no man might buy or sell, save he that had the mark, or the name of the beast, or the number of his name. Rev. 13:17.

The time is coming when we cannot sell at any price. The decree will soon go forth prohibiting men to buy or sell of any man save him that hath the mark of the beast.[65]

In the last great conflict of the controversy with Satan those who are loyal to God will see every earthly support cut off. Because they refuse to break His law in obedience to earthly powers, they will be forbidden to buy or sell.[66]

Religious powers, allied to heaven by profession, and claiming to have the characteristics of a lamb, will show by their acts that they have the heart of a dragon and that they are instigated and controlled by Satan. The time is coming when God's people will feel the hand of persecution because they keep holy the seventh day.[67]

There is a time coming when commandment-keepers can neither buy nor sell. Make haste to dig out your buried talents. If God has intrusted you with money, show yourselves faithful to your trust; unwrap your napkin, and send your talents to the exchangers, that when Christ shall come, He may receive His own with interest. In the last extremity, before this work shall close, thousands will be cheerfully laid upon the altar. Men and women will feel it a blessed privilege to share in the work of preparing souls to stand in the great day of God, and they will give hundreds as readily as dollars are given now. If the love of Christ were burning in the hearts of His professed people, we would see the same spirit manifested to-day. Did they but realize how near is the end of all work for the salvation of souls, they would sacrifice their possessions as freely as did the members of the early church. They would work for the advancement of God's cause as earnestly as worldly men labor to acquire riches. Tact and skill would be exercised, and earnest and unselfish labor put forth to acquire means, not to hoard, but to pour into the treasury of the Lord.[68]

WORK THE CITIES FROM OUTPOSTS

Wherefore come out from among them, and be ye separate, saith the Lord, and touch not the unclean thing; and I will receive you. 2 Cor. 6:17.

As God's commandment-keeping people, we must leave the cities. As did Enoch, we must work in the cities but not dwell in them.[69]

As far as possible, our institutions should be located away from the cities. . . . It is not God's will that His people shall settle in the cities, where there is constant turmoil and confusion. Their children should be spared this; for the whole system is demoralized by the hurry and rush and noise. The Lord desires His people to move into the country, where they can settle on the land, and raise their own fruit and vegetables, and where their children can be brought in direct contact with the works of God in nature. Take your families away from the cities is my message.

The truth must be spoken, whether men will hear, or whether men will forbear. The cities are filled with temptation. We should plan our work in such a way as to keep our young people as far as possible from this contamination.

The cities are to be worked from outposts. Said the messenger of God, "Shall not the cities be warned? Yes; not by God's people living in them, but by their visiting them, to warn them of what is coming upon the earth."[70]

When iniquity abounds in a nation, there is always to be heard some voice giving warning and instruction, as the voice of Lot was heard in Sodom. Yet Lot could have preserved his family from many evils had he not made his home in this wicked, polluted city. All that Lot and his family did in Sodom could have been done by them, even if they had lived in a place some distance away from the city. Enoch walked with God, and yet he did not live in the midst of any city polluted with every kind of violence and wickedness, as did Lot in Sodom.[71]

He [Enoch] did not make his abode with the wicked. . . . He placed himself and his family where the atmosphere would be as pure as possible. Then at times he went forth to the inhabitants of the world with his God-given message. . . . After proclaiming his message, he always took back with him to his place of retirement some who had received the warning.[72]

RELIEF OF PHYSICAL SUFFERING

And as ye go, preach, saying, The kingdom of heaven is at hand. Heal the sick, cleanse the lepers, raise the dead, cast out devils: freely ye have received, freely give. Matt. 10:7, 8.

Perilous times are before us. The whole world will be involved in perplexity and distress, disease of every kind will be upon the human family, and such ignorance as now prevails concerning the laws of health would result in great suffering and the loss of many lives that might be saved. . . .

As religious aggression subverts the liberties of our nation, those who would stand for freedom of conscience will be placed in unfavorable positions. For their own sake, they should, while they have opportunity, become intelligent in regard to disease, its causes, prevention, and cure. And those who do this will find a field of labor anywhere. There will be suffering ones, plenty of them, who will need help, not only among those of our own faith, but largely among those who know not the truth.[73]

The medical work done in connection with the giving of the third angel's message, is to accomplish wonderful results. It is to be a sanctifying, unifying work, corresponding to the work which the great Head of the church sent forth the first disciples to do.

Calling these disciples together, Christ gave them their commission: . . . "And as ye go, preach, saying, The kingdom of heaven is at hand. Heal the sick, cleanse the lepers, raise the dead, cast out devils: freely ye have received, freely give." "Behold, I send you forth as sheep in the midst of wolves: be ye therefore wise as serpents, and harmless as doves." Matthew 10:7, 8, 16.

It is well for us to read this chapter and let its instruction prepare us for our labors. The early disciples were going forth on Christ's errands, under His commission. His spirit was to prepare the way before them. They were to feel that with such a message to give, such blessings to impart, they should receive a welcome in the homes of the people.[74]

God reaches hearts through the relief of physical suffering. A seed of truth is dropped into the mind, and is watered by God. Much patience may be required before this seed shows signs of life, but at last it springs up, and bears fruit unto eternal life.

How slow men are to understand God's preparation for the day of His power![75]

THE SUNDAY LAW IS INVOKED

Ye shall be hated of all nations for my name's sake. Matt. 24:9.

As the movement for Sunday enforcement becomes more bold and decided, the law will be invoked against commandment keepers. They will be threatened with fines and imprisonment, and some will be offered positions of influence, and other rewards and advantages, as inducements to renounce their faith. But their steadfast answer is: "Show us from the word of God our error." . . . Those who are arraigned before the courts make a strong vindication of the truth, and some who hear them are led to take their stand to keep all the commandments of God. Thus light will be brought before thousands who otherwise would know nothing of these truths.

Conscientious obedience to the word of God will be treated as rebellion. Blinded by Satan, the parent will exercise harshness and severity toward the believing child; the master or mistress will oppress the commandment-keeping servant. Affection will be alienated; children will be disinherited and driven from home. The words of Paul will be literally fulfilled: "All that will live godly in Christ Jesus shall suffer persecution." 2 Timothy 3:12. As the defenders of truth refuse to honor the Sunday-sabbath, some of them will be thrust into prison, some will be exiled, some will be treated as slaves. . . .

In this time of persecution the faith of the Lord's servants will be tried. They have faithfully given the warning, looking to God and to His word alone. God's Spirit, moving upon their hearts, has constrained them to speak. . . . Yet when the storm of opposition and reproach bursts upon them, some, overwhelmed with consternation, will be ready to exclaim: "Had we foreseen the consequences of our words, we would have held our peace." They are hedged in with difficulties. Satan assails them with fierce temptations. The work which they have undertaken seems far beyond their ability to accomplish. They are threatened with destruction. The enthusiasm which animated them is gone; yet they cannot turn back. Then, feeling their utter helplessness, they flee to the Mighty One for strength.[76]

PROTESTANTISM UNITES WITH THE PAPACY

And the ten horns which thou sawest are ten kings, which have received no kingdom as yet; but receive power as kings one hour with the beast. These have one mind, and shall give their power and strength unto the beast. Rev. 17:12, 13.

As we approach the last crisis, it is of vital moment that harmony and unity exist among the Lord's instrumentalities. The world is filled with storm and war and variance. Yet under one head—the papal power—the people will unite to oppose God in the person of His witnesses.[77]

What is it that gives its kingdom to this power? Protestantism, a power which, while professing to have the temper and spirit of a lamb and to be allied to Heaven, speaks with the voice of a dragon. It is moved by a power from beneath.[78]

"These have one mind." There will be a universal bond of union, one great harmony, a confederacy of Satan's forces. "And shall give their power and strength unto the beast." Thus is manifested the same arbitrary, oppressive power against religious liberty, freedom to worship God according to the dictates of conscience, as was manifested by the papacy, when in the past it persecuted those who dared to refuse to conform with the religious rites and ceremonies of Romanism.

In the warfare to be waged in the last days there will be united, in opposition to God's people, all the corrupt powers that have apostatized from allegiance to the law of Jehovah. In this warfare the Sabbath of the fourth commandment will be the great point at issue; for in the Sabbath commandment the great Lawgiver identifies Himself as the Creator of the heavens and the earth.[79]

Through the two great errors, the immortality of the soul and Sunday sacredness, Satan will bring the people under his deceptions. While the former lays the foundation of spiritualism, the latter creates a bond of sympathy with Rome. The Protestants of the United States will be foremost in stretching their hands across the gulf to grasp the hand of spiritualism; they will reach over the abyss to clasp hands with the Roman power; and under the influence of this threefold union, this country will follow in the steps of Rome in trampling on the rights of conscience.[80]

TWO GREAT CLASSES OF CHRISTIANS

I saw one of his heads as it were wounded to death; and his deadly wound was healed: and all the world wondered after the beast. Rev. 13:3.

In homage to the Papacy the United States will not be alone. The influence of Rome in the countries that once acknowledged her dominion, is still far from being destroyed.[81]

In the last conflict the Sabbath will be the special point of controversy throughout all Christendom. Secular rulers and religious leaders will unite to enforce the observance of the Sunday; and as milder measures fail, the most oppressive laws will be enacted. It will be urged that the few who stand in opposition to an institution of the church and a law of the land ought not to be tolerated. . . . Romanism in the Old World, and apostate Protestantism in the New, will pursue a similar course toward those who honor the divine precepts.[82]

The so-called Christian world is to be the theater of great and decisive actions. Men in authority will enact laws controlling the conscience, after the example of the Papacy. Babylon will make all nations drink of the wine of the wrath of her fornication. Every nation will be involved. [Rev. 18:3-7 quoted.]

The warning of the third angel [of Revelation 14] . . . is represented in the prophecy as being proclaimed with a loud voice, by an angel flying in the midst of heaven; and it will command the attention of the world.

In the issue of the contest all Christendom will be divided into two great classes—those who keep the commandments of God and the faith of Jesus, and those who worship the beast and his image and receive his mark. Although church and state will unite their power to compel "all, both small and great, rich and poor, free and bond" (Revelation 13:16), to receive "the mark of the beast," yet the people of God will not receive it. The prophet of Patmos beholds "them that had gotten the victory over the beast, and over his image, and over his mark, and over the number of his name, stand on the sea of glass, having the harps of God" and singing the song of Moses and the Lamb. Revelation 15:2, 3.[84]

CONFUSION OF MANY VOICES

And I heard another voice from heaven, saying, Come out of her, my people, that ye be not partakers of her sins, and that ye receive not of her plagues. Rev. 18:4.

In the last work for the warning of the world, two distinct calls are made to the churches. The second angel's message is, "Babylon is fallen, is fallen, that great city, because she made all nations drink of the wine of the wrath of her fornication." And in the loud cry of the third angel's message a voice is heard from heaven saying, "Come out of her, my people, that ye be not partakers of her sins, and that ye receive not of her plagues. For her sins have reached unto heaven, and God hath remembered her iniquities."[85]

As God called the children of Israel out of Egypt, that they might keep His Sabbath, so He calls His people out of Babylon, that they may not worship the beast or his image. . . .

After the truth has been proclaimed as a witness to all nations, every conceivable power of evil will be set in operation, and minds will be confused by many voices crying, "Lo, here is Christ, Lo, He is there. This is the truth, I have the message from God, He has sent me with great light." Then there will be a removing of the landmarks, and an attempt to tear down the pillars of our faith. A more decided effort will be made to exalt the false sabbath, and to cast contempt upon God Himself by supplanting the day He has blessed and sanctified. This false sabbath is to be enforced by an oppressive law. . . . But while Satan works with his lying wonders, the time will be fulfilled foretold in the Revelation, and the mighty angel that shall lighten the earth with his glory, will proclaim the fall of Babylon, and call upon God's people to forsake her.[86]

When do her sins reach unto heaven? When the law of God is finally made void by legislation. Then the extremity of God's people is His opportunity to show who is the governor of heaven and earth. As a Satanic power is stirring up the elements from beneath, God will send light and power to His people, that the message of truth may be proclaimed to all the world.[87]

THE THREEFOLD UNION
OF RELIGION

And I saw three unclean spirits like frogs come out of the mouth of the dragon, and out of the mouth of the beast, and out of the mouth of the false prophet. For they are the spirits of devils, working miracles, which go forth unto the kings of the earth and of the whole world, to gather them to the battle of that great day of God Almighty. Rev. 16:13, 14.

By the decree enforcing the institution of the papacy in violation of the law of God, our nation [the United States] will disconnect herself fully from righteousness. When Protestantism shall stretch her hand across the gulf to grasp the hand of the Roman power, when she shall reach over the abyss to clasp hands with spiritualism, when, under the influence of this threefold union, our country shall repudiate every principle of its Constitution as a Protestant and republican government, and shall make provision for the propagation of papal falsehoods and delusions, then we may know that the time has come for the marvelous working of Satan and that the end is near.[1]

Through the two great errors, the immortality of the soul and Sunday sacredness, Satan will bring the people under his deceptions. While the former lays the foundation of spiritualism, the latter creates a bond of sympathy with Rome. The Protestants of the United States will be foremost in stretching their hands across the gulf to grasp the hand of spiritualism; they will reach over the abyss to clasp hands with the Roman power; and under the influence of this threefold union, this country will follow in the steps of Rome in trampling on the rights of conscience. . . .

Papists, Protestants, and worldlings will alike accept the form of godliness without the power, and they will see in this union a grand movement for the conversion of the world and the ushering in of the long-expected millennium.[2]

When our nation [the United States] shall so abjure the principles of its government as to enact a Sunday law, Protestantism will in this act join hands with popery; it will be nothing else than giving life to the tyranny which has long been eagerly watching its opportunity to spring again into active despotism.[3]

SATAN AND THE THREEFOLD UNION

And they worshipped the dragon which gave power unto the beast. Rev. 13:4.

"He had two horns like a lamb, and he spake as a dragon." Though professing to be followers of the Lamb of God, men become imbued with the spirit of the dragon. They profess to be meek and humble but they speak and legislate with the spirit of Satan, showing by their actions that they are the opposite of what they profess to be. This lamb-like power unites with the dragon in making war upon those who keep the commandments of God and have the testimony of Jesus Christ. And Satan unites with Protestants and Papists, acting in consort with them as the god of this world, dictating to men as if they were the subjects of his kingdom, to be handled and governed and controlled as he pleases. If men will not agree to trample under foot the commandments of God, the spirit of the dragon is revealed. They are imprisoned, brought before councils, and fined. "He causeth all, both small and great, rich and poor, free and bond, to receive a mark in their right hand, or in their foreheads." "He had power to give life unto the image of the beast, that the image of the beast should both speak, and cause that as many as would not worship the image of the beast should be killed." Thus Satan usurps the prerogatives of Jehovah. The man of sin sits in the seat of God, proclaiming himself to be God, and acting above God.

There is a marked contrast between those who bear the seal of God and those who worship the beast and his image. The Lord's faithful servants will receive the bitterest persecution from false teachers, who will not hear the word of God, and who prepare stumbling blocks to put in the way of those who would hear. But God's people are not to fear. Satan cannot go beyond his limit. The Lord will be the defense of His people. He regards the injury done to His servants for the truth's sake as done to Himself. When the last decision has been made, when all have taken sides, either for Christ and the commandments or for the great apostate, God will arise in His power, and the mouths of those who have blasphemed against Him will be forever stopped. Every opposing power will receive its punishment.[4]

THE CORRUPTION OF TRUTH

Then if any man shall say unto you, Lo, here is Christ, or there; believe it not. Matt. 24:23.

Before the last developments of the work of apostasy there will be a confusion of faith. There will not be clear and definite ideas concerning the mystery of God. One truth after another will be corrupted.[5]

After the truth has been proclaimed as a witness to all nations, every conceivable power of evil will be set in operation, and minds will be confused by many voices crying, "Lo, here is Christ; lo, He is there. This is the truth, I have the message from God, He has sent me with great light." Then there will be a removing of the landmarks, and an attempt to tear down the pillars of our faith. A more decided effort will be made to exalt the false sabbath, and to cast contempt upon God Himself by supplanting the day He has blessed and sanctified. This false sabbath is to be enforced by an oppressive law.[6]

In the future, deception of every kind is to arise, and we want solid ground for our feet. We want solid pillars for the building. Not one pin is to be removed from that which the Lord has established. The enemy will bring in false theories, such as the doctrine that there is no sanctuary. This is one of the points on which there will be a departing from the faith.[7]

There will be false dreams and false visions, which have some truth, but lead away from the original faith. The Lord has given men a rule by which to detect them: "To the law and to the testimony: if they speak not according to this word, it is because there is no light in them" (Isa. 8:20).[8]

As we near the end of time, falsehood will be so mingled with truth, that only those who have the guidance of the Holy Spirit will be able to distinguish truth from error. We need to make every effort to keep the way of the Lord. We must in no case turn from His guidance to put our trust in man. The Lord's angels are appointed to keep strict watch over those who put their faith in the Lord, and these angels are to be our special help in every time of need. Every day we are to come to the Lord with full assurance of faith, and to look to Him for wisdom. . . . Those who are guided by the Word of the Lord will discern with certainty between falsehood and truth, between sin and righteousness.[9]

THE UNITED STATES IN PROPHECY

I beheld another beast coming up out of the earth; and he had two horns like a lamb, and he spake as a dragon. Rev. 13:11.

One nation, and only one, meets the specifications of this prophecy; it points unmistakably to the United States of America.[10]

Here is a striking figure of the rise and growth of our own nation. And the lamb-like horns, emblems of innocence and gentleness, well represent the character of our government, as expressed in its two fundamental principles, Republicanism and Protestantism.[11]

The Lord has done more for the United States than for any other country upon which the sun shines. Here He provided an asylum for His people, where they could worship Him according to the dictates of conscience. Here Christianity has progressed in its purity. The life-giving doctrine of the one Mediator between God and man has been freely taught. God designed that this country should ever remain free for all people to worship Him in accordance with the dictates of conscience. He designed that its civil institutions, in their expansive productions, should represent the freedom of gospel privileges.

But the enemy of all righteousness has designs upon God's purpose for this country. He will bring in enterprises that will lead men to forget that there is a God. Worldliness and covetousness, which is idolatry, will prevail through the working of the archdeceiver, till the law of God, in all its bearings, shall be made void.[12]

I have been shown that Satan is stealing a march upon us. The law of God, through the agency of Satan, is to be made void. In our land of boasted freedom, religious liberty will come to an end.[13]

When our nation, in its legislative councils, shall enact laws to bind the consciences of men in regard to their religious privileges, enforcing Sunday observance, and bringing oppressive power to bear against those who keep the seventh-day Sabbath, the law of God will, to all intents and purposes, be made void in our land; and national apostasy will be followed by national ruin.[14]

PERSECUTION BY PROTESTANTS AND CATHOLICS

Ye shall be hated of all men for my name's sake: but he that endureth to the end shall be saved. Matt. 10:22.

There is no necessity for thinking that we cannot endure persecution; we shall have to go through terrible times.[15]

The persecutions of Protestants by Romanism, by which the religion of Jesus Christ was almost annihilated, will be more than rivaled when Protestantism and popery are combined.[16]

The commandment-keeping people of God erelong will be placed in a most trying position; but all those who have walked in the light, and diffused the light, will realize that God interposes in their behalf. When everything looks most forbidding, then the Lord will reveal His power to His faithful ones. When the nation for which God has worked in such a marvelous manner, and over which He has spread the shield of Omnipotence, abandons Protestant principles, and through its legislature gives countenance and support to Romanism in limiting religious liberty, then God will work in His own power for His people that are true. The tyranny of Rome will be exercised, but Christ is our refuge.[17]

When the leading churches of the United States, uniting upon such points of doctrine as are held by them in common, shall influence the state to enforce their decrees and to sustain their institutions, then Protestant America will have formed an image of the Roman hierarchy, and the infliction of civil penalties upon dissenters will inevitably result.[18]

The Scriptures teach that popery is to regain its lost supremacy, and that the fires of persecution will be rekindled through the time-serving concessions of the so-called Protestant world. In this time of peril we can stand only as we have the truth and the power of God. . . . The prospect of being brought into personal danger and distress, need not cause despondency, but should quicken the vigor and hopes of God's people; for the time of their peril is the season for God to grant them clearer manifestations of his power.

PERSECUTED FOR CHRIST'S SAKE

All that will live godly in Christ Jesus shall suffer persecution. 2 Tim. 3:12.

As Christ was hated without cause, so will His people be hated because they are obedient to the commandments of God. If He who was pure, holy, and undefiled, who did good and only good in our world, was treated as a base criminal and condemned to death, His disciples must expect but similar treatment, however faultless may be their life and blameless their character.

Human enactments, laws manufactured by satanic agencies under a plea of goodness and restriction of evil, will be exalted, while God's holy commandments are despised and trampled underfoot. And all who prove their loyalty by obedience to the law of Jehovah must be prepared to be arrested, to be brought before councils that have not for their standard the high and holy law of God.[20]

Those who live during the last days of this earth's history will know what it means to be persecuted for the truth's sake. In the courts injustice will prevail. The judges will refuse to listen to the reasons of those who are loyal to the commandments of God, because they know that arguments in favor of the fourth commandment are unanswerable. They will say, "We have a law, and by our law he ought to die." God's law is nothing to them. "Our law" with them is supreme. Those who respect this human law will be favored, but those who will not bow to the idol sabbath will have no favors shown them.[21]

In summer there is no noticeable difference between evergreens and other trees; but when the blasts of winter come, the evergreens remain unchanged, while other trees are stripped of their foliage. So the falsehearted professor may not now be distinguished from the real Christian, but the time is just upon us when the difference will be apparent. Let opposition arise, let bigotry and intolerance again bear sway, let persecution be kindled, and the halfhearted and hypocritical will waver and yield the faith; but the true Christian will stand firm as a rock, his faith stronger, his hope brighter, than in days of prosperity.[22]

FORMER BRETHREN WORST PERSECUTORS

Then shall many be offended, and shall betray one another, and shall hate one another. Matt. 24:10.

As the storm approaches, a large class who have professed faith in the third angel's message, but have not been sanctified through obedience to the truth, abandon their position and join the ranks of the opposition. By uniting with the world and partaking of its spirit, they have come to view matters in nearly the same light; and when the test is brought, they are prepared to choose the easy, popular side. Men of talent and pleasing address, who once rejoiced in the truth, employ their powers to deceive and mislead souls. They become the most bitter enemies of their former brethren. When Sabbathkeepers are brought before the courts to answer for their faith, these apostates are the most efficient agents of Satan to misrepresent and accuse them, and by false reports and insinuations to stir up the rulers against them.[23]

The season of distress before God's people will call for a faith that will not falter. His children must make it manifest that He is the only object of their worship, and that no consideration, not even that of life itself, can induce them to make the least concession to false worship.[24]

At that time the gold will be separated from the dross. . . . Many a star that we have admired for its brilliance will then go out in darkness. Those who have assumed the ornaments of the sanctuary, but are not clothed with Christ's righteousness, will then appear in the shame of their own nakedness.

Among earth's inhabitants, scattered in every land, there are those who have not bowed the knee to Baal. Like the stars of heaven, which appear only at night, these faithful ones will shine forth when darkness covers the earth and gross darkness the people. . . . In the hour of deepest apostasy, when Satan's supreme effort is made to cause "all, both small and great, rich and poor, free and bond," to receive, under penalty of death, the sign of allegiance to a false rest day, these faithful ones . . . will "shine as lights in the world.". . . Philippians 2:15. The darker the night, the more brilliantly will they shine.[25]

BETRAYED BY FRIENDS AND RELATIVES

A man's foes shall be they of his own household. Matt. 10:36.

When the law of God is made void, and the church is sifted by the fiery trials that are to try all that live upon the earth, a great proportion of those who are supposed to be genuine will give heed to seducing spirits, and will turn traitors and betray sacred trusts. They will prove our very worst persecutors. "Of your own selves shall men arise, speaking perverse things, to draw away disciples after them;" and many will give heed to seducing spirits.[26]

Those who apostatize in time of trial will bear false witness and betray their brethren, to secure their own safety. They will tell where their brethren are concealed, putting the wolves on their track. Christ has warned us of this, that we may not be surprised at the cruel, unnatural course pursued by friends and relatives.[27]

We shall find that we must let loose of all hands except the hand of Jesus Christ. Friends will prove treacherous, and will betray us. Relatives, deceived by the enemy, will think they do God service in opposing us and putting forth the utmost efforts to bring us into hard places, hoping we will deny our faith. But we may trust our hand in the hand of Christ amid darkness and peril.[28]

The followers of Christ must expect to encounter sneers. They will be reviled; their words and their faith will be misrepresented. Coldness and contempt may be harder to endure than martyrdom. . . .

Parents will turn harshly against their children who accept unpopular truth. Those who conscientiously serve God will be accused of rebellion. Property that was willed to children or other relatives who believe the present truth will be given into other hands. Guardians will rob orphans and widows of their just dues. Those who depart from evil will make themselves a prey through laws enacted to compel the conscience. Men will take to themselves property to which they have no right. The words of the apostle will be verified in the near future: "All that will live godly in Christ Jesus shall suffer persecution." [29]

UNDER THREAT OF DEATH

For if thou altogether holdest thy peace at this time, then shall there enlargement and deliverance arise to the Jews from another place; but thou and thy father's house shall be destroyed: and who knoweth whether thou art come to the kingdom for such a time as this? Esther 4:14.

Wonderful events are soon to open before the world. The end of all things is at hand. The time of trouble is about to come upon the people of God. Then it is that the decree will go forth forbidding those who keep the Sabbath of the Lord to buy or sell, and threatening them with punishment, and even death, if they do not observe the first day of the week as the Sabbath.[30]

The decree which is to go forth against the people of God will be very similar to that issued by Ahasuerus against the Jews in the time of Esther. . . . Satan instigated the scheme in order to rid the earth of those who preserved the knowledge of the true God. But his plots were defeated by a counterpower that reigns among the children of men. . . .

The Protestant world today see in the little company keeping the Sabbath a Mordecai in the gate. His character and conduct, expressing reverence for the law of God, are a constant rebuke to those who have cast off the fear of the Lord and are trampling upon His Sabbath; the unwelcome intruder must by some means be put out of the way.

The same masterful mind that plotted against the faithful in ages past is still seeking to rid the earth of those who fear God and obey His law. Satan will excite indignation against the humble minority who conscientiously refuse to accept popular customs and traditions. Men of position and reputation will join with the lawless and the vile to take counsel against the people of God. . . . Not having a "Thus saith the Scriptures" to bring against the advocates of the Bible Sabbath, they will resort to oppressive enactments to supply the lack. . . . On this battlefield comes the last great conflict of the controversy between truth and error. And we are not left in doubt as to the issue. Now, as in the days of Mordecai, the Lord will vindicate His truth and His people.[31]

MARTYRS IN THE LAST DAYS

They shall put you out of the synagogues: yea, the time cometh, that whosoever killeth you will think that he doeth God service. John 16:2.

Every individual in our world will be arrayed under one of two banners.[32]

The two armies will stand distinct and separate, and this distinction will be so marked that many who shall be convinced of truth will come on the side of God's commandment-keeping people. When this grand work is to take place in the battle, prior to the last closing conflict, many will be imprisoned, many will flee for their lives from cities and towns, and many will be martyrs for Christ's sake in standing in defense of the truth.[33]

By the decree enforcing the institution of the papacy in violation of the law of God, our nation [the United States] will disconnect herself fully from righteousness. . . .

As the approach of the Roman armies was a sign to the disciples of the impending destruction of Jerusalem, so may this apostasy be a sign to us that the limit of God's forbearance is reached, that the measure of our nation's iniquity is full, and that the angel of mercy is about to take her flight, never to return. The people of God will then be plunged into those scenes of affliction and distress which prophets have described as the time of Jacob's trouble. The cries of the faithful, persecuted ones ascend to heaven. And as the blood of Abel cried from the ground, there are voices also crying to God from martyrs' graves, from the sepulchers of the sea, from mountain caverns, from convent vaults: "How long, O Lord, holy and true, dost thou not judge and avenge our blood on them that dwell on the earth?" [34]

When the fifth seal was opened, John the Revelator in vision saw beneath the altar the company that were slain for the Word of God and the testimony of Jesus Christ. After this came the scenes described in the eighteenth of Revelation, when those who are faithful and true are called out from Babylon.[35]

Christ will restore the life taken; for He is the Life-giver: He will beautify the righteous with immortal life.[36]

THE SHAKING TIME

And because iniquity shall abound, the love of many shall wax cold. Matt. 24:12.

Just as soon as the people of God are sealed in their foreheads—it is not any seal or mark that can be seen, but a settling into the truth, both intellectually and spiritually, so they cannot be moved—just as soon as God's people are sealed and prepared for the shaking, it will come. Indeed, it has begun already; the judgments of God are now upon the land, to give us warning, that we may know what is coming.[37]

The days are fast approaching when there will be great perplexity and confusion. Satan, clothed in angel robes, will deceive, if possible, the very elect. There will be gods many and lords many. Every wind of doctrine will be blowing. . . .

The mark of the beast will be urged upon us. Those who have step by step yielded to worldly demands and conformed to worldly customs will not find it a hard matter to yield to the powers that be, rather than subject themselves to derision, insult, threatened imprisonment, and death. The contest is between the commandments of God and the commandments of men. In this time the gold will be separated from the dross in the church. True godliness will be clearly distinguished from the appearance and tinsel of it. Many a star that we have admired for its brilliancy will then go out in darkness. Chaff like a cloud will be borne away on the wind, even from places where we see only floors of rich wheat. All who assume the ornaments of the sanctuary, but are not clothed with Christ's righteousness, will appear in the shame of their own nakedness.[38]

But there are men who will receive the truth, and these will take the places made vacant by those who become offended and leave the truth. . . .

Men of true Christian principle will take their place, and will become faithful, trustworthy householders, to advocate the word of God in its true bearings, and in its simplicity. The Lord will work so that the disaffected ones will be separated from the true and loyal ones. . . . The ranks will not be diminished. Those who are firm and true will close up the vacancies that are made by those who become offended and apostatize.[39]

A VIEW OF THE SHAKING

For in my jealousy and in the fire of my wrath have I spoken, Surely in that day there shall be a great shaking in the land of Israel. Eze. 38:19.

I saw some, with strong faith and agonizing cries, pleading with God. Their countenances were pale and marked with deep anxiety, expressive of their internal struggle. Firmness and great earnestness was expressed in their countenances; large drops of perspiration fell from their foreheads. . . .

Evil angels crowded around, pressing darkness upon them to shut out Jesus from their view, that their eyes might be drawn to the darkness that surrounded them, and thus they be led to distrust God and murmur against Him. Their only safety was in keeping their eyes directed upward. Angels of God had charge over His people, and as the poisonous atmosphere of evil angels was pressed around these anxious ones, the heavenly angels were continually wafting their wings over them to scatter the thick darkness.

As the praying ones continued their earnest cries, at times a ray of light from Jesus came to them, to encourage their hearts and light up their countenances. Some, I saw, did not participate in this work of agonizing and pleading. They seemed indifferent and careless. . . . The angels of God . . . went to the aid of the earnest, praying ones. . . . But His angels left those who made no effort to help themselves, and I lost sight of them.

I asked the meaning of the shaking I had seen and was shown that it would be caused by the straight testimony called forth by the counsel of the True Witness to the Laodiceans. . . .

My attention was then turned to the company I had seen, who were mightily shaken. . . . The company of guardian angels around them had been doubled, and they were clothed with an armor from their head to their feet. . . .

I heard those clothed with the armor speak forth the truth with great power. It had effect. . . . I asked what had made this great change. An angel answered, "It is the latter rain, the refreshing from the presence of the Lord, the loud cry of the third angel." [40]

UNITY AND SEPARATION UNDER THE LOUD CRY

Arise, shine; for thy light is come, and the glory of the Lord is risen upon thee. For, behold, the darkness shall cover the earth, and gross darkness the people: but the Lord shall arise upon thee, and his glory shall be seen upon thee. Isa. 60:1, 2.

As trials thicken around us, both separation and unity will be seen in our ranks. Some who are now ready to take up weapons of warfare will in times of real peril make it manifest that they have not built upon the solid rock; they will yield to temptation. Those who have had great light and precious privileges, but have not improved them, will, under one pretext or another, go out from us. Not having received the love of the truth, they will be taken in the delusions of the enemy; they will give heed to seducing spirits and doctrines of devils, and will depart from the faith. But, on the other hand, when the storm of persecution really breaks upon us, the true sheep will hear the true Shepherd's voice. Self-denying efforts will be put forth to save the lost, and many who have strayed from the fold will come back to follow the great Shepherd. The people of God will draw together and present to the enemy a united front. In view of the common peril, strife for supremacy will cease; there will be no disputing as to who shall be accounted greatest. No one of the true believers will say: "I am of Paul; and I of Apollos; and I of Cephas." The testimony of one and all will be: "I cleave unto Christ; I rejoice in Him as my personal Saviour." [41]

As the third angel's message swells into a loud cry, great power and glory will attend its proclamation. The faces of God's people will shine with the light of heaven.[42]

Many of the rulers are those whom Satan controls; but . . . God has His agents, even among the rulers. And some of them will yet be converted to the truth. . . . A few of God's agents will have power to bear down a great mass of evil. Thus the work will go on until the third message has done its work, and at the loud cry of the third angel, these agents will have an opportunity to receive the truth, and some of them will be converted, and endure with the saints through the time of trouble.[43]

THE CHURCH APPEARS ABOUT TO FALL

But Zion said, The Lord hath forsaken me, and my Lord hath forgotten me. Can a woman forget her sucking child, that she should not have compassion on the son of her womb? yea, they may forget, yet will I not forget thee. Isa. 49:14, 15.

Satan will work his miracles to deceive; he will set up his power as supreme. The church may appear as about to fall, but it does not fall. It remains, while the sinners in Zion will be sifted out—the chaff separated from the precious wheat. This is a terrible ordeal, but nevertheless it must take place. None but those who have been overcoming by the blood of the Lamb and the word of their testimony will be found with the loyal and true, without spot or stain of sin, without guile in their mouths. . . . The remnant that purify their souls by obeying the truth gather strength from the trying process, exhibiting the beauty of holiness amid the surrounding apostasy.[44]

I know that the Lord loves His church. It is not to be disorganized or broken up into independent atoms. There is not the least consistency in this; there is not the least evidence that such a thing will be. Those who shall heed this false message and try to leaven others will be deceived and prepared to receive advanced delusions, and they will come to nought.[45]

I am encouraged and blessed as I realize that the God of Israel is still guiding His people, and that He will continue to be with them, even to the end.[46]

We cannot now step off the foundation that God has established. We cannot now enter into any new organization; for this would mean apostasy from the truth.[47]

The church, soon to enter upon her most severe conflict, will be the object most dear to God upon earth. The confederacy of evil will be stirred with power from beneath, and Satan will cast all the reproach possible upon the chosen ones whom he cannot deceive and delude with his satanic inventions and falsehoods. But exalted "to be a Prince and a Saviour, for to give repentance to Israel, and remission of sins," will Christ, our representative and head, close His heart, or withdraw His hand, or falsify His promise? No; never, never.[48]

THE PURIFICATION OF THE CHURCH

And he shall sit as a refiner and purifier of silver: and he shall purify the sons of Levi, and purge them as gold and silver, that they may offer unto the Lord an offering in righteousness. Mal. 3:3.

The time is upon us when the miracle-working power of the archdeceiver will be more decidedly revealed. And his deceptions will increase in their delusive attraction, so that they will perplex, and if possible, deceive, the very elect. The prince of darkness with his evil angels is working upon the Christian world, inducing those who profess the name of Christ to stand under the banner of darkness, to make war with those who keep the commandments of God, and have the faith of Jesus.

An apostate church will unite with the powers of earth and hell to place upon the forehead or in the hand, the mark of the beast, and prevail upon the children of God to worship the beast and his image. They will seek to compel them to renounce their allegiance to God's law, and yield homage to the papacy. Then will come the times which will try men's souls; for the confederacy of apostasy will demand that the loyal subjects of God shall renounce the law of Jehovah, and repudiate the truth of His word. Then will the gold be separated from the dross, and it will be made apparent who are the godly, who are the loyal and true, and who are the disloyal, the dross and the tinsel. What clouds of chaff will then be borne away by the fan of God! Where now our eyes can discover only rich floors of wheat, will be chaff blown away with the fan of God. Every one who is not centered in Christ will fail to stand the test and ordeal of that day. While those who are clothed with Christ's righteousness will stand firm to truth and duty, those who have trusted in their own righteousness will be ranged under the black banner of the prince of darkness. Then it will be seen whether the choice is for Christ or Belial.

Those who have been self-distrustful, who have been so circumstanced that they have not dared to face stigma and reproach, will at last openly declare themselves for Christ and His law; while many who have appeared to be flourishing trees, but who have borne no fruit, will go with the multitude to do evil, and will receive the mark of apostasy in the forehead or in the hand.[49]

SATAN PERSONATES CHRIST—I

Take heed that ye be not deceived: for many shall come in my name, saying, I am Christ; and the time draweth near: go ye not therefore after them. Luke 21:8.

"In this age antichrist will appear as the true Christ, and then the law of God will be fully made void in the nations of our world. Rebellion against God's holy law will be fully ripe. But the true leader of all this rebellion is Satan clothed as an angel of light. Men will be deceived and will exalt him to the place of God, and deify him. But Omnipotence will interpose, and to the apostate churches that unite in the exaltation of Satan, the sentence will go forth, 'Therefore shall her plagues come in one day, death, and mourning, and famine; and she shall be utterly burned with fire: for strong is the Lord God who judgeth her.' " [50]

Disguised as an angel of light, he [Satan] will walk the earth as a wonder-worker. In beautiful language he will present lofty sentiments. Good words will be spoken by him, and good deeds performed. Christ will be personified, but on one point there will be a marked distinction. Satan will turn the people from the law of God. [51]

He will declare that the Sabbath has been changed from the seventh to the first day of the week; and as lord of the first day of the week he will present this spurious sabbath as a test of loyalty to him. [52]

It is impossible to give any idea of the experience of the people of God who shall be alive upon the earth when celestial glory and a repetition of the persecutions of the past are blended. They will walk in the light proceeding from the throne of God. By means of the angels there will be constant communication between heaven and earth. And Satan, surrounded by evil angels, and claiming to be God, will work miracles of all kinds, to deceive, if possible, the very elect. God's people will not find their safety in working miracles, for Satan will counterfeit the miracles that will be wrought. God's tried and tested people will find their power in the sign spoken of in Exodus 31:12-18. They are to take their stand on the living word: "It is written." This is the only foundation upon which they can stand securely. [53]

SATAN PERSONATES CHRIST—II

And no marvel; for Satan himself is transformed into an angel of light. 2 Cor. 11:14.

Satan is preparing his deceptions that in his last campaign against the people of God, they may not understand that it is he. "And no marvel; for Satan himself is transformed into an angel of light." . . . Satan will go to the extent of his power to harass, tempt, and mislead God's people.

He who dared to face, and tempt, and taunt our Lord, and who had power to take Him in his arms and carry Him to a pinnacle of the temple, and up into an exceeding high mountain, will exercise his power to a wonderful degree upon the present generation, who are far inferior in wisdom to their Lord, and who are almost wholly ignorant of his subtlety and strength.

In a marvelous manner will he affect the bodies of those who are naturally inclined to do his bidding.[54]

He will come personating Jesus Christ, working mighty miracles; and men will fall down and worship him as Jesus Christ.

We shall be commanded to worship this being, whom the world will glorify as Christ. What shall we do?—Tell them that Christ has warned us against just such a foe, who is man's worst enemy, yet who claims to be God; and that when Christ shall make His appearance, it will be with power and great glory, accompanied by ten thousand times ten thousand angels and thousands of thousands; and that when He shall come, we shall know His voice.[55]

The time is coming when Satan will work miracles right in your sight, claiming that he is Christ; and if your feet are not firmly established upon the truth of God, then you will be led away from your foundation.[56]

Satan is determined to keep up the warfare to the end. Coming as an angel of light, claiming to be the Christ, he will deceive the world. But his triumph will be short. No storm or tempest can move those whose feet are planted on the principles of eternal truth. They will be able to stand in this time of almost universal apostasy.[57]

SATANIC MIRACLES—I

There shall arise false Christs, and false prophets, and shall shew great signs and wonders; insomuch that, if it were possible, they shall deceive the very elect. Matt. 24:24.

The enemy is preparing to deceive the whole world by his miracle-working power. He will assume to personate the angels of light, to personate Jesus Christ.[58]

So far as his power extends, he will perform actual miracles. Says the Scripture: "He . . . deceiveth them that dwell on the earth by the means of those miracles which he had power to do," not merely those which he pretends to do. Something more than mere impostures is brought to view in this scripture. But there is a limit beyond which Satan cannot go, and here he calls deception to his aid and counterfeits the work which he has not power actually to perform. In the last days he will appear in such a manner as to make men believe him to be Christ come the second time into the world. He will indeed transform himself into an angel of light.[59]

He will come personating Jesus Christ, working mighty miracles; and men will fall down and worship him as Jesus Christ. We shall be commanded to worship this being, whom the world will glorify as Christ.[60]

Just before us is "the hour of temptation, which shall come upon all the world, to try them that dwell upon the earth." Revelation 3:10. All whose faith is not firmly established upon the word of God will be deceived and overcome. Satan works "with all deceivableness of unrighteousness" to gain control of the children of men, and his deceptions will continually increase. But he can gain his object only as men voluntarily yield to his temptations. Those who are earnestly seeking a knowledge of the truth and are striving to purify their souls through obedience, thus doing what they can to prepare for the conflict, will find, in the God of truth, a sure defense. "Because thou hast kept the word of my patience, I also will keep thee" (verse 10), is the Saviour's promise. He would sooner send every angel out of heaven to protect His people than leave one soul that trusts in Him to be overcome by Satan.[61]

207

SATANIC MIRACLES—II

And he doeth great wonders, so that he maketh fire come down from heaven on the earth in the sight of men. Rev. 13:13.

As the people of God approach the perils of the last days, Satan holds earnest consultation with his angels as to the most successful plan of overthrowing their faith. He sees that the popular churches are already lulled to sleep by his deceptive power. By pleasing sophistry and lying wonders he can continue to hold them under his control. Therefore he directs his angels to lay their snares especially for those who are looking for the second advent of Christ and endeavoring to keep all the commandments of God.[62]

We are warned that in the last days he will work with signs and lying wonders. And he will continue these wonders until the close of probation, that he may point to them as evidence that he is an angel of light and not of darkness.[63]

Satan will come in to deceive if possible the very elect. He claims to be Christ, and he is coming in, pretending to be the great medical missionary. He will cause fire to come down from heaven in the sight of men to prove that he is God.[64]

It is the lying wonders of the devil that will take the world captive, and he will cause fire to come down from heaven in the sight of men. He is to work miracles; and this wonderful, miracle-working power is to sweep in the whole world.[65]

Some will be tempted to receive these wonders as from God. The sick will be healed before us. Miracles will be performed in our sight. Are we prepared for the trial which awaits us when the lying wonders of Satan shall be more fully exhibited? Will not many souls be ensnared and taken? By departing from the plain precepts and commandments of God, and giving heed to fables, the minds of many are preparing to receive these lying wonders. We must all now seek to arm ourselves for the contest in which we must soon engage. Faith in God's word, prayerfully studied and practically applied, will be our shield from Satan's power and will bring us off conquerors through the blood of Christ.[66]

GOD'S PEOPLE BROUGHT TO THE TEST

Many will say to me in that day, Lord, Lord, have we not prophesied in thy name? and in thy name have cast out devils? and in thy name done many wonderful works? And then will I profess unto them, I never knew you: depart from me, ye that work iniquity. Matt. 7:22, 23.

We need not be deceived. Wonderful scenes, with which Satan will be closely connected, will soon take place. God's Word declares that Satan will work miracles. He will make people sick, and then will suddenly remove from them his satanic power. They will then be regarded as healed. These works of apparent healing will bring Seventh-day Adventists to the test. Many who have had great light will fail to walk in the light, because they have not become one with Christ.[67]

I saw our people in great distress, weeping, and praying, pleading the sure promises of God, while the wicked were all around us, mocking us, and threatening to destroy us. They ridiculed our feebleness, they mocked at the smallness of our numbers, and taunted us with words calculated to cut deep. They charged us with taking an independent position from all the rest of the world. They had cut off our resources so that we could not buy nor sell, and referred to our abject poverty and stricken condition. They could not see how we could live without the world; we were dependent upon the world, and we must concede to the customs, practices, and laws of the world, or go out of it. If we were the only people in the world whom the Lord favored the appearances were awfully against us. They declared that they had the truth, that miracles were among them, that angels from heaven talked with them, and walked with them, that great power, and signs and wonders were performed among them, and this was the Temporal Millennium, which they had been expecting so long. The whole world was converted and in harmony with the Sunday law, and this little feeble people stood out in defiance of the laws of the land, and the laws of God, and claimed to be the only ones right on the earth.[68]

God's people will not find their safety in working miracles, for Satan would counterfeit any miracle that might be worked.... They are to take their stand on the living Word—"It is written."[69]

SIGHTS OF A SUPERNATURAL CHARACTER

Great earthquakes shall be in divers places, and famines, and pestilences; and fearful sights and great signs shall there be from heaven. Luke 21:11.

As we near the close of time, there will be greater and still greater external parade of heathen power; heathen deities will manifest their signal power, and will exhibit themselves before the cities of the world; and this delineation has already begun to be fulfilled.[70]

The Saviour's prophecy concerning the visitation of judgments upon Jerusalem is to have another fulfillment, of which that terrible desolation was but a faint shadow. In the fate of the chosen city we may behold the doom of a world that has rejected God's mercy and trampled upon His law.[71]

Signs and wonders appeared, foreboding disaster and doom. In the midst of the night an unnatural light shone over the temple and the altar. Upon the clouds at sunset were pictured chariots and men of war gathering for battle.[72]

Last Friday morning [August 24, 1906], just before I awoke, a very impressive scene was presented before me. I seemed to awake from sleep but was not in my home. From the windows I could behold a terrible conflagration. Great balls of fire were falling upon houses, and from these balls fiery arrows were flying in every direction. It was impossible to check the fires that were kindled, and many places were being destroyed. The terror of the people was indescribable.[73]

Fearful sights of a supernatural character will soon be revealed in the heavens, in token of the power of miracle-working demons. The spirits of devils will go forth to the kings of the earth and to the whole world, to fasten them in deception, and urge them on to unite with Satan in his last struggle against the government of heaven. By these agencies, rulers and subjects will be alike deceived. Persons will arise pretending to be Christ Himself, and claiming the title and worship which belong to the world's Redeemer. They will perform wonderful miracles of healing and will profess to have revelations from heaven contradicting the testimony of the Scriptures.[74]

THE SEAL OF GOD AND THE MARK OF THE BEAST

Bind up the testimony, seal the law among my disciples. Isa. 8:16.

The living righteous will receive the seal of God prior to the close of probation.[75]

The sign, or seal, of God is revealed in the observance of the seventh-day Sabbath, the Lord's memorial of creation. . . . The mark of the beast is the opposite of this—the observance of the first day of the week.[76]

Sundaykeeping is not yet the mark of the beast, and will not be until the decree goes forth causing men to worship this idol sabbath. The time will come when this day will be the test, but that time has not come yet.[77]

No one has yet received the mark of the beast. The testing time has not yet come. There are true Christians in every church, not excepting the Roman Catholic communion. None are condemned until they have had the light and have seen the obligation of the fourth commandment. But when the decree shall go forth enforcing the counterfeit sabbath, and the loud cry of the third angel shall warn men against the worship of the beast and his image, the line will be clearly drawn between the false and the true. Then those who still continue in transgression will receive the mark of the beast.[78]

If the light of truth has been presented to you, revealing the Sabbath of the fourth commandment, and showing that there is no foundation in the Word of God for Sunday observance, and yet you still cling to the false sabbath, refusing to keep holy the Sabbath which God calls "my holy day," you receive the mark of the beast. When does this take place? When you obey the decree that commands you to cease from labor on Sunday and worship God, while you know that there is not a word in the Bible showing Sunday to be other than a common working day, you consent to receive the mark of the beast, and refuse the seal of God.[79]

In a little while every one who is a child of God will have His seal placed upon him. O that it may be placed upon our foreheads! Who can endure the thought of being passed by when the angel goes forth to seal the servants of God in their foreheads?[80]

THE SEALING AND THE LATTER RAIN

Nevertheless the foundation of God standeth sure, having this seal, The Lord knoweth them that are his. And, Let every one that nameth the name of Christ depart from iniquity. 2 Tim. 2:19.

Before the work is closed up and the sealing of God's people is finished, we shall receive the outpouring of the Spirit of God. Angels from heaven will be in our midst.[81]

Our heavenly Father claims not at our hands that which we cannot perform. He desires His people to labor earnestly to carry out His purpose for them. They are to pray for power, expect power, and receive power, that they may grow up into the full stature of men and women in Christ Jesus.

Not all members of the church are cultivating personal piety; therefore they do not understand their personal responsibility. They do not realize that it is their privilege and duty to reach the high standard of Christian perfection. . . . Are we looking forward to the latter rain, confidently hoping for a better day, when the church shall be endued with power from on high and thus fitted for work? The latter rain will never refresh and invigorate the indolent, who do not use the powers God has given them.

We are in great need of the pure, life-giving atmosphere that nurtures and invigorates the spiritual life. We need greater earnestness. The solemn message given us to give to the world is to be proclaimed with greater fervency, even with an intensity that will impress unbelievers, leading them to see that the Most High is working with us, that He is the source of our efficiency and strength. . . .

Are you using all your powers in an effort to bring the lost sheep back to the fold? There are thousands upon thousands in ignorance who might be warned. Pray as you have never prayed before for the power of Christ. Pray for the inspiration of His Spirit, that you may be filled with a desire to save those who are perishing. Let the prayer ascend to heaven, "God be merciful unto us, and bless us; and cause his face to shine upon us; that thy way may be known upon earth, thy saving health among all nations" (Ps. 67:1, 2).[82]

THE REMNANT AND THE SEALING

And the Lord said unto Satan, The Lord rebuke thee, O Satan; even the Lord that hath chosen Jerusalem rebuke thee: is not this a brand plucked out of the fire? Zech. 3:2.

The remnant church will be brought into great trial and distress. Those who keep the commandments of God and the faith of Jesus, will feel the ire of the dragon and his hosts. Satan numbers the world as his subjects; he has gained control of the apostate churches. But here is a little company that are resisting his supremacy. If he could blot them from the earth, his triumph would be complete. As he influenced the heathen nations to destroy Israel, so in the near future he will stir up the wicked powers of earth to destroy the people of God. All will be required to render obedience to human edicts in violation of the divine law. Those who will be true to God and to duty will be menaced, denounced, and proscribed. They will be betrayed "both by parents, and brethren, and kinsfolks, and friends."

Their only hope is in the mercy of God; their only defense will be prayer. As Joshua was pleading before the Angel, so the remnant church, with brokenness of heart and earnest faith, will plead for pardon and deliverance through Jesus their Advocate. . . .

Satan urges before God his accusations against them, declaring that they have by their sins forfeited the divine protection, and claiming the right to destroy them as transgressors. . . .

But while the followers of Christ have sinned, they have not given themselves to the control of evil. They have put away their sins, and have sought the Lord in humility and contrition, and the divine Advocate pleads in their behalf. . . .

The people of God are sighing and crying for the abominations done in the land. With tears they warn the wicked of their danger in trampling upon the divine law, and with unutterable sorrow they humble themselves before the Lord on account of their own transgressions. The wicked mock their sorrow, ridicule their solemn appeals, and sneer at what they term their weakness. But the anguish and humiliation of God's people is unmistakable evidence that they are regaining the strength and nobility of character lost in consequence of sin. . . .

While Satan was urging his accusations, holy angels, unseen, were passing to and fro, placing upon them the seal of the living God.[83]

ALL NATIONS FOLLOW AMERICA'S LEAD

When all the people heard the sound of the cornet, flute, harp, sackbut, psaltery, and all kinds of musick, all the people, the nations, and the languages, fell down and worshipped the golden image that Nebuchadnezzar the king had set up. Dan. 3:7.

History will be repeated. False religion will be exalted. The first day of the week, a common working day, possessing no sanctity whatever, will be set up as was the image at Babylon. All nations and tongues and peoples will be commanded to worship this spurious sabbath. This is Satan's plan to make of no account the day instituted by God, and given to the world as a memorial of creation.

The decree enforcing the worship of this day is to go forth to all the world.[84]

As America, the land of religious liberty, shall unite with the papacy in forcing the conscience and compelling men to honor the false sabbath, the people of every country on the globe will be led to follow her example.[85]

Foreign nations will follow the example of the United States. Though she leads out, yet the same crisis will come upon our people in all parts of the world.[86]

Nations will be stirred to their very center. Support will be withdrawn from those who proclaim God's only standard of righteousness, the only sure test of character. And all who will not bow to the decree of the national councils and obey the national laws to exalt the sabbath instituted by the man of sin, to the disregard of God's holy day, will feel, not the oppressive power of popery alone, but of the Protestant world, the image of the beast.[87]

The season of distress before God's people will call for a faith that will not falter. His children must make it manifest that He is the only object of their worship, and that no consideration, not even that of life itself, can induce them to make the least concession to false worship. To the loyal heart the commands of sinful, finite men will sink into insignificance beside the word of the eternal God. Truth will be obeyed though the result be imprisonment or exile or death.[88]

THE BEGINNING OF THE END

Evil on evil! says the Lord the Eternal—it is coming, the hour has come, the hour is striking, and striking at you, the hour and the end! Eze. 7:5, 6, Moffatt.

Fearful is the issue to which the world is to be brought. The powers of earth, uniting to war against the commandments of God, will decree that all, "both small and great, rich and poor, free and bond," shall conform to the customs of the church by observance of the false sabbath. All who refuse compliance will be visited with civil penalties, and it will finally be declared that they are deserving of death. On the other hand, the law of God enjoining the Creator's rest day demands obedience, and threatens wrath against all who transgress its precepts.

With the issue thus clearly brought before him, whosoever shall trample upon God's law to obey a human enactment, receives the mark of the beast; he accepts the sign of allegiance to the power which he chooses to obey instead of God. . . .

The Sabbath will be the great test of loyalty; for it is the point of truth especially controverted. When the final test shall be brought to bear upon men, then the line of distinction will be drawn between those who serve God and those who serve Him not. While the observance of the false sabbath in compliance with the law of the state, contrary to the fourth commandment, will be an avowal of an allegiance to a power that is in opposition to God, the keeping of the true Sabbath, in obedience to God's law, is an evidence of loyalty to the Creator. While one class, by accepting the sign of submission to earthly powers, receive the mark of the beast, the other, choosing the token of allegiance to divine authority, receive the seal of God.

Heretofore those who presented the truths of the third angel's message have been often regarded as mere alarmists. . . . But as the question of enforcing Sunday observance is widely agitated, the event so long doubted and disbelieved is seen to be approaching, and the third message will produce an effect which it could not have had before.[89]

NATIONAL RUIN FOLLOWS NATIONAL APOSTASY

The earth also is defiled under the inhabitants thereof; because they have transgressed the laws, changed the ordinance, broken the everlasting covenant. Isa. 24:5.

The people of the United States have been a favored people; but when they restrict religious liberty, surrender Protestantism, and give countenance to popery, the measure of their guilt will be full, and "national apostasy" will be registered in the books of heaven. The result of this apostasy will be national ruin.[90]

By the decree enforcing the institution of the papacy in violation of the law of God, our nation will disconnect herself fully from righteousness. When Protestantism shall stretch her hand across the gulf to grasp the hand of the Roman power, when she shall reach over the abyss to clasp hands with spiritualism, when, under the influence of this threefold union, our country shall repudiate every principle of its Constitution as a Protestant and republican government, and shall make provision for the propagation of papal falsehoods and delusions, then we may know that the time has come for the marvelous working of Satan and that the end is near.[91]

Through spiritualism, Satan appears as a benefactor of the race, healing the diseases of the people, and professing to present a new and more exalted system of religious faith; but at the same time he works as a destroyer. . . .

While appearing to the children of men as a great physician who can heal all their maladies, he will bring disease and disaster, until populous cities are reduced to ruin and desolation. . . .

And then the great deceiver will persuade men that those who serve God are causing these evils.[92]

As men depart further and further from God, Satan is permitted to have power over the children of disobedience. He hurls destruction among men. There is calamity by land and sea. Property and life are destroyed by fire and flood. Satan resolves to charge this upon those who refuse to bow to the idol which he has set up. His agents point to Seventh-day Adventists as the cause of the trouble. "These people stand out in defiance of law," they say. "They desecrate Sunday. Were they compelled to obey the law for Sunday observance, there would be a cessation of these terrible judgments." [93]

THE WORLD AGAINST GOD'S PEOPLE

The dragon was wroth with the woman, and went to make war with the remnant of her seed, which keep the commandments of God, and have the testimony of Jesus Christ. Rev. 12:17.

Our people have been regarded as too insignificant to be worthy of notice, but a change will come. The Christian world is now making movements which will necessarily bring commandment-keeping people into prominence.[94]

The whole world is to be stirred with enmity against Seventh-day Adventists, because they will not yield homage to the papacy, by honoring Sunday, the institution of this antichristian power. It is the purpose of Satan to cause them to be blotted from the earth, in order that his supremacy of the world may not be disputed.[95]

Every position of truth taken by our people will bear the criticism of the greatest minds; the highest of the world's great men will be brought in contact with truth, and therefore every position we take should be critically examined and tested by the Scriptures. Now we seem to be unnoticed, but this will not always be. Movements are at work to bring us to the front, and if our theories of truth can be picked to pieces by historians or the world's greatest men, it will be done.

We must individually know for ourselves what is truth, and be prepared to give a reason of the hope that we have with meekness and fear, not in a proud, boasting, self-sufficiency, but with the spirit of Christ. We are nearing the time when we shall stand individually alone to answer for our belief.[96]

We shall be attacked on every point; we shall be tried to the utmost. We do not want to hold our faith simply because it was handed down to us by our fathers. Such a faith will not stand the terrible test that is before us. We want to know why we are Seventh-day Adventists, what real reason we have for coming out from the world as a separate and distinct people. . . .

The powers of darkness will open their batteries upon us; and all who are indifferent and careless, who have set their affections on their earthly treasure, and who have not cared to understand God's dealings with His people, will be ready victims. No power but a knowledge of the truth as it is in Jesus, will ever make us steadfast; but with this, one may chase a thousand, and two put ten thousand to flight.[97]

THE ANGEL OF REVELATION 18

And after these things I saw another angel come down from heaven, having great power; and the earth was lightened with his glory. Rev. 18:1.

The prophecies in the eighteenth of Revelation will soon be fulfilled. During the proclamation of the third angel's message, "another angel" is to "come down from heaven, having great power," and the earth is to be "lightened with his glory." The Spirit of the Lord will so graciously bless consecrated human instrumentalities that men, women, and children will open their lips in praise and thanksgiving, filling the earth with the knowledge of God, and with His unsurpassed glory, as the waters cover the sea.

Those who have held the beginning of their confidence firm unto the end will be wide-awake during the time that the third angel's message is proclaimed with great power. During the loud cry, the church, aided by the providential interpositions of her exalted Lord, will diffuse the knowledge of salvation so abundantly that light will be communicated to every city and town. The earth will be filled with the knowledge of salvation. So abundantly will the renewing Spirit of God have crowned with success the intensely active agencies, that the light of present truth will be seen flashing everywhere.[98]

There is to be, at this period, a series of events which will reveal that God is Master of the situation. The truth will be proclaimed in clear, unmistakable language. As a people, we must prepare the way of the Lord, under the overruling guidance of the Holy Spirit. The gospel is to be given in its purity. The stream of living water is to deepen and widen in its course. In all fields, nigh and afar off, men will be called from the plow and from the more common commercial business vocations that largely occupy the mind, and will be educated in connection with men of experience. As they learn to labor effectively, they will proclaim the truth with power. Through most wonderful workings of divine providence, mountains of difficulties will be removed, and cast into the sea. The message that means so much to the dwellers upon the earth will be heard and understood. Men will know what is truth. Onward, and still onward the work will advance, until the whole earth shall have been warned. And then shall the end come.[99]

THE EARLY AND THE LATTER RAIN

Be glad then, ye children of Zion, and rejoice in the Lord your God: for he hath given you the former rain moderately, and he will cause to come down for you the rain, the former rain, and the latter rain in the first month. Joel 2:23.

There is to be in the churches a wonderful manifestation of the power of God, but it will not move upon those who have not humbled themselves before the Lord, and opened the door of their heart by confession and repentance. In the manifestation of that power which lightens the earth with the glory of God, they will see only something which in their blindness they think dangerous, something which will arouse their fears, and they will brace themselves to resist it. Because the Lord does not work according to their ideas and expectations, they will oppose the work. "Why," they say, "should we not know the Spirit of God, when we have been in the work so many years?" Because they did not respond to the warnings, the entreaties, of the messages of God, but persistently said, "I am rich, and increased with goods, and have need of nothing."

Talent, long experience, will not make men channels of light unless they place themselves under the bright beams of the Sun of Righteousness, and are called, and chosen, and prepared by the endowment of the Holy Spirit. When men who handle sacred things will humble themselves under the mighty hand of God, the Lord will lift them up. He will make them men of discernment—men rich in the grace of His Spirit. Their strong, selfish traits of character and their stubbornness will be seen in the light shining from the Light of the world. "I will come unto thee quickly, and will remove thy candlestick out of his place, except thou repent." If you seek the Lord with all your heart, He will be found of you.[100]

There must be no neglect of the grace represented by the former rain. Only those who are living up to the light they have will receive greater light. Unless we are daily advancing in the exemplification of the active Christian virtues, we shall not recognize the manifestations of the Holy Spirit in the latter rain. It may be falling on hearts all around us, but we shall not discern or receive it.[101]

HIGH TIME TO AWAKE!

And that, knowing the time, that now it is high time to awake out of sleep: for now is our salvation nearer than when we believed. The night is far spent, the day is at hand: let us therefore cast off the works of darkness, and let us put on the armour of light. Rom. 13:11, 12.

The great controversy is nearing its end. Every report of calamity by sea or land is a testimony to the fact that the end of all things is at hand. Wars and rumors of wars declare it. Is there a Christian whose pulse does not beat with quickened action as he anticipates the great events opening before us? The Lord is coming. We hear the footsteps of an approaching God.[102]

This knowledge of the nearness of Christ's coming should not be allowed to lose its force, and we become careless and inattentive, and fall into slumber—into an insensibility and indifference to realities. In slumber we are in an unreal world, and not sensible of the things which are taking place around us. . . .

There are those who have the blazing light of truth shining all around them, and yet are insensible to it. They are enchanted by the enemy, held under a spell by his bewitching power. They are not preparing for that great day which is soon to come to our world. They seem utterly insensible to religious truth.

Are there not some youth who are awake? Those who see that the night cometh, and also the morning, should work with untiring energy to arouse their sleeping associates. Can they not feel their peril, pray for them, and show them by their own life and character that they believe themselves that Christ is soon to come? . . . The rapidly diminishing space of time between us and eternity should more deeply impress us. Every day that passes makes one less left us to complete our work of perfecting character. . . .

As long as there are many asleep, many sporting away the precious hours in careless indifference, as it were, upon the very brink of the eternal world, those who do believe must be sober, must be awake, must be earnest and diligent, and watch unto prayer. . . .

Have you, dear youth, your lamps trimmed and burning?[103]

"IN THESE HOURS OF PROBATION"

I have heard thee in a time accepted, and in the day of salvation have I succoured thee: behold, now is the accepted time; behold, now is the day of salvation. 2 Cor. 6:2.

We believe without a doubt that Christ is soon coming. This is not a fable to us; it is a reality. We have no doubt, neither have we had a doubt for years, that the doctrines we hold today are present truth, and that we are nearing the judgment. We are preparing to meet Him who, escorted by a retinue of holy angels, is to appear in the clouds of heaven to give the faithful and the just the finishing touch of immortality. When He comes He is not to cleanse us of our sins, to remove from us the defects in our characters, or to cure us of the infirmities of our tempers and dispositions. If wrought for us at all, this work will all be accomplished before that time. When the Lord comes, those who are holy will be holy still. Those who have preserved their bodies and spirits in holiness, in sanctification and honor, will then receive the finishing touch of immortality. But those who are unjust, unsanctified, and filthy will remain so forever. No work will then be done for them to remove their defects and give them holy characters. The Refiner does not then sit to pursue His refining process and remove their sins and their corruption. This is all to be done in these hours of probation. It is *now* that this work is to be accomplished for us.

We embrace the truth of God with our different faculties, and as we come under the influence of that truth, it will accomplish the work for us which is necessary to give us a moral fitness for the kingdom of glory and for the society of the heavenly angels. We are now in God's workshop. Many of us are rough stones from the quarry. But as we lay hold upon the truth of God, its influence affects us. It elevates us and removes from us every imperfection and sin, of whatever nature. Thus we are prepared to see the King in His beauty and finally to unite with the pure and heavenly angels in the kingdom of glory. It is here that this work is to be accomplished for us, here that our bodies and spirits are to be fitted for immortality.[1]

THE SUBSTANCE OF MORAL CHARACTER

Not boasting of things without our measure, that is, of other men's labours; but having hope, when your faith is increased, that we shall be enlarged by you. 2 Cor. 10:15.

You should keep off from Satan's enchanted ground and not allow your minds to be swayed from allegiance to God. Through Christ you may and should be happy and should acquire habits of self-control. Even your thoughts must be brought into subjection to the will of God and your feelings under the control of reason and religion. Your imagination was not given you to be allowed to run riot and have its own way without any effort at restraint or discipline. If the thoughts are wrong the feelings will be wrong, and the thoughts and feelings combined make up the moral character. . . . If you yield to your impressions and allow your thoughts to run in a channel of suspicion, doubt, and repining you will be among the most unhappy of mortals. . . .

Dear Sister F, you have a diseased imagination; and you dishonor God by allowing your feelings to have complete control of your reason and judgment. You have a determined will, which causes the mind to react upon the body, unbalancing the circulation and producing congestion in certain organs; and you are sacrificing health to your feelings.

You are making a mistake, which, if not corrected, will not end with wrecking your own happiness merely. You are doing positive injury, not only to yourself, but to the other members of your family. . . . You have . . . let your highly wrought imagination control reason. . . . Had you no power over your feelings, this would not be sin; but it will not answer thus to yield to the enemy. Your will needs to be sanctified and subdued instead of being arrayed in opposition to that of God. . . .

Man has been placed in a world of sorrow, care, and perplexity. He is placed here to be tested and proved, as were Adam and Eve, that he may develop a right character and bring harmony out of discord and confusion. There is much for us to do that is essential. . . . And there is much for us to enjoy. Through Christ we are brought into connection with God. His mercies place us under continual obligation; feeling unworthy of His favors, we are to appreciate even the least of them.[2]

CHARACTER A QUALITY OF THE SOUL

No mention shall be made of coral, or of pearls: for the price of wisdom is above rubies. Job 28:18.

A character formed according to the divine likeness is the only treasure that we can take from this world to the next. Those who are under the instruction of Christ in this world will take every divine attainment with them to the heavenly mansions. And in heaven we are continually to improve. . . .

Mental ability and genius are not character, for these are often possessed by those who have the very opposite of a good character. Reputation is not character. True character is a quality of the soul, revealing itself in the conduct.

A good character is a capital of more value than gold or silver. It is unaffected by panics or failures, and in that day when earthly possessions shall be swept away, it will bring rich returns. Integrity, firmness, and perseverance are qualities that all should seek earnestly to cultivate; for they clothe the possessor with a power which is irresistible—a power which makes him strong to do good, strong to resist evil, strong to bear adversity.

Strength of character consists of two things—power of will and power of self-control. Many youth mistake strong, uncontrolled passion for strength of character; but the truth is that he who is mastered by his passions is a weak man. The real greatness and nobility of the man is measured by his powers to subdue his feelings, not by the power of his feelings to subdue him. The strongest man is he who, while sensitive to abuse, will yet restrain passion and forgive his enemies.

If it were considered as important that the young possess a beautiful character and amiable disposition as it is that they imitate the fashions of the world in dress and deportment, we would see hundreds where there is one today coming upon the stage of active life prepared to exert an ennobling influence upon society.[3]

CHRIST OUR HELPER AND REDEEMER

As by one man's disobedience many were made sinners, so by the obedience of one shall many be made righteous. Rom. 5:19.

Because man fallen could not overcome Satan with his human strength, Christ came from the royal courts of heaven to help him with His human and divine strength combined. Christ knew that Adam in Eden, with his superior advantages, might have withstood the temptations of Satan, and conquered him. He also knew that it was not possible for man, out of Eden, separated from the light and love of God since the Fall, to resist the temptations of Satan in his own strength. In order to bring hope to man, and save him from complete ruin, He humbled Himself to take man's nature, that, with His divine power combined with the human, He might reach man where he is. He obtains for the fallen sons and daughters of Adam that strength which it is impossible for them to gain for themselves, that in His name they may overcome the temptations of Satan. . . .

Adam and Eve in Eden were placed under most favorable circumstances. . . . They were without the condemnation of sin. . . . The Author of their existence was their teacher. But they fell beneath the power and temptations of the artful foe. Four thousand years had Satan been at work against the government of God, and he had obtained strength and experience from determined practice. Fallen men had not the advantages of Adam in Eden. They had been separating from God for four thousand years. The wisdom to understand, and power to resist, the temptations of Satan had become less and less, until Satan seemed to reign triumphant in the earth. Appetite and passion, the love of the world and presumptuous sins, were the great branches of evil out of which every species of . . . corruption grew.[4]

Our lives may seem a tangle; but as we commit ourselves to the wise Master Worker, He will bring out the pattern of life and character that will be to His own glory. And that character which expresses the glory—character—of Christ, will be received into the Paradise of God.[5]

Everyone who by faith obeys God's commandments, will reach the condition of sinlessness in which Adam lived before his transgression.[6]

HIGH SPIRITUAL STATE ATTAINABLE

Now unto him that is able to keep you from falling, and to present you faultless before the presence of his glory with exceeding joy. Jude 24.

Christ was obedient to every requirement of the law. . . .

By His perfect obedience He has made it possible for every human being to obey God's commandments. When we submit ourselves to Christ, the heart is united with His heart, the will is merged in His will, the mind becomes one with His mind, the thoughts are brought into captivity to Him; we live His life. This is what it means to be clothed with the garment of His righteousness. Then as the Lord looks upon us He sees, not the fig-leaf garment, not the nakedness and deformity of sin, but His own robe of righteousness, which is perfect obedience to the law of Jehovah.[7]

Through the plan of redemption, God has provided means for subduing every sinful trait, and resisting every temptation, however strong.[8]

The strongest temptation is no excuse for sin. However great the pressure brought to bear upon the soul, transgression is our own act. It is not in the power of earth or hell to compel any one to sin. The will must consent, the heart must yield, or passion cannot overbear reason, nor iniquity triumph over righteousness.[9]

If you will stand under the bloodstained banner of Prince Emmanuel, faithfully doing His service, you need never yield to temptation; for One stands by your side who is able to keep you from falling.[10]

We need not retain one sinful propensity. . . . [Eph. 2:1-6 quoted.] . . .

As we partake of the divine nature, hereditary and cultivated tendencies to wrong are cut away from the character, and we are made a living power for good. Ever learning of the divine Teacher, daily partaking of His nature, we cooperate with God in overcoming Satan's temptations. God works, and man works, that man may be one with Christ as Christ is one with God. Then we sit together with Christ in heavenly places. The mind rests with peace and assurance in Jesus.[11]

REACHING THE HEIGHT OF CHRISTIAN PERFECTION

Now unto him that is able to do exceeding abundantly above all that we ask or think, according to the power that worketh in us. Eph. 3:20.

If you make God your strength, you may, under the most discouraging circumstances, attain a height and breadth of Christian perfection which you hardly think it possible to reach. Your thoughts may be elevated, you may have noble aspirations, clear perceptions of truth, and purposes of action which shall raise you above all sordid motives.

Both thought and action will be necessary if you would attain to perfection of character. While brought in contact with the world, you should be on your guard that you do not seek too ardently for the applause of men and live for their opinion. . . . Cultivate the grace of humility, and hang your helpless souls upon Christ. . . . In the midst of confusion and temptation in the worldly crowd you may, with perfect sweetness, keep the independence of the soul.

If you are in daily communion with God you will learn to place His estimate upon men, and the obligations resting upon you to bless suffering humanity will meet with a willing response. You are not your own; your Lord has sacred claims upon your supreme affections and the very highest services of your life. He has a right to use you, in your body and in your spirit, to the fullest extent of your capabilities, for His own honor and glory. Whatever crosses you may be required to bear, . . . you are to accept without a murmur. . . .

Many are without God and without hope in the world. They are guilty, corrupt, and degraded, enslaved by Satan's devices. Yet these are the ones whom Christ came from heaven to redeem. They are subjects for tenderest pity, sympathy, and tireless effort; for they are on the verge of ruin. They suffer from ungratified desires, disordered passions, and the condemnation of their own consciences; they are miserable in every sense of the word, for they are losing their hold on this life and have no prospect for the life to come.

You have an important field of labor, and you should be active and vigilant, rendering cheerful and unqualified obedience to the Master's calls.[12]

PERFECTION IN THE HUMAN SPHERE

Be ye therefore perfect, even as your Father which is in heaven is perfect. Matt. 5:48.

Our Saviour understood all about human nature, and He says to every human being, "Be ye therefore perfect, even as your Father which is in heaven is perfect." As God is perfect in His sphere, so man is to be perfect in his sphere. Those who receive Christ are among the number to whom the words so full of hope are spoken, "As many as received him, to them gave he power to become the sons of God, even to them that believe on his name." These words declare to us that we should be content with nothing less than the best and highest character, a character formed after the divine similitude. When such a character is possessed, the life, the faith, the purity of the religion, is an instructive example to others.[13]

But those who are waiting to behold a magical change in their characters without determined effort on their part to overcome sin, will be disappointed. We have no reason to fear while looking to Jesus, no reason to doubt but that He is able to save to the uttermost all that come unto Him; but we may constantly fear lest our old nature will again obtain the supremacy, that the enemy shall devise some snare whereby we shall again become his captives. We are to work out our own salvation with fear and trembling, for it is God that worketh in you to will and to do of His good pleasure. With our limited powers we are to be as holy in our sphere as God is holy in His sphere. To the extent of our ability, we are to make manifest the truth and love and excellence of the divine character. As wax takes the impression of the seal, so the soul is to take the impression of the Spirit of God and retain the image of Christ.

We are to grow daily in spiritual loveliness. We shall fail often in our efforts to copy the divine pattern. We shall often have to bow down to weep at the feet of Jesus, because of our shortcomings and mistakes; but we are not to be discouraged; we are to pray more fervently, believe more fully, and try again with more steadfastness to grow into the likeness of our Lord. As we distrust our own power, we shall trust the power of our Redeemer, and render praise to God, who is the health of our countenance, and our God.[14]

HONORABLE IN MOTIVE AND ACTION

Be ye kind one to another, tenderhearted, forgiving one another, even as God for Christ's sake hath forgiven you. Eph. 4:32.

Principle, right, honesty, should ever be cherished. Honesty will not tarry where policy is harbored. They will never agree; one is of Baal, the other of God. The Master requires His servants to be honorable in motive and action. . . . Those who choose honesty as their companion will embody it in all their acts. To a large class, these men are not pleasing, but to God they are beautiful.

Satan is working to crowd himself in everywhere. He would put asunder very friends. There are men who are ever talking and gossiping and bearing false witness, who sow the seeds of discord and engender strife. Heaven looks upon this class as Satan's most efficient servants. But the man who is injured is in a far less dangerous position than when fawned upon and extolled for a few of his efforts which appear successful. The commendation of apparent friends is more dangerous than reproach.

Every man who praises himself brushes the luster from his best efforts. A truly noble character will not stoop to resent the false accusations of enemies; every word spoken falls harmless, for it strengthens that which it cannot overthrow. The Lord would have His people closely united with Himself, the God of patience and love. All should manifest in their lives the love of Christ. Let none venture to belittle the reputation or the position of another; this is egotism. . . .

Never speak disparagingly of any man, for he may be great in the sight of the Lord, while those who feel great may be lightly esteemed of God because of the perversity of their hearts. Our only safety is to lie low at the foot of the cross, be little in our own eyes, and trust in God; for He alone has power to make us great. . . .

The judgment and ability of all are needed now. Every man's work is of sufficient importance to demand that it be performed with care and fidelity. One man cannot do the work of all. Each has his respective place and his special work, and each should realize that the manner in which his work is done must stand the test of the judgment.[15]

OVERCOMING BAD HABITS

Keep thyself pure. 1 Tim. 5:22.

To know what constitutes purity of mind, soul, and body is an important part of education.

When the character is lacking in purity, when sin has become a part of the character, it has a bewitching power that is equal to the intoxicating glass of liquor. The power of self-control and reason is overborne by practices that defile the whole being; and if these sinful practices are continued, the brain is enfeebled and diseased, and loses its balance. Such ones are a curse to themselves and to all who have any connection with them. . . .

Bad habits are more easily formed than good habits, and the bad habits are given up with more difficulty. The natural depravity of the heart accounts for this well-known fact—that it takes far less labor to demoralize the youth, to corrupt their ideas of moral and religious character, than to engraft upon their character the enduring, pure, and uncorrupted habits of righteousness and truth. Self-indulgence, love of pleasure, enmity, pride, self-esteem, envy, jealousy, will grow spontaneously, without example and teaching. In our present fallen state all that is needed is to give up the mind and character to its natural tendencies. In the natural world, give up a field to itself and you will see it covered with briers and thorns; but if it yields precious grain or beautiful flowers, care and unremitting labor must be applied.

Now we present before you the necessity of constant resistance to evil. All heaven is interested in men and women whom God has valued so much as to give His beloved Son to die to redeem them. No other creature that God has made is capable of such improvement, such refinement, such nobility as man. Then when men become blunted by their own debasing passions, sunken in vice, what a specimen for God to look upon! Man cannot conceive what he may be and what he may become. Through the grace of Christ he is capable of constant mental progress. Let the light of truth shine into his mind and the love of God be shed abroad in his heart and he may, through the grace Christ has died to impart to him, be a man of power—a child of earth but an heir of immortality.[16]

SANCTIFICATION OF THE WHOLE MAN

Be renewed in the spirit of your mind; and that ye put on the new man, which after God is created in righteousness and true holiness. Eph. 4:23, 24.

The truth must sanctify the whole man—his mind, his thoughts, his heart, his strength. His vital powers will not be consumed upon his own lustful practices. These must be overcome, or they will overcome him. . . . The thoughts need purifying. What might not men and women have been had they realized that the treatment of the body has everything to do with the vigor and purity of mind and heart.

The true Christian obtains an experience which brings holiness. He is without a spot of guilt upon the conscience, or a taint of corruption upon the soul. The spirituality of the law of God, with its limiting principles, is brought into his life. The light of truth irradiates his understanding. A glow of perfect love for the Redeemer clears away the miasma which has interposed between his soul and God. The will of God has become his will, pure, elevated, refined, and sanctified. His countenance reveals the light of heaven. His body is a fit temple for the Holy Spirit. Holiness adorns his character. God can commune with him; for soul and body are in harmony with God. . . .

God would have us realize that He has a right to mind, soul, body, and spirit—to all that we possess. We are His by creation and by redemption. As our Creator, He claims our entire service. As our Redeemer, He has a claim of love as well as of right—of love without a parallel. This claim we should realize every moment of our existence. . . . Our bodies, our souls, our lives, are His, not only because they are His free gift, but because He constantly supplies us with His benefits, and gives us strength to use our faculties. . . . He says, "As many as received him, to them gave he power to become the sons of God, even to them that believe on his name." . . .

Those who are sons of God will represent Christ in character. Their works will be perfumed by the infinite tenderness, compassion, love, and purity of the Son of God. And the more completely mind and body are yielded to the Holy Spirit, the greater will be the fragrance of our offering to Him.[17]

IN HARMONY WITH HIS LAW

Give me understanding, and I shall keep thy law; yea, I shall observe it with my whole heart. Ps. 119:34.

In the new birth the heart is brought into harmony with God, as it is brought into accord with His law. When this mighty change has taken place in the sinner, he has passed from death unto life, from sin unto holiness, from transgression and rebellion to obedience and loyalty. . . .

Erroneous theories of sanctification, . . . springing from neglect or rejection of the divine law, have a prominent place in the religious movements of the day. These theories are both false in doctrine and dangerous in practical results; and the fact that they are so generally finding favor, renders it doubly essential that all have a clear understanding of what the Scriptures teach upon this point.

True sanctification is a Bible doctrine. The apostle Paul, in his letter to the Thessalonian church, declares: "This is the will of God, even your sanctification." And he prays: "The very God of peace sanctify you wholly" (1 Thess. 4:3; 5:23). The Bible clearly teaches what sanctification is and how it is to be attained. The Saviour prayed for His disciples: "Sanctify them through thy truth: thy word is truth" (John 17:17, 19). And Paul teaches that believers are to be "sanctified by the Holy Ghost" (Rom. 15:16). What is the work of the Holy Spirit? Jesus told His disciples: "When he, the Spirit of truth, is come, he will guide you into all truth" (John 16:13). And the psalmist says: "Thy law is the truth." By the Word and the Spirit of God are opened to men the great principles of righteousness embodied in His law. And since the law of God is "holy, and just, and good," a transcript of the divine perfection, it follows that a character formed by obedience to that law will be holy. Christ is a perfect example of such a character. He says: "I have kept my Father's commandments." "I do always those things that please him" (John 15:10; 8:29). The followers of Christ are to become like Him—by the grace of God to form characters in harmony with the principles of His holy law. This is Bible sanctification.

This work can be accomplished only through faith in Christ, by the power of the indwelling Spirit of God.[18]

COUNTERFEIT SANCTIFICATION

He that saith, I know him, and keepeth not his commandments, is a liar, and the truth is not in him. But whoso keepeth his word, in him verily is the love of God perfected: hereby know we that we are in him. 1 John 2:4, 5.

The sanctification now gaining prominence in the religious world carries with it a spirit of self-exaltation and a disregard for the law of God that mark it as foreign to the religion of the Bible. Its advocates teach that sanctification is an instantaneous work, by which, through faith alone, they attain to perfect holiness. "Only believe," say they, "and the blessing is yours." No further effort on the part of the receiver is supposed to be required. At the same time they deny the authority of the law of God, urging that they are released from obligation to keep the commandments. But is it possible for men to be holy, in accord with the will and character of God, without coming into harmony with the principles which are an expression of His nature and will . . . ?

The desire for an easy religion that requires no striving, no self-denial, no divorce from the follies of the world, has made the doctrine of faith, and faith only, a popular doctrine; but what saith the word of God? Says the apostle James: "What doth it profit, my brethren, though a man say he hath faith, and have not works? can faith save him? . . . Wilt thou know, O vain man, that faith without works is dead? . . ."

The testimony of the word of God is against this ensnaring doctrine of faith without works. It is not faith that claims the favor of Heaven without complying with the conditions upon which mercy is to be granted, it is presumption; for genuine faith has its foundation in the promises and provisions of the Scriptures.

Let none deceive themselves with the belief that they can become holy while willfully violating one of God's requirements. The commission of a known sin silences the witnessing voice of the Spirit and separates the soul from God. . . . "He that saith, I know him, and keepeth not his commandments, is a liar, and the truth is not in him. But whoso keepeth his word, in him verily is the love of God perfected" (1 John 2:4, 5).[19]

IMPRESSIONS, FEELINGS, AND DRUGS

Through thy precepts I get understanding: therefore I hate every false way. Ps. 119:104.

There are many restless spirits who will not submit to discipline, system, and order. They think that their liberties would be abridged were they to lay aside their own judgment and submit to the judgment of those of experience. The work of God will not progress unless there is a disposition to submit to order and expel the reckless, disorderly spirit of fanaticism from their meetings.

Impressions and feelings are no sure evidence that a person is led by the Lord. Satan will, if he is unsuspected, give feelings and impressions. These are not safe guides. All should thoroughly acquaint themselves with the evidences of our faith, and the great study should be how they can adorn their profession and bear fruit to the glory of God. . . .

For some time he [a patient at the Battle Creek Sanitarium] had thought he was obtaining new light. He was very ill, and must soon die. . . . Those to whom he presented his views listened to him eagerly, and some thought him inspired. . . . To many his reasoning seemed to be without a flaw. They told of his powerful exhortations in his sickroom. Most wonderful views passed before him. But what was the source of his inspiration? It was the morphine given him to relieve his pain.[20]

The poisons contained in many so-called remedies create habits and appetites that mean ruin to both soul and body. Many of the popular nostrums called patent medicines, and even some of the drugs dispensed by physicians, act a part in laying the foundation of the liquor habit, the opium habit, the morphine habit, that are so terrible a curse to society.[21]

If the blessing that those who claim to be sanctified have received, leads them to rely upon some particular emotion, and they declare there is no need of searching the Scriptures that they may know God's revealed will, then the supposed blessing is a counterfeit, for it leads its possessors to place value on their own unsanctified emotions and fancies, and to close their ears to the voice of God in His word.[22]

233

DRUMS, DANCING, AND NOISE

Let all things be done decently and in order. 1 Cor. 14:40.

The things you have described . . . the Lord has shown me would take place just before the close of probation. Every uncouth thing will be demonstrated. There will be shouting, with drums, music, and dancing. The senses of rational beings will become so confused that they cannot be trusted to make right decisions. And this is called the moving of the Holy Spirit.

The Holy Spirit never reveals itself in such methods, in such a bedlam of noise. This is an invention of Satan to cover up his ingenious methods for making of none effect the pure, sincere, elevating, ennobling, sanctifying truth for this time. . . . A bedlam of noise shocks the senses and perverts that which if conducted aright might be a blessing. The powers of Satanic agencies blend with the din and noise, to have a carnival, and this is termed the Holy Spirit's working. . . . Those participating in the supposed revival receive impressions which lead them adrift. They cannot tell what they formerly knew regarding Bible principles.

No encouragement should be given to this kind of worship. The same kind of influence came in after the passing of the time in 1844. The same kind of representations were made. Men became excited, and were worked by a power thought to be the power of God. . . .

Men and women, supposed to be guided by the Holy Spirit, held meetings in a state of nudity. They talked about holy flesh. They said they were beyond the power of temptation, and they sang, and shouted, and made all manner of noisy demonstrations. . . . Satan was moulding the work, and sensuality was the result. The cause of God was dishonored. Truth, sacred truth, was leveled in the dust by human agencies. . . .

I bore my testimony, declaring that these fanatical movements, this din and noise, were inspired by the spirit of Satan, who was working miracles to deceive if possible the very elect.

We need to be on our guard, to maintain a close connection with Christ, that we be not deceived by Satan's devices. The Lord desires to have in His service order and discipline, not excitement and confusion.[23]

NO ROOM FOR BOASTING

Then said I, Woe is me! for I am undone; because I am a man of unclean lips, and I dwell in the midst of a people of unclean lips: for mine eyes have seen the King, the Lord of hosts. Isa. 6:5.

Those who experience the sanctification of the Bible will manifest a spirit of humility. Like Moses, they have had a view of the awful majesty of holiness, and they see their own unworthiness in contrast with the purity and exalted perfection of the Infinite One.

The prophet Daniel was an example of true sanctification. His long life was filled up with noble service for his Master. He was a man "greatly beloved" (Dan. 10:11) of Heaven. Yet instead of claiming to be pure and holy, this honored prophet identified himself with the really sinful of Israel as he pleaded before God in behalf of his people: "We do not present our supplications before thee for our righteousnesses, but for thy great mercies." "We have sinned, we have done wickedly." He declares: "I was speaking, and praying, and confessing my sin and the sin of my people. . . ." (Dan. 9:18, 15, 20).

When Job heard the voice of the Lord out of the whirlwind, he exclaimed: "I abhor myself, and repent in dust and ashes" (Job 42:6). It was when Isaiah saw the glory of the Lord, and heard the cherubim crying, "Holy, holy, holy, is the Lord of hosts," that he cried out, "Woe is me! for I am undone" (Isa. 6:3, 5). Paul, after he was caught up into the third heaven and heard things which it was not possible for a man to utter, speaks of himself as "less than the least of all saints" (2 Cor. 12:2-4, margin; Eph. 3:8). It was the beloved John, who leaned on Jesus' breast and beheld His glory, that fell as one dead before the feet of the angel (Rev. 1:17).

There can be no self-exaltation, no boastful claim to freedom from sin, on the part of those who walk in the shadow of Calvary's cross. They feel that it was their sin which caused the agony that broke the heart of the Son of God, and this thought will lead them to self-abasement. Those who live nearest to Jesus discern most clearly the frailty and sinfulness of humanity, and their only hope is in the merit of a crucified and risen Saviour.[24]

235

SALVATION DAY BY DAY

Let him that thinketh he standeth take heed lest he fall. 1 Cor. 10:12.

Peter's fall was not instantaneous, but gradual. Self-confidence led him to the belief that he was saved, and step after step was taken in the downward path, until he could deny his Master. Never can we safely put confidence in self or feel, this side of heaven, that we are secure against temptation. Those who accept the Saviour, however sincere their conversion, should never be taught to say or to feel that they are saved. This is misleading. Every one should be taught to cherish hope and faith; but even when we give ourselves to Christ and know that He accepts us, we are not beyond the reach of temptation. . . . Only he who endures the trial will receive the crown of life (James 1:12).

Those who accept Christ, and in their first confidence say, I am saved, are in danger of trusting to themselves. . . . We are admonished, "Let him that thinketh he standeth take heed lest he fall" (1 Cor. 10:12). Our only safety is in constant distrust of self, and dependence on Christ.

There are many who profess Christ, but who never become mature Christians. They admit that man is fallen, that his faculties are weakened, that he is unfitted for moral achievement, but they say that Christ has borne all the burden, all the suffering, all the self-denial, and they are willing to let Him bear it. They say that there is nothing for them to do but to believe; but Christ said, "If any man will come after me, let him deny himself, and take up his cross, and follow me" (Matt. 16:24). . . .

We are never to rest in a satisfied condition, and cease to make advancement, saying, "I am saved." When this idea is entertained, the motives for watchfulness, for prayer, for earnest endeavor to press onward to higher attainments, cease to exist. No sanctified tongue will be found uttering these words till Christ shall come, and we enter in through the gates into the city of God. Then, with the utmost propriety, we may give glory to God and to the Lamb for eternal deliverance.[25]

THE MEANING OF CONVERSION

If any man be in Christ, he is a new creature: old things are passed away; behold, all things are become new. 2 Cor. 5:17.

The old nature, born of blood and the will of the flesh, cannot inherit the kingdom of God. The old ways, the hereditary tendencies, the former habits, must be given up; for grace is not inherited. The new birth consists in having new motives, new tastes, new tendencies. Those who are begotten unto a new life by the Holy Spirit, have become partakers of the divine nature, and in all their habits and practices they will give evidence of their relationship to Christ. When men who claim to be Christians retain all their natural defects of character and disposition, in what does their position differ from that of the worldling? They do not appreciate the truth as a sanctifier, a refiner. They have not been born again. . . .

A genuine conversion changes hereditary and cultivated tendencies to wrong. The religion of God is a firm fabric, composed of innumerable threads, and woven together with tact and skill. Only the wisdom which comes from God can make this fabric complete. There are a great many kinds of cloth which at first have a fine appearance, but they cannot endure the test. They wash out. The colors are not fast. Under the heat of summer they fade away and are lost. The cloth cannot endure rough handling.

So it is with the religion of many. When the warp and woof of character will not stand the test of trial, the material of which it is composed is worthless. The efforts made to patch the old with a new piece do not better the condition of things; for the old, flimsy material breaks away from the new, leaving the rent much larger than before. Patching will not do. The only way is to discard the old garment altogether, and procure one entirely new.

Christ's plan is the only safe one. He declares, "Behold, I make all things new." "If any man be in Christ, he is a new creature." . . . The patchwork religion is not of the least value with God. He requires the whole heart.[26]

Jesus gave His life . . . for us, and shall we not give Him our best affections, our holiest aspirations, our fullest service?[27]

SANCTIFICATION IS FOR SABBATHKEEPERS

Remember the sabbath day, to keep it holy. . . . The seventh day is the sabbath of the Lord thy God: in it thou shalt not do any work. Ex. 20:8-10.

God has declared in His Word that the seventh day is a sign between Him and His chosen people—a sign of their loyalty. . . .

The seventh day is God's chosen day. He has not left this matter to be remodeled by priest or ruler. It is of too great importance to be left to human judgment. God saw that men would study their own convenience, and choose a day best suited to their inclinations, a day bearing no divine authority; and He has stated plainly that the seventh day is the Sabbath of the Lord.

Every man in God's world is under the laws of His government. God has placed the Sabbath in the bosom of the Decalogue, and has made it the criterion of obedience. Through it we may learn of His power, as displayed in His works and His Word. . . .

Men could not place themselves more decidedly in opposition to God's work and to His law than by upholding a day that is without one evidence of sanctity, and professing to worship Him on that day. Those who have corrupted the law by substituting a false sabbath for the holy Sabbath of God, and who compel the observance of this false sabbath, exalt themselves above God, and honor the spurious above the genuine.

Sanctification is claimed by professed Christians who ignore God's holy rest day for a spurious sabbath. But God declares that the sanctification coming from Him is bestowed on those only who honor Him by obeying His commands. The sanctification claimed by those who continue in transgression is a spurious sanctification. Thus the religious world is deceived by the enemy of God and man. . . .

Men have sought out many inventions. They have taken a common day, upon which God has placed no sanctity, and have clothed it with sacred prerogatives. They have declared it to be a holy day, but this does not give it a vestige of sanctity. They dishonor God by accepting human institutions and presenting to the world as the Christian Sabbath a day which has no "Thus saith the Lord" for its authority.[28]

238

SOUND THE NOTE OF ALARM

In all thy ways acknowledge him, and he shall direct thy paths. Prov. 3:6.

In all our ways we should acknowledge God, and He will direct our paths. We should consult His Word with humble hearts, ask His counsel, and give up our will to His. We can do nothing without God.

There is the highest reason for us to prize the true Sabbath and stand in its defense, for it is the sign which distinguishes the people of God from the world. The commandment that the world makes void is the one to which, for this very reason, God's people will give greater honor. It is when the unbelieving cast contempt upon the Word of God that the faithful Calebs are called for. It is then that they will stand firm at the post of duty, without parade, and without swerving because of reproach. The unbelieving spies stood ready to destroy Caleb. He saw the stones in the hands of those who had brought a false report, but this did not deter him; he had a message, and he would bear it. The same spirit will be manifested today by those who are true to God.

The psalmist says, "They have made void thy law. Therefore I love thy commandments above gold; yea, above fine gold" (Ps. 119:126, 127). When men press close to the side of Jesus, when Christ is abiding in their hearts by faith, their love for the commandments of God grows stronger in proportion to the contempt which the world heaps upon His holy precepts. It is at this time that the true Sabbath must be brought before the people by both pen and voice. As the fourth commandment and those who observe it are ignored and despised, the faithful feel that it is the time not to hide their faith but to exalt the law of Jehovah by unfurling the banner on which is inscribed the message of the third angel, the commandments of God and the faith of Jesus.

Let not those who have the truth as it is in Jesus give sanction, even by their silence, to the work of the mystery of iniquity. Let them never cease to sound the note of alarm. . . . The truth must not be hid, it must not be denied or disguised, but fully avowed, and boldly proclaimed.[29]

THE PURE MARK OF TRUTH

The Lord said unto him, Go through the midst of the city, through the midst of Jerusalem, and set a mark upon the foreheads of the men that sigh and that cry for all the abominations that be done in the midst thereof. Eze. 9:4.

Mark this point with care: Those who receive the pure mark of truth, wrought in them by the power of the Holy Ghost, represented by a mark by the man in linen, are those "that sigh and that cry for all the abominations that be done" in the church.[30]

The class who do not feel grieved over their own spiritual declension, nor mourn over the sins of others, will be left without the seal of God. . . .

Not all who profess to keep the Sabbath will be sealed. There are many even among those who teach the truth to others who will not receive the seal of God in their foreheads. They had the light of truth, they knew their Master's will, they understood every point of our faith, but they had not corresponding works. . . .

Not one of us will ever receive the seal of God while our characters have one spot or stain upon them. It is left with us to remedy the defects in our characters, to cleanse the soul temple of every defilement. Then the latter rain will fall upon us as the early rain fell upon the disciples. . . .

What are you doing, brethren, in the great work of preparation? Those who are uniting with the world are receiving the worldly mold and preparing for the mark of the beast. Those who are distrustful of self, who are humbling themselves before God and purifying their souls by obeying the truth—these are receiving the heavenly mold and preparing for the seal of God in their foreheads. When the decree goes forth and the stamp is impressed, their character will remain pure and spotless for eternity.

Now is the time to prepare. The seal of God will never be placed upon the forehead of an impure man or woman. It will never be placed upon the forehead of the ambitious, world-loving man or woman. It will never be placed upon the forehead of men or women of false tongues or deceitful hearts. All who receive the seal must be without spot before God—candidates for heaven.[31]

WHO RECEIVE THE SEAL?

And in their mouth was found no guile: for they are without fault before the throne of God. Rev. 14:5.

Only those who receive the seal of the living God will have the passport through the gates of the Holy City. . . .

The seal of the living God will be placed upon those only who bear a likeness to Christ in character.

As wax takes the impression of the seal, so the soul is to take the impression of the Spirit of God and retain the image of Christ.

Many will not receive the seal of God because they do not keep His commandments or bear the fruits of righteousness.

The great mass of professing Christians will meet with bitter disappointment in the day of God. They have not upon their foreheads the seal of the living God. Lukewarm and half-hearted, they dishonor God far more than the avowed unbeliever. They grope in darkness, when they might be walking in the noonday light of the Word, under the guidance of One who never errs. . . .

Those whom the Lamb shall lead by the fountains of living waters, and from whose eyes He shall wipe away all tears, will be those now receiving the knowledge and understanding revealed in the Bible, the Word of God. . . .

We are to copy no human being. There is no human being wise enough to be our criterion. We are to look to the man Christ Jesus, who is complete in the perfection of righteousness and holiness. He is the author and finisher of our faith. He is the pattern man. His experience is the measure of the experience that we are to gain. His character is our model. Let us, then, take our minds off the perplexities and the difficulties of this life, and fix them on Him, that by beholding we may be changed into His likeness. We may behold Christ to good purpose. We may safely look to Him; for He is all-wise. As we look to Him and think of Him, He will be formed within, the hope of glory.

Let us strive with all the power that God has given us to be among the hundred and forty-four thousand.[32]

TIME OF SEALING SOON OVER

I must work the works of him that sent me, while it is day: the night cometh, when no man can work. John 9:4.

The sealing time is very short, and will soon be over. Now is the time, while the four angels are holding the four winds, to make our calling and election sure.[33]

I was pointed down to the time when the third angel's message was closing. The power of God had rested upon His people; they had accomplished their work and were prepared for the trying hour before them.

They had received the latter rain, or refreshing from the presence of the Lord, and the living testimony had been revived. The last great warning had sounded everywhere, and it had stirred up and enraged the inhabitants of the earth who would not receive the message.

I saw angels hurrying to and fro in heaven. An angel with a writer's inkhorn by his side returned from the earth and reported to Jesus that his work was done, and the saints were numbered and sealed. Then I saw Jesus . . . throw down the censer. He raised His hands, and with a loud voice said, *"It is done."* [34]

I also saw that many do not realize what they must be in order to live in the sight of the Lord without a high priest in the sanctuary through the time of trouble. Those who receive the seal of the living God and are protected in the time of trouble must reflect the image of Jesus fully.

I saw that many were neglecting the preparation so needful and were looking to the time of "refreshing" and the "latter rain" to fit them to stand in the day of the Lord and to live in His sight. Oh, how many I saw in the time of trouble without a shelter![35]

When Jesus leaves the sanctuary, then they who are holy and righteous will be holy and righteous still; for all their sins will then be blotted out, and they will be sealed with the seal of the living God. But those that are unjust and filthy will be unjust and filthy still; for then there will be no Priest in the sanctuary to offer their sacrifices, their confessions, and their prayers before the Father's throne. Therefore what is done to rescue souls from the coming storm of wrath must be done before Jesus leaves the most holy place of the heavenly sanctuary.[36]

ANGELS CAN READ GOD'S MARK

I saw another angel ascending from the east, having the seal of the living God: and he cried with a loud voice to the four angels, to whom it was given to hurt the earth and the sea, saying, Hurt not the earth, neither the sea, nor the trees, till we have sealed the servants of our God in their foreheads. Rev. 7:2, 3.

Everything in the world is in an unsettled state. The nations are angry, and great preparations for war are being made. Nation is plotting against nation, and kingdom against kingdom. The great day of God is hasting greatly. But although the nations are mustering their forces for war and bloodshed, the command to the angels is still in force, that they hold the four winds until the servants of God are sealed in their foreheads.[37]

As yet the four winds are held until the servants of God shall be sealed in their foreheads. Then the powers of earth will marshal their forces for the last great battle. How carefully we should improve the little remaining period of our probation![38]

Minds that have been given up to loose thought need to change. . . . The thoughts must be centered upon God. Now is the time to put forth earnest effort to overcome the natural tendencies of the carnal heart.[39]

Just before we entered it [the time of trouble], we all received the seal of the living God. Then I saw the four angels cease to hold the four winds. And I saw famine, pestilence and sword, nation rose against nation, and the whole world was in confusion.[40]

What is the seal of the living God, which is placed in the foreheads of His people? It is a mark which angels, but not human eyes, can read; for the destroying angel must see this mark of redemption. The intelligent mind has seen the sign of the cross of Calvary in the Lord's adopted sons and daughters. The sin of the transgression of the law of God is taken away. They have on the wedding garment, and are obedient and faithful to all God's commands.[41]

The Lord will not excuse those who know the truth if they do not in word and deed obey His commands.[42]

A SIGN THAT DISTINGUISHES GOD'S PEOPLE

Moreover also I gave them my sabbaths, to be a sign between me and them, that they might know that I am the Lord that sanctify them. Eze. 20:12.

As the Sabbath was the sign that distinguished Israel when they came out of Egypt to enter the earthly Canaan, so it is the sign that now distinguishes God's people as they come out from the world to enter the heavenly rest.

The observance of the Sabbath is the means ordained by God of preserving a knowledge of Himself and of distinguishing between His loyal subjects and the transgressors of His law.

It [the Sabbath] belongs to Christ. . . . Since He made all things, He made the Sabbath. By Him it was set apart as a memorial of the work of creation. It points to Him as both the Creator and the Sanctifier. It declares that He who created all things in heaven and in earth, and by whom all things hold together, is the head of the church, and that by His power we are reconciled to God. For, speaking of Israel, He said, "I gave them my sabbaths, to be a sign between me and them, that they might know that I am the Lord that sanctify them"—make them holy. Then the Sabbath is a sign of Christ's power to make us holy. And it is given to all whom Christ makes holy. As a sign of His sanctifying power, the Sabbath is given to all who through Christ become a part of the Israel of God. . . .

To all who receive the Sabbath as a sign of Christ's creative and redeeming power, it will be a delight. Seeing Christ in it, they delight themselves in Him. The Sabbath points them to the works of creation as an evidence of His mighty power in redemption. While it calls to mind the lost peace of Eden, it tells of peace restored through the Saviour. And every object in nature repeats His invitation, "Come unto me, all ye that labour and are heavy laden, and I will give you rest." Matt. 11:28.

The Sabbath is a golden clasp that unites God and His people.[43]

IMPORTANCE AND GLORY OF THE SABBATH

I will cause thee to ride upon the high places of the earth, and feed thee with the heritage of Jacob thy father: for the mouth of the Lord hath spoken it. Isa. 58:14.

Sabbath we had a sweet, glorious time. . . . We were made to rejoice and glorify God for His exceeding goodness unto us. . . . I was taken off in vision. . . .

I saw that we sensed and realized but little of the importance of the Sabbath, to what we yet should realize and know of its importance and glory. I saw we knew not what it was yet to ride upon the high places of the earth and to be fed with the heritage of Jacob. But when the refreshing and latter rain shall come from the presence of the Lord and the glory of His power we shall know what it is to be fed with the heritage of Jacob and ride upon the high places of the earth. Then shall we see the Sabbath more in its importance and glory. But we shall not see it in all its glory and importance until the covenant of peace is made with us at the voice of God, and the pearly gates of the New Jerusalem are thrown open and swing back on their glittering hinges and the glad and joyful voice of the lovely Jesus is heard richer than any music that ever fell on mortal ear bidding us enter. [I saw] that we had a perfect right in the city for we had kept the commandmen*s of God, and heaven, sweet heaven is our home.[44]

I saw the ten commandments written on them [the tables of stone] with the finger of God. On one table were four, and on the other six. The four on the first table shone brighter than the other six. But the fourth, the Sabbath commandment, shone above them all; for the Sabbath was set apart to be kept in honor of God's holy name. The holy Sabbath looked glorious—a halo of glory was all around it. I saw that the Sabbath commandment was not nailed to the cross. If it was, the other nine commandments were; and we are at liberty to break them all, as well as to break the fourth. . . .

I saw that the holy Sabbath is, and will be, the separating wall between the true Israel of God and unbelievers; and that the Sabbath is the great question to unite the hearts of God's dear, waiting saints.[45]

THE SABBATH IS GOD'S MARK

Hallow my sabbaths; and they shall be a sign between me and you, that ye may know that I am the Lord your God. Eze. 20:20.

The Israelites placed over their doors a signature of blood, to show that they were God's property. So the children of God in this age will bear the signature God has appointed. They will place themselves in harmony with God's holy law. A mark is placed upon every one of God's people just as verily as a mark was placed over the doors of the Hebrew dwellings, to preserve the people from the general ruin. God declares, "I gave them my sabbaths, to be a sign between me and them, that they might know that I am the Lord that sanctify them." [46]

Every soul in our world is the Lord's property, by creation and by redemption. Each individual soul is on trial for his life. Has he given to God that which belongs to Him? Has he surrendered to God all that is His as His purchased possession? All who cherish the Lord as their portion in this life will be under His control, and will receive the sign, the mark of God, which shows them to be God's special possession. Christ's righteousness will go before them, and the glory of the Lord will be their rereward. The Lord protects every human being who bears His sign.

"And the Lord spake unto Moses, saying, Speak thou also unto the children of Israel, saying, Verily my sabbaths ye shall keep: for it is a sign between me and you throughout your generations; that ye may know that I am the Lord that doth sanctify you. . . . Six days may work be done; but in the seventh is the sabbath of rest, holy to the Lord: whosoever doeth any work in the sabbath day, he shall surely be put to death. Wherefore the children of Israel shall keep the sabbath, to observe the sabbath throughout their generations, for a perpetual covenant. It is a sign between me and the children of Israel for ever: for in six days the Lord made heaven and earth, and on the seventh day he rested, and was refreshed."

This recognition of God is of the highest value to every human being. All who love and serve Him are very precious in His sight. He would have them stand where they are worthy representatives of the truth as it is in Jesus.[47]

STUDY THE SUBJECT OF THE SANCTUARY

And he said unto me, Unto two thousand and three hundred days; then shall the sanctuary be cleansed. Dan. 8:14.

We should be earnest students of prophecy; we should not rest until we become intelligent in regard to the subject of the sanctuary, which is brought out in the visions of Daniel and John. This subject sheds great light on our present position and work, and gives us unmistakable proof that God has led us in our past experience. It explains our disappointment in 1844, showing us that the sanctuary to be cleansed was not the earth, as we had supposed, but that Christ then entered into the most holy apartment of the heavenly sanctuary, and is there performing the closing work of His priestly office, in fulfillment of the words of the angel to the prophet Daniel.

The 2300 days had been found to begin when the commandment of Artaxerxes for the restoration and building of Jerusalem, went into effect, in the autumn of B.C. 457. Taking this as the starting point, there was perfect harmony in the application of all the events foretold in the explanation of that period in Daniel 9:25-27. . . . The seventy weeks, or 490 years, were to pertain especially to the Jews. At the expiration of this period, the nation sealed its rejection of Christ by the persecution of His disciples, and the apostles turned to the Gentiles, A.D. 34. The first 490 years of the 2300 having then ended, 1810 years would remain. From A.D. 34, 1810 years extend to 1844. "Then," said the angel, "shall the sanctuary be cleansed."

Our faith in reference to the messages of the first, second, and third angels was correct. The great waymarks we have passed are immovable. Although the hosts of hell may try to tear them from their foundation, and triumph in the thought that they have succeeded, yet they do not succeed. These pillars of truth stand firm as the eternal hills, unmoved by all the efforts of men combined with those of Satan and his host. We can learn much, and should be constantly searching the Scriptures to see if these things are so.[48]

CLEANSING OF THE SANCTUARY

I saw in the night visions, and, behold, one like the Son of man came with the clouds of heaven, and came to the Ancient of days, and they brought him near before him. Dan. 7:13.

After His ascension, our Saviour began His work as our high priest. Says Paul, "Christ is not entered into the holy places made with hands, which are the figures of the true; but into heaven itself, now to appear in the presence of God for us." Heb. 9:24. . . .

For eighteen centuries this work of ministration continued in the first apartment of the sanctuary. The blood of Christ, pleaded in behalf of penitent believers, secured their pardon and acceptance with the Father, yet their sins still remained upon the books of record. As in the typical service there was a work of atonement at the close of the year, so before Christ's work for the redemption of men is completed, there is a work of atonement for the removal of sin from the sanctuary. This is the service which began when the 2300 days ended. At that time . . . our High Priest entered the most holy, to perform the last division of His solemn work—to cleanse the sanctuary. . . .

The coming of Christ as our high priest to the most holy place, for the cleansing of the sanctuary, brought to view in Daniel 8:14; the coming of the Son of man to the Ancient of days, as presented in Daniel 7:13; and the coming of the Lord to His temple, foretold by Malachi, are descriptions of the same event; and this is also represented by the coming of the bridegroom to the marriage, described by Christ in the parable of the ten virgins, of Matthew 25.

The cleansing of the sanctuary . . . involves a work of investigation—a work of judgment. This work must be performed prior to the coming of Christ to redeem His people; for when He comes, His reward is with Him to give to every man according to his works.

In the day of final reckoning, position, rank, or wealth will not alter by a hair's breadth the case of any one. By the all-seeing God, men will be judged by what they are in purity, in nobility, in love for Christ.[49]

INSTRUCTION
FROM THE SANCTUARY IN HEAVEN

Let us draw near with a true heart in full assurance of faith, having our hearts sprinkled from an evil conscience. Heb. 10:22.

"And, behold, one like the Son of man came with the clouds of heaven, and came to the Ancient of days, and they brought him near before him." Dan. 7:13. . . . The coming of Christ here described is not His second coming to the earth. He comes to the Ancient of days in heaven to receive dominion, and glory, and a kingdom, which will be given Him at the close of His work as a mediator. It is this coming, and not His second advent to the earth, that was foretold in prophecy to take place at the termination of the 2300 days in 1844. Attended by heavenly angels, our great High Priest enters the holy of holies, and there appears in the presence of God . . . to perform the work of investigative judgment, and to make an atonement for all who are shown to be entitled to its benefits.[50]

May the Lord give us to see the need of drinking from the living fountain of the water of life. Its pure streams will refresh and heal us and refresh all connected with us. Oh, if the hearts were only subdued by the Spirit of God! If the eye were single to God's glory, what a flood of heavenly light would pour upon the soul. He who spake as never man spake was an educator upon earth. After His resurrection He was an educator to the lonely, disappointed disciples traveling to Emmaus, and to those assembled in the upper chamber. He opened to them the Scriptures concerning Himself and caused their hearts to bound with a holy, new and sacred hope and joy.

From the Holy of Holies, there goes on the grand work of instruction. The angels of God are communicating to men. Christ officiates in the sanctuary. We do not follow Him into the sanctuary as we should. Christ and angels work in the hearts of the children of men. The church above united with the church below is warring the good warfare upon the earth. There must be a purifying of the soul here upon the earth, in harmony with Christ's cleansing of the sanctuary in heaven.[51]

God's people are now to have their eyes fixed on the heavenly sanctuary, where . . . our great High Priest . . . is interceding for His people.[52]

JUDGING THE CASES OF THE LIVING

Remember therefore how thou hast received and heard, and hold fast, and repent. If therefore thou shalt not watch, I will come on thee as a thief, and thou shalt not know what hour I will come upon thee. Rev. 3:3.

At the time appointed for the judgment—the close of the 2300 days, in 1844—began the work of investigation and blotting out of sins. All who have ever taken upon themselves the name of Christ must pass its searching scrutiny. Both the living and the dead are to be judged "out of those things which were written in the books, according to their works." Rev. 20:12.

Said the Judge: "All will be justified by their faith and judged by their works."

Sins that have not been repented of and forsaken will not be pardoned, and blotted out of the books of record, but will stand to witness against the sinner in the day of God. . . .

There is earnest warfare before all who would subdue the evil tendencies that strive for the mastery. The work of preparation is an individual work. We are not saved in groups. The purity and devotion of one will not offset the want of these qualities in another. Though all nations are to pass in judgment before God, yet He will examine the case of each individual with as close and searching scrutiny as if there were not another being upon the earth. Every one must be tested, and found without spot or wrinkle or any such thing.

The judgment is now passing in the sanctuary above. For many years this work has been in progress. Soon—none know how soon—it will pass to the cases of the living. In the awful presence of God our lives are to come up in review. At this time above all others it behooves every soul to heed the Saviour's admonition, "Watch and pray: for ye know not when the time is." Mark 13:33. "If therefore thou shalt not watch, I will come on thee as a thief, and thou shalt not know what hour I will come upon thee." Rev. 3:3.[53]

THE INVESTIGATIVE JUDGMENT

Some men's sins are open beforehand, going before to judgment; and some men they follow after. 1 Tim. 5:24.

The work of the investigative judgment and the blotting out of sins is to be accomplished before the second advent of the Lord. Since the dead are to be judged out of the things written in the books, it is impossible that the sins of men should be blotted out until after the judgment at which their cases are to be investigated. . . . When the investigative judgment closes, Christ will come, and His reward will be with Him to give to every man as his work shall be.

All are to be judged according to the things written in the books, and to be rewarded as their works have been. This judgment does not take place at death.

In the typical service the high priest, having made the atonement for Israel, came forth and blessed the congregation. So Christ, at the close of His work as mediator, will appear, "without sin unto salvation," to bless His waiting people with eternal life. As the priest, in removing the sins from the sanctuary, confessed them upon the head of the scapegoat, so Christ will place all these sins upon Satan, the originator and instigator of sin. The scapegoat, bearing the sins of Israel, was sent away "unto a land not inhabited;" so Satan, bearing the guilt of all the sins which he has caused God's people to commit, will be for a thousand years confined to the earth, which will then be desolate, without inhabitant, and he will at last suffer the full penalty of sin in the fires that shall destroy all the wicked.

A few, yes, only a few, of the vast number who people the earth will be saved unto life eternal, while the masses who have not perfected their souls in obeying the truth will be appointed to the second death.

While the sins of penitent believers are being removed from the sanctuary, there is to be a special work of purification, of putting away of sin, among God's people upon earth.[54]

STANDING BEFORE COURTS AND COUNCILS

I will speak of thy testimonies also before kings, and will not be ashamed. Ps. 119:46.

In the great closing work we shall meet with perplexities that we know not how to deal with, but let us not forget that the three great powers of heaven are working, that a divine hand is on the wheel, and that God will bring His purposes to pass.[1]

The time will come when we shall be brought before councils and before thousands for His name's sake, and each one will have to give the reason of his faith.[2]

Every position of truth taken by our people will bear the criticism of the greatest minds; the highest of the world's great men will be brought in contact with truth, and therefore every position we take should be critically examined and tested by the Scriptures. Now we seem to be unnoticed, but this will not always be. Movements are at work to bring us to the front, and if our theories of truth can be picked to pieces by historians or the world's greatest men, it will be done.[3]

The Lord Jesus will give the disciples a tongue and wisdom that their adversaries can neither gainsay nor resist. Those who could not by reasoning overcome satanic delusions, will bear an affirmative testimony that will baffle supposedly learned men. Words will come from the lips of the unlearned with such convincing power and wisdom that conversions will be made to the truth. Thousands will be converted under their testimony.

Why should the illiterate man have this power, which the learned man has not? The illiterate one, through faith in Christ, has come into the atmosphere of pure, clear truth, while the learned man has turned away from the truth. The poor man is Christ's witness. He cannot appeal to histories or to so-called high science, but he gathers from the Word of God powerful evidence. The truth that he speaks under the inspiration of the Spirit, is so pure and remarkable and carries with it a power so indisputable, that his testimony cannot be gainsaid.[4]

WITNESSING BEFORE THE GREAT MEN OF THE EARTH

And ye shall be brought before governors and kings for my sake, for a testimony against them and the Gentiles. Matt. 10:18.

The time is not far off when the people of God will be called upon to give their testimony before the rulers of the earth. Not one in twenty has a realization of what rapid strides we are making toward the great crisis in our history. . . . There is no time for vanity, for trifling, for engaging the mind in unimportant matters.[5]

Kings, governors, and great men will hear of you through the reports of those who are at enmity with you, and your faith and character will be misrepresented before them. But those who are falsely accused will have an opportunity to appear in the presence of their accusers to answer for themselves. They will have the privilege of bringing the light before those who are called the great men of the earth, and if you have studied the Bible, if you are ready to give an answer to every man that asketh you of the hope that is in you with meekness and fear, your enemies will not be able to gainsay your wisdom.

You now have an opportunity to attain to the greatest intellectual power through the study of the Word of God. But if you are indolent, and fail to dig deep in the mines of truth, you will not be ready for the crisis that is soon to come upon us. O that you would realize that each moment is golden. If you live by every word that proceedeth out of the mouth of God, you will not be found unprepared.[6]

You know not where you may be called upon to give your witness of truth. Many will have to stand in the legislative courts; some will have to stand before kings and before the learned of the earth, to answer for their faith. Those who have only a superficial understanding of truth will not be able clearly to expound the Scriptures, and give definite reasons for their faith. They will become confused, and will not be workmen that need not to be ashamed. Let no one imagine that he has no need to study, because he is not to preach in the sacred desk. You know not what God may require of you.[7]

253

PREPARE TO MEET THY GOD

Therefore thus will I do unto thee, O Israel: and because I will do this unto thee, prepare to meet thy God, O Israel. Amos 4:12.

Many do not realize what they must be in order to live in the sight of the Lord without a high priest in the sanctuary through the time of trouble. Those who receive the seal of the living God and are protected in the time of trouble must reflect the image of Jesus fully.[8]

Their robes must be spotless, their characters must be purified from sin by the blood of sprinkling. Through the grace of God and their own diligent effort, they must be conquerors in the battle with evil. While the investigative judgment is going forward in heaven, while the sins of penitent believers are being removed from the sanctuary, there is to be a special work of purification, of putting away of sin, among God's people upon earth.[9]

I saw that many were neglecting the preparation so needful and were looking to the time of "refreshing" and the "latter rain" to fit them to stand in the day of the Lord and to live in His sight. Oh, how many I saw in the time of trouble without a shelter! They had neglected the needful preparation; therefore they could not receive the refreshing that all must have to fit them to live in the sight of a holy God.[10]

Those who refuse to be hewed by the prophets and fail to purify their souls in obeying the whole truth, and who are willing to believe that their condition is far better than it really is, will come up to the time of the falling of the plagues, and then see that they needed to be hewed and squared for the building. . . .

I saw that none could share the "refreshing" unless they obtain the victory over every besetment, over pride, selfishness, love of the world, and over every wrong word and action. We should, therefore, be drawing nearer and nearer to the Lord and be earnestly seeking that preparation necessary to enable us to stand in the battle in the day of the Lord. Let all remember that God is holy and that none but holy beings can ever dwell in His presence.[11]

PROMISE OF DIVINE HELP

But when they deliver you up, take no thought how or what ye shall speak: for it shall be given you in that same hour what ye shall speak. Matt. 10:19.

The servants of Christ are to prepare no set speech to present when brought to trial for their faith. Their preparation is to be made day by day, in treasuring up in their hearts the precious truths of God's Word, in feeding upon the teaching of Christ, and through prayer strengthening their faith; then, when brought into trial, the Holy Spirit will bring to their remembrance the very truths that will reach the hearts of those who shall come to hear. God will flash the knowledge obtained by diligent searching of the Scriptures, into their memory at the very time when it is needed.[12]

You are now to get ready for the time of trial. Now you are to know whether your feet are planted on the Eternal Rock. You must have an individual experience, and not depend upon others for your light. When you are brought to the test, how do you know that you will not be alone, with no earthly friend at your side? Will you then be able to realize that Christ is your support? Will you be able to recall the promise, "Lo, I am with you alway, even unto the end of the world"? There will be invisible ones all about you bent upon your destruction. Satan and his agents will seek in every way to make you waver from your steadfastness to God and His truth. But if you have an eye single to His glory, you need not take thought as to how you shall witness for His truth.[13]

Young men and women, are you growing up to the full stature of men and women in Christ, so that when the crisis comes, you cannot be separated from the Source of your strength? If we would stand during the time of test, we must now, in the time of peace, be gaining a living experience in the things of God. We must now learn to understand what are the deep movings of the Spirit of God. Christ must be our all and in all, the Alpha and Omega, the first and the last, the beginning and the end.[14]

ANOTHER PENTECOST COMING!

I will make them and the places round about my hill a blessing; and I will cause the shower to come down in his season; there shall be showers of blessing. Eze. 34:26.

Under the figure of the early and the latter rain, that falls in Eastern lands at seedtime and harvest, the Hebrew prophets foretold the bestowal of spiritual grace in extraordinary measure upon God's church. The outpouring of the Spirit in the days of the apostles was the beginning of the early, or former, rain, and glorious was the result. . . . But near the close of earth's harvest, a special bestowal of spiritual grace is promised to prepare the church for the coming of the Son of man. This outpouring of the Spirit is likened to the falling of the latter rain.[15]

The great work of the gospel is not to close with less manifestation of the power of God than marked its opening. The prophecies which were fulfilled in the outpouring of the former rain at the opening of the gospel are again to be fulfilled in the latter rain at its close. . . .

Servants of God, with their faces lighted up and shining with holy consecration, will hasten from place to place to proclaim the message from heaven. By thousands of voices, all over the earth, the warning will be given. Miracles will be wrought, the sick will be healed, and signs and wonders will follow the believers. Satan also works with lying wonders, even bringing down fire from heaven in the sight of men. Revelation 13:13. Thus the inhabitants of the earth will be brought to take their stand.

The message will be carried not so much by argument as by the deep conviction of the Spirit of God. The arguments have been presented. The seed has been sown, and now it will spring up and bear fruit. . . . Now the rays of light penetrate everywhere, the truth is seen in its clearness, and the honest children of God sever the bands which have held them. Family connections, church relations, are powerless to stay them now. Truth is more precious than all besides. Notwithstanding the agencies combined against the truth, a large number take their stand upon the Lord's side.[16]

THE BATTLE OF ARMAGEDDON JOINS

These shall make war with the Lamb, and the Lamb shall overcome them: for he is Lord of lords, and King of kings: and they that are with him are called, and chosen, and faithful. Rev. 17:14.

We need to study the pouring out of the seventh vial. The powers of evil will not yield up the conflict without a struggle. But Providence has a part to act in the battle of Armageddon. When the earth is lighted with the glory of the angel of Revelation eighteen, the religious elements, good and evil, will awake from slumber, and the armies of the living God will take the field.[17]

Four mighty angels hold back the powers of this earth till the servants of God are sealed in their foreheads. The nations of the world are eager for conflict; but they are held in check by the angels. When this restraining power is removed, there will come a time of trouble and anguish. Deadly instruments of warfare will be invented. Vessels, with their living cargo, will be entombed in the great deep. All who have not the spirit of truth will unite under the leadership of satanic agencies. But they are to be kept under control till the time shall come for the great battle of Armageddon.[18]

Every form of evil is to spring into intense activity. Evil angels unite their powers with evil men, and as they have been in constant conflict and attained an experience in the best modes of deception and battle, and have been strengthening for centuries, they will not yield the last great final contest without a desperate struggle. All the world will be on one side or the other of the question. The battle of Armageddon will be fought, and that day must find none of us sleeping. Wide awake we must be, as wise virgins having oil in our vessels with our lamps. . . .

The power of the Holy Ghost must be upon us, and the Captain of the Lord's host will stand at the head of the angels of heaven to direct the battle. Solemn events before us are yet to transpire. Trumpet after trumpet is to be sounded, vial after vial poured out one after another upon the inhabitants of the earth. Scenes of stupendous interest are right upon us.[19]

FUTURE EVENTS COME IN ORDER

But ye, brethren, are not in darkness, that that day should overtake you as a thief. 1 Thess. 5:4.

I saw that Jesus would not leave the most holy place until every case was decided either for salvation or destruction, and that the wrath of God could not come until Jesus had finished His work in the most holy place, laid off His priestly attire, and clothed Himself with the garments of vengeance. Then Jesus will step out from between the Father and man, and God will keep silence no longer, but pour out His wrath on those who have rejected His truth. I saw that the anger of the nations, the wrath of God, and the time to judge the dead were separate and distinct, one following the other, also that Michael had not stood up, and that the time of trouble, such as never was, had not yet commenced. The nations are now getting angry, but when our High Priest has finished His work in the sanctuary, He will stand up, put on the garments of vengeance, and then the seven last plagues will be poured out.

I saw that the four angels would hold the four winds until Jesus' work was done in the sanctuary, and then will come the seven last plagues. These plagues enraged the wicked against the righteous; they thought that we had brought the judgments of God upon them, and that if they could rid the earth of us, the plagues would then be stayed. A decree went forth to slay the saints, which caused them to cry day and night for deliverance. This was the time of Jacob's trouble. Then all the saints cried out with anguish of spirit, and were delivered by the voice of God.[20]

Before His crucifixion the Saviour explained to His disciples that He was to be put to death and to rise again from the tomb. . . . But the disciples were looking for temporal deliverance from the Roman yoke, and they could not tolerate the thought that He in whom all their hopes centered should suffer an ignominious death. . . . So in the prophecies the future is opened before us as plainly as it was opened to the disciples by the words of Christ. The events connected with the close of probation and the work of preparation for the time of trouble, are clearly presented. But multitudes have no more understanding of these important truths than if they had never been revealed.[21]

A LITTLE TIME OF PEACE

**For when they shall say, Peace and safety; then sudden de-
struction cometh upon them, as travail upon a woman with
child; and they shall not escape. 1 Thess. 5:3.**

While the work of salvation is closing, trouble will be coming
on the earth, and the nations will be angry, yet held in check so
as not to prevent the work of the third angel. At that time the
"latter rain," or refreshing from the presence of the Lord, will
come, to give power to the loud voice of the third angel, and
prepare the saints to stand in the period when the seven last
plagues shall be poured out.[22]

I was shown the inhabitants of the earth in the utmost confusion. War, bloodshed, privation, want, famine, and pestilence
were abroad in the land. As these things surrounded God's
people, they began to press together, and to cast aside their little
difficulties. Self-dignity no longer controlled them; deep humility took its place. Suffering, perplexity, and privation caused
reason to resume its throne, and the passionate and unreasonable man became sane, and acted with discretion and wisdom.

My attention was then called from the scene. There seemed
to be a little time of peace. Once more the inhabitants of the
earth were presented before me; and again everything was in
the utmost confusion. Strife, war, and bloodshed, with famine
and pestilence, raged everywhere. Other nations were engaged
in this war and confusion. War caused famine. Want and bloodshed caused pestilence. And then men's hearts failed them for
fear, "and for looking after those things which are coming on
the earth." [23]

Angels are now restraining the winds of strife, until the
world shall be warned of its coming doom; but a storm is gathering, ready to burst upon the earth, and when God shall bid
His angels loose the winds, there will be such a scene of strife
as no pen can picture. . . .

A moment of respite has been graciously given us of God.
Every power lent us of heaven is to be used in doing the work
assigned us by the Lord for those who are perishing in ignorance.[24]

THE PEACE AND SAFETY CRY

They have healed also the hurt of the daughter of my people slightly, saying, Peace, peace; when there is no peace. Jer. 6:14.

Papists, Protestants, and worldlings will . . . see in this union a grand movement for the conversion of the world and the ushering in of the long-expected millennium.[25]

"The day of the Lord will come as a thief in the night; in the which the heavens shall pass away with a great noise, and the elements shall melt with fervent heat, the earth also and the works that are therein shall be burned up." 2 Peter 3:10. When the reasoning of philosophy has banished the fear of God's judgments; when religious teachers are pointing forward to long ages of peace and prosperity, and the world are absorbed in their rounds of business and pleasure, planting and building, feasting and merrymaking, rejecting God's warnings and mocking His messengers—then it is that sudden destruction cometh upon them, and they shall not escape. 1 Thessalonians 5:3.[26]

Like the dwellers in the vale of Siddim, the people are dreaming of prosperity and peace. "Escape for thy life," is the warning from the angels of God; but other voices are heard saying, "Be not excited; there is no cause for alarm." The multitudes cry, "Peace and safety," while Heaven declares that swift destruction is about to come upon the transgressor. On the night prior to their destruction, the cities of the plain rioted in pleasure and derided the fears and warnings of the messenger of God; but those scoffers perished in the flames; that very night the door of mercy was forever closed to the wicked, careless inhabitants of Sodom. God will not always be mocked; He will not long be trifled with. "Behold, the day of the Lord cometh, cruel both with wrath and fierce anger, to lay the land desolate: and he shall destroy the sinners thereof out of it." Isaiah 13:9. The great mass of the world will reject God's mercy, and will be overwhelmed in swift and irretrievable ruin. But those who heed the warning shall dwell "in the secret place of the most High," and "abide under the shadow of the Almighty." His truth shall be their shield and buckler.[27]

GOD'S WORK IS FINISHED

And this gospel of the kingdom shall be preached in all the world for a witness unto all nations; and then shall the end come. Matt. 24:14.

The solemn, sacred message of warning must be proclaimed in the most difficult fields and in the most sinful cities, in every place where the light of the great threefold gospel message has not yet dawned. Every one is to hear the last call to the marriage supper of the Lamb. From town to town, from city to city, from country to country, the message of present truth is to be proclaimed, not with outward display, but in the power of the Spirit.[28]

The message of the renewing power of God's grace will be carried to every country and clime, until the truth shall belt the world. Of the number of them that shall be sealed will be those who have come from every nation and kindred and tongue and people. From every country will be gathered men and women who will stand before the throne of God and before the Lamb, crying, "Salvation to our God which sitteth upon the throne, and unto the Lamb." Revelation 7:10.[29]

The whole earth is to be illuminated with the glory of God's truth. The light is to shine to all lands and all peoples. And it is from those who have received the light that it is to shine forth. The daystar has risen upon us, and we are to flash its light upon the pathway of those in darkness.

A crisis is right upon us. We must now by the Holy Spirit's power proclaim the great truths for these last days. It will not be long before everyone will have heard the warning and made his decision. Then shall the end come.[30]

The truth contained in the first, second, and third angels' messages must go to every nation, kindred, tongue, and people; it must lighten the darkness of every continent, and extend to the islands of the sea. There must be no delay in this work.

Our watchword is to be, Onward, ever onward! Angels of heaven will go before us to prepare the way. Our burden for the regions beyond can never be laid down till the whole earth is lightened with the glory of the Lord.[31]

GOD INTERVENES ON BEHALF OF HIS PEOPLE

Hear, all ye people; hearken, O earth, and all that therein is: and let the Lord God be witness against you, the Lord from his holy temple. For, behold, the Lord cometh forth out of his place, and will come down, and tread upon the high places of the earth. Micah 1:2, 3.

It is in a crisis that character is revealed. . . . The great final test comes at the close of human probation, when it will be too late for the soul's need to be supplied.[32]

God keeps a reckoning with the nations. Through every century of this world's history evil workers have been treasuring up wrath against the day of wrath; and when the time fully comes that iniquity shall have reached the stated boundary of God's mercy, His forbearance will cease. When the accumulated figures in heaven's record books shall mark the sum of transgression complete, wrath will come, unmixed with mercy, and then it will be seen what a tremendous thing it is to have worn out the divine patience. This crisis will be reached when the nations shall unite in making void God's law.

The days will come when the righteous will be stirred to zeal for God because of the abounding iniquity. None but divine power can stay the arrogance of Satan united with evil men; but in the hour of the church's greatest danger most fervent prayer will be offered in her behalf by the faithful remnant, and God will hear and answer at the very time when the guilt of the transgressor has reached its height. He will "avenge his own elect, which cry day and night unto him, though he bear long with them." [33]

The substitution of the false for the true is the last act in the drama. When this substitution becomes universal, God will reveal Himself. When the laws of men are exalted above the laws of God, when the powers of this earth try to force men to keep the first day of the week, know that the time has come for God to work. He will arise in His majesty, and will shake terribly the earth. He will come out of His place to punish the inhabitants of the world for their iniquity. The earth shall disclose her blood, and shall no more cover her slain.[34]

HUMAN PROBATION CLOSES

He that is unjust, let him be unjust still: and he which is filthy, let him be filthy still: and he that is righteous, let him be righteous still: and he that is holy, let him be holy still. Rev. 22:11.

When the work of the investigative judgment closes, the destiny of all will have been decided for life or death. Probation is ended a short time before the appearing of the Lord in the clouds of heaven.[35]

Scoffers pointed to the things of nature—to the unvarying succession of the seasons, to the blue skies that had never poured out rain, to the green fields refreshed by the soft dews of night—and they cried out: "Doth he not speak parables?" In contempt they declared the preacher of righteousness to be a wild enthusiast; and they went on, more eager in their pursuit of pleasure, more intent upon their evil ways, than before. But their unbelief did not hinder the predicted event. God bore long with their wickedness, giving them ample opportunity for repentance; but at the appointed time His judgments were visited upon the rejecters of His mercy.

Christ declares that there will exist similar unbelief concerning His second coming. As the people of Noah's day "knew not until the flood came, and took them all away; so," in the words of our Saviour, "shall also the coming of the Son of man be." Matthew 24:39. When the professed people of God are uniting with the world, living as they live, and joining with them in forbidden pleasures; when the luxury of the world becomes the luxury of the church; when the marriage bells are chiming, and all are looking forward to many years of worldly prosperity—then, suddenly as the lightning flashes from the heavens, will come the end of their bright visions and delusive hopes.[36]

The events connected with the close of probation and the work of preparation for the time of trouble, are clearly presented. But multitudes have no more understanding of these important truths than if they had never been revealed. Satan watches to catch away every impression that would make them wise unto salvation, and the time of trouble will find them unready.[37]

CLOSE OF PROBATION PASSES UNNOTICED

But of the times and the seasons, brethren, ye have no need that I write unto you. For yourselves know perfectly that the day of the Lord so cometh as a thief in the night. 1 Thess. 5:1, 2.

The righteous and the wicked will still be living upon the earth in their mortal state—men will be planting and building, eating and drinking, all unconscious that the final, irrevocable decision has been pronounced in the sanctuary above. Before the flood, after Noah entered the ark, God shut him in, and shut the ungodly out; but for seven days the people, knowing not that their doom was fixed, continued their careless, pleasure-loving life, and mocked the warnings of impending judgment. "So," says the Saviour, "shall also the coming of the Son of man be." Silently, unnoticed as the midnight thief, will come the decisive hour which marks the fixing of every man's destiny, the final withdrawal of mercy's offer to guilty men.[38]

The people are fast being lulled to a fatal security, to be awakened only by the outpouring of the wrath of God.[39]

The Lord in judgment will at the close of time walk through the earth, the fearful plagues will begin to fall. Then those who have despised God's word, those who have lightly esteemed it, shall wander from sea to sea, and from the north even to the east; they shall run to and fro to seek the word of the Lord and shall not find it. . . . The ministers of God will have done their last work, offered their last prayers, shed their last bitter tear for a rebellious church and an ungodly people.[40]

The eye of Jesus, looking down the ages, was fixed upon our time when He said, "If thou hadst known, even thou, at least in this thy day, the things which belong unto thy peace!" It is still thy day, O church of God, whom He has made the depositary of His law. This day of trust and probation is drawing to a close. The sun is fast westering. Can it be that it will set and thou wilt not know "the things which belong unto thy peace!"? Must the irrevocable sentence be passed, "But now they are hid from thine eyes" (Luke 19:42)? [41]

A TIME OF TROUBLE SUCH AS NEVER WAS

And at that time shall Michael stand up, the great prince which standeth for the children of thy people: and there shall be a time of trouble, such as never was since there was a nation even to that same time: and at that time thy people shall be delivered, every one that shall be found written in the book. Dan. 12:1.

When the third angel's message closes, mercy no longer pleads for the guilty inhabitants of the earth. The people of God have accomplished their work. They have received "the latter rain," "the . . . refreshing . . . from the presence of the Lord," and they are prepared for the trying hour before them. Angels are hastening to and fro in heaven. An angel returning from the earth announces that his work is done; the final test has been brought upon the world, and all who have proved themselves loyal to the divine precepts have received "the seal of the living God." Then Jesus ceases His intercession in the sanctuary above. He lifts His hands and with a loud voice says, "It is done." . . .

When He leaves the sanctuary, darkness covers the inhabitants of the earth. In that fearful time the righteous must live in the sight of a holy God without an intercessor. The restraint which has been upon the wicked is removed, and Satan has entire control of the finally impenitent. God's long-suffering has ended. The world has rejected His mercy, despised His love, and trampled upon His law. The wicked have passed the boundary of their probation; the Spirit of God, persistently resisted, has been at last withdrawn. Unsheltered by divine grace, they have no protection from the wicked one. Satan will then plunge the inhabitants of the earth into one great, final trouble. As the angels of God cease to hold in check the fierce winds of human passion, all the elements of strife will be let loose. The whole world will be involved in ruin more terrible than that which came upon Jerusalem of old.[42]

Those only who have clean hands and pure hearts will stand in that trying time. . . . Now is the time, while the four angels are holding the four winds, to make our calling and election sure.[43]

THE FOUR WINDS LOOSED

Hurt not the earth, neither the sea, nor the trees, till we have sealed the servants of our God in their foreheads. Rev. 7:3.

Angels are belting the world, refusing Satan his claims to supremacy, made because of the vast multitude of his adherents. We hear not the voices, we see not with the natural sight the work of these angels, but their hands are linked about the world, and with sleepless vigilance they are keeping the armies of Satan at bay till the sealing of God's people shall be accomplished.[44]

John sees the elements of nature—earthquake, tempest, and political strife—represented as being held by four angels. These winds are under control until God gives the word to let them go. There is the safety of God's church. The angels of God do His bidding, holding back the winds of the earth, that the winds should not blow on the earth, nor on the sea, nor on any tree, until the servants of God should be sealed in their foreheads.[45]

The present is a time of overwhelming interest to all living. Rulers and statesmen, men who occupy positions of trust and authority, thinking men and women of all classes, have their attention fixed upon the events taking place about us. They are watching the strained, restless relations that exist among the nations. They observe the intensity that is taking possession of every earthly element, and they realize that something great and decisive is about to take place—that the world is on the verge of a stupendous crisis.

Angels are now restraining the winds of strife, until the world shall be warned of its coming doom; but a storm is gathering, ready to burst upon the earth, and when God shall bid His angels loose the winds, there will be such a scene of strife as no pen can picture. . . .

A moment of respite has been graciously given us of God. Every power lent us of heaven is to be used in doing the work assigned us by the Lord for those who are perishing in ignorance. The warning message is to be sounded in all parts of the world. . . . A great work is to be done, and this work has been entrusted to those who know the truth for this time.[46]

SEVEN LAST PLAGUES BEGIN TO FALL

And I heard a great voice out of the temple saying to the seven angels, Go your ways, and pour out the vials of the wrath of God upon the earth. Rev. 16:1.

When Christ ceases His intercession in the sanctuary, the unmingled wrath threatened against those who worship the beast and his image and receive his mark (Revelation 14:9, 10), will be poured out. The plagues upon Egypt when God was about to deliver Israel were similar in character to those more terrible and extensive judgments which are to fall upon the world just before the final deliverance of God's people. Says the revelator, in describing those terrific scourges: "There fell a noisome and grievous sore upon the men which had the mark of the beast, and upon them which worshipped his image." The sea "became as the blood of a dead man: and every living soul died in the sea." And "the rivers and fountains of waters . . . became blood." Terrible as these inflictions are, God's justice stands fully vindicated. The angel of God declares: "Thou art righteous, O Lord, . . . because thou hast judged thus. For they have shed the blood of saints and prophets, and thou hast given them blood to drink; for they are worthy." Revelation 16:2-6. By condemning the people of God to death, they have as truly incurred the guilt of their blood as if it had been shed by their hands. . . .

In the plague that follows, power is given to the sun "to scorch men with fire. And men were scorched with great heat." Verses 8, 9. . . .

These plagues are not universal, or the inhabitants of the earth would be wholly cut off. Yet they will be the most awful scourges that have ever been known to mortals. All the judgments upon men, prior to the close of probation, have been mingled with mercy. The pleading blood of Christ has shielded the sinner from receiving the full measure of his guilt; but in the final judgment, wrath is poured out unmixed with mercy.[47]

The bolts of God's wrath are soon to fall, and when He shall begin to punish the transgressors, there will be no period of respite until the end. The storm of God's wrath is gathering, and those only will stand who are sanctified through the truth in the love of God. They shall be hid with Christ in God till the desolation shall be overpast.[48]

THE DEATH DECREE ISSUED

And he had power to . . . cause that as many as would not worship the image of the beast should be killed. Rev. 13:15.

When Jesus leaves the most holy, His restraining Spirit is withdrawn from rulers and people. They are left to the control of evil angels. Then such laws will be made by the counsel and direction of Satan, that unless time should be very short, no flesh could be saved.[49]

I saw that the four angels would hold the four winds until Jesus' work was done in the sanctuary, and then will come the seven last plagues. These plagues enraged the wicked against the righteous; they thought that we had brought the judgments of God upon them, and that if they could rid the earth of us, the plagues would then be stayed. A decree went forth to slay the saints, which caused them to cry day and night for deliverance. This was the time of Jacob's trouble.[50]

I saw the leading men of the earth consulting together, and Satan and his angels busy around them. I saw a writing, copies of which were scattered in different parts of the land, giving orders that unless the saints should yield their peculiar faith, give up the Sabbath, and observe the first day of the week, the people were at liberty after a certain time to put them to death.[51]

Though a general decree has fixed the time when commandment keepers may be put to death, their enemies will in some cases anticipate the decree, and before the time specified, will endeavor to take their lives. But none can pass the mighty guardians stationed about every faithful soul. Some are assailed in their flight from the cities and villages; but the swords raised against them break and fall powerless as a straw. Others are defended by angels in the form of men of war.[52]

Could men see with heavenly vision, they would behold companies of angels that excel in strength stationed about those who have kept the word of Christ's patience. With sympathizing tenderness, angels have witnessed their distress and have heard their prayers. They are waiting the word of their Commander to snatch them from their peril. But they must wait yet a little longer. The people of God must drink of the cup and be baptized with the baptism.[53]

MARKED FOR DEATH

The letters were sent by posts into all the king's provinces, to destroy, to kill, and to cause to perish, all Jews, both young and old, little children and women, in one day. Esther 3:13.

The decree that will finally go forth against the remnant people of God will be very similar to that issued by Ahasuerus against the Jews.[54]

When the protection of human laws shall be withdrawn from those who honor the law of God, there will be, in different lands, a simultaneous movement for their destruction. As the time appointed in the decree draws near, the people will conspire to root out the hated sect. It will be determined to strike in one night a decisive blow, which shall utterly silence the voice of dissent and reproof.[55]

The decree will go forth that they must disregard the Sabbath of the fourth commandment, and honor the first day, or lose their lives; but they will not yield, and trample under their feet the Sabbath of the Lord, and honor an institution of papacy. Satan's host and wicked men will surround them, and exult over them, because there will seem to be no way of escape for them.[56]

When this time of trouble comes, every case is decided; there is no longer probation, no longer mercy for the impenitent. The seal of the living God is upon His people. This small remnant, unable to defend themselves in the deadly conflict with the powers of earth that are marshaled by the dragon host, make God their defense. The decree has been passed by the highest earthly authority that they shall worship the beast and receive his mark under pain of persecution and death.[57]

I saw the saints suffering great mental anguish. They seemed to be surrounded by the wicked inhabitants of the earth. Every appearance was against them. Some began to fear that God had at last left them to perish by the hand of the wicked. . . .

It was an hour of fearful, terrible agony to the saints. Day and night they cried unto God for deliverance. To outward appearance, there was no possibility of their escape. The wicked had already begun to triumph, crying out, "Why doesn't your God deliver you out of our hands? Why don't you go up and save your lives?" But the saints heeded them not.[58]

269

ANGELIC PROTECTION IN THE TIME OF TROUBLE

Come, my people, enter thou into thy chambers, and shut thy doors about thee: hide thyself as it were for a little moment, until the indignation be overpast. Isa. 26:20.

In the day of fierce trial He [Christ] will say, "Come, my people, enter thou into thy chambers, and shut thy doors about thee: hide thyself as it were for a little moment, until the indignation be overpast." What are the chambers in which they are to hide? They are the protection of Christ and holy angels. The people of God are not at this time all in one place. They are in different companies, and in all parts of the earth.[59]

I saw the saints leaving the cities and villages, and associating together in companies, and living in the most solitary places. Angels provided them food and water, while the wicked were suffering from hunger and thirst.[60]

During the night a very impressive scene passed before me. There seemed to be great confusion and the conflict of armies. A messenger from the Lord stood before me, and said, "Call your household. I will lead you; follow me." He led me down a dark passage, through a forest, then through the clefts of mountains, and said, "Here you are safe." There were others who had been led to this retreat. The heavenly messenger said, "The time of trouble has come as a thief in the night, as the Lord warned you it would come."[61]

In the time of trouble just before the coming of Christ, the righteous will be preserved through the ministration of heavenly angels; but there will be no security for the transgressor of God's law. Angels cannot then protect those who are disregarding one of the divine precepts.[62]

In the closing period of earth's history the Lord will work mightily in behalf of those who stand steadfastly for the right. . . . In the midst of the time of trouble—trouble such as has not been since there was a nation—His chosen ones will stand unmoved. Satan with all the hosts of evil cannot destroy the weakest of God's saints. Angels that excel in strength will protect them, and in their behalf Jehovah will reveal Himself as a "God of gods," able to save to the uttermost those who have put their trust in Him.[63]

THE WICKED DURING THE PLAGUES

Behold, the days come, saith the Lord God, that I will send a famine in the land, not a famine of bread, nor a thirst for water, but of hearing the words of the Lord: and they shall wander from sea to sea, and from the north even to the east, they shall run to and fro to seek the word of the Lord, and shall not find it. Amos 8:11, 12.

And as mercy's sweet voice died away, fear and horror seized the wicked. With terrible distinctness they heard the words, "Too late! too late!" [64]

Christ [on the cross] felt much as sinners will feel when the vials of God's wrath shall be poured out upon them. Black despair like the pall of death will gather about their guilty souls, and then they will realize to the fullest extent the sinfulness of sin. [65]

Those who had not prized God's Word were hurrying to and fro, wandering from sea to sea, and from the north to the east, to seek the Word of the Lord. Said the angel, "They shall not find it. There is a famine in the land; not a famine of bread, nor a thirst for water, but for hearing the words of the Lord. What would they not give for one word of approval from God! . . .

Many of the wicked were greatly enraged as they suffered the effects of the plagues. It was a scene of fearful agony. Parents were bitterly reproaching their children, and children their parents, brothers their sisters, and sisters their brothers. . . . The people turned upon their ministers with bitter hate and reproached them, saying, "You have not warned us. You told us that all the world was to be converted, and cried, Peace, peace, to quiet every fear that was aroused. You have not told us of this hour; and those who warned us of it you declared to be fanatics and evil men, who would ruin us." But I saw that the ministers did not escape the wrath of God. Their suffering was tenfold greater than that of their people. [66]

In the time when God's judgments are falling without mercy, oh, how enviable to the wicked will be the position of those who abide "in the secret place of the most High"—the pavilion in which the Lord hides all who have loved Him and have obeyed His commandments! [67]

THE TIME OF JACOB'S TROUBLE

Alas! for that day is great, so that none is like it: it is even the time of Jacob's trouble; but he shall be saved out of it. Jer. 30:7.

I saw that the four angels would hold the four winds until Jesus' work was done in the sanctuary, and then will come the seven last plagues. These plagues enraged the wicked against the righteous; they thought that we had brought the judgments of God upon them, and that if they could rid the earth of us, the plagues would then be stayed. A decree went forth to slay the saints, which caused them to cry day and night for deliverance. This was the time of Jacob's trouble.[68]

As Satan influenced Esau to march against Jacob, so he will stir up the wicked to destroy God's people in the time of trouble. And as he accused Jacob, he will urge his accusations against the people of God. He numbers the world as his subjects; but the little company who keep the commandments of God are resisting his supremacy. If he could blot them from the earth, his triumph would be complete. He sees that holy angels are guarding them, and he infers that their sins have been pardoned; but he does not know that their cases have been decided in the sanctuary above. He has an accurate knowledge of the sins which he has tempted them to commit, and he presents these before God in the most exaggerated light, representing this people to be just as deserving as himself of exclusion from the favor of God. He declares that the Lord cannot in justice forgive their sins and yet destroy him and his angels. He claims them as his prey and demands that they be given into his hands to destroy.

As Satan accuses the people of God on account of their sins, the Lord permits him to try them to the uttermost. Their confidence in God, their faith and firmness, will be severely tested. As they review the past, their hopes sink; for in their whole lives they can see little good. They are fully conscious of their weakness and unworthiness. Satan endeavors to terrify them with the thought that their cases are hopeless, that the stain of their defilement will never be washed away. He hopes so to destroy their faith that they will yield to his temptations and turn from their allegiance to God.[69]

WHY THE TIME OF TROUBLE

**God is our refuge and strength, a very present help in trouble.
Ps. 46:1.**

Though God's people will be surrounded by enemies who
are bent upon their destruction, yet the anguish which they
suffer is not a dread of persecution for the truth's sake; they
fear that every sin has not been repented of, and that through
some fault in themselves they will fail to realize the fulfillment of the Saviour's promise: I "will keep thee from the
hour of temptation, which shall come upon all the world."
Revelation 3:10. If they could have the assurance of pardon
they would not shrink from torture or death; but should
they prove unworthy, and lose their lives because of their
own defects of character, then God's holy name would be reproached.

On every hand they hear the plottings of treason and see
the active working of rebellion; and there is aroused within
them an intense desire, an earnest yearning of soul, that this
great apostasy may be terminated and the wickedness of the
wicked may come to an end. But while they plead with God
to stay the work of rebellion, it is with a keen sense of self-
reproach that they themselves have no more power to resist
and urge back the mighty tide of evil. They feel that had
they always employed all their ability in the service of Christ,
going forward from strength to strength, Satan's forces would
have less power to prevail against them.

They afflict their souls before God, pointing to their past
repentance of their many sins, and pleading the Saviour's
promise: "Let him take hold of my strength, that he may make
peace with me; and he shall make peace with me." Isaiah 27:5.
Their faith does not fail because their prayers are not immediately answered. Though suffering the keenest anxiety, terror,
and distress, they do not cease their intercessions. They lay
hold of the strength of God as Jacob laid hold of the Angel; and
the language of their souls is: "I will not let thee go, except
thou bless me." [70]

The time of trouble is the crucible that is to bring out Christlike characters. It is designed to lead the people of God to renounce Satan and his temptations. [71]

GOD'S EYE IS UPON HIS PEOPLE

Shall not God avenge his own elect, which cry day and night unto him, though he bear long with them? I tell you that he will avenge them speedily. Luke 18:7, 8.

In the time of trouble, if the people of God had unconfessed sins to appear before them while tortured with fear and anguish, they would be' overwhelmed; despair would cut off their faith, and they could not have confidence to plead with God for deliverance. But while they have a deep sense of their unworthiness, they have no concealed wrongs to reveal. Their sins have gone beforehand to judgment and have been blotted out, and they cannot bring them to remembrance. . . .

Those professed Christians who come up to that last fearful conflict unprepared will, in their despair, confess their sins in words of burning anguish, while the wicked exult over their distress. . . .

Jacob's history is also an assurance that God will not cast off those who have been deceived and tempted and betrayed into sin, but who have returned unto Him with true repentance. While Satan seeks to destroy this class, God will send His angels to comfort and protect them in the time of peril. The assaults of Satan are fierce and determined, his delusions are terrible; but the Lord's eye is upon His people, and His ear listens to their cries. Their affliction is great, the flames of the furnace seem about to consume them; but the Refiner will bring them forth as gold tried in the fire. God's love for His children during the period of their severest trial is as strong and tender as in the days of their sunniest prosperity; but it is needful for them to be placed in the furnace of fire; their earthliness must be consumed, that the image of Christ may be perfectly reflected.

The season of distress and anguish before us will require a faith that can endure weariness, delay, and hunger—a faith that will not faint though severely tried. The period of probation is granted to all to prepare for that time. . . . All who will lay hold of God's promises, as he [Jacob] did, and be as earnest and persevering as he was, will succeed as he succeeded.[72]

THE GREAT TIME OF TROUBLE

In those days shall be affliction, such as was not from the beginning of the creation which God created unto this time, neither shall be. Mark 13:19.

The time of trouble such as never was, is soon to open upon us; and we shall need an experience which we do not now possess, and which many are too indolent to obtain. It is often the case that trouble is greater in anticipation than in reality; but this is not true of the crisis before us. The most vivid presentation cannot reach the magnitude of the ordeal. And now, while the precious Saviour is making an atonement for us, we should seek to become perfect in Christ. God's providence is the school in which we are to learn the meekness and lowliness of Jesus. The Lord is ever setting before us, not the way we would choose, which is easier and pleasanter to us, but the true aims of life. None can neglect or defer this work but at the most fearful peril to their souls.

The apostle John in vision heard a loud voice in Heaven exclaiming, "Woe to the inhabiters of the earth and of the sea! for the devil is come down unto you, having great wrath, because he knoweth that he hath but a short time." Fearful are the scenes which call forth this exclamation from the heavenly voice. The wrath of Satan increases as his time grows short, and his work of deceit and destruction reaches its culmination in the time of trouble. God's long-suffering has ended. The world has rejected His mercy, despised His love, and trampled upon His law. The wicked have passed the boundary of their probation, and the Lord withdraws His protection, and leaves them to the mercy of the leader they have chosen. Satan will have power over those who have yielded themselves to his control, and he will plunge the inhabitants of the earth into one great, final trouble. As the angels of God cease to hold in check the fierce winds of human passion, all the elements of strife will be let loose. The whole world will be involved in ruin more terrible than that which came upon Jerusalem of old.[73]

In the midst of the time of trouble—trouble such as has not been since there was a nation—His [God's] chosen ones will stand unmoved. Satan with all the hosts of evil cannot destroy the weakest of God's saints.[74]

THE CROWNING ACT OF DECEPTION

Because thou hast kept the word of my patience, I also will keep thee from the hour of temptation, which shall come upon all the world, to try them that dwell upon the earth. Rev. 3:10.

As the second appearing of our Lord Jesus Christ draws near, satanic agencies are moved from beneath. Satan will not only appear as a human being, but he will personate Jesus Christ; and the world who has rejected the truth will receive him as the Lord of lords and King of kings.[75]

The wrath of Satan increases as his time grows short, and his work of deceit and destruction will reach its culmination in the time of trouble. . . .

As the crowning act in the great drama of deception, Satan himself will personate Christ. The church has long professed to look to the Saviour's advent as the consummation of her hopes. Now the great deceiver will make it appear that Christ has come. In different parts of the earth, Satan will manifest himself among men as a majestic being of dazzling brightness, resembling the description of the Son of God given by John in the Revelation. Revelation 1:13-15. The glory that surrounds him is unsurpassed by anything that mortal eyes have yet beheld. The shout of triumph rings out upon the air: "Christ has come! Christ has come!" The people prostrate themselves in adoration before him, while he lifts up his hands and pronounces a blessing upon them, as Christ blessed His disciples when He was upon the earth. His voice is soft and subdued, yet full of melody. In gentle, compassionate tones he presents some of the same gracious, heavenly truths which the Saviour uttered; he heals the diseases of the people, and then, in his assumed character of Christ, he claims to have changed the Sabbath to Sunday, and commands all to hallow the day which he has blessed. He declares that those who persist in keeping holy the seventh day are blaspheming his name by refusing to listen to his angels sent to them with light and truth. This is the strong, almost overmastering delusion. Like the Samaritans who were deceived by Simon Magus, the multitudes, from the least to the greatest, give heed to these sorceries, saying: This is "the great power of God." Acts 8:10.

But the people of God will not be misled. The teachings of this false christ are not in accordance with the Scriptures.[76]

NO MARTYRS AFTER PROBATION CLOSES

He shall call upon me, and I will answer him: I will be with him in trouble; I will deliver him, and honour him. Ps. 91:15.

The people of God will not be free from suffering; but while persecuted and distressed, while they endure privation and suffer for want of food they will not be left to perish. . . .

Yet to human sight it will appear that the people of God must soon seal their testimony with their blood as did the martyrs before them. They themselves begin to fear that the Lord has left them to fall by the hand of their enemies. It is a time of fearful agony. Day and night they cry unto God for deliverance. . . .

The eye of God, looking down the ages, was fixed upon the crisis which His people are to meet, when earthly powers shall be arrayed against them. Like the captive exile, they will be in fear of death by starvation or by violence. But the Holy One who divided the Red Sea before Israel, will manifest His mighty power and turn their captivity. "They shall be mine, saith the Lord of hosts, in that day when I make up my jewels; and I will spare them, as a man spareth his own son that serveth him." Malachi 3:17. If the blood of Christ's faithful witnesses were shed at this time, it would not, like the blood of the martyrs, be as seed sown to yield a harvest for God. Their fidelity would not be a testimony to convince others of the truth; for the obdurate heart has beaten back the waves of mercy until they return no more. If the righteous were now left to fall a prey to their enemies, it would be a triumph for the prince of darkness. Says the psalmist: "In the time of trouble he shall hide me in his pavilion: in the secret of his tabernacle shall he hide me." Psalm 27:5. Christ has spoken: "Come, my people, enter thou into thy chambers, and shut thy doors about thee: hide thyself as it were for a little moment, until the indignation be overpast. For, behold, the Lord cometh out of his place to punish the inhabitants of the earth for their iniquity." Isaiah 26:20, 21. Glorious will be the deliverance of those who have patiently waited for His coming and whose names are written in the book of life.[77]

GOD'S PEOPLE DELIVERED

Thus saith the Lord, Even the captives of the mighty shall be taken away, and the prey of the terrible shall be delivered: for I will contend with him that contendeth with thee, and I will save thy children. Isa. 49:25.

When the protection of human laws shall be withdrawn from those who honor the law of God, there will be, in different lands, a simultaneous movement for their destruction. As the time appointed in the decree draws near, the people will conspire to root out the hated sect. It will be determined to strike in one night a decisive blow, which shall utterly silence the voice of dissent and reproof.

The people of God—some in prison cells, some hidden in solitary retreats in the forests and the mountains—still plead for divine protection, while in every quarter companies of armed men, urged on by hosts of evil angels, are preparing for the work of death. It is now, in the hour of utmost extremity, that the God of Israel will interpose for the deliverance of His chosen. . . .

With shouts of triumph, jeering, and imprecation, throngs of evil men are about to rush upon their prey, when, lo, a dense blackness, deeper than the darkness of the night, falls upon the earth. Then a rainbow, shining with the glory from the throne of God, spans the heavens and seems to encircle each praying company. The angry multitudes are suddenly arrested. Their mocking cries die away. The objects of their murderous rage are forgotten. With fearful forebodings they gaze upon the symbol of God's covenant and long to be shielded from its overpowering brightness.

By the people of God a voice, clear and melodious, is heard saying, "Look up," and lifting their eyes to the heavens, they behold the bow of promise. The black, angry clouds that covered the firmament are parted, and like Stephen they look up steadfastly into heaven and see the glory of God and the Son of man seated upon His throne.[78]

While all the world is plunged in darkness, there will be light in every dwelling of the saints. They will catch the first light of His second appearing.[79]

MIDNIGHT DELIVERANCE

In a moment shall they [the wicked] die, and the people shall be troubled at midnight, and pass away: and the mighty shall be taken away without hand. Job 34:20.

He [God] has always chosen extremities, when there seemed no possible chance for deliverance from Satan's workings, for the manifestation of His power.[80]

It is at midnight that God manifests His power for the deliverance of His people. The sun appears, shining in its strength. Signs and wonders follow in quick succession. The wicked look with terror and amazement upon the scene, while the righteous behold with solemn joy the tokens of their deliverance. Everything in nature seems turned out of its course. The streams cease to flow. Dark, heavy clouds come up and clash against each other. In the midst of the angry heavens is one clear space of indescribable glory, whence comes the voice of God like the sound of many waters, saying: "It is done." Revelation 16:17.[81]

The powers of heaven will be shaken at the voice of God. Then the sun, moon, and stars will be moved out of their places. They will not pass away, but be shaken by the voice of God.

Dark, heavy clouds came up and clashed against each other. The atmosphere parted and rolled back; then we could look up through the open space in Orion, whence came the voice of God.[82]

Now in regard to the coming of the Son of man, this will not take place until after the mighty earthquake shakes the earth after the people have heard the voice of God. They are in despair and trouble such as never was since there was a nation, and in this the people of God will suffer affliction. The clouds of heaven will clash and there will be darkness. Then that voice comes from heaven and the clouds begin to roll back like a scroll, and there is the bright, clear sign of the Son of man. The children of God know what that cloud means.[83]

The 144,000 triumphed. Their faces were lighted up with the glory of God.[84]

When the voice of God turns the captivity of His people, there is a terrible awakening of those who have lost all in the great conflict of life.[85]

The day of wrath to the enemies of God is the day of final deliverance to His church.[86]

GOD OVERTURNS NATURE

And the seventh angel poured out his vial into the air; and there came a great voice out of the temple of heaven, from the throne, saying, It is done. And there were voices, and thunders, and lightnings; and there was a great earthquake, such as was not since men were upon the earth, so mighty an earthquake, and so great. Rev. 16:17, 18.

We need to study the pouring out of the seventh vial. The powers of evil will not yield up the conflict without a struggle.[87]

In the midst of the angry heavens is one clear space of indescribable glory, whence comes the voice of God like the sound of many waters, saying: "It is done." Revelation 16:17.

That voice shakes the heavens and the earth. There is a mighty earthquake, "such as was not since men were upon the earth, so mighty an earthquake, and so great." Verses 17, 18. The firmament appears to open and shut. The glory from the throne of God seems flashing through. The mountains shake like a reed in the wind, and ragged rocks are scattered on every side. There is a roar as of a coming tempest. The sea is lashed into fury. There is heard the shriek of a hurricane like the voice of demons upon a mission of destruction. The whole earth heaves and swells like the waves of the sea. Its surface is breaking up. Its very foundations seem to be giving way. Mountain chains are sinking. Inhabited islands disappear. The seaports that have become like Sodom for wickedness are swallowed up by the angry waters. Babylon the great has come in remembrance before God, "to give unto her the cup of the wine of the fierceness of his wrath." Great hailstones, every one "about the weight of a talent," are doing their work of destruction. Verses 19, 21. The proudest cities of the earth are laid low. The lordly palaces, upon which the world's great men have lavished their wealth in order to glorify themselves, are crumbling to ruin before their eyes. Prison walls are rent asunder, and God's people, who have been held in bondage for their faith, are set free.[88]

THE SPECIAL RESURRECTION

And many of them that sleep in the dust of the earth shall awake, some to everlasting life, and some to shame and everlasting contempt. Dan. 12:2.

It was at midnight that God chose to deliver His people. As the wicked were mocking around them, suddenly the sun appeared, shining in his strength, and the moon stood still. . . . Dark, heavy clouds came up and clashed against each other. But there was one clear place of settled glory, whence came the voice of God like many waters, shaking the heavens and the earth. There was a mighty earthquake. The graves were opened, and those who had died in faith under the third angel's message, keeping the Sabbath, came forth from their dusty beds, glorified, to hear the covenant of peace that God was to make with those who had kept His law.[89]

Those who sleep in Jesus will be called from their prison house . . . to a glorious immortality. . . . He has risen, dear friends, and in your despondency you may know . . . that Jesus is by your side to give you peace.

I know what I am talking about. I have seen the time when I thought the waves were going over my head; in that time I felt my Saviour precious to me. When my eldest son was taken from me I felt my grief was very great, but Jesus came to my side and I felt His peace in my soul. The cup of consolation was placed to my lips.

And then he who had stood by my side for thirty-six years . . . was taken. We had labored together side by side in the ministry, but we had to fold the hands of the warrior and lay him down to rest in the silent grave. Again my grief seemed very great, but after all came the cup of consolation. Jesus is precious to me. He walked by my side . . . and He will walk by your side. When our friends go into the grave they are beautiful to us. It may be our father or mother that we lay away: when they come forth those wrinkles are all gone but the figure is there, and we know them. . . .

We want to be prepared to meet these dear friends as they come forth in the resurrection morning. . . . Shall we lay hold upon the hope set before us in the gospel that we shall be like Him, for we shall see Him as He is?[90]

THE SPECIAL RESURRECTION OF THE UNJUST

Behold, he cometh with clouds; and every eye shall see him, and they also which pierced him: and all kindreds of the earth shall wail because of him. Even so, Amen. Rev. 1:7.

"They also which pierced him" (Revelation 1:7), those that mocked and derided Christ's dying agonies, and the most violent opposers of His truth and His people, are raised to behold Him in His glory and to see the honor placed upon the loyal and obedient.[1]

[At His trial], Caiaphas, raising his right hand toward heaven, addressed Jesus in the form of a solemn oath: "I adjure thee by the living God, that thou tell us whether thou be the Christ, the Son of God." . . .

Every ear was bent to listen, and every eye was fixed on His face as He answered, "Thou hast said." A heavenly light seemed to illuminate His pale countenance as He added, "Nevertheless I say unto you, Hereafter shall ye see the Son of man sitting on the right hand of power, and coming in the clouds of heaven."

For a moment the divinity of Christ flashed through His guise of humanity. The high priest quailed before the penetrating eyes of the Saviour. . . . For a moment he felt as if standing before the eternal Judge, whose eye, which sees all things, was reading his soul, bringing to light mysteries supposed to be hidden with the dead.

The scene passed from the priest's vision. . . . Rending his robe, . . . he demanded that . . . the prisoner be condemned for blasphemy. "What further need have we of witnesses?" he said; "behold, now ye have heard his blasphemy. What think ye?" And they all condemned Him.[2]

Thus the Jewish leaders made their choice. Their decision was registered in the book which John saw in the hand of Him that sat upon the throne, the book which no man could open. In all its vindictiveness this decision will appear before them in the day when this book is unsealed by the Lion of the tribe of Judah.[3]

When Christ comes the second time, not as a prisoner surrounded by a rabble will they see Him. They will see Him as heaven's King. . . . Then the priests and rulers will remember distinctly the scene in the judgment hall. Every circumstance will appear before them as if written in letters of fire.[4]

THE ELEMENTS MELT WITH FERVENT HEAT

The day of the Lord will come as a thief in the night; in the which the heavens shall pass away with a great noise, and the elements shall melt with fervent heat, the earth also and the works that are therein shall be burned up. 2 Peter 3:10.

In the day of the Lord, just before the coming of Christ, God will send lightnings from Heaven in His wrath, which will unite with fire in the earth. The mountains will burn like a furnace, and will pour forth terrible streams of lava, destroying gardens and fields, villages and cities; and as they pour their melted ore, rocks and heated mud into the rivers, will cause them to boil like a pot, and send forth massive rocks and scatter their broken fragments upon the land with indescribable violence. Whole rivers will be dried up. The earth will be convulsed, and there will be dreadful eruptions and earthquakes everywhere. God will plague the wicked inhabitants of the earth until they are destroyed from off it.[5]

The earth shall reel to and fro like a drunkard, and be removed as a cottage. The elements shall be in flames, and the heavens shall be rolled together as a scroll.[6]

The earth's crust will be rent by the outbursts of the elements concealed in the bowels of the earth. These elements, once broken loose, will sweep away the treasures of those who for years have been adding to their wealth by securing large possessions at starvation prices from those in their employ.[7]

The great general conflagration is but just ahead, when all this wasted labor of life will be swept away in a night and day.[8]

There will be . . . great destruction of human life. But as in the days of the great deluge Noah was preserved in the ark that God had prepared for him, so in these days of destruction and calamity, God will be the refuge of His believing ones. Through the psalmist He declares, "Because thou hast made the Lord, which is my refuge, even the most High, thy habitation; there shall no evil befall thee, neither shall any plague come nigh thy dwelling." "For in the time of trouble he shall hide me in his pavilion. . . ." Then shall we not make the Lord our surety and our defense?[9]

We should be preparing for the mansions that Christ has gone to prepare for them that love Him. There is a rest from earth's conflict.[10]

A GRAPHIC ILLUSTRATION OF THE SEVENTH PLAGUE

Hast thou seen the treasures of the hail, which I have reserved against the time of trouble? Job 38:22, 23.

Byron Belden, Sarah Belden, and Sister May Lacey accompanied me to my appointment at Prospect [Australia]. As we left the [meeting] house we saw a storm coming . . . so portentous that we drove as fast with our colts as we dared. When we were almost home the fury of the gale struck. Large hailstones began to fall—as large as a hen's egg. . . . [They] frightened the young horse, for they were striking her with terrible force. •.

I said, "Byron, get out at once. . . . Go to her head; talk to her. Let the horses know it is not you that are beating them." He jumped out at this suggestion. I said, "May Lacey and Sarah, get out." They did. . . . I got out next, May and Sarah helping me. . . . The wind was blowing with such force that hats were taken from our heads and cushions were blown from the wagon. The heavy carriage cushions, umbrellas, and heavy carriage robes were blown into the field, and were flying in every direction. . . .

What a scene! Sister Belden, May Lacey, and I reached the house hatless. . . . Byron was with the poor terror-stricken new horse. . . . We could only lift up our hearts to God for His help. . . .

This is the sharpest experience I have ever had in a carriage in a storm. . . . I thought of the day when the judgment of God would be poured out upon the world, when blackness and horrible darkness would clothe the heavens as sackcloth of hair. . . . My imagination anticipated what it must be in that period when the Lord's mighty voice shall give commission to His angels, "Go your ways, and pour out the vials of the wrath of God upon the earth." . . .

Revelation 6 and 7 are full of meaning. Terrible are the judgments of God revealed. The seven angels stood before God to receive their commission. To them were given seven trumpets. The Lord was going forth to punish the inhabitants of the earth. . . .

When the plagues of God shall come upon the earth hail will fall upon the wicked about the weight of a talent.[11]

THE EARTH FLEES FROM ITS MAKER

Therefore I will shake the heavens, and the earth shall remove out of her place, in the wrath of the Lord of hosts, and in the day of his fierce anger. And it shall be as the chased roe, and as a sheep that no man taketh up. Isa. 13:13, 14.

Thick clouds still cover the sky; yet the sun now and then breaks through, appearing like the avenging eye of Jehovah. Fierce lightnings leap from the heavens, enveloping the earth in a sheet of flame. Above the terrific roar of thunder, voices, mysterious and awful, declare the doom of the wicked. The words spoken are not comprehended by all; but they are distinctly understood by the false teachers. Those who a little before were so reckless, so boastful and defiant, so exultant in their cruelty to God's commandment-keeping people, are now overwhelmed with consternation and shuddering in fear. Their wails are heard above the sound of the elements. Demons acknowledge the deity of Christ and tremble before His power, while men are supplicating for mercy and groveling in abject terror. . . .

Through a rift in the clouds there beams a star whose brilliancy is increased fourfold in contrast with the darkness. It speaks hope and joy to the faithful, but severity and wrath to the transgressors of God's law. Those who have sacrificed all for Christ are now secure, hidden as in the secret of the Lord's pavilion. They have been tested, and before the world and the despisers of truth they have evinced their fidelity to Him who died for them. A marvelous change has come over those who have held fast their integrity in the very face of death. They have been suddenly delivered from the dark and terrible tyranny of men transformed to demons. Their faces, so lately pale, anxious, and haggard, are now aglow with wonder, faith, and love. Their voices rise in triumphant song: "God is our refuge and strength, a very present help in trouble. Therefore will not we fear, though the earth be removed, and though the mountains be carried into the midst of the sea; though the waters thereof roar and be troubled, though the mountains shake with the swelling thereof." Psalm 46:1-3.[12]

GOD'S LAW APPEARS IN THE HEAVENS

The heavens shall declare his righteousness: for God is judge himself. Ps. 50:6.

The clouds sweep back, and the starry heavens are seen, unspeakably glorious in contrast with the black and angry firmament on either side. The glory of the celestial city streams from the gates ajar.[13]

In the temple will be seen the ark of the testament in which were placed the two tables of stone, on which are written God's law. These tables of stone will be brought forth from their hiding place, and on them will be seen the Ten Commandments engraved by the finger of God. These tables of stone now lying in the ark of the testament will be a convincing testimony to the truth and binding claims of God's law.[14]

Sacrilegious minds and hearts have thought they were mighty enough to change the times and laws of Jehovah; but, safe in the archives of heaven, in the ark of God, are the original commandments, written upon the two tables of stone. No potentate of earth has power to draw forth those tables from their sacred hiding place beneath the mercy seat.[15]

There appears against the sky a hand holding two tables of stone folded together. Says the prophet: "The heavens shall declare his righteousness: for God is judge himself." Psalm 50:6. That holy law, God's righteousness, that amid thunder and flame was proclaimed from Sinai as the guide of life, is now revealed to men as the rule of judgment. The hand opens the tables, and there are seen the precepts of the Decalogue, traced as with a pen of fire. The words are so plain that all can read them. Memory is aroused, the darkness of superstition and heresy is swept from every mind, and God's ten words, brief, comprehensive, and authoritative, are presented to the view of all the inhabitants of the earth.

It is impossible to describe the horror and despair of those who have trampled upon God's holy requirements. . . .

The enemies of God's law, from the ministers down to the least among them, have a new conception of truth and duty. Too late they see that the Sabbath of the fourth commandment is the seal of the living God.[16]

THE DAY AND HOUR
OF CHRIST'S COMING ANNOUNCED

But of that day and hour knoweth no man, no, not the angels of heaven, but my Father only. Matt. 24:36.

The voice of God is heard from heaven, declaring the day and hour of Jesus' coming, and delivering the everlasting covenant to His people. Like peals of loudest thunder His words roll through the earth.[17]

He spoke one sentence, and then paused, while the words were rolling through the earth. The Israel of God stood with their eyes fixed upward, listening to the words as they came from the mouth of Jehovah and rolled through the earth like peals of loudest thunder. It was awfully solemn. At the end of every sentence the saints shouted, "Glory! Hallelujah!"[18]

The living saints, 144,000 in number, knew and understood the voice, while the wicked thought it was thunder and an earthquake.[19]

The Israel of God stand listening, with their eyes fixed upward. Their countenances are lighted up with His glory, and shine as did the face of Moses when he came down from Sinai. The wicked cannot look upon them. And when the blessing is pronounced on those who have honored God by keeping His Sabbath holy, there is a mighty shout of victory.[20]

Then commenced the jubilee, when the land should rest.[21]

A glorious light shone upon them [the saints]. How beautiful they then looked! All marks of care and weariness were gone, and health and beauty were seen in every countenance. Their enemies, the heathen around them, fell like dead men; they could not endure the light that shone upon the delivered, holy ones. This light and glory remained upon them, until Jesus was seen in the clouds of heaven.[22]

And I saw a flaming cloud come where Jesus stood. Then Jesus . . . took His place on the cloud which carried Him to the East, where it first appeared to the saints on earth—a small black cloud which was the sign of the Son of man. While the cloud was passing from the Holiest to the East, which took a number of days, the synagogue of Satan worshipped at the saints' feet.[23]

GLEAMS OF THE GOLDEN MORNING

For as the lightning cometh out of the east, and shineth even unto the west; so shall also the coming of the Son of man be. Matt. 24:27.

While all the world is plunged in darkness, there will be light in every dwelling of the saints. They will catch the first light of His second appearing.[24]

Soon there appears in the east a small black cloud, about half the size of a man's hand. It is the cloud which surrounds the Saviour and which seems in the distance to be shrouded in darkness. The people of God know this to be the sign of the Son of man. In solemn silence they gaze upon it as it draws nearer the earth, becoming lighter and more glorious, until it is a great white cloud, its base a glory like consuming fire, and above it the rainbow of the covenant. Jesus rides forth as a mighty conqueror. Not now a "man of sorrows," to drink the bitter cup of shame and woe, He comes, victor in heaven and earth, to judge the living and the dead. "Faithful and True," "in righteousness he doth judge and make war." And "the armies which were in heaven" (Revelation 19:11, 14) follow Him. With anthems of celestial melody the holy angels, a vast, unnumbered throng, attend Him on His way. The firmament seems filled with radiant forms—"ten thousand times ten thousand, and thousands of thousands." No human pen can portray the scene; no mortal mind is adequate to conceive its splendor. "His glory covered the heavens, and the earth was full of his praise. And his brightness was as the light." Habakkuk 3:3, 4. As the living cloud comes still nearer, every eye beholds the Prince of life. No crown of thorns now mars that sacred head; but a diadem of glory rests on His holy brow. His countenance outshines the dazzling brightness of the noonday sun. "And he hath on his vesture and on his thigh a name written, KING OF KINGS, AND LORD OF LORDS." Revelation 19:16.[25]

With uplifted heads, with the bright beams of the Sun of Righteousness shining upon them, with rejoicing that their redemption draweth nigh, they [the living saints], go forth to meet the Bridegroom, saying, "Lo, this is our God; we have waited for him, and he will save us." [26]

288

THE SECOND COMING OF CHRIST

Our God shall come, and shall not keep silence: a fire shall devour before him, and it shall be very tempestuous round about him. He shall call to the heavens from above, and to the earth, that he may judge his people. Ps. 50:3, 4.

Soon our eyes were drawn to the east, for a small black cloud had appeared, about half as large as a man's hand, which we all knew was the sign of the Son of man. We all in solemn silence gazed on the cloud as it drew nearer and became lighter, glorious, and still more glorious, till it was a great white cloud. The bottom appeared like fire; a rainbow was over the cloud, while around it were ten thousand angels, singing a most lovely song; and upon it sat the Son of man.[27]

When it first appeared in the distance, this cloud looked very small. The angel said that it was the sign of the Son of man. As it drew nearer the earth, we could behold the excellent glory and majesty of Jesus as He rode forth to conquer.[28]

His hair was white and curly and lay on His shoulders; and upon His head were many crowns. His feet had the appearance of fire; in His right hand was a sharp sickle; in His left, a silver trumpet. His eyes were as a flame of fire, which searched His children through and through. Then all faces gathered paleness, and those that God had rejected gathered blackness. Then we all cried out, "Who shall be able to stand? Is my robe spotless?" Then the angels ceased to sing, and there was some time of awful silence, when Jesus spoke: "Those who have clean hands and pure hearts shall be able to stand; My grace is sufficient for you." At this our faces lighted up, and joy filled every heart. And the angels struck a note higher and sang again, while the cloud drew still nearer the earth.[29]

The earth trembled before Him, the heavens departed as a scroll when it is rolled together, and every mountain and island were moved out of their places. "And the kings of the earth, and the great men, and the rich men, and the chief captains, and the mighty men, and every bondman, and every free man, hid themselves in the dens and in the rocks of the mountains." [30]

IN THE DENS AND CAVES
OF THE EARTH

And they shall go into the holes of the rocks, and into the caves of the earth, for fear of the Lord, and for the glory of his majesty, when he ariseth to shake terribly the earth. Isa. 2:19.

The hidden ones have been scattered because of man's enmity against the law of Jehovah. They have been oppressed by all the powers of the earth. They have been scattered in the dens and caves of the earth through the violence of their adversaries, because they are true and obedient to Jehovah's laws. But deliverance comes to the people of God. To their enemies God will show Himself a God of just retribution. . . .

From the dens and the caves of the earth, that have been the secret hiding places of God's people, they are called forth as His witnesses, true and faithful.

The people who have braved out their rebellion will fulfill the description given in Revelation 6:15-17. In these very caves and dens they find the very statement of truth in the letters and in the publications as witness against them. The shepherds who lead the sheep in false paths will hear the charge made against them, "It was you who made light of truth. It was you who told us that God's law was abrogated, that it was a yoke of bondage. It was you who voiced the false doctrines when I was convicted that these Seventh-day Adventists had the truth. The blood of our souls is upon your priestly garments. . . . Now will you pay the ransom for my soul? . . . What shall we do who listened to your garbling of the Scriptures and your turning into a lie the truth which if obeyed would have saved us?"

When Christ comes to take vengeance on those who have educated and trained the people to trample on God's Sabbath, to tear down His memorial, and tread down with their feet the feed of His pastures, lamentations will be in vain. Those who trusted in the false shepherds had the word of God to search for themselves, and they find that God will judge every man who has had the truth and turned from the light because it involved self-denial and the cross. Rocks and mountains cannot screen them from the indignation of Him that sitteth on the throne and from the wrath of the Lamb.[31]

CHRIST'S APPEARANCE AT HIS SECOND COMING

We look for the Saviour, the Lord Jesus Christ: who shall change our vile body, that it may be fashioned like unto his glorious body, according to the working whereby he is able even to subdue all things unto himself. Phil. 3:20, 21.

Christ had ascended to heaven in the form of humanity. The disciples had beheld the cloud receive Him. The same Jesus who had walked and talked and prayed with them; who had broken bread with them; who had been with them in their boats on the lake; and who had that very day toiled with them up the ascent of Olivet—the same Jesus had now gone to share His Father's throne. And the angels had assured them that the very One whom they had seen go up into heaven, would come again even as He had ascended.[32]

The glory of Christ's humanity did not appear when He was upon the earth. . . . That same humanity now appears as He descends from heaven, robed in glory, triumphant, exalted.[33]

Christ will come in His own glory, in the glory of His Father, and in the glory of the holy angels. Ten thousand times ten thousand and thousands of thousands of angels, the beautiful, triumphant sons of God, possessing surpassing loveliness and glory, will escort Him on His way. In the place of a crown of thorns, He will wear a crown of glory—a crown within a crown. In the place of that old purple robe, He will be clothed in a garment of whitest white, "so as no fuller on earth can white" (Mark 9:3) it. And on His vesture and on His thigh a name will be written, "KING OF KINGS, AND LORD OF LORDS." Rev. 19:16.[34]

All heaven will be emptied of the angels, while the waiting saints will be looking for Him and gazing into heaven, as were the men of Galilee when He ascended from the Mount of Olivet. Then only those who are holy, those who have followed fully the meek Pattern, will with rapturous joy exclaim as they behold Him, "Lo, this is our God; we have waited for him, and he will save us." And they will be changed "in a moment, in the twinkling of an eye, at the last trump"—that trump which wakes the sleeping saints, and calls them forth from their dusty beds, clothed with glorious immortality, and shouting, "Victory! Victory over death and the grave!"[35]

291

JUDGMENT AT THE SECOND ADVENT

I charge thee therefore before God, and the Lord Jesus Christ, who shall judge the quick and the dead at his appearing and his kingdom. 2 Tim. 4:1.

The judgment scene will take place in the presence of all the worlds; for in this judgment the government of God will be vindicated, and His law will stand forth as "holy, and just, and good." Then every case will be decided, and sentence will be passed upon all. Sin will not then appear attractive, but will be seen in all its hideous magnitude.[36]

No human language can portray the scenes of the second coming of the Son of man in the clouds of heaven. He is to come with His own glory, and with the glory of the Father and of the holy angels. He will come clad in the robe of light, which He has worn from the days of eternity. Angels will accompany Him. Ten thousand times ten thousand will escort Him on His way. The sound of the trumpet will be heard, calling the sleeping dead from the grave. The voice of Christ will penetrate the tomb, and pierce the ears of the dead, "and all that are in the graves . . . shall come forth."

"And before him shall be gathered all nations." The very One who died for man is to judge him in the last day: for the Father "hath committed all judgment unto the Son: . . . and hath given him authority to execute judgment also, because he is the Son of man." What a day that will be, when those who rejected Christ will look upon Him whom their sins have pierced.[37]

At His second coming, conviction will be brought to every heart. Those who have turned from Him to the trivial things of this earth, seeking selfish interests and worldly honor, will in the day of His coming acknowledge their mistake. These are the ones spoken of by the Revelator as "all kindreds of the earth," who "shall wail because of him." . . .

"And they also which pierced him." These words apply not only to the men who pierced Christ when He hung on the cross of Calvary, but to those who by evil-speaking and wrong-doing are piercing Him to-day.[38]

THEY THAT PIERCED HIM

Ye shall see the Son of man sitting on the right hand of power, and coming in the clouds of heaven. Mark 14:62.

As they [the Jewish rulers] gaze upon His glory, there flashes before their minds the memory of the Son of Man clad in the garb of humanity. They remember how they treated Him, how they refused Him, and pressed close to the side of the great apostate. The scenes of Christ's life appear before them in all their clearness. All He did, all He said, the humiliation to which He descended to save them from the taint of sin, rises before them in condemnation.

They behold Him riding into Jerusalem, and see Him break into an agony of tears over the impenitent city that would not receive His message. His voice, which was heard in invitation, in entreaty, in tones of tender solicitude, seems again to fall upon their ears. The scene in the garden of Gethsemane rises before them, and they hear Christ's amazing prayer, "Father, if it be possible, let this cup pass from me."

Again they hear the voice of Pilate, saying, "I find in him no fault at all." They see the shameful scene in the judgment hall, when Barabbas stood by the side of Christ, and they had the privilege of choosing the guiltless One. They hear again the words of Pilate, "Whom will ye that I release unto you? Barabbas, or Jesus which is called Christ?" They hear the response, "Away with this man, and release unto us Barabbas." To the question of Pilate, "What shall I do then with Jesus?" the answer comes, "Let him be crucified."

Again they see their Sacrifice bearing the reproach of the cross. They hear the loud, triumphant tones tauntingly exclaim, "If thou be the Son of God, come down from the cross." "He saved others; himself he cannot save."

Now they behold Him not in the garden of Gethsemane, not in the judgment hall, not on the cross of Calvary. The signs of His humiliation have passed away, and they look upon the face of God—the face they spit upon, the face which priests and rulers struck with the palms of their hands. Now the truth in all its vividness is revealed to them.[39]

THE WICKED SLAY EACH OTHER

I will call for a sword against him throughout all my mountains, saith the Lord God: every man's sword shall be against his brother. Eze. 38:21.

The wicked are filled with regret, not because of their sinful neglect of God and their fellow men, but because God has conquered. They lament that the result is what it is; but they do not repent of their wickedness. They would leave no means untried to conquer if they could. . . .

Ministers and people see that they have not sustained the right relation to God. They see that they have rebelled against the Author of all just and righteous law. The setting aside of the divine precepts gave rise to thousands of springs of evil, discord, hatred, iniquity, until the earth became one vast field of strife, one sink of corruption. This is the view that now appears to those who rejected truth and chose to cherish error. No language can express the longing which the disobedient and disloyal feel for that which they have lost forever—eternal life. Men whom the world has worshiped for their talents and eloquence now see these things in their true light. They realize what they have forfeited by transgression, and they fall at the feet of those whose fidelity they have despised and derided, and confess that God has loved them.

The people see that they have been deluded. They accuse one another of having led them to destruction; but all unite in heaping their bitterest condemnation upon the ministers. Unfaithful pastors have prophesied smooth things; they have led their hearers to make void the law of God and to persecute those who would keep it holy. Now, in their despair, these teachers confess before the world their work of deception. The multitudes are filled with fury. "We are lost!" they cry, "and you are the cause of our ruin"; and they turn upon the false shepherds. The very ones that once admired them most will pronounce the most dreadful curses upon them. The very hands that once crowned them with laurels will be raised for their destruction. The swords which were to slay God's people are now employed to destroy their enemies. Everywhere there is strife and bloodshed.[40]

THE WRATH OF THE LAMB

The kings of the earth, and the great men, and the rich men, and the chief captains, and the mighty men, and every bondman, and every free man, hid themselves in the dens and in the rocks of the mountains; and said to the mountains and rocks, Fall on us, and hide us from the face of him that sitteth on the throne, and from the wrath of the Lamb. Rev. 6:15, 16.

The derisive jests have ceased. Lying lips are hushed into silence. The clash of arms, the tumult of battle, "with confused noise, and garments rolled in blood" (Isaiah 9:5), is stilled. Nought now is heard but the voice of prayer and the sound of weeping and lamentation. The cry bursts forth from lips so lately scoffing: "The great day of his wrath is come; and who shall be able to stand?" The wicked pray to be buried beneath the rocks of the mountains rather than meet the face of Him whom they have despised and rejected.

That voice which penetrates the ear of the dead, they know. How often have its plaintive, tender tones called them to repentance. How often has it been heard in the touching entreaties of a friend, a brother, a Redeemer. To the rejecters of His grace no other could be so full of condemnation, so burdened with denunciation, as that voice which has so long pleaded: "Turn ye, turn ye from your evil ways; for why will ye die?" Ezekiel 33:11. Oh, that it were to them the voice of a stranger! Says Jesus: "I have called, and ye refused; I have stretched out my hand, and no man regarded; but ye have set at nought all my counsel, and would none of my reproof." Proverbs 1:24, 25. That voice awakens memories which they would fain blot out—warnings despised, invitations refused, privileges slighted. . . .

In the lives of all who reject truth there are moments when conscience awakens, when memory presents the torturing recollection of a life of hypocrisy and the soul is harassed with vain regrets. But what are these compared with the remorse of that day . . . when "destruction cometh as a whirlwind"! Proverbs 1:27. Those who would have destroyed Christ and His faithful people now witness the glory which rests upon them.[41]

GOD INTERVENES IN ARMAGEDDON

A noise shall come even to the ends of the earth; for the Lord hath a controversy with the nations, he will plead with all flesh; he will give them that are wicked to the sword, saith the Lord. Jer. 25:31.

For six thousand years the great controversy has been in progress; the Son of God and His heavenly messengers have been in conflict with the power of the evil one, to warn, enlighten, and save the children of men. Now all have made their decisions; the wicked have fully united with Satan in his warfare against God. The time has come for God to vindicate the authority of His downtrodden law. Now the controversy is not alone with Satan, but with men. "The Lord hath a controversy with the nations"; "He will give them that are wicked to the sword."

The mark of deliverance has been set upon those "that sigh and that cry for all the abominations that be done." Now the angel of death goes forth, represented in Ezekiel's vision by the men with the slaughtering weapons, to whom the command is given: "Slay utterly old and young, both maids, and little children, and women: but come not near any man upon whom is the mark; and begin at my sanctuary." Says the prophet: "They began at the ancient men which were before the house." Ezekiel 9:1-6. The work of destruction begins among those who have professed to be the spiritual guardians of the people. The false watchmen are the first to fall. There are none to pity or to spare. Men, women, maidens, and little children perish together.

"The Lord cometh out of his place to punish the inhabitants of the earth for their iniquity: the earth also shall disclose her blood, and shall no more cover her slain." Isaiah 26:21. . . . In the mad strife of their own fierce passions, and by the awful outpouring of God's unmingled wrath, fall the wicked inhabitants of the earth—priests, rulers, and people, rich and poor, high and low. "And the slain of the Lord shall be at that day from one end of the earth even unto the other end of the earth: they shall not be lamented, neither gathered, nor buried." Jeremiah 25:33.[42]

THE NATURE OF THE FINAL BATTLE

The Lord hath opened his armoury, and hath brought forth the weapons of his indignation. Jer. 50:25.

At His own will God summons the forces of nature to overthrow the might of His enemies—"fire, and hail; snow, and vapours; stormy wind fulfilling his word." Psalm 148:8. When the heathen Amorites had set themselves to resist His purposes, God interposed, casting down "great stones from heaven" upon the enemies of Israel. We are told of a greater battle to take place in the closing scenes of earth's history, when Jehovah "hath opened his armoury, and hath brought forth the weapons of his indignation." Jeremiah 50:25. "Hast thou," he inquires, "entered into the treasures of the snow? or hast thou seen the treasures of the hail, which I have reserved against the time of trouble, against the day of battle and war?" Job 38:22, 23.

The revelator describes the destruction that is to take place when the "great voice out of the temple of heaven" announces, "It is done." He says, "There fell upon men a great hail out of heaven, every stone about the weight of a talent." Revelation 16:17, 21.[43]

In the last scenes of this earth's history, war will rage.[44]

The powers of evil will not yield up the conflict without a struggle. But Providence has a part to act in the battle of Armageddon.[45]

The Captain of the Lord's host will stand at the head of the angels of heaven to direct the battle.[46]

He on whose vesture is written the name, King of kings and Lord of lords, leads forth the armies of heaven on white horses, clothed in fine linen, clean and white.[47]

When He shall come to the earth again, He will shake "not the earth only, but also heaven." "The earth shall reel to and fro like a drunkard, and shall be removed like a cottage." "The heavens shall be rolled together as a scroll"; "the elements shall melt with fervent heat, the earth also and the works that are therein shall be burned up." But "the Lord will be the hope of his people, and the strength of the children of Israel." Heb. 12:26; Isa. 24:20; 34:4; 2 Peter 3:10; Joel 3:16.[48]

BE YE ALSO READY

Be ye also ready: for in such an hour as ye think not the Son of man cometh. Matt. 24:44.

Suppose that today Christ should appear in the clouds of heaven, who . . . would be ready to meet Him? Suppose we should be translated into the kingdom of heaven just as we are. Would we be prepared to unite with the saints of God, to live in harmony with the royal family, the children of the heavenly King? What preparation have you made for the judgment? Have you made your peace with God? . . . Are you seeking to help those around you, those in your home, those in your neighborhood, those with whom you come in contact that are not keeping the commandments of God? . . . Remember that profession is worthless without a practice that enters into the daily life. God knows whether we are keeping His law in truth. He knows just what we are doing, just what we are thinking and saying. Are we getting ready to meet the King? When He comes in the clouds of heaven with power and great glory, will you be able to say, "Lo, this is our God; we have waited for him, and he will save us" (Isa. 25:9)? To those who can say this Christ will say, "Come up higher. Upon this earth you have loved Me. You have loved to do My will. You can now enter the Holy City and receive the crown of everlasting life."

If it were possible for us to be admitted into heaven as we are, how many of us would be able to look upon God? How many of us have on the wedding garment? How many of us are without spot or wrinkle or any such thing? . . .

This is our washing and ironing time—the time when we are to cleanse our robes of character in the blood of the Lamb. John says, "Behold the Lamb of God, which taketh away the sin of the world" (John 1:29). . . . Shall we not let our sins go? . . .

I entreat you, brethren and sisters, to labor earnestly to secure the crown of everlasting life. The reward will be worth the conflict, worth the effort. . . . In the race in which we are running, everyone may receive the reward offered—a crown of everlasting life. I want this crown; I mean by God's help to have it. I mean to hold fast to the truth, that I may see the King in His beauty.[49]

THE GENERAL RESURRECTION OF THE RIGHTEOUS

Awake and sing, ye that dwell in dust: for thy dew is as the dew of herbs, and the earth shall cast out the dead. Isa. 26:19.

The King of kings descends upon the cloud, wrapped in flaming fire. The heavens are rolled together as a scroll, the earth trembles before Him, and every mountain and island is moved out of its place. . . .

Amid the reeling of the earth, the flash of lightning, and the roar of thunder, the voice of the Son of God calls forth the sleeping saints. He looks upon the graves of the righteous, then, raising His hands to heaven, He cries: "Awake, awake, awake, ye that sleep in the dust, and arise!" Throughout the length and breadth of the earth the dead shall hear that voice, and they that hear shall live. And the whole earth shall ring with the tread of the exceeding great army of every nation, kindred, tongue, and people. From the prison house of death they come, clothed with immortal glory, crying: "O death, where is thy sting? O grave, where is thy victory?" 1 Corinthians 15:55. And the living righteous and the risen saints unite their voices in a long, glad shout of victory.

All come forth from their graves the same in stature as when they entered the tomb. . . . But all arise with the freshness and vigor of eternal youth. . . . The mortal, corruptible form, devoid of comeliness, once polluted with sin, becomes perfect, beautiful, and immortal. All blemishes and deformities are left in the grave. . . .

The living righteous are changed "in a moment, in the twinkling of an eye." At the voice of God they were glorified; now they are made immortal and with the risen saints are caught up to meet their Lord in the air. Angels "gather together his elect from the four winds, from one end of heaven to the other."[50]

As the little infants come forth immortal from their dusty beds, they immediately wing their way to their mothers' arms.[51]

Friends long separated by death are united, nevermore to part, and with songs of gladness ascend together to the City of God.[52]

VICTORY OF THE SLEEPING SAINTS

Marvel not at this: for the hour is coming, in the which all that are in the graves shall hear his voice, and shall come forth; they that have done good, unto the resurrection of life; and they that have done evil, unto the resurrection of damnation. John 5:28, 29.

The Life-giver will call up His purchased possession in the first resurrection, and until that triumphant hour, when the last trump shall sound and the vast army shall come forth to eternal victory, every sleeping saint will be kept in safety and will be guarded as a precious jewel, who is known to God by name. By the power of the Saviour that dwelt in them while living and because they were partakers of the divine nature, they are brought forth from the dead.[53]

"The hour is coming," Christ said, "in the which all that are in the graves shall hear his voice, and shall come forth." That voice is to resound through all the habitations of the dead; and every saint who sleeps in Jesus will awake and leave his prison-house. Then the virtue of character we have received from Christ's righteousness will ally us to true greatness of the highest order.[54]

The victory of the sleeping saints will be glorious on the morning of the resurrection. . . . The Life-giver will crown with immortality all who come forth from the grave.[55]

There stands the risen host. The last thought was of death and its pangs. The last thoughts they had were of the grave and the tomb, but now they proclaim, "O death, where is thy sting? O grave, where is thy victory?" . . . Here they stand and the finishing touch of immortality is put upon them and they go up to meet their Lord in the air. . . . There are the columns of angels on either side; . . . then the angelic choir strike the note of victory and the angels in the two columns take up the song and the redeemed host join as though they had been singing the song on the earth, and they have been. Oh, what music! There is not an inharmonious note. Every voice proclaims, "Worthy is the Lamb that was slain." He sees the travail of His soul, and is satisfied.[56]

MYSTERIES OF THE RESURRECTION

For I know that my redeemer liveth, and that he shall stand at the latter day upon the earth: and though after my skin worms destroy this body, yet in my flesh shall I see God: whom I shall see for myself, and mine eyes shall behold, and not another; though my reins be consumed within me. Job 19:25-27.

Our personal identity is preserved in the resurrection, though not the same particles of matter or material substance as went into the grave. The wondrous works of God are a mystery to man. The spirit, the character of man, is returned to God, there to be preserved. In the resurrection every man will have his own character. God in His own time will call forth the dead, giving again the breath of life, and bidding the dry bones live. The same form will come forth, but it will be free from disease and every defect. It lives again bearing the same individuality of features, so that friend will recognize friend. There is no law of God in nature which shows that God gives back the same identical particles of matter which composed the body before death. God shall give the righteous dead a body that will please Him.

Paul illustrates this subject by the kernel of grain sown in the field. The planted kernel decays, but there comes forth a new kernel. The natural substance in the grain that decays is never raised as before, but God giveth it a body as it hath pleased Him. A much finer material will compose the human body, for it is a new creation, a new birth. It is sown a natural body, it is raised a spiritual body.[57]

He [the believer] may die, as Christ died, but the life of the Saviour is in him. His life is hid with Christ in God. "I am come that they might have life," Jesus said, "and that they might have it more abundantly." He carries on the great process by which believers are made one with Him in this present life, to be one with Him throughout all eternity. . . .

At the last day He will raise them as a part of Himself. . . . Christ became one with us in order that we might become one with Him in divinity.[58]

LIFE ETERNAL BEGINS NOW

This is the record, that God hath given to us eternal life, and this life is in his Son. 1 John 5:11.

The resurrection of Jesus was a sample of the final resurrection of all who sleep in Him.[59]

He [the Christian] may die; but the life of Christ is in him, and at the resurrection of the just he will rise to newness of life.[60]

"In him [Christ] was life; and the life was the light of men." It is not physical life that is here specified, but immortality, the life which is exclusively the property of God. The Word, who was with God, and who was God, had this life. Physical life is something which each individual receives. It is not eternal or immortal; for God, the Life-giver, takes it again. Man has no control over his life. But the life of Christ was unborrowed. No one can take this life from Him. "I lay it down of myself," He said. In Him was life, original, unborrowed, underived. This life is not inherent in man. He can possess it only through Christ.[61]

While bearing human nature, He [Christ] was dependent upon the Omnipotent for His life. In His humanity, He laid hold of the divinity of God; and this every member of the human family has the privilege of doing. . . .

If we repent of our transgression, and receive Christ as the Life-giver, . . . we become one with Him, and our will is brought into harmony with the divine will. We become partakers of the life of Christ, which is eternal. We derive immortality from God by receiving the life of Christ, for in Christ dwells all the fulness of the Godhead bodily. This life is the mystical union and coöperation of the divine with the human.[62]

Christ became one flesh with us, in order that we might become one spirit with Him. It is by virtue of this union that we are to come forth from the grave—not merely as a manifestation of the power of Christ, but because, through faith, His life has become ours. Those who see Christ in His true character, and receive Him into the heart, have everlasting life. It is through the Spirit that Christ dwells in us; and the Spirit of God, received into the heart by faith, is the beginning of the life eternal.[63]

WE SHALL RECOGNIZE EACH OTHER

Then shall I know even as also I am known. 1 Cor. 13:12.

We shall know our friends, even as the disciples knew Jesus. They may have been deformed, diseased, or disfigured, in this mortal life, and they rise in perfect health and symmetry; yet in the glorified body their identity will be perfectly preserved. . . . In the face radiant with the light shining from the face of Jesus, we shall recognize the lineaments of those we love.[64]

The redeemed will meet and recognize those whose attention they have directed to the uplifted Saviour. What blessed converse they have with these souls! "I was a sinner," it will be said, "without God and without hope in the world, and you came to me and drew my attention to the precious Saviour as my only hope. . . ." Others will say, "I was a heathen in heathen lands. You left your friends and comfortable home and came to teach me how to find Jesus and believe in Him as the only true God. I demolished my idols and worshiped God, and now I see Him face to face. I am saved, eternally saved, ever to behold Him whom I love. . . ."

Others will express their gratitude to those who fed the hungry and clothed the naked. "When despair bound my soul in unbelief, the Lord sent you to me," they say, "to speak words of hope and comfort. You brought me food for my physical necessities, and you opened to me the Word of God, awakening me to my spiritual needs. You treated me as a brother. You sympathized with me in my sorrows, and restored my bruised and wounded soul, so that I could grasp the hand of Christ that was reached out to save me. In my ignorance you taught me patiently that I had a Father in heaven who cared for me. You read to me the precious promises of God's Word. You inspired in me the faith that He would save me. My heart was softened, subdued, broken, as I contemplated the sacrifice which Christ had made for me. . . . I am here, saved, eternally saved, ever to live in His presence and to praise Him who gave His life for me."

What rejoicing there will be as these redeemed ones meet and greet those who have had a burden in their behalf! And those who have lived, not to please themselves, but to be a blessing to the unfortunate who have so few blessings—how their hearts will thrill with satisfaction![65]

THE BLESSED HOPE

Looking for that blessed hope, and the glorious appearing of the great God and our Saviour Jesus Christ. Titus 2:13.

Jesus said He would go away and prepare mansions for us, that where He is there we may be also. We shall ever dwell with and enjoy the light of His precious countenance. My heart leaps with joy at the cheering prospect. We are almost home. Heaven, sweet heaven! It is our eternal home. I am glad every moment that Jesus lives, and because He lives we shall live also. My soul says, Praise the Lord. There is a fullness in Jesus, a supply for each, for all, and why should we die for bread or starve in foreign lands?

I hunger, I thirst for salvation, for entire conformity to the will of God. We have a good hope through Jesus. It is sure and steadfast and entereth into that within the veil. It yields us consolation in affliction, it gives us joy amid anguish, disperses the gloom around us, and causes us to look through it all to immortality and eternal life. . . . Earthly treasures are no inducement to us, for while we have this hope it reaches clear above the treasures of earth that are passing away and takes hold of the immortal inheritance, the treasures that are durable, incorruptible, undefiled, and that fade not away. . . .

Our mortal bodies may die and be laid away in the grave. Yet the blessed hope lives on until the resurrection, when the voice of Jesus calls forth the sleeping dust. We shall then enjoy the fullness of the blessed, glorious hope. We know in whom we have believed. We have not run in vain, neither labored in vain. A rich, a glorious reward is before us; it is the prize for which we run, and if we persevere with courage we shall surely obtain it. . . .

There is salvation for us, and why do we stay away from the fountain? Why not come and drink that our souls may be refreshed, invigorated, and may flourish in God? Why do we cling so closely to earth? There is something better than earth for us to talk about and think of. We can be in a heavenly frame of mind. Oh, let us dwell upon Jesus' lovely, spotless character, and by beholding we shall become changed to the same image. Be of good courage. Have faith in God.[66]

TRANSLATION OF THE RIGHTEOUS

For the Lord himself shall descend from heaven with a shout, with the voice of the archangel, and with the trump of God: and the dead in Christ shall rise first: then we which are alive and remain shall be caught up together with them in the clouds, to meet the Lord in the air: and so shall we ever be with the Lord. 1 Thess. 4:16, 17.

Soon appeared the great white cloud. It looked more lovely than ever before. On it sat the Son of man. At first we did not see Jesus on the cloud, but as it drew near the earth we could behold His lovely person. . . . The voice of the Son of God called forth the sleeping saints, clothed with glorious immortality. The living saints were changed in a moment and were caught up with them into the cloudy chariot. It looked all over glorious as it rolled upward. On either side of the chariot were wings, and beneath it wheels. And as the chariot rolled upward, the wheels cried, "Holy," and the wings, as they moved, cried, "Holy," and the retinue of holy angels around the cloud cried, "Holy, holy, holy, Lord God Almighty!" And the saints in the cloud cried, "Glory! Alleluia!" [67]

We all entered the cloud together, and were seven days ascending to the sea of glass, when Jesus brought the crowns, and with His own right hand placed them on our heads. He gave us harps of gold and palms of victory. Here on the sea of glass the 144,000 stood in a perfect square. Some of them had very bright crowns, others not so bright. Some crowns appeared heavy with stars, while others had but few. All were perfectly satisfied with their crowns. And they were all clothed with a glorious white mantle from their shoulders to their feet. Angels were all about us as we marched over the sea of glass to the gate of the city. Jesus raised His mighty, glorious arm, laid hold of the pearly gate, swung it back on its glittering hinges, and said to us, "You have washed your robes in My blood, stood stiffly for My truth, enter in." We all marched in and felt that we had a perfect right in the city. [68]

A voice, richer than any music that ever fell on mortal ear, will be heard saying, "Come, ye blessed of my Father, inherit the kingdom prepared for you from the foundation of the world." [69]

THE EARTH DEPOPULATED

I beheld the earth, and, lo, it was without form, and void; and the heavens, and they had no light. I beheld the mountains, and, lo, they trembled, and all the hills moved lightly. I beheld, and, lo, there was no man, and all the birds of the heavens were fled. Jer. 4:23-25.

At the coming of Christ the wicked are blotted from the face of the whole earth—consumed with the spirit of His mouth and destroyed by the brightness of His glory. Christ takes His people to the City of God, and the earth is emptied of its inhabitants. "Behold, the Lord maketh the earth empty, and maketh it waste, and turneth it upside down, and scattereth abroad the inhabitants thereof." "The land shall be utterly emptied, and utterly spoiled: for the Lord hath spoken this word." "Because they have transgressed the laws, changed the ordinance, broken the everlasting covenant. Therefore hath the curse devoured the earth, and they that dwell therein are desolate: therefore the inhabitants of the earth are burned." Isaiah 24:1, 3, 5, 6.

The whole earth appears like a desolate wilderness. The ruins of cities and villages destroyed by the earthquake, uprooted trees, ragged rocks thrown out by the sea or torn out of the earth itself, are scattered over its surface, while vast caverns mark the spot where the mountains have been rent from their foundations.

Now the event takes place foreshadowed in the last solemn service of the Day of Atonement. When the ministration in the holy of holies had been completed, and the sins of Israel had been removed from the sanctuary by virtue of the blood of the sin offering, then the scapegoat was presented alive before the Lord; and in the presence of the congregation the high priest confessed over him "all the iniquities of the children of Israel, and all their transgressions in all their sins, putting them upon the head of the goat." Leviticus 16:21. In like manner when the work of atonement in the heavenly sanctuary has been completed then in the presence of God and heavenly angels and the host of the redeemed the sins of God's people will be placed upon Satan; he will be declared guilty of all the evil which he has caused them to commit.[70]

SATAN IS BOUND

And I saw an angel come down from heaven, having the key of the bottomless pit and a great chain in his hand. And he laid hold on the dragon, that old serpent, which is the Devil, and Satan, and bound him a thousand years. Rev. 20:1, 2.

The revelator foretells the banishment of Satan and the condition of chaos and desolation to which the earth is to be reduced, and he declares that this condition will exist for a thousand years. After presenting the scenes of the Lord's second coming and the destruction of the wicked, the prophecy continues: "I saw an angel come down from heaven, having the key of the bottomless pit and a great chain in his hand. And he laid hold on the dragon, that old serpent, which is the Devil, and Satan, and bound him a thousand years, and cast him into the bottomless pit, and shut him up, and set a seal upon him, that he should deceive the nations no more, till the thousand years should be fulfilled: and after that he must be loosed a little season." Revelation 20:1-3.

That the expression "bottomless pit" represents the earth in a state of confusion and darkness is evident from other scriptures. Concerning the condition of the earth "in the beginning," the Bible record says that it "was without form, and void; and darkness was upon the face of the deep." Genesis 1:2. Prophecy teaches that it will be brought back, partially at least, to this condition. Looking forward to the great day of God, the prophet Jeremiah declares: "I beheld the earth, and, lo, it was without form, and void; and the heavens, and they had no light. I beheld the mountains, and, lo, they trembled, and all the hills moved lightly. I beheld, and, lo, there was no man, and all the birds of the heavens were fled. I beheld, and, lo, the fruitful place was a wilderness, and all the cities thereof were broken down." Jeremiah 4:23-26.

Here is to be the home of Satan with his evil angels for a thousand years. Limited to the earth, he will not have access to other worlds to tempt and annoy those who have never fallen. It is in this sense that he is bound: there are none remaining, upon whom he can exercise his power. He is wholly cut off from the work of deception and ruin which for so many centuries has been his sole delight.[71]

307

FAMILIES WILL BE REUNITED

Thus saith the Lord; Refrain thy voice from weeping, and thine eyes from tears: for thy work shall be rewarded, saith the Lord; and they shall come again from the land of the enemy. And there is hope in thine end, saith the Lord, that thy children shall come again to their own border. Jer. 31:16, 17.

Christ is coming with clouds and with great glory. A multitude of shining angels will attend Him. He will come to raise the dead, and to change the living saints from glory to glory. He will come to honor those who have loved Him, and kept His commandments, and to take them to Himself. He has not forgotten them nor His promise. There will be a relinking of the family chain.[72]

The day of God will reveal how much the world owes to godly mothers. . . .

When the judgment shall sit, and the books shall be opened; when the "well done" of the great Judge is pronounced, and the crown of immortal glory is placed upon the brow of the victor, many will raise their crowns in sight of the assembled universe, and pointing to their mother say: "She made me all I am through the grace of God. Her instruction, her prayers, have been blessed to my eternal salvation."[73]

With joy unutterable, parents see the crown, the robe, the harp, given to their children. The days of hope and fear are ended. The seed sown with tears and prayers may have seemed to be sown in vain, but their harvest is reaped with joy at last. Their children have been redeemed.[74]

Oh, wonderful redemption! long talked of, long hoped for, contemplated with eager anticipation, but never fully understood.[75]

To His faithful followers Christ has been a daily companion and familiar friend. They have lived in close contact, in constant communion with God. Upon them the glory of the Lord has risen. In them the light of the knowledge of the glory of God in the face of Jesus Christ has been reflected. Now they rejoice in the undimmed rays of the brightness and glory of the King in His majesty. They are prepared for the communion of heaven; for they have heaven in their hearts.[76]

CROWNS BEING PREPARED FOR THE FAITHFUL

I have fought a good fight, I have finished my course, I have kept the faith: henceforth there is laid up for me a crown of righteousness, which the Lord, the righteous judge, shall give me at that day: and not to me only, but unto all them also that love his appearing. 2 Tim. 4:7, 8.

When the Lord makes up His jewels, the true, the frank, the honest, will be looked upon with pleasure. Angels are employed in making crowns for such ones, and upon these star-gemmed crowns will be reflected, with splendor, the light which radiates from the throne of God.[77]

Talk of heavenly things. Talk of Jesus, His loveliness and glory, and of His undying love for you, and let your heart flow out in love and gratitude to Him, who died to save you. O, get ready to meet your Lord in peace. Those who are ready will soon receive an unfading crown of life, and will dwell forever in the kingdom of God, with Christ, with angels, and with those who have been redeemed by the precious blood of Christ.[78]

A crown of glory . . . is laid up for us who wait, and love, and long for, the appearing of the Saviour.

It is the waiting ones who are to be crowned with glory, honor, and immortality. You need not talk . . . of the honors of the world, or the praise of its great ones. They are all vanity. Let but the finger of God touch them, and they would soon go back to dust again. I want honor that is lasting, honor that is immortal, honor that will never perish; a crown that is richer than any crown that ever decked the brow of a monarch.[79]

In that day the redeemed will shine forth in the glory of the Father and His Son. The angels of heaven, touching their golden harps, will welcome the King, and those who are the trophies of His victory—those who have been washed and made white in the blood of the Lamb. A song of triumph will peal forth, filling all heaven. Christ has conquered. He enters the heavenly courts accompanied by His redeemed ones, the witnesses that His mission of suffering and self-sacrifice has not been in vain.[80]

A CROWN FOR EVERY CHILD OF GOD

Blessed is the man that endureth temptation: for when he is tried, he shall receive the crown of life, which the Lord hath promised to them that love him. James 1:12.

I saw a very great number of angels bring from the city glorious crowns—a crown for every saint, with his name written thereon. As Jesus called for the crowns, angels presented them to Him, and with His own right hand the lovely Jesus placed the crowns on the heads of the saints. In the same manner the angels brought the harps, and Jesus presented them also to the saints. The commanding angels first struck the note, and then every voice was raised in grateful, happy praise, and every hand skillfully swept over the strings of the harp, sending forth melodious music in rich and perfect strains. . . .

Within the city there was everything to feast the eye. Rich glory they beheld everywhere. Then Jesus looked upon His redeemed saints; their countenances were radiant with glory; and as He fixed His loving eyes upon them, He said, with His rich, musical voice, "I behold the travail of My soul, and am satisfied. This rich glory is yours to enjoy eternally. Your sorrows are ended. There shall be no more death, neither sorrow nor crying, neither shall there be any more pain." . . .

I then saw Jesus leading His people to the tree of life. . . . Upon the tree of life was most beautiful fruit, of which the saints could partake freely; in the city was a most glorious throne, from which proceeded a pure river of water of life, clear as crystal. On each side of this river was the tree of life, and on the banks of the river were other beautiful trees bearing fruit. . . .

Language is altogether too feeble to attempt a description of heaven. As the scene rises before me, I am lost in amazement. Carried away with the surpassing splendor and excellent glory, I lay down the pen, and exclaim, "Oh, what love! what wondrous love!" The most exalted language fails to describe the glory of heaven or the matchless depths of a Saviour's love.[81]

OUR REDEMPTION DRAWETH NIGH

When these things begin to come to pass, then look up, and lift up your heads; for your redemption draweth nigh. Luke 21:28.

The coming of Christ is nearer than when we first believed. The great controversy is nearing its end. The judgments of God are in the land. They speak in solemn warning, saying: "Be ye also ready: for in such an hour as ye think not the Son of man cometh." Matthew 24:44. . . .

We are living in the closing scenes of this earth's history. Prophecy is fast fulfilling. The hours of probation are fast passing. We have no time—not a moment—to lose. Let us not be found sleeping on guard. Let no one say in his heart or by his works: "My lord delayeth his coming." Let the message of Christ's soon return sound forth in earnest words of warning. Let us persuade men and women everywhere to repent and flee from the wrath to come. . . .

The Lord is soon to come, and we must be prepared to meet Him in peace. Let us be determined to do all in our power to impart light to those around us. We are not to be sad, but cheerful, and we are to keep the Lord Jesus ever before us. He is soon coming, and we must be ready and waiting for His appearing. Oh, how glorious it will be to see Him and be welcomed as His redeemed ones! Long have we waited, but our hope is not to grow dim. If we can but see the King in His beauty we shall be forever blessed. I feel as if I must cry aloud: "Homeward bound!" We are nearing the time when Christ will come in power and great glory to take His ransomed ones to their eternal home. . . .

Long have we waited for our Saviour's return. But nonetheless sure is the promise. Soon we shall be in our promised home. There Jesus will lead us beside the living stream flowing from the throne of God and will explain to us the dark providences through which on this earth He brought us in order to perfect our characters. There we shall behold with undimmed vision the beauties of Eden restored. Casting at the feet of the Redeemer the crowns that He has placed on our heads, and touching our golden harps, we shall fill all heaven with praise to Him that sitteth on the throne.[82]

HIS REWARD IS WITH HIM

Behold, I come quickly; and my reward is with me, to give every man according as his work shall be. Rev. 22:12.

Our work here is soon to close, and every man will receive his reward according to his own labor. I was shown the saints' reward, the immortal inheritance, and saw that those who had endured the most for the truth's sake will not think they have had a hard time, but will count heaven cheap enough.[83]

Every day bears its burden of record of unfulfilled duties, of neglect, of selfishness, of deception, of fraud, of overreaching. What an amount of evil works is accumulating for the final judgment! When Christ shall come, "His reward is with him, and his work before him," to render to every man according as his works have been. What a revelation will then be made! What confusion of face to some as the acts of their lives are revealed upon the pages of history![84]

Every good and every wrong act, and its influence upon others, is traced out by the Searcher of hearts, to whom every secret is revealed. And the reward will be according to the motives which prompted the action.[85]

The coming of Christ is near and hasteth greatly. The time in which to labor is short, and men and women are perishing. . . .

We need the converting power of God to take hold of us, that we may understand the needs of a perishing world. The burden of my message to you is: Get ready, get ready to meet the Lord. Trim your lamps, and let the light of truth shine forth into the byways and the hedges. There is a world to be warned of the near approach of the end of all things. . . .

Let us seek a new conversion. We need the presence of the Holy Spirit of God with us, that our hearts may be softened and that we may not bring a harsh spirit into the work. I pray that the Holy Spirit may take full possession of our hearts. Let us act like children of God who are looking to Him for counsel, ready to work out His plans wherever presented. God will be glorified by such a people, and those who witness our zeal will say: Amen and amen.[86]

THE CAPTIVITY OF SATAN AND HIS ANGELS

The angels which kept not their first estate, but left their own habitation, he hath reserved in everlasting chains under darkness unto the judgment of the great day. Jude 6.

The earth looked like a desolate wilderness. Cities and villages, shaken down by the earthquake, lay in heaps. Mountains had been moved out of their places, leaving large caverns. Ragged rocks, thrown out by the sea, or torn out of the earth itself, were scattered all over its surface. Large trees had been uprooted and were strewn over the land. Here is to be the home of Satan with his evil angels for a thousand years.

Here he will be confined, to wander up and down over the broken surface of the earth and see the effects of his rebellion against God's law. For a thousand years he can enjoy the fruit of the curse which he has caused. Limited alone to the earth, he will not have the privilege of ranging to other planets, to tempt and annoy those who have not fallen. During this time, Satan suffers extremely. Since his fall his evil traits have been in constant exercise. But he is then to be deprived of his power, and left to reflect upon the part which he has acted since his fall, and to look forward with trembling and terror to the dreadful future, when he must suffer for all the evil that he has done and be punished for all the sins that he has caused to be committed.

I heard shouts of triumph from the angels and from the redeemed saints, which sounded like ten thousand musical instruments, because they were to be no more annoyed and tempted by Satan and because the inhabitants of other worlds were delivered from his presence and his temptations.[1]

To God's people the captivity of Satan will bring gladness and rejoicing. Says the prophet: "It shall come to pass in the day that Jehovah shall give thee rest from thy sorrow, and from thy trouble, and from the hard service wherein thou wast made to serve, that thou shalt take up this parable against the king of Babylon [here representing Satan], and say, How hath the oppressor ceased! . . . Jehovah hath broken the staff of the wicked, the scepter of the rulers; that smote the peoples in wrath with a continual stroke, that ruled the nations in anger, with a persecution that none restrained." Verses 3-6, R.V.[2]

WE SHALL MEET OUR GUARDIAN ANGELS

He shall give his angels charge over thee, to keep thee in all thy ways. Ps. 91:11.

Not until the providences of God are seen in the light of eternity shall we understand what we owe to the care and interposition of His angels. Celestial beings have taken an active part in the affairs of men. They have appeared in garments that shone as the lightning; they have come as men, in the garb of wayfarers. They have accepted the hospitalities of human homes; they have acted as guides to benighted travelers. They have thwarted the spoiler's purpose and turned aside the stroke of the destroyer.

Though the rulers of this world know it not, yet often in their councils angels have been spokesmen. Human eyes have looked upon them. Human ears have listened to their appeals. In the council hall and the court of justice, heavenly messengers have pleaded the cause of the persecuted and oppressed. They have defeated purposes and arrested evils that would have brought wrong and suffering to God's children. To the students in the heavenly school, all this will be unfolded.

Every redeemed one will understand the ministry of angels in his own life. The angel who was his guardian from his earliest moment; the angel who watched his steps, and covered his head in the day of peril; the angel who was with him in the valley of the shadow of death, who marked his resting place, who was the first to greet him in the resurrection morning—what will it be to hold converse with him, and to learn the history of divine interposition in the individual life, of heavenly co-operation in every work for humanity![3]

With the word of God in his hands, every human being, wherever his lot in life may be cast, may have such companionship as he shall choose. In its pages he may hold converse with the noblest and best of the human race, and may listen to the voice of the Eternal as He speaks with men. As he studies and meditates upon the themes into which "the angels desire to look" (1 Peter 1:12), he may have their companionship.[4]

314

WELCOME TO THE CITY OF GOD

His lord said unto him, Well done, good and faithful servant; thou hast been faithful over a few things, I will make thee ruler over many things: enter thou into the joy of thy lord. Matt. 25:23.

With unutterable love, Jesus welcomes His faithful ones to the joy of their Lord. The Saviour's joy is in seeing, in the kingdom of glory, the souls that have been saved by His agony and humiliation. And the redeemed will be sharers in His joy, as they behold, among the blessed, those who have been won to Christ through their prayers, their labors, and their loving sacrifice. As they gather about the great white throne, gladness unspeakable will fill their hearts, when they behold those whom they have won for Christ, and see that one has gained others, and these still others, all brought into the haven of rest, there to lay their crowns at Jesus' feet and praise Him through the endless cycles of eternity.

As the ransomed ones are welcomed to the City of God, there rings out upon the air an exultant cry of adoration. The two Adams are about to meet. The Son of God is standing with outstretched arms to receive the father of our race—the being whom He created, who sinned against his Maker, and for whose sin the marks of the crucifixion are borne upon the Saviour's form. As Adam discerns the prints of the cruel nails, he does not fall upon the bosom of his Lord, but in humiliation casts himself at His feet, crying: "Worthy, worthy is the Lamb that was slain!" Tenderly the Saviour lifts him up and bids him look once more upon the Eden home from which he has so long been exiled.

After his expulsion from Eden, Adam's life on earth was filled with sorrow. Every dying leaf, every victim of sacrifice, every blight upon the fair face of nature, every stain upon man's purity, was a fresh reminder of his sin. . . . With patient humility he bore, for nearly a thousand years, the penalty of transgression. Faithfully did he repent of his sin and trust in the merits of the promised Saviour, and he died in the hope of a resurrection. The Son of God redeemed man's failure and fall; and now, through the work of the atonement, Adam is reinstated in his first dominion.[5]

315

UNSPEAKABLE GLADNESS

Jesus . . . for the joy that was set before him endured the cross, despising the shame, and is seated at the right hand of the throne of God. Heb. 12:2, R.S.V.

"These things have I spoken unto you," said Christ, "that my joy might remain in you, and that your joy might be full." John 15:11.

Ever before Him, Christ saw the result of His mission. His earthly life, so full of toil and self-sacrifice, was cheered by the thought that He would not have all this travail for nought. By giving His life for the life of men, He would restore in humanity the image of God. He would lift us up from the dust, reshape the character after the pattern of His own character, and make it beautiful with His own glory.

Christ saw of the travail of His soul and was satisfied. He viewed the expanse of eternity and saw the happiness of those who through His humiliation should receive pardon and everlasting life. He was wounded for their transgressions, bruised for their iniquities. The chastisement of their peace was upon Him, and with His stripes they were healed. He heard the shout of the redeemed. He heard the ransomed ones singing the song of Moses and the Lamb. Although the baptism of blood must first be received, although the sins of the world were to weigh upon His innocent soul, although the shadow of an unspeakable woe was upon Him; yet for the joy that was set before Him He chose to endure the cross and despised the shame.

This joy all His followers are to share. However great and glorious hereafter, our reward is not all to be reserved for the time of final deliverance. Even here we are by faith to enter into the Saviour's joy.[6]

To those who receive Him, He gives power to become the sons of God, that at last God may receive them as His, to dwell with Him throughout eternity. If, during this life, they are loyal to God, they will at last "see His face; and His name shall be in their foreheads." Revelation 22:4. And what is the happiness of heaven but to see God? What greater joy could come to the sinner saved by the grace of Christ than to look upon the face of God and know Him as Father?[7]

THE GRATITUDE OF THE REDEEMED

The King shall answer and say unto them, Verily I say unto you, Inasmuch as ye have done it unto one of the least of these my brethren, ye have done it unto me. Matt. 25:40.

Every action of ours in befriending God's people will be rewarded as done unto Himself.[8]

What satisfaction will every reaper have, when the clear, musical voice of Jesus shall be heard, saying, "Come, ye blessed of my Father, inherit the kingdom prepared for you from the foundation of the world." "Enter thou into the joy of thy lord."

The Redeemer is glorified because He has not died in vain. With glad, rejoicing hearts, those who have been colaborers with God see of the travail of their soul for perishing, dying sinners, and are satisfied. The anxious hours they have spent, the perplexing circumstances they have had to meet, the sorrow of heart because some refused to see and receive the things which make for their peace, are forgotten. The self-denial they have practiced in order to support the work, is remembered no more. As they look upon the souls they sought to win to Jesus, and see them saved, eternally saved—monuments of God's mercy and of a Redeemer's love—there ring through the arches of heaven shouts of praise and thanksgiving.[9]

There is a heaven before us, and among its inhabitants there will be no strife. . . .

We shall greet the holy family of the redeemed, and hear the words of Christ, "Come, ye blessed of my Father, inherit the kingdom prepared for you from the foundation of the world." We shall touch our golden harps, and heaven will ring with rich music. We shall cast our glittering crowns at His feet, and give glory to Him who has overcome in our behalf.

There may be some things here that we do not understand. Some things in the Bible may appear to us mysterious, because they are beyond our finite comprehension. But as our Saviour leads us by the living waters, He will make clear to our minds that which was not before clearly understood.[10]

HEAVEN IS CHEAP ENOUGH

He shall see his seed, he shall prolong his days, and the pleasure of the Lord shall prosper in his hand. He shall see of the travail of his soul, and shall be satisfied. Isa. 53:10, 11.

The love of God is without measure, without comparison! It is infinite. . . . When we contemplate the dignity and glory of Christ we see how great was that love that prompted the sacrifice made upon the cross of Calvary for the redemption of a lost world. This theme will fill the saints with wonder and amazement through eternal ages, and why should we not meditate upon it here in this world? . . .

O the mystery of godliness—God manifest in the flesh! This mystery increases as we try to comprehend it. It is incomprehensible, and yet human beings will allow worldly, earthly things to intercept the faint view it is possible for mortals to have of Jesus and His matchless love. . . . How can we be enthusiastic over earthly, common things and not be stirred with this picture—the cross of Calvary, the love that is revealed in the death of God's dear Son . . . ?

All this humiliation and anguish were endured to bring back the wanderers, guilty and thankless, to the Father's house. O the home of the blest—I cannot afford to lose it! I shall, if saved in the kingdom of God, be constantly discerning new depths in the plan of salvation. All the redeemed saints will see and appreciate as never before the love of the Father and the Son, and songs of praise will burst forth from immortal tongues. He loved us, He gave His life for us. With glorified bodies, with enlarged capacities, with hearts made pure, with lips undefiled, we shall sing the riches of redeeming love. There will be no suffering ones in heaven, no skeptics whom we must labor to convince of the reality of eternal things, no prejudices to uproot, but all will be susceptible to that love which passeth knowledge. Rest, thank God, there is a rest for the people of God, where Jesus will lead the redeemed into green pastures, by the streams of living waters which make glad the city of our God. Then the prayer of Jesus to His Father will be answered: "I will that they also, whom thou hast given me, be with me where I am." [11]

HOME AT LAST!

Well done, thou good and faithful servant: . . . enter thou into the joy of thy lord. Matt. 25:21.

As your senses delight in the attractive loveliness of the earth, think of the world that is to come, that shall never know the blight of sin and death; where the face of nature will no more wear the shadow of the curse. Let your imagination picture the home of the saved, and remember that it will be more glorious than your brightest imagination can portray. In the varied gifts of God in nature we see but the faintest gleaming of His' glory. It is written, "Eye hath not seen, nor ear heard, neither have entered into the heart of man, the things which God hath prepared for them that love him." 1 Corinthians 2:9.[12]

By and by the gates of heaven will be thrown open to admit God's children, and from the lips of the King of glory the benediction will fall on their ears like richest music, "Come, ye blessed of my Father, inherit the kingdom prepared for you from the foundation of the world." Matthew 25:34.

Then the redeemed will be welcomed to the home that Jesus is preparing for them.[13]

Then I saw Jesus lead the redeemed company to the gate of the city. He laid hold of the gate and swung it back on its glittering hinges and bade the nations that had kept the truth enter in. Within the city there was everything to feast the eye. Rich glory they beheld everywhere. Then Jesus looked upon His redeemed saints; their countenances were radiant with glory; and as He fixed His loving eyes upon them, He said, with His rich, musical voice, "I behold the travail of My soul, and am satisfied. This rich glory is yours to enjoy eternally. Your sorrows are ended. There shall be no more death, neither sorrow nor crying, neither shall there be any more pain." . . .

Language is altogether too feeble to attempt a description of heaven. As the scene rises before me, I am lost in amazement. Carried away with the surpassing splendor and excellent glory, I lay down the pen, and exclaim, "Oh, what love! what wondrous love!" The most exalted language fails to describe the glory of heaven or the matchless depths of a Saviour's love.[14]

SURPRISES WHEN WE GET TO HEAVEN

The Lord seeth not as man seeth; for man looketh on the outward appearance, but the Lord looketh on the heart. 1 Sam. 16:7.

Often we regard as hopeless subjects the very ones whom Christ is drawing to Himself. . . . Many will be in heaven who their neighbors supposed would never enter there. Man judges from appearance, but God judges the heart.[15]

Some among the redeemed will have laid hold of Christ in the last hours of life, and in heaven instruction will be given to these, who, when they died, did not understand perfectly the plan of salvation.[16]

To Jesus in His agony on the cross there came one gleam of comfort. It was the prayer of the penitent thief. . . . In Jesus, bruised, mocked, and hanging upon the cross, he sees the Lamb of God, that taketh away the sin of the world. Hope is mingled with anguish in his voice as the helpless, dying soul casts himself upon a dying Saviour. "Lord, remember me," he cries, "when thou comest into thy kingdom." Quickly the answer came. . . . Verily I say unto thee today, Thou shalt be with Me in paradise.[17]

Such faith may be represented by the eleventh hour laborers who receive as much reward as do those who have labored for many hours. The thief asked in faith, in penitence, in contrition. He asked in earnestness, as if he fully realized that Jesus could save him if He would.[18]

Those whom Christ commends in the judgment may have known little of theology, but they have cherished His principles. . . . Among the heathen are those who worship God ignorantly, those to whom the light is never brought by human instrumentality, yet they will not perish. Though ignorant of the written law of God, they have heard His voice speaking to them in nature, and have done the things that the law required. Their works are evidence that the Holy Spirit has touched their hearts, and they are recognized as the children of God.

How surprised and gladdened will be the lowly among the nations, and among the heathen, to hear from the lips of the Saviour, "Inasmuch as ye have done it unto one of the least of these my brethren, ye have done it unto me"! How glad will be the heart of Infinite Love as His followers look up with surprise and joy at His words of approval! [19]

SATISFYING ANSWERS

As the heavens are higher than the earth, so are my ways higher than your ways, and my thoughts than your thoughts. Isa. 55:9.

Our plans are not always God's plans. . . .

In His loving care and interest for us, often He who understands us better than we understand ourselves refuses to permit us selfishly to seek the gratification of our own ambition. . . . Often our plans fail that God's plans for us may succeed. . . .

In the future life the mysteries that here have annoyed and disappointed us will be made plain. We shall see that our seemingly unanswered prayers and disappointed hopes have been among our greatest blessings.[20]

We are not now sufficiently advanced in spiritual attainments to comprehend the mysteries of God. But when we shall compose the family of heaven, these mysteries will be unfolded before us. . . .

Then much will be revealed in explanation of matters upon which God now keeps silence because we have not gathered up and appreciated that which has been made known of the eternal mysteries. The ways of Providence will be made clear; the mysteries of grace through Christ will be unfolded. That which the mind cannot now grasp, which is hard to be understood, will be explained. We shall see order in that which has seemed unexplainable; wisdom in everything withheld; goodness and gracious mercy in everything imparted. Truth will be unfolded to the mind, free from obscurity, in a single line, and its brightness will be endurable. The heart will be made to sing for joy. Controversies will be forever ended, and all difficulties will be solved.[21]

All that has perplexed us in the providences of God will in the world to come be made plain. The things hard to be understood will then find explanation. The mysteries of grace will unfold before us. Where our finite minds discovered only confusion and broken promises, we shall see the most perfect and beautiful harmony. We shall know that infinite love ordered the experiences that seemed most trying. As we realize the tender care of Him who makes all things work together for our good, we shall rejoice with joy unspeakable and full of glory.[22]

SET YOUR AFFECTIONS ON THINGS ABOVE

Set your affection on things above, not on things on the earth. Col. 3:2.

When God's people take their eyes off the things of this world and place them on heaven and heavenly things they will be a peculiar people, because they will see the mercy and goodness and compassion that God has shown to the children of men. His love will call forth a response from them, and their lives will show to those around them that the Spirit of God is controlling them, that they are setting their affections on things above, not on the things of the earth.

In thinking of heaven, we may put our imagination to the utmost stretch and think the loftiest thoughts that we are capable of thinking, and our minds will grow weary in the effort to comprehend the breadth and depth and height of the subject. It is impossible for our minds to take in the great themes of eternity. It is impossible for us even to make an effort to understand these things without the effort affecting our whole character for good and having an uplifting influence on our minds. As we think of how Christ came to our world to die for fallen man, we understand something of the price that was paid for our redemption, and we realize that there is no true goodness or greatness apart from God.

Only by the light shining from the cross of Calvary can we know to what depths of sin and degradation the human race has fallen through sin. Only by the length of the chain let down from heaven to draw us up can we know the depths to which we had sunk. And it is only by keeping the unseen realities in view that we can understand anything of the wonderful theme of redemption.[23]

We are almost home; we shall soon hear the voice of the Saviour richer than any music, saying, Your warfare is accomplished. Enter into the joy of thy Lord. Blessed, blessed benediction; I want to hear it from His immortal lips. I want to praise Him; I want to honor Him that sitteth on the throne. I want my voice to echo and re-echo through the courts of heaven. Will you be there? . . . God help us, and fill us with all fullness and power, and then we can taste of the joys of the world to come.[24]

THE REWARD OF THE REDEEMED

If any man's work abide . . . , he shall receive a reward. 1 Cor. 3:14.

Glorious will be the reward bestowed when the faithful workers gather about the throne of God and of the Lamb. When John in his mortal state beheld the glory of God, he fell as one dead; he was not able to endure the sight. But when the children of God shall have put on immortality, they will "see him as he is." 1 John 3:2. They will stand before the throne, accepted in the Beloved. All their sins have been blotted out, all their transgressions borne away. Now they can look upon the undimmed glory of the throne of God. They have been partakers with Christ in His sufferings, they have been workers together with Him in the plan of redemption, and they are partakers with Him in the joy of seeing souls saved in the kingdom of God, there to praise God through all eternity.[25]

In that day the redeemed will shine forth in the glory of the Father and the Son. The angels, touching their golden harps, will welcome the King and His trophies of victory. . . . A song of triumph will peal forth, filling all heaven. Christ has conquered. He enters the heavenly courts, accompanied by His redeemed ones, the witnesses that His mission of suffering and sacrifice has not been in vain. . . .

There are homes for the pilgrims of earth. There are robes for the righteous, with crowns of glory and palms of victory. All that has perplexed us in the providences of God will in the world to come be made plain. The things hard to be understood will then find explanation. The mysteries of grace will unfold before us. Where our finite minds discovered only confusion and broken promises, we shall see the most perfect and beautiful harmony. We shall know that infinite love ordered the experiences that seemed most trying. As we realize the tender care of Him who makes all things work together for our good, we shall rejoice with joy unspeakable and full of glory.[26]

I urge you to prepare for the coming of Christ in the clouds of heaven. . . . Prepare for the judgment, that when Christ shall come, to be admired in all them that believe, you may be among those who will meet Him in peace.[27]

EYE HATH NOT SEEN, NOR EAR HEARD

Eye hath not seen, nor ear heard, neither have entered into the heart of man, the things which God hath prepared for them that love him. 1 Cor. 2:9.

Those who truly love God will desire so to improve the talents that He has given them, that they may be a blessing to others. And by and by the gates of heaven will be thrown wide open to admit them, and from the lips of the King of Glory the benediction will fall upon their ear like richest music, "Come, ye blessed of my Father, inherit the kingdom prepared for you from the foundation of the world" (Matt. 25:34). Thus the redeemed will be welcomed to the mansions that Jesus is preparing for them. There their companions will not be the vile of earth, but those who through divine aid have formed perfect characters. Every sinful tendency, every imperfection, has been removed by the blood of Christ; and the excellence and brightness of His glory, far exceeding the brightness of the sun in its meridian splendor, is imparted to them. And the moral beauty, the perfection of His character, shines through them in worth far exceeding this outward splendor. They are without fault before the great white throne, sharing the dignity and privileges of the angels.

"Eye hath not seen, nor ear heard, neither have entered into the heart of man, the things which God hath prepared for them that love him." In view of the glorious inheritance which may be his, "What shall a man give in exchange for his soul?" (Matt. 16:26). He may be poor; yet he possesses in himself a wealth and dignity that the world could never bestow. The soul, redeemed and cleansed from sin, with all its noble powers dedicated to the service of God, is of surpassing worth.[28]

To dwell forever in this home of the blest, to bear in soul, body, and spirit, not the dark traces of sin and the curse, but the perfect likeness of our Creator, and through ceaseless ages to advance in wisdom, in knowledge, and in holiness, ever exploring new fields of thought, ever finding new wonders and new glories, ever increasing in capacity to know and to enjoy and to love, and knowing that there is still beyond us joy and love and wisdom infinite—such is the object to which the Christian's hope is pointing.[29]

LIFE-GIVING FRUIT

In the midst of the street of it, and on either side of the river, was there the tree of life, which bare twelve manner of fruits, and yielded her fruit every month: and the leaves of the tree were for the healing of the nations. Rev. 22:2.

The fruit of the tree of life in the Garden of Eden possessed supernatural virtue. To eat of it was to live forever. Its fruit was the antidote of death. . . .

After the entrance of sin the heavenly Husbandman transplanted the tree of life to the Paradise above.[30]

The redeemed saints, who have loved God and kept His commandments here, will enter in through the gates of the city, and have right to the tree of life. They will eat freely of it as our first parents did before their fall. The leaves of that immortal widespread tree will be for the healing of the nations. All their woes will then be gone. Sickness, sorrow, and death they will never again feel, for the leaves of the tree of life have healed them. Jesus will then see of the travail of His soul and be satisfied, when the redeemed, who have been subject to sorrow, toil, and afflictions, who have groaned beneath the curse, are gathered up around that tree of life to eat of its immortal fruit, that our first parents forfeited all right to, by breaking God's commands. There will be no danger of their ever losing right to the tree of life again, for he that tempted our first parents to sin will be destroyed by the second death.[31]

Obedience to all the commandments of God was the condition of eating of the tree of life. Adam fell by disobedience. . . .

Obedience through Jesus Christ gives to man perfection of character and a right to that tree of life. The conditions of again partaking of the fruit of the tree are plainly stated in the testimony of Jesus Christ to John: "Blessed are they that do his commandments, that they may have right to the tree of life, and may enter in through the gates into the city." [32]

Restored to the tree of life in the long-lost Eden, the redeemed will "grow up" to the full stature of the race in its primeval glory. The last lingering traces of the curse of sin will be removed, and Christ's faithful ones will appear in "the beauty of the Lord our God," in mind and soul and body reflecting the perfect image of their Lord. Oh, wonderful redemption! long talked of, long hoped for, contemplated with eager anticipation, but never fully understood.[33]

THE BOW-CIRCLED THRONE

Behold, a throne was set in heaven, and one sat on the throne. And he that sat was to look upon like a jasper and a sardine stone: and there was a rainbow round about the throne, in sight like unto an emerald. Rev. 4:2, 3.

In the rainbow above the throne is an everlasting testimony that "God so loved the world, that he gave his only begotten Son, that whosoever believeth in him should not perish, but have everlasting life." . . .

As the bow in the cloud is formed by the union of the sunlight and the shower, so the rainbow encircling the throne represents the combined power of mercy and justice. It is not justice alone that is to be maintained; for this would eclipse the glory of the rainbow of promise above the throne; men could see only the penalty of the law. Were there no justice, no penalty, there would be no stability to the government of God. It is the mingling of judgment and mercy that makes salvation complete. . . .

Mercy invites us to enter through the gates into the city of God, and justice is satisfied to accord to every obedient soul full privileges as a member of the royal family, a child of the heavenly King. If we were defective in character, we could not pass the gates that mercy has opened to the obedient; for justice stands at the entrance, and demands holiness in all who would see God.

Were justice extinct, and were it possible for divine mercy to open the gates to the whole race, irrespective of character, there would be a worse condition of disaffection and rebellion in heaven than before Satan was expelled. The peace, happiness, and harmony of heaven would be broken. The change from earth to heaven will not change men's character; the happiness of the redeemed in heaven results from the character formed in this life after the image of Christ. The saints in heaven will first have been saints on earth.

The salvation that Christ made such a sacrifice to gain for man is that which is alone of value; for it is that which saves from sin. . . . Thus the law of God is not weakened by the gospel, but the power of sin is broken, and the scepter of mercy is extended to the penitent sinner. . . . God will never forget His people in their struggle against evil. Let Jesus be our theme.[34]

WE SHALL SEE THE KING

Thine eyes shall see the king in his beauty: they shall behold the land that is very far off. Isa. 33:17.

If we desire to see the King in His beauty we must here behave worthily. We must outgrow our childishness. When provocation comes let us be silent. There are times when silence is eloquence. We are to reveal the patience and kindness and forbearance that will make us worthy of being called sons and daughters of God. We are to trust Him, and believe on Him, and rely upon Him. We are to follow in Christ's steps. "If any man will come after me," He says, "let him deny himself, and take up his cross daily, and follow me" (Luke 9:23). . . . It may be a heavy cross to keep silent when you ought to. It may be a painful discipline, but let me assure you that silence does much more to overcome evil than a storm of angry words.

Here in this world we are to learn what we must be in order to have a place in the heavenly courts. We are to learn the lessons that Christ desires to teach us, that we may be prepared to be taken to the higher school in the courts above, where the Saviour will lead us beside the river of life, explaining to us many things that here we could not comprehend. . . . There we shall see the glory of God as we have never seen it here. We get but a glimpse of the glory now, because we do not follow on to know the Lord.[35]

Every right principle, every truth learned in an earthly school, will advance us just that much in the heavenly school. As Christ walked and talked with His disciples during His ministry on this earth, so will He teach us in the school above, leading us beside the river of living waters, and revealing to us truths that in this life must remain hidden mysteries because of the limitations of the human mind, so marred by sin. In the heavenly school we shall have opportunity to attain, step by step, to the greatest heights of learning. There, as children of the heavenly King, we shall ever dwell with the members of the royal family; there we shall see the King in His beauty, and behold His matchless charms.[36]

Long have we waited, but our hope is not to grow dim. If we can but see the King in His beauty we shall be forever blessed.[37]

327

THE ONE HUNDRED FORTY-FOUR THOUSAND

I looked, and, lo, a Lamb stood on the mount Sion, and with him an hundred forty and four thousand, having his Father's name written in their foreheads. Rev. 14:1.

Upon the crystal sea before the throne, that sea of glass as it were mingled with fire—so resplendent is it with the glory of God—are gathered the company that have "gotten the victory over the beast, and over his image, and over his mark, and over the number of his name." With the Lamb upon Mount Zion, "having the harps of God," they stand, the hundred and forty and four thousand that were redeemed from among men; and there is heard, as the sound of many waters, and as the sound of a great thunder, "the voice of harpers harping with their harps." And they sing "a new song" before the throne, a song which no man can learn save the hundred and forty and four thousand. It is the song of Moses and the Lamb—a song of deliverance.

None but the hundred and forty-four thousand can learn that song; for it is the song of their experience—an experience such as no other company have ever had. "These are they which follow the Lamb whithersoever he goeth." These, having been translated from the earth, from among the living, are counted as "the firstfruits unto God and to the Lamb." Revelation 15:2, 3; 14:1-5. "These are they which came out of great tribulation;" they have passed through the time of trouble such as never was since there was a nation; they have endured the anguish of the time of Jacob's trouble; they have stood without an intercessor through the final outpouring of God's judgments. But they have been delivered, for they have "washed their robes, and made them white in the blood of the Lamb." "In their mouth was found no guile: for they are without fault" before God. "Therefore are they before the throne of God, and serve him day and night in his temple: and he that sitteth on the throne shall dwell among them."

They have seen the earth wasted with famine and pestilence, the sun having power to scorch men with great heat, and they themselves have endured suffering, hunger, and thirst. But "they shall hunger no more, neither thirst any more; neither shall the sun light on them, nor any heat." Revelation 7:14-16.[38]

328

THE GREAT MULTITUDE OF THE REDEEMED

After this I beheld, and, lo, a great multitude, which no man could number, of all nations, and kindreds, and people, and tongues, stood before the throne, and before the Lamb, clothed with white robes, and palms in their hands. Rev. 7:9.

All classes, all nations and kindreds and people and tongues will stand before the throne of God and the Lamb with their spotless robes and jeweled crowns. Said the angel, These are they that have come up through great tribulation and have washed their robes and made them white, while the lovers of pleasure more than lovers of God, the self-indulgent and disobedient, have lost both worlds. They have neither the things of this life nor the immortal life.

That triumphant throng, with songs of victory and with crowns and harps, have trodden in the fiery furnace of earthly affliction when it was heated and intensely hot. From destitution, from hunger and torture, they come, from deep self-denial and bitter disappointments. Look upon them now as conquerors, no longer poor, no longer in sorrow, in affliction and hated of all men for Christ's sake. Behold their heavenly garments, white and shining, richer than any kingly robe. Look by faith upon their jeweled crowns; never did such a diadem deck the brow of any earthly monarch.

Listen to their voices as they sing loud hosannas and as they wave the palm branches of victory. Rich music fills heaven as their voices sing forth these words: "Worthy, worthy is the Lamb that was slain and rose again forevermore. Salvation unto our God which sitteth upon the throne, and unto the Lamb." And the angelic host, angels and archangels, covering cherub and glorious seraph, echo back the refrain of that joyous, triumphant song saying, "Amen: Blessing, and glory, and wisdom, and thanksgiving, and honour, and power, and might, be unto our God for ever and ever" (Rev. 7:12).

Oh, in that day it will be discovered that the righteous were the wise ones, while the sinful and disobedient were fools. . . . Shame and everlasting contempt is their portion. Those who have been colaborers for Christ will then be near the throne of God, girt with purity and the garments of eternal righteousness.[39]

THE SOUL WINNER'S REWARD

They that be wise shall shine as the brightness of the firmament; and they that turn many to righteousness as the stars for ever and ever. Dan. 12:3.

When I think of those words of Daniel, I find myself waking up in the night and repeating them over and over: "And they that be wise shall shine as the brightness of the firmament; and they that turn many to righteousness as the stars for ever and ever." Look at the sun and the stars marshaled in the heavens, and known by their names. The Lord says, They that turn many to righteousness shall shine as the stars forever and ever.[40]

In order to determine how important are the interests involved in the conversion of the soul from error to truth, we must appreciate the value of immortality; we must realize how terrible are the pains of the second death; we must comprehend the honor and glory awaiting the ransomed, and understand what it is to live in the presence of Him who died that He might elevate and ennoble man, and give to the overcomer a royal diadem.

The worth of a soul cannot be fully estimated by finite minds. How gratefully will the ransomed and glorified ones remember those who were instrumental in their salvation! No one will then regret his self-denying efforts and persevering labors, his patience, forbearance, and earnest heart yearnings for souls that might have been lost had he neglected his duty or become weary in well-doing.

Now these white-robed ones are gathered into the fold of the Great Shepherd. The faithful worker and the soul saved through his labor are greeted by the Lamb in the midst of the throne, and are led to the tree of life and to the fountain of living waters. With what joy does the servant of Christ behold these redeemed ones, who are made to share the glory of the Redeemer! How much more precious is heaven to those who have been faithful in the work of saving souls! "And they that be wise shall shine as the brightness of the firmament; and they that turn many to righteousness as the stars." [41]

What is done through the cooperation of men with God is a work that shall never perish, but endure through the eternal ages.[42]

THINK ON HEAVENLY THINGS

These are they which came out of great tribulation, and have washed their robes, and made them white in the blood of the Lamb. Rev. 7:14.

John, while in vision, saw a company clothed in white robes. . . . They were seen in the temple of God. This will be the result for all who will lay hold of the merits of Christ and wash their robes in His blood. Every provision has been made so that we can sit with Christ upon His throne, but the condition is that we be in harmony with the law of God. . . .

We cannot afford to lose heaven. We ought to have our conversation on heavenly things. There there is no death nor pain. Why are we so reluctant to talk of these things? Why do we dwell upon earthly things? The apostle exhorts us to have our conversation in heaven. "For our conversation is in heaven; from whence also we look for the Saviour, the Lord Jesus Christ" (Phil. 3:20). . . . Christ will soon return to gather those who are prepared, and take them to this glorious place. "So Christ was once offered to bear the sins of many; and unto them that look for him shall he appear the second time without sin unto salvation" (Heb. 9:28).

Do we love to think of this event or do we want to put it off? . . . The more we talk of Jesus, the more we shall reflect His divine image. By beholding we become transformed. We need to bring Christ into our religious experience. When you assemble together, let the conversation be on Christ and His salvation. . . . The more we talk of Jesus the more of His matchless charms we shall behold.[43]

Those who take no pleasure in thinking and talking of God in this life, will not enjoy the life that is to come, where God is ever present, dwelling among His people. But those who love to think of God will be in their element, breathing in the atmosphere of heaven. Those who on earth love the thought of heaven will be happy in its holy associations and pleasures. . . . "And there shall be no more curse: but the throne of God and of the Lamb shall be in it; and his servants shall serve him: and they shall see his face; and his name shall be in their foreheads" (Rev. 22:3, 4).[44]

THE GLORIES OF THE HEAVENLY WORLD

Since the beginning of the world men have not heard, nor perceived by the ear, neither hath the eye seen, O God, beside thee, what he hath prepared for him that waiteth for him. Isa. 64:4.

Many have longed to penetrate into the glories of the future world and to have the secrets of eternal mysteries disclosed to them, but they knock in vain. That which is revealed is for us and for our children. . . . The Great Revealer hath opened to our intelligence many things that are essential in order that we may understand the heavenly attractions and have respect to the recompense of the reward. . . .

The unfoldings of Jesus in reference to heavenly things are of a character that only the spiritual mind can appreciate. The imagination may summon its utmost powers in order to picture the glories of heaven, but "eye hath not seen, nor ear heard, neither have entered into the heart of man, the things which God hath prepared for them that love him" (1 Cor. 2:9). The heavenly intelligences are all around us. . . . Angels of light create a heavenly atmosphere about the soul, lifting us toward the unseen and eternal. We cannot behold their forms with our natural sight; only by the spiritual vision can we discern heavenly things. Our human powers would be extinguished by the inexpressible glory of the angels of light. The spiritual ear alone can distinguish the harmony of heavenly voices. It is not Christ's plan to excite the emotions by brilliant descriptions. . . . He has with sufficient distinctness presented Himself, the way, the truth, and the life, as the only means whereby salvation is to be obtained. No more than this is really required.

He might bring the human soul to the threshold of heaven, and through the open door show us its inner glory flooding the heavenly sanctuary and shining out through its portals; but we must behold it by faith, not with the natural eyes. He does not forget that we are His human agents, to work the works of God in a world all seared and marred with the curse. It is in this world, that is clothed with moral darkness like the pall of death, where darkness covers the earth and gross darkness the people, that we are to walk in the light of heaven.[45]

LOOK AT THINGS ETERNAL

We look not at the things which are seen, but at the things which are not seen: for the things which are seen are temporal; but the things which are not seen are eternal. 2 Cor. 4:18.

If the church will put on the robe of Christ's righteousness, withdrawing from all allegiance with the world, there is before her the dawn of a bright and glorious day. God's promise to her will stand fast forever. . . . Truth, passing by those who despise and reject it, will triumph. Although at times apparently retarded, its progress has never been checked. . . . Endowed with divine energy, it will cut its way through the strongest barriers and triumph over every obstacle.

What sustained the Son of God during His life of toil and sacrifice? He saw the results of the travail of His soul and was satisfied. Looking into eternity, He beheld the happiness of those who through His humiliation had received pardon and everlasting life. His ear caught the shout of the redeemed. He heard the ransomed ones singing the song of Moses and the Lamb.

We may have a vision of the future, the blessedness of heaven. In the Bible are revealed visions of the future glory, scenes pictured by the hand of God, and these are dear to His church. By faith we may stand on the threshold of the eternal city, and hear the gracious welcome given to those who in this life co-operate with Christ, regarding it as an honor to suffer for His sake. As the words are spoken, "Come, ye blessed of my Father," they cast their crowns at the feet of the Redeemer, exclaiming, "Worthy is the Lamb that was slain to receive power, and riches, and wisdom, and strength, and honour, and glory, and blessing. . . . Honour, and glory, and power, be unto him that sitteth upon the throne, and unto the Lamb for ever and ever." Matthew 25:34; Revelation 5:12, 13.

There the redeemed greet those who led them to the Saviour, and all unite in praising Him who died that human beings might have the life that measures with the life of God. The conflict is over. Tribulation and strife are at an end. Songs of victory fill all heaven as the ransomed ones take up the joyful strain, Worthy, worthy is the Lamb that was slain, and lives again, a triumphant conqueror.[46]

333

BLESSED ARE THEY THAT WASH THEIR ROBES

Blessed are they that wash their robes, that they may have the right to come to the tree of life, and may enter in by the gates into the city. Rev. 22:14, R.V.

Do we expect to get to heaven at last and join the heavenly choir? Just as we go into the grave we will come up, as far as the character is concerned. . . . Now is the time for washing and ironing. . . .

John saw the throne of God and around that throne a company, and he inquired, Who are these? The answer came, "These are they which . . . have washed their robes, and made them white in the blood of the Lamb" (Rev. 7:14). Christ leads them to the fountains of living waters, and there is the tree of life and there is the precious Saviour. Here is presented to us a life that measures with the life of God. There is no pain, sorrow, sickness, or death there. All is peace and harmony and love. . . .

Now is the time to receive grace and strength and power to combine with our human efforts that we can form characters for everlasting life. When we do this we will find that the angels of God will minister unto us, and we shall be heirs of God and joint heirs with Jesus Christ. And when the last trump shall sound, and the dead shall be called from their prison house and changed in a moment, in the twinkling of an eye, the crowns of immortal glory shall be placed upon the heads of the overcomers. The pearly gates will swing back for the nations that have kept the truth and they will enter in. The conflict is ended.

"Come, ye blessed of my Father, inherit the kingdom prepared for you from the foundation of the world" (Matt. 25:34). Do we want this benediction? I do, and I believe you do. May God help you that you may fight the battles of this life and gain a victory day by day and at last be among the number that shall cast their crowns at Jesus' feet and touch the golden harps and fill all heaven with sweetest music. I want you to love my Jesus. . . . Do not reject my Saviour, for He has paid an infinite price for you. I see in Jesus matchless charms, and I want you to see these charms.[47]

THE MILLENNIAL JUDGMENT

Know ye not that we shall judge angels? how much more things that pertain to this life? 1 Cor. 6:3.

During the thousand years between the first and the second resurrection the judgment of the wicked takes place. The apostle Paul points to this judgment as an event that follows the second advent. "Judge nothing before the time, until the Lord come, who both will bring to light the hidden things of darkness, and will make manifest the counsels of the hearts." 1 Corinthians 4:5. Daniel declares that when the Ancient of Days came, "judgment was given to the saints of the most High." Daniel 7:22. At this time the righteous reign as kings and priests unto God. John in the Revelation says: "I saw thrones, and they sat upon them, and judgment was given unto them." "They shall be priests of God and of Christ, and shall reign with him a thousand years." Revelation 20:4, 6. It is at this time that, as foretold by Paul, "the saints shall judge the world." 1 Corinthians 6:2. In union with Christ they judge the wicked, comparing their acts with the statute book, the Bible, and deciding every case according to the deeds done in the body. Then the portion which the wicked must suffer is meted out, according to their works; and it is recorded against their names in the book of death.

Satan also and evil angels are judged by Christ and His people. Says Paul: "Know ye not that we shall judge angels?" Verse 3. And Jude declares that "the angels which kept not their first estate, but left their own habitation, he hath reserved in everlasting chains under darkness unto the judgment of the great day." Jude 6.

At the close of the thousand years the second resurrection will take place. Then the wicked will be raised from the dead and appear before God for the execution of "the judgment written." Thus the revelator, after describing the resurrection of the righteous, says: "The rest of the dead lived not again until the thousand years were finished." Revelation 20:5. And Isaiah declares, concerning the wicked: "They shall be gathered together, as prisoners are gathered in the pit, and shall be shut up in the prison, and *after many days shall they be visited.*" Isaiah 24:22.[48]

335

CHRIST AGAIN RETURNS TO THE EARTH

Enoch also, the seventh from Adam, prophesied of these, saying, Behold, the Lord cometh with ten thousands of his saints, to execute judgment upon all. Jude 14, 15.

At the close of the thousand years, Christ again returns to the earth. He is accompanied by the host of the redeemed and attended by a retinue of angels. As He descends in terrific majesty He bids the wicked dead arise to receive their doom. They come forth, a mighty host, numberless as the sands of the sea. What a contrast to those who were raised at the first resurrection! The righteous were clothed with immortal youth and beauty. The wicked bear the traces of disease and death.

Every eye in that vast multitude is turned to behold the glory of the Son of God. With one voice, the wicked hosts exclaim: "Blessed is he that cometh in the name of the Lord!" It is not love to Jesus that inspires this utterance. The force of truth urges the words from unwilling lips. As the wicked went into their graves, so they come forth with the same enmity to Christ and the same spirit of rebellion. They are to have no new probation in which to remedy the defects of their past lives. Nothing would be gained by this. A lifetime of transgression has not softened their hearts. A second probation, were it given them, would be occupied as was the first in evading the requirements of God and exciting rebellion against Him.

Christ descends upon the Mount of Olives, whence, after His resurrection, He ascended, and where angels repeated the promise of His return. Says the prophet: "The Lord my God shall come, and all the saints with thee." "And his feet shall stand in that day upon the mount of Olives, which is before Jerusalem on the east, and the mount of Olives shall cleave in the midst thereof, . . . and there shall be a very great valley." "And the Lord shall be king over all the earth: in that day shall there be one Lord, and his name one." Zechariah 14:5, 4, 9. As the New Jerusalem, in its dazzling splendor, comes down out of heaven, it rests upon the place purified and made ready to receive it, and Christ, with His people and the angels, enters the Holy City.[49]

SATAN LOOSED FROM HIS PRISON

When the thousand years are expired, Satan shall be loosed out of his prison, and shall go out to deceive the nations which are in the four quarters of the earth. Rev. 20:7, 8.

At the close of the thousand years the second resurrection will take place. Then the wicked will be raised from the dead and appear before God for the execution of "the judgment written." Thus the revelator, after describing the resurrection of the righteous, says: "The rest of the dead lived not again until the thousand years were finished." Revelation 20:5. And Isaiah declares, concerning the wicked: "They shall be gathered together, as prisoners are gathered in the pit, and shall be shut up in the prison, and *after many days shall they be visited."* Isaiah 24:22.[50]

Now Satan prepares for a last mighty struggle for the supremacy. While deprived of his power and cut off from his work of deception, the prince of evil was miserable and dejected; but as the wicked dead are raised and he sees the vast multitudes upon his side, his hopes revive, and he determines not to yield the great controversy. He will marshal all the armies of the lost under his banner and through them endeavor to execute his plans. The wicked are Satan's captives. In rejecting Christ they have accepted the rule of the rebel leader. They are ready to receive his suggestions and to do his bidding. Yet, true to his early cunning, he does not acknowledge himself to be Satan. He claims to be the prince who is the rightful owner of the world and whose inheritance has been unlawfully wrested from him. He represents himself to his deluded subjects as a redeemer, assuring them that his power has brought them forth from their graves and that he is about to rescue them from the most cruel tyranny. The presence of Christ having been removed, Satan works wonders to support his claims. He makes the weak strong and inspires all with his own spirit and energy. He proposes to lead them against the camp of the saints and to take possession of the City of God. With fiendish exultation he points to the unnumbered millions who have been raised from the dead and declares that as their leader he is well able to overthrow the city and regain his throne and his kingdom.[51]

THE WICKED PREPARE TO ATTACK THE NEW JERUSALEM

Satan . . . shall go out to deceive the nations . . . to gather them together to battle. Rev. 20:7, 8.

In that vast throng are multitudes of the long-lived race that existed before the Flood; men of lofty stature and giant intellect, who, yielding to the control of fallen angels, devoted all their skill and knowledge to the exaltation of themselves; men whose wonderful works of art led the world to idolize their genius, but whose cruelty and evil inventions, defiling the earth and defacing the image of God, caused Him to blot them from the face of His creation. There are kings and generals who conquered nations, valiant men who never lost a battle, proud, ambitious warriors whose approach made kingdoms tremble. In death these experienced no change. As they come up from the grave, they resume the current of their thoughts just where it ceased. They are actuated by the same desire to conquer that ruled them when they fell.

Satan consults with his angels, and then with these kings and conquerors and mighty men. They look upon the strength and numbers on their side, and declare that the army within the city is small in comparison with theirs, and that it can be overcome. They lay their plans to take possession of the riches and glory of the New Jerusalem. All immediately begin to prepare for battle. Skillful artisans construct implements of war. Military leaders, famed for their success, marshal the throngs of warlike men into companies and divisions.

At last the order to advance is given, and the countless host moves on—an army such as was never summoned by earthly conquerors, such as the combined forces of all ages since war began on earth could never equal. Satan, the mightiest of warriors, leads the van, and his angels unite their forces for this final struggle. Kings and warriors are in his train, and the multitudes follow in vast companies, each under its appointed leader. With military precision the serried ranks advance over the earth's broken and uneven surface to the City of God. By command of Jesus, the gates of the New Jerusalem are closed, and the armies of Satan surround the city and make ready for the onset.[52]

THE LAST JUDGMENT

I saw the dead, small and great, stand before God; and the books were opened: . . . and the dead were judged out of those things which were written in the books, according to their works. Rev. 20:12.

Now Christ again appears to the view of His enemies. Far above the city, upon a foundation of burnished gold, is a throne, high and lifted up. Upon this throne sits the Son of God, and around Him are the subjects of His kingdom. The power and majesty of Christ no language can describe, no pen portray. The glory of the Eternal Father is enshrouding His Son. The brightness of His presence fills the City of God, and flows out beyond the gates, flooding the whole earth with its radiance.

Nearest the throne are those who were once zealous in the cause of Satan, but who, plucked as brands from the burning, have followed their Saviour with deep, intense devotion. Next are those who perfected Christian characters in the midst of falsehood and infidelity, those who honored the law of God when the Christian world declared it void, and the millions, of all ages, who were martyred for their faith. And beyond is the "great multitude, which no man could number, of all nations, and kindreds, and people, and tongues, . . . before the throne, and before the Lamb, clothed with white robes, and palms in their hands." Revelation 7:9. . . .

The redeemed raise a song of praise that echoes and re-echoes through the vaults of heaven: "Salvation to our God which sitteth upon the throne, and unto the Lamb." Verse 10. And angel and seraph unite their voices in adoration. . . .

In the presence of the assembled inhabitants of earth and heaven the final coronation of the Son of God takes place. And now, invested with supreme majesty and power, the King of kings pronounces sentence upon the rebels against His government and executes justice upon those who have transgressed His law and oppressed His people. . . .

As soon as the books of record are opened, and the eye of Jesus looks upon the wicked, they are conscious of every sin which they have ever committed.[53]

EVERY WORK WILL BE BROUGHT INTO JUDGMENT

God shall bring every work into judgment, with every secret thing, whether it be good, or whether it be evil. Eccl. 12:14.

In the case of each individual there is a process going forward which is far more wonderful than that which transfers the features to the polished plate of the artist. The art of the photographer merely imprints the likeness on perishable substance; but in the life-record the character is faithfully delineated, and this record, however dark, can never be effaced except by the blood of the atoning Sacrifice.[54]

Angels of God are taking a daguerreotype of the character just as accurately as the artist takes the likeness of the human features; and . . . it is from this that we are to be judged![55]

When the Judgment shall sit, and the books shall be opened, there will be many astonishing disclosures. Men will not then appear as they appear to the human eyes and finite judgments. Secret sins will then be laid open to the view of all. Motives and intentions which have been hidden in the dark chambers of the heart will be revealed.[56]

All will appear as a real life-picture.[57]

In that solemn and awful hour the unfaithfulness of the husband will be opened to the wife, and the unfaithfulness of the wife, to the husband. Parents will then learn, for the first time, what was the real character of their children, and children will see the errors and mistakes that marked the lives of their parents. The man who robbed his neighbor through false representations, is not to escape with his ill-gotten gains. God has an exact record in His books, of every unjust account and every unfair dealing.[58]

Memory will be true and vivid in condemnation of the guilty one, who in that day is found wanting. The mind will recall all the thoughts and acts of the past; the whole life will come in review like the scenes in a panorama.[59]

CHRIST IS JUDGE

The Father judgeth no man, but hath committed all judgment unto the Son. John 5:22.

In His teachings, Christ sought to impress men with the certainty of the coming judgment, and with its publicity. This is not the judgment of a few individuals, or even of a nation, but of a whole world of human intelligences, of accountable beings. It is to be held in the presence of other worlds, that the love, the integrity, the service, of man for God, may be honored to the highest degree. There will be no lack of glory and honor. . . . The law of God will be revealed in its majesty; and those who have stood in defiant rebellion against its holy precepts will understand that the law that they have discarded, and despised, and trampled underfoot is God's standard of character. . . .

In this speck of a world, the heavenly universe manifests the greatest interest; for Jesus paid an infinite price for the souls of its inhabitants. . . .

God has committed all judgment unto the Son, for without controversy He is God manifest in the flesh.

God designed that the Prince of sufferers in humanity should be judge of the whole world. He who came from the heavenly courts to save man from eternal death; . . . He who submitted to be arraigned before an earthly tribunal, and who suffered the ignominious death of the cross—He alone is to pronounce the sentence of reward or of punishment. He who submitted to the suffering and humiliation of the cross here, in the counsel of God is to have the fullest compensation, and ascend the throne acknowledged by all the heavenly universe as the King of saints. He has undertaken the work of salvation, and shown before unfallen worlds and the heavenly family that the work He has begun He is able to complete. . . .

In the day of final punishment and reward, both saints and sinners will recognize in Him who was crucified the Judge of all living. . . . Solemn will be the day of final decision. . . . Probationary time is granted us, opportunities and privileges are given us, to make our calling and election sure. How we should prize this precious time, and improve every talent God has given, that we may be faithful stewards over ourselves.[60]

REWARDS AND PUNISHMENTS

Then shall the King say unto them on his right hand, Come, ye blessed of my Father, inherit the kingdom prepared for you from the foundation of the world. Matt. 25:34.

The Saviour presents before us the scene of the last judgment when the reward is given to those upon His right hand, and the sentence of condemnation to those upon His left hand. The righteous are represented as wondering what they have done for which they are to be so liberally rewarded. They had had the abiding presence of Christ in their hearts; they had been imbued with His Spirit, and without conscious effort on their part; they had been serving Christ in the person of His saints, and had thereby gained the sure reward. But they had not had in view the reward they were to receive, and the expectation of it had been no part of the motive that had actuated their service. What they did was done from love to Christ and to their fellow-men, and Christ identifies Himself with suffering humanity, and accounts that all deeds done in sympathy and compassion and love to men, are done to Him. . . .

In a subordinate sense we should all have respect unto the recompense of the reward. But while we appreciate the promise of blessing, we should have perfect confidence in Jesus Christ, believing that He will do right, and give us reward according as our works have been. The gift of God is eternal life, but Jesus would have us not so anxious concerning rewards, as that we may do the will of God because it is right to do it, irrespective of all gain. . . .

Those who will receive the most abundant reward will be those who have mingled with their activity and zeal, gracious, tender pity for the poor, the orphan, the oppressed, and the afflicted. . . . There are about us those who have a meek and lowly spirit, the spirit of Christ, who do many little things to help those around them, and who think nothing of it; they will be astonished at last to find that Christ has noticed the kind word spoken to the disheartened, and taken account of the smallest gift given for the relief of the poor, that cost the giver some self-denial. The Lord measures the spirit, and rewards accordingly, and the pure, humble, childlike spirit of love makes the offering precious in His sight.[61]

THE PANORAMIC SCENE ABOVE THE HOLY CITY

We must all appear before the judgment seat of Christ; that every one may receive the things done in his body, according to that he hath done, whether it be good or bad. 2 Cor. 5:10.

Above the throne is revealed the cross; and like a panoramic view appear the scenes of Adam's temptation and fall, and the successive steps in the great plan of redemption. The Saviour's lowly birth; His early life of simplicity and obedience; His baptism in Jordan; the fast and temptation in the wilderness; His public ministry, unfolding to men heaven's most precious blessings; the days crowded with deeds of love and mercy, the nights of prayer and watching in the solitude of the mountains; the plottings of envy, hate, and malice which repaid His benefits; the awful, mysterious agony in Gethsemane beneath the crushing weight of the sins of the whole world; His betrayal into the hands of the murderous mob; the fearful events of that night of horror—the unresisting prisoner, forsaken by His best-loved disciples, rudely hurried through the streets of Jerusalem; the Son of God exultingly displayed before Annas, arraigned in the high priest's palace, in the judgment hall of Pilate, before the cowardly and cruel Herod, mocked, insulted, tortured, and condemned to die—all are vividly portrayed.

And now before the swaying multitude are revealed the final scenes—the patient Sufferer treading the path to Calvary; the Prince of heaven hanging upon the cross; the haughty priests and the jeering rabble deriding His expiring agony; the supernatural darkness; the heaving earth, the rent rocks, the open graves, marking the moment when the world's Redeemer yielded up His life.

The awful spectacle appears just as it was. Satan, his angels, and his subjects have no power to turn from the picture of their own work. Each actor recalls the part which he performed. . . . All behold the enormity of their guilt. They vainly seek to hide from the divine majesty of His countenance, outshining the glory of the sun, while the redeemed cast their crowns at the Saviour's feet, exclaiming: "He died for me!" [1]

343

HISTORICAL PERSONS PRESENT AT THE JUDGMENT

I have sworn by myself, . . . That unto me every knee shall bow, every tongue shall swear. Surely, shall one say, in the Lord have I righteousness and strength: even to him shall men come; and all that are incensed against him shall be ashamed. Isa. 45:23, 24.

Amid the ransomed throng are the apostles of Christ, the heroic Paul, the ardent Peter, the loved and loving John, and their truehearted brethren, and with them the vast host of martyrs; while outside the walls, with every vile and abominable thing, are those by whom they were persecuted, imprisoned, and slain. There is Nero, that monster of cruelty and vice, beholding the joy and exaltation of those whom he once tortured, and in whose extremest anguish he found satanic delight. His mother is there to witness the result of her own work; to see how the evil stamp of character transmitted to her son, the passions encouraged and developed by her influence and example, have borne fruit in crimes that caused the world to shudder.[2]

There . . . [is] the proud, ambitious Napoleon, whose approach had caused kingdoms to tremble.[3]

There are papist priests and prelates, who claimed to be Christ's ambassadors, yet employed the rack, the dungeon, and the stake to control the consciences of His people. There are the proud pontiffs who exalted themselves above God and presumed to change the law of the Most High. Those pretended fathers of the church have an account to render to God from which they would fain be excused. Too late they are made to see that the Omniscient One is jealous of His law and that He will in no wise clear the guilty. They learn now that Christ identifies His interest with that of His suffering people; and they feel the force of His own words: "Inasmuch as ye have done it unto one of the least of these my brethren, ye have done it unto me." Matthew 25:40.

The whole wicked world stand arraigned at the bar of God on the charge of high treason against the government of heaven. They have none to plead their cause; they are without excuse; and the sentence of eternal death is pronounced against them.[4]

THE WICKED ACKNOWLEDGE GOD'S JUSTICE

We shall all stand before the judgment seat of Christ. For it is written, As I live, saith the Lord, every knee shall bow to me, and every tongue shall confess to God. Rom. 14:10, 11.

As if entranced, the wicked have looked upon the coronation of the Son of God. They see in His hands the tables of the divine law, the statutes which they have despised and transgressed. They witness the outburst of wonder, rapture, and adoration from the saved; and as the wave of melody sweeps over the multitudes without the city, all with one voice exclaim, "Great and marvellous are thy works, Lord God Almighty; just and true are thy ways, thou King of saints" (Revelation 15:3); and, falling prostrate, they worship the Prince of life.

Satan seems paralyzed as he beholds the glory and majesty of Christ. He who was once a covering cherub remembers whence he has fallen. A shining seraph, "son of the morning;" how changed, how degraded! From the council where once he was honored, he is forever excluded. He sees another now standing near to the Father, veiling His glory. He has seen the crown placed upon the head of Christ by an angel of lofty stature and majestic presence, and he knows that the exalted position of this angel might have been his.

Memory recalls the home of his innocence and purity. . . . As Satan looks upon his kingdom, the fruit of his toil, he sees only failure and ruin. . . .

The time has now come when the rebellion is to be finally defeated and the history and character of Satan disclosed. In his last great effort to dethrone Christ, destroy His people, and take possession of the City of God, the archdeceiver has been fully unmasked. Those who have united with him see the total failure of his cause. . . . He is the object of universal abhorrence.

Satan sees that his voluntary rebellion has unfitted him for heaven. He has trained his powers to war against God; the purity, peace, and harmony of heaven would be to him supreme torture. His accusations against the mercy and justice of God are now silenced. The reproach which he has endeavored to cast upon Jehovah rests wholly upon himself. And now Satan bows down and confesses the justice of his sentence.[5]

345

GOD'S CHARACTER VINDICATED

Great and marvellous are thy works, Lord God Almighty; just and true are thy ways, thou King of saints. Rev. 15:3.

Every question of truth and error in the long-standing controversy has now been made plain. The results of rebellion, the fruits of setting aside the divine statutes, have been laid open to the view of all created intelligences. The working out of Satan's rule in contrast with the government of God has been presented to the whole universe. Satan's own works have condemned him. God's wisdom, His justice, and His goodness stand fully vindicated. It is seen that all His dealings in the great controversy have been conducted with respect to the eternal good of His people and the good of all the worlds that He has created. . . . The history of sin will stand to all eternity as a witness that with the existence of God's law is bound up the happiness of all the beings He has created. With all the facts of the great controversy in view, the whole universe, both loyal and rebellious, with one accord declare: "Just and true are thy ways, thou King of saints."

Before the universe has been clearly presented the great sacrifice made by the Father and the Son in man's behalf. The hour has come when Christ occupies His rightful position and is glorified above principalities and powers and every name that is named. It was for the joy that was set before Him—that He might bring many sons unto glory—that He endured the cross and despised the shame. And inconceivably great as was the sorrow and the shame, yet greater is the joy and the glory. He looks upon the redeemed, renewed in His own image, every heart bearing the perfect impress of the divine, every face reflecting the likeness of their King. He beholds in them the result of the travail of His soul, and He is satisfied. Then, in a voice that reaches the assembled multitudes of the righteous and the wicked, He declares: "Behold the purchase of My blood! For these I suffered, for these I died, that they might dwell in My presence throughout eternal ages." And the song of praise ascends from the white-robed ones about the throne: "Worthy is the Lamb that was slain to receive power, and riches, and wisdom, and strength, and honour, and glory, and blessing." Revelation 5:12.[6]

SIN AND SINNERS DESTROYED

Behold, the day cometh, that shall burn as an oven; and all the proud, yea, and all that do wickedly, shall be stubble: and the day that cometh shall burn them up, saith the Lord of hosts, that it shall leave them neither root nor branch. Mal. 4:1.

Notwithstanding that Satan has been constrained to acknowledge God's justice and to bow to the supremacy of Christ, his character remains unchanged. The spirit of rebellion, like a mighty torrent, again bursts forth. Filled with frenzy, he determines not to yield the great controversy. The time has come for a last desperate struggle against the King of heaven. He rushes into the midst of his subjects and endeavors to inspire them with his own fury and arouse them to instant battle. But of all the countless millions whom he has allured into rebellion, there are none now to acknowledge his supremacy. His power is at an end. The wicked are filled with the same hatred of God that inspires Satan; but they see that their case is hopeless, that they cannot prevail against Jehovah. Their rage is kindled against Satan and those who have been his agents in deception, and with the fury of demons they turn upon them.

Saith the Lord: "Because thou hast set thine heart as the heart of God; behold, therefore I will bring strangers upon thee, the terrible of the nations: and they shall draw their swords against the beauty of thy wisdom, and they shall defile thy brightness. They shall bring thee down to the pit." "I will destroy thee, O covering cherub, from the midst of the stones of fire. . . . I will cast thee to the ground, I will lay thee before kings, that they may behold thee. . . . I will bring thee to ashes upon the earth in the sight of all them that behold thee. . . . Thou shalt be a terror, and never shalt thou be any more." Ezekiel 28:6-8, 16-19. . . .

Fire comes down from God out of heaven. The earth is broken up. The weapons concealed in its depths are drawn forth. Devouring flames burst from every yawning chasm. The very rocks are on fire. The day has come that shall burn as an oven. The elements melt with fervent heat, the earth also, and the works that are therein are burned up.[7]

347

ONLY ONE REMINDER OF SIN

Behold, the righteous shall be recompensed in the earth: much more the wicked and the sinner. Prov. 11:31.

The wicked receive their recompense in the earth. Proverbs 11:31. They "shall be stubble: and the day that cometh shall burn them up, saith the Lord of hosts." Malachi 4:1. Some are destroyed as in a moment, while others suffer many days. All are punished "according to their deeds." The sins of the righteous having been transferred to Satan, he is made to suffer not only for his own rebellion, but for all the sins which he has caused God's people to commit. His punishment is to be far greater than that of those whom he has deceived. After all have perished who fell by his deceptions, he is still to live and suffer on. In the cleansing flames the wicked are at last destroyed, root and branch—Satan the root, his followers the branches.[8]

Satan and all who have joined him in rebellion will be cut off. . . . Then "the wicked shall not be: yea, thou shalt diligently consider his place, and it shall not be"; "they shall be as though they had not been." Ps. 37:10; Obadiah 16.[9]

The justice of God is satisfied, and the saints and all the angelic host say with a loud voice, Amen.

While the earth is wrapped in the fire of God's vengeance, the righteous abide safely in the Holy City. Upon those that had part in the first resurrection, the second death has no power. (Rev. 20:6.) While God is to the wicked a consuming fire, He is to His people both a sun and a shield. (Ps. 84:11.)[10]

The fire that consumes the wicked purifies the earth. Every trace of the curse is swept away. No eternally burning hell will keep before the ransomed the fearful consequences of sin.

One reminder alone remains: our Redeemer will ever bear the marks of His crucifixion. . . .

All that was lost by sin has been restored. . . . God's original purpose in the creation of the earth is fulfilled as it is made the eternal abode of the redeemed. "The righteous shall inherit the land, and dwell therein for ever." Psalm 37:29.[11]

WE BELONG TO THE ROYAL FAMILY

Beloved, now are we the sons of God, and it doth not yet appear what we shall be: but we know that, when he shall appear, we shall be like him; for we shall see him as he is. 1 John 3:2.

Can any earthly promotion confer honor equal to this—to be sons of God, children of the heavenly King, members of the royal family? . . . The nobility of earth are but men; they die, and return to dust; and there is no lasting satisfaction in their praise and honor. But the honor that comes from God is lasting. To be heirs of God and joint heirs with Christ, is to be entitled to unsearchable riches—treasures of such value that in comparison with them the gold and silver, the gems and precious stones of earth, sink into insignificance.[12]

To have fellowship with the Father and His Son Jesus Christ is to be ennobled and elevated, and made a partaker of joys unspeakable and full of glory. Food, clothing, station, and wealth may have their value; but to have a connection with God and to be a partaker of His divine nature is of priceless value. Our lives should be hid with Christ in God; and although it "doth not yet appear what we shall be," "when Christ, who is our life, shall appear," "we shall be like him; for we shall see him as he is." The princely dignity of the Christian character will shine forth as the sun, and the beams of light from the face of Christ will be reflected upon those who have purified themselves even as He is pure. The privilege of becoming sons of God is cheaply purchased, even at the sacrifice of everything we possess, be it life itself.[13]

When John in his mortal state beheld the glory of God, he fell as one dead; he was not able to endure the sight. But when the children of God shall have put on immortality, they will "see him as he is." They will stand before the throne, accepted in the Beloved. All their sins have been blotted out, all their transgressions borne away. Now they can look upon the undimmed glory of the throne of God. They have been partakers with Christ in His sufferings, they have been workers together with Him in the plan of redemption, and they are partakers with Him in the joy of seeing souls saved in the kingdom of God, there to praise God through all eternity.[14]

SATISFYING EMPLOYMENT

My Father worketh hitherto, and I work. John 5:17.

Heaven is a place of interested activity; yet to the weary and heavy laden, to those who have fought the good fight of faith, it will be a glorious rest; for the youth and vigor of immortality will be theirs, and against sin and Satan they will no longer have to contend. To these energetic workers a state of eternal indolence would be irksome. It would be no heaven to them.[15]

To the dwellers in Eden was committed the care of the garden, "to dress it and to keep it." Their occupation was not wearisome, but pleasant and invigorating. God appointed labor as a blessing to man, to occupy his mind, to strengthen his body, and to develop his faculties. In mental and physical activity Adam found one of the highest pleasures of his holy existence. . . .

Those who regard work as a curse, attended though it be with weariness and pain, are cherishing an error. The rich often look down with contempt upon the working classes, but this is wholly at variance with God's purpose in creating man. What are the possessions of even the most wealthy in comparison with the heritage given to the lordly Adam? Yet Adam was not to be idle. Our Creator, who understands what is for man's happiness, appointed Adam his work. The true joy of life is found only by the working men and women.[16]

Work is constantly being done in heaven. There are no idlers there. "My Father worketh hitherto," said Christ, "and I work." We cannot suppose that when the final triumph shall come, and we have the mansions prepared for us, idleness will be our portion—that we shall rest in a blissful, do-nothing state.[17]

God designs that all shall be workers. The toiling beast of burden answers the purpose of its creation better than does the indolent man. God is a constant worker. The angels are workers; they are ministers of God to the children of men. Those who look forward to a heaven of inactivity will be disappointed, for the economy of heaven provides no place for the gratification of indolence. But to the weary and heavy-laden rest is promised. It is the faithful servant who will be welcomed from his labors to the joy of his Lord.[18]

THE NEW HEAVENS AND THE NEW EARTH

What manner of persons ought ye to be in all holy conversation and godliness, looking for and hasting unto the coming of the day of God, wherein the heavens being on fire shall be dissolved, and the elements shall melt with fervent heat? Nevertheless we, according to his promise, look for new heavens and a new earth, wherein dwelleth righteousness. 2 Peter 3:11-13.

The feet of the wicked will never desecrate the earth made new. Fire will come down from God out of heaven and devour them—burn them up root and branch. Satan is the root, and his children are the branches.[19]

The same fire from God that consumed the wicked purified the whole earth. The broken, ragged mountains melted with fervent heat, the atmosphere also, and all the stubble was consumed. Then our inheritance opened before us, glorious and beautiful, and we inherited the whole earth made new.[20]

"I saw a new heaven and a new earth: for the first heaven and the first earth were passed away." Revelation 21:1. The fire that consumes the wicked purifies the earth. Every trace of the curse is swept away. No eternally burning hell will keep before the ransomed the fearful consequences of sin.[21]

The sea divides friends. It is a barrier between us and those whom we love. Our associations are broken up by the broad, fathomless ocean. In the new earth there will be no more sea, and there shall pass there "no galley with oars." In the past many who have loved and served God have been bound by chains to their seats in galleys, compelled to serve the purpose of cruel, hardhearted men. The Lord has looked upon their suffering in sympathy and compassion. Thank God, in the earth made new there will be no fierce torrents, no engulfing ocean, no restless, murmuring waves.[22]

Let all that is beautiful in our earthly home remind us of the crystal river and green fields, the waving trees and the living fountains, the shining city and the white-robed singers, of our heavenly home—that world of beauty which no artist can picture, no mortal tongue describe. "Eye hath not seen, nor ear heard, neither have entered into the heart of man, the things which God hath prepared for them that love him." [23]

351

NO MORE DEATH—EVER!

God shall wipe away all tears from their eyes; and there shall be no more death, neither sorrow, nor crying, neither shall there be any more pain: for the former things are passed away. Rev. 21:4.

As we enter the kingdom of God, there to spend eternity, the trials and the difficulties and the perplexities that we have had here will sink into insignificance.[24]

In the home of the redeemed there will be no tears, no funeral trains, no badges of mourning. "The inhabitant shall not say, I am sick: the people that dwell therein shall be forgiven their iniquity." Isaiah 33:24. One rich tide of happiness will flow and deepen as eternity rolls on. . . .

Let us consider most earnestly the blessed hereafter. Let our faith pierce through every cloud of darkness and behold Him who died for the sins of the world. He has opened the gates of paradise to all who receive and believe on Him. To them He gives power to become the sons and daughters of God. Let the afflictions which pain us so grievously become instructive lessons, teaching us to press forward toward the mark of the prize of our high calling in Christ. Let us be encouraged by the thought that the Lord is soon to come. Let this hope gladden our hearts. . . .

We are homeward bound. He who loved us so much as to die for us hath builded for us a city. The New Jerusalem is our place of rest. There will be no sadness in the city of God. No wail of sorrow, no dirge of crushed hopes and buried affections, will evermore be heard. Soon the garments of heaviness will be changed for the wedding garment. Soon we shall witness the coronation of our King. Those whose lives have been hidden with Christ, those who on this earth have fought the good fight of faith, will shine forth with the Redeemer's glory in the kingdom of God.

It will not be long till we shall see Him in whom our hopes of eternal life are centered. And in His presence, all the trials and sufferings of this life will be as nothingness. . . . Look up, look up, and let your faith continually increase. Let this faith guide you along the narrow path that leads through the gates of the city of God into the great beyond, the wide, unbounded future of glory that is for the redeemed.[25]

INHERITANCE OF THE SAVED

My people shall dwell in a peaceable habitation, and in sure dwellings, and in quiet resting places. Isa. 32:18.

In the Bible the inheritance of the saved is called "a country." Hebrews 11:14-16. There the heavenly Shepherd leads His flock to fountains of living waters. The tree of life yields its fruit every month, and the leaves of the tree are for the service of the nations. There are ever-flowing streams, clear as crystal, and beside them waving trees cast their shadows upon the paths prepared for the ransomed of the Lord. There the wide-spreading plains swell into hills of beauty, and the mountains of God rear their lofty summits. On those peaceful plains, beside those living streams, God's people, so long pilgrims and wanderers, shall find a home. . . .

There, "the wilderness and the solitary place shall be glad for them; and the desert shall rejoice, and blossom as the rose." "Instead of the thorn shall come up the fir tree, and instead of the brier shall come up the myrtle tree." "The wolf also shall dwell with the lamb, and the leopard shall lie down with the kid; . . . and a little child shall lead them." "They shall not hurt nor destroy in all my holy mountain," saith the Lord. Isaiah 35:1; 55:13; 11:6, 9.[26] There man will be restored to his lost kingship, and the lower order of beings will again recognize his sway; the fierce will become gentle, and the timid trustful.[27]

Pain cannot exist in the atmosphere of heaven. There will be no more tears, no funeral trains, no badges of mourning. "There shall be no more death, neither sorrow, nor crying: . . . for the former things are passed away." "The inhabitant shall not say, I am sick: the people that dwell therein shall be forgiven their iniquity." Revelation 21:4; Isaiah 33:24.[28]

There the Eden life will be lived, the life in garden and field. "They shall build houses, and inhabit them; and they shall plant vineyards, and eat the fruit of them. They shall not build, and another inhabit; they shall not plant, and another eat: for as the days of a tree are the days of my people, and mine elect shall long enjoy the work of their hands." Isaiah 65:21, 22.[29]

GARDEN OF EDEN RESTORED

To him that overcometh will I give to eat of the tree of life, which is in the midst of the paradise of God. Rev. 2:7.

The Garden of Eden remained upon the earth long after man had become an outcast from its pleasant paths. The fallen race were long permitted to gaze upon the home of innocence, their entrance barred only by the watching angels. At the cherubim-guarded gate of Paradise the divine glory was revealed. Hither came Adam and his sons to worship God. Here they renewed their vows of obedience to that law the transgression of which had banished them from Eden. When the tide of iniquity overspread the world, and the wickedness of men determined their destruction by a flood of waters, the hand that had planted Eden withdrew it from the earth. But in the final restitution, when there shall be "a new heaven and a new earth" (Revelation 21:1), it is to be restored more gloriously adorned than at the beginning.

Then they that have kept God's commandments shall breathe in immortal vigor beneath the tree of life; and through unending ages the inhabitants of sinless worlds shall behold, in that garden of delight, a sample of the perfect work of God's creation, untouched by the curse of sin—a sample of what the whole earth would have become, had man but fulfilled the Creator's glorious plan.[30]

Adam is reinstated in his first dominion. Transported with joy, he beholds the trees that were once his delight—the very trees whose fruit he himself had gathered in the days of his innocence and joy. He sees the vines that his own hands have trained, the very flowers that he once loved to care for. His mind grasps the reality of the scene; he comprehends that this is indeed Eden restored.[31]

Restored to the tree of life in the long-lost Eden, the redeemed will "grow up" (Malachi 4:2) to the full stature of the race in its primeval glory. The last lingering traces of the curse of sin will be removed, and Christ's faithful ones will appear in "the beauty of the Lord our God," in mind and soul and body reflecting the perfect image of their Lord. Oh, wonderful redemption! long talked of, long hoped for, contemplated with eager anticipation, but never fully understood.[32]

GLORIES OF THE ETERNAL WORLD

Thou wilt shew me the path of life: in thy presence is fulness of joy; at thy right hand there are pleasures for evermore. Ps. 16:11.

The glory of the eternal world has been opened before me. I want to tell you that Heaven is worth winning. It should be the aim of your life to fit yourself for association with the redeemed, with holy angels, and with Jesus, the world's Redeemer. If we could have but one view of the celestial city, we would never wish to dwell on earth again. There are beautiful landscapes on earth, and I enjoy all these prospects of loveliness in nature. I associate them with the Creator. But I know that if I love God, and keep His commandments, there is a far more exceeding and eternal weight of glory reserved in Heaven for me.[33]

This earth, . . . purified with fire, then . . . will be much more beautiful. The grass will be living green, and will never wither. There will be roses and lilies, and all kinds of flowers there. They will never blight or fade, or lose their beauty and fragrance.

The lion, we should much dread and fear here, will then lie down with the lamb, and everything in the New Earth will be peace and harmony. The trees of the New Earth will be straight and lofty, without deformity.

The saints will have crowns of glory upon their heads, and harps of gold in their hands. They will play upon the golden harp, and sing redeeming love, and make melody unto God. Their former trials and suffering in this world will be forgotten and lost amid the glories of the New Earth.[34]

Let all that is beautiful in our earthly home remind us of the crystal river and green fields, the waving trees and the living fountains, the shining city and the white-robed singers, of our heavenly home—that world of beauty which no artist can picture and no mortal tongue describe.[35] Let your imagination picture the home of the saved, and remember that it will be more glorious than your brightest imagination can portray.[36]

Human language is inadequate to describe the reward of the righteous. It will be known only to those who behold it.[37]

AT HOME IN THE NEW JERUSALEM

Be ye glad and rejoice for ever in that which I create: for, behold, I create Jerusalem a rejoicing, and her people a joy. Isa. 65:18.

There is the New Jerusalem, the metropolis of the glorified new earth, "a crown of glory in the hand of the Lord, and a royal diadem in the hand of thy God." "Her light was like unto a stone most precious, even like a jasper stone, clear as crystal." "The nations of them which are saved shall walk in the light of it: and the kings of the earth do bring their glory and honour into it." Saith the Lord: "I will rejoice in Jerusalem, and joy in my people.". . .

In the City of God "there shall be no night." None will need or desire repose. There will be no weariness in doing the will of God and offering praise to His name. We shall ever feel the freshness of the morning and shall ever be far from its close. "And they need no candle, neither light of the sun; for the Lord God giveth them light." The light of the sun will be superseded by a radiance which is not painfully dazzling, yet which immeasurably surpasses the brightness of our noontide. The glory of God and the Lamb floods the Holy City with unfading light. The redeemed walk in the sunless glory of perpetual day.

"I saw no temple therein: for the Lord God Almighty and the Lamb are the temple of it." The people of God are privileged to hold open communion with the Father and the Son. "Now we see through a glass, darkly." We behold the image of God reflected, as in a mirror, in the works of nature and in His dealings with men; but then we shall see Him face to face, without a dimming veil between. We shall stand in His presence and behold the glory of His countenance.[38]

There we shall know even as also we are known. There the loves and sympathies that God has planted in the soul will find truest and sweetest exercise. The pure communion with holy beings, the harmonious social life with the blessed angels and with the faithful ones of all ages, the sacred fellowship that binds together "the whole family in heaven and earth"—all are among the experiences of the hereafter.[39]

THE IMMORTAL INHERITANCE

Giving thanks to the Father, who has qualified us to share in the inheritance of the saints in light. Col. 1:12, R.S.V.

The ransom has been paid, and it is possible for all to come to God, and through a life of obedience to attain unto everlasting life. Then how sad it is that men turn from the immortal inheritance, and live for the gratification of pride, for selfishness and display, and . . . lose the blessing which they might have both in this life and in the life to come. They might enter into the palaces of heaven, and associate on terms of freedom and equality with Christ and heavenly angels, and with the princes of God; and yet, incredible as it may seem, they turn from heavenly attractions.

The Creator of all worlds proposes to love those who believe in His only-begotten Son as their personal Saviour, even as He loves His Son. Even here and now His gracious favor is bestowed upon us to this marvelous extent. He has given to men the gift of the Light and Majesty of heaven, and with Him He has bestowed all the treasures of heaven. Much as He has promised us for the life to come, He also bestows princely gifts upon us in this life, and as subjects of His grace, He would have us enjoy everything that will ennoble, expand, and elevate our characters. It is His design to fit us for the heavenly courts above.

But Satan is contending for the souls of men. . . . He would not have them catch a glimpse of the future honor, the eternal glories, laid up for those who shall be inhabitants of heaven, or have a taste of the experience that gives a foretaste of the happiness of heaven. . . .

Those who accept Christ as their Saviour have the promise of the life that now is, and that which is to come. . . . The lowliest disciple of Christ may become an inhabitant of heaven, an heir of God to an inheritance incorruptible, and that fadeth not away. O that every one might make choice of the heavenly gift, become an heir of God to that inheritance whose title is secure from any destroyer, world without end! O, choose not the world, but choose the better inheritance! Press, urge your way toward the mark for the prize of your high calling in Christ Jesus.[40]

357

THE CHURCH TRIUMPHANT

I saw as it were a sea of glass mingled with fire: and them that had gotten the victory over the beast, and over his image, and over his mark, and over the number of his name, stand on the sea of glass, having the harps of God. Rev. 15:2.

Now the church is militant. Now we are confronted with a world in darkness, almost wholly given over to idolatry. But the day is coming when the battle will have been fought, the victory won. The will of God is to be done on earth as it is done in heaven. The nations of the saved will know no other law than the law of heaven. All will be a happy, united family, clothed with the garments of praise and thanksgiving—the robe of Christ's righteousness. All nature, in its surpassing loveliness, will offer to God a tribute of praise and adoration. The world will be bathed in the light of heaven. The light of the moon will be as the light of the sun, and the light of the sun will be sevenfold greater than it is now. The years will move on in gladness. Over the scene the morning stars will sing together, and the sons of God will shout for joy, while God and Christ will unite in proclaiming, "There shall be no more sin, neither shall there be any more death.". . .

Stand on the threshold of eternity and hear the gracious welcome given to those who in this life have co-operated with Christ, regarding it as a privilege and an honor to suffer for His sake. With the angels, they cast their crowns at the feet of the Redeemer, exclaiming, "Worthy is the Lamb that was slain to receive power, and riches, and wisdom, and strength, and honour, and glory, and blessing. . . . Honour, and glory, and power, be unto Him that sitteth upon the throne, and unto the Lamb for ever and ever." Revelation 5:12, 13.

There the redeemed ones greet those who directed them to the uplifted Saviour. They unite in praising Him who died that human beings might have the life that measures with the life of God. The conflict is over. All tribulation and strife are at an end. Songs of victory fill all heaven, as the redeemed stand around the throne of God. All take up the joyful strain, "Worthy is the Lamb that was slain" and hath redeemed us to God.[41]

358

UNEXPECTED RECOMPENSE

Whatsoever good thing any man doeth, the same shall he receive of the Lord. Eph. 6:8.

In this life our work for God often seems to be almost fruitless. Our efforts to do good may be earnest and persevering, yet we may not be permitted to witness their results. To us the effort may seem to be lost. But the Saviour assures us that our work is noted in heaven, and that the recompense cannot fail.[42]

The poor widow who cast her two mites into the Lord's treasury little knew what she was doing. Her example of self-sacrifice has acted and reacted upon thousands of hearts in every land and in every age. It has brought to the treasury of God gifts from the high and the low, the rich and the poor. It has helped to sustain missions, to establish hospitals, to feed the hungry, clothe the naked, heal the sick, and preach the gospel to the poor. Multitudes have been blessed through her unselfish deed. And the outworking of all these lines of influence she, in the day of God, will be permitted to see. So with Mary's precious gift to the Saviour. How many have been inspired to loving service by the memory of that broken alabaster box! And how she will rejoice as she beholds all this![43]

"Verily I say unto you," Christ declared, "Wheresoever this gospel shall be preached throughout the whole world, this also that she hath done shall be spoken of for a memorial of her." Looking into the future, the Saviour spoke with certainty concerning His gospel. It was to be preached throughout the world. And as far as the gospel extended, Mary's gift would shed its fragrance, and hearts would be blessed through her unstudied act. Kingdoms would rise and fall; the names of monarchs and conquerors would be forgotten; but this woman's deed would be immortalized upon the pages of sacred history. Until time should be no more, that broken alabaster box would tell the story of the abundant love of God for a fallen race.[44]

Every impulse of the Holy Spirit leading men to goodness and to God is noted in the books of heaven, and in the day of God everyone who has given himself as an instrument for the Holy Spirit's working will be permitted to behold what his life has wrought.[45]

NEW EARTH ACTIVITIES

They shall build houses, and inhabit them; and they shall plant vineyards, and eat the fruit of them. They shall not build, and another inhabit; they shall not plant, and another eat: for as the days of a tree are the days of my people, and mine elect shall long enjoy the work of their hands. Isa. 65:21, 22.

We cannot suppose that when the final triumph shall come, and we have the mansions prepared for us, idleness will be our portion—that we shall rest in a blissful, do-nothing state.[46]

In the earth made new, the redeemed will engage in the occupations and pleasures that brought happiness to Adam and Eve in the beginning. The Eden life will be lived, the life in garden and field. "They shall build houses, and inhabit them; and they shall plant vineyards, and eat the fruit of them. They shall not build, and another inhabit; they shall not plant, and another eat: for as the days of a tree are the days of my people, and mine elect shall long enjoy the work of their hands." Isaiah 65: 21, 22.[47]

There I saw most glorious houses, that had the appearance of silver, supported by four pillars set with pearls most glorious to behold. These were to be inhabited by the saints. In each was a golden shelf. I saw many of the saints go into the houses, take off their glittering crowns and lay them on the shelf, then go out into the field by the houses to do something with the earth; not as we have to do with the earth here; no, no. A glorious light shone all about their heads, and they were continually shouting and offering praises to God.[48]

Every faculty will be developed, every capacity increased. The acquirement of knowledge will not weary the mind or exhaust the energies. There the grandest enterprises may be carried forward, the loftiest aspirations reached, the highest ambitions realized; and still there will arise new heights to surmount, new wonders to admire, new truths to comprehend, fresh objects to call forth the powers of mind and soul and body.[49]

INCOMPARABLE MUSIC

The ransomed of the Lord shall return, and come to Zion with songs and everlasting joy upon their heads: they shall obtain joy and gladness, and sorrow and sighing shall flee away. Isa. 35:10.

There will be music there, and song, such music and song as, save in the visions of God, no mortal ear has heard or mind conceived.

"As well the singers as the players on instruments shall be there." "They shall lift up their voice, they shall sing for the majesty of the Lord." "For the Lord shall comfort Zion: . . . He will make her wilderness like Eden, and her desert like the garden of the Lord; joy and gladness shall be found therein, thanksgiving, and the voice of melody." [50]

I have been shown the order, the perfect order, of heaven, and have been enraptured as I listened to the perfect music there. After coming out of vision, the singing here has sounded very harsh and discordant. I have seen companies of angels, who stood in a hollow square, everyone having a harp of gold. At the end of the harp was an instrument to turn to set the harp or change the tunes. Their fingers did not sweep over the strings carelessly, but they touched different strings to produce different sounds. There is one angel who always leads, who first touches the harp and strikes the note, then all join in the rich, perfect music of heaven. It cannot be described. It is melody, heavenly, divine, while from every countenance beams the image of Jesus, shining with glory unspeakable. [51]

What a song that will be when the ransomed of the Lord meet . . . ! All heaven is filled with rich music, and with songs of praise to the Lamb. Saved, everlastingly saved, in the kingdom of glory! To have a life that measures with the life of God—that is the reward. [52]

Language is altogether too feeble to attempt a description of heaven. As the scene rises before me, I am lost in amazement. Carried away with the surpassing splendor and excellent glory, I lay down the pen, and exclaim, "Oh, what love! what wondrous love!" The most exalted language fails to describe the glory of heaven or the matchless depths of a Saviour's love. [53]

OUR SAVIOUR'S HIGHEST HONOR

And one shall say unto him, What are these wounds in thine hands? Then he shall answer, Those with which I was wounded in the house of my friends. Zech. 13:6.

"I saw a new heaven and a new earth: for the first heaven and the first earth were passed away." Revelation 21:1. The fire that consumes the wicked purifies the earth. Every trace of the curse is swept away. . . .

One reminder alone remains: Our Redeemer will ever bear the marks of His crucifixion. Upon His wounded head, upon His side, His hands and feet, are the only traces of the cruel work that sin has wrought. Says the prophet, beholding Christ in His glory: "He had bright beams coming out of his side: and there was the hiding of his power." Habakkuk 3:4, margin. That pierced side whence flowed the crimson stream that reconciled man to God—there is the Saviour's glory, there "the hiding of his power.". . . And the tokens of His humiliation are His highest honor; through the eternal ages the wounds of Calvary will show forth His praise and declare His power.[54]

The cross of Christ will be the science and the song of the redeemed through all eternity. In Christ glorified they will behold Christ crucified. Never will it be forgotten that He whose power created and upheld the unnumbered worlds through the vast realms of space, the Beloved of God, the Majesty of heaven, He whom cherub and shining seraph delighted to adore—humbled Himself to uplift fallen man; that He bore the guilt and shame of sin, and the hiding of His Father's face, till the woes of a lost world broke His heart and crushed out His life on Calvary's cross. That the Maker of all worlds, the Arbiter of all destinies, should lay aside His glory and humiliate Himself from love to man will ever excite the wonder and adoration of the universe. As the nations of the saved look upon their Redeemer and behold the eternal glory of the Father shining in His countenance; as they behold His throne, which is from everlasting to everlasting, and know that His kingdom is to have no end, they break forth in rapturous song: "Worthy, worthy is the Lamb that was slain, and hath redeemed us to God by His own most precious blood!"[55]

THE SCHOOL OF THE HEREAFTER

Behold, the dwelling of God is with men. He will dwell with them. Rev. 21:3, R.S.V.

Between the school established in Eden at the beginning and the school of the hereafter there lies the whole compass of this world's history—the history of human transgression and suffering, of divine sacrifice, and of victory over death and sin. Not all the conditions of that first school of Eden will be found in the school of the future life. No tree of knowledge of good and evil will afford opportunity for temptation. No tempter is there, no possibility of wrong. Every character has withstood the testing of evil, and none are longer susceptible to its power. . . . Restored to His presence, man will again, as at the beginning, be taught of God.[56]

Our lifework here is a preparation for the life eternal. The education begun here will not be completed in this life; it will be going forward through all eternity—ever progressing, never completed.[57]

Every right principle, every truth learned in an earthly school, will advance us just that much in the heavenly school. As Christ walked and talked with His disciples during His ministry on this earth, so will He teach us in the school above, leading us beside the river of living waters and revealing to us truths that in this life must remain hidden mysteries because of the limitations of the human mind, so marred by sin.[58]

The history of the inception of sin; of fatal falsehood in its crooked working; of truth that . . . has met and conquered error—all will be made manifest. The veil that interposes between the visible and the invisible world will be drawn aside, and wonderful things will be revealed.[59]

Every faculty will be developed, every capacity increased. The acquirement of knowledge will not weary the mind or exhaust the energies. There the grandest enterprises may be carried forward, the loftiest aspirations reached, the highest ambitions realized; and still there will arise new heights to surmount, new wonders to admire, new truths to comprehend, fresh objects to call forth the powers of mind and soul and body.[60]

CHRIST WILL BE OUR TEACHER

My people shall know my name: . . . they shall know in that day that I am he that doth speak: behold, it is I. Isa. 52:6.

Restored to His presence, man will again, as at the beginning, be taught of God.[61]

We have not the slightest idea of what will then be opened before us. With Christ we shall walk beside the living waters. He will unfold to us the beauty and glory of nature. He will reveal what He is to us, and what we are to Him. Truth we cannot know now, because of finite limitations, we shall know hereafter.[62]

In the world to come Christ will lead the redeemed beside the river of life and will teach them wonderful lessons of truth. He will unfold to them the mysteries of nature. They will see that a master hand holds the world in position. They will behold the skill displayed by the great Artist in coloring the flowers of the field, and will learn of the purposes of the merciful Father, who dispenses every ray of light, and with the holy angels the redeemed will acknowledge in songs of grateful praise God's supreme love to an unthankful world.[63]

There will be open to the student, history of infinite scope and of wealth inexpressible. . . . The history of the inception of sin; of fatal falsehood in its crooked working; of truth that, swerving not from its own straight lines, has met and conquered error—all will be made manifest. The veil that interposes between the visible and the invisible world will be drawn aside, and wonderful things will be revealed.[64]

With unutterable delight we shall enter into the joy and the wisdom of unfallen beings. We shall share the treasures gained through ages upon ages spent in contemplation of God's handiwork. And the years of eternity, as they roll, will continue to bring more glorious revelations. "Exceeding abundantly above all that we ask or think" (Ephesians 3:20) will be, forever and forever, the impartation of the gifts of God.[65]

We must get an education here that will enable us to live with God through the eternal ages. The education we begin here will be perfected in heaven. We will only just enter a higher grade.[66]

OUR STUDY IN AGES TO COME

That in the ages to come he might shew the exceeding riches of his grace in his kindness toward us through Christ Jesus. Eph. 2:7.

The science of redemption is the science of all sciences; the science that is the study of the angels, and of all the intelligences of the unfallen worlds; the science that engages the attention of our Lord and Saviour; the science that enters into the purpose brooded in the mind of the Infinite—"kept in silence through times eternal"; the science that will be the study of God's redeemed throughout the endless ages. This is the highest study in which it is possible for man to engage. As no other study can, it will quicken the mind, and uplift the soul. . . .

The theme of redemption is one that angels desire to look into; it will be the science and the song of the redeemed throughout the ceaseless ages of eternity. Is it not worthy of careful thought and study now? . . .

The study of the incarnation of Christ, His atoning sacrifice and mediatorial work, will employ the mind of the diligent student as long as time shall last; and, looking to heaven with its unnumbered years, he will exclaim, "Great is the mystery of godliness."

In eternity we shall learn that which, had we received the enlightenment that it was possible to obtain here, would have opened our understanding. The themes of redemption will employ the hearts and minds and tongues of the redeemed through the everlasting ages. They will understand the truths which Christ longed to open to His disciples, but which they did not have faith to grasp. Forever and forever new views of the perfection and glory of Christ will appear. Through endless ages the faithful Householder will bring forth from His treasures things new and old.[67]

If it were possible for us to attain to a full understanding of God and His truth, there would be for us no further discovery of truth, no greater knowledge, no further development. . . . Thank God, it is not so. Since God is infinite, and in Him are all the treasures of wisdom, we may to all eternity be ever searching, ever learning, yet never exhaust the riches of His wisdom, His goodness, or His power.[68]

INEXHAUSTIBLE THEMES

Of which salvation the prophets have enquired and searched diligently, who prophesied of the grace that should come unto you: searching what, or what manner of time the Spirit of Christ which was in them did signify, when it testified beforehand the sufferings of Christ, and the glory that should follow. . . . Which things the angels desire to look into. 1 Peter 1:10-12.

In this life we can only begin to understand the wonderful theme of redemption. With our finite comprehension we may consider most earnestly the shame and the glory, the life and the death, the justice and the mercy, that meet in the cross; yet with the utmost stretch of our mental powers we fail to grasp its full significance. The length and the breadth, the depth and the height, of redeeming love are but dimly comprehended. The plan of redemption will not be fully understood, even when the ransomed see as they are seen and know as they are known; but through the eternal ages new truth will continually unfold to the wondering and delighted mind. Though the griefs and pains and temptations of earth are ended and the cause removed, the people of God will ever have a distinct, intelligent knowledge of what their salvation has cost. . . .

The mystery of the cross explains all other mysteries. In the light that streams from Calvary the attributes of God which had filled us with fear and awe appear beautiful and attractive. Mercy, tenderness, and parental love are seen to blend with holiness, justice, and power. While we behold the majesty of His throne, high and lifted up, we see His character in its gracious manifestations, and comprehend, as never before, the significance of that endearing title, "Our Father."

It will be seen that He who is infinite in wisdom could devise no plan for our salvation except the sacrifice of His Son. The compensation for this sacrifice is the joy of peopling the earth with ransomed beings, holy, happy, and immortal. The result of the Saviour's conflict with the powers of darkness is joy to the redeemed, redounding to the glory of God throughout eternity. And such is the value of the soul that the Father is satisfied with the price paid; and Christ Himself, beholding the fruits of His great sacrifice, is satisfied.[69]

Through all eternity the ransomed host will be His chief glory.[70]

THE UNIVERSE OUR FIELD OF STUDY

O Lord, how manifold are thy works! in wisdom hast thou made them all: the earth is full of thy riches. Ps. 104:24.

The knowledge of God's works and ways we can only begin to obtain in this world; the study will be continued throughout eternity. God has provided for man subjects of thought which will bring into activity every faculty of the mind. We may read the character of the Creator in the heavens above and the earth beneath, filling the heart with gratitude and thanksgiving. Every nerve and sense will respond to the expressions of God's love in His marvelous works.[71]

There, when the veil that darkens our vision shall be removed, and our eyes shall behold that world of beauty of which we now catch glimpses through the microscope; when we look on the glories of the heavens, now scanned afar through the telescope; when, the blight of sin removed, the whole earth shall appear in "the beauty of the Lord our God," what a field will be open to our study! There the student of science may read the records of creation and discern no reminders of the law of evil. He may listen to the music of nature's voices and detect no note of wailing or undertone of sorrow. In all created things he may trace one handwriting—in the vast universe behold "God's name writ large," and not in earth or sea or sky one sign of ill remaining.[72]

The redeemed throng will range from world to world, and much of their time will be employed in searching out the mysteries of redemption. And throughout the whole stretch of eternity, this subject will be continually opening to their minds. The privileges of those who overcome by the blood of the Lamb and the word of their testimony are beyond comprehension.[73]

All the treasures of the universe will be open to the study of God's children. With unutterable delight we shall enter into the joy and the wisdom of unfallen beings. We shall share the treasures gained through ages upon ages spent in contemplation of God's handiwork. And the years of eternity, as they roll, will continue to bring more glorious revelations. "Exceeding abundantly above all that we ask or think" will be, forever and forever, the impartation of the gifts of God.[74]

WORLDS UPON WORLDS TO BE VISITED

Thus saith the Lord. . . . I, even my hands, have stretched out the heavens, and all their host have I commanded. Isa. 45: 11, 12.

Many seem to have the idea that this world and the heavenly mansions constitute the universe of God. Not so.[75]

God has worlds upon worlds that are obedient to His law. These worlds are conducted with reference to the glory of the Creator. As the inhabitants of these worlds see the great price that has been paid to ransom man, they are filled with amazement.[76]

The Lord has given me a view of other worlds. Wings were given me, and an angel attended me from the city to a place that was bright and glorious. The grass of the place was living green, and the birds there warbled a sweet song. The inhabitants of the place were of all sizes; they were noble, majestic, and lovely. They bore the express image of Jesus, and their countenances beamed with holy joy, expressive of the freedom and happiness of the place.

I asked one of them why they were so much more lovely than those on the earth. The reply was, "We have lived in strict obedience to the commandments of God, and have not fallen by disobedience, like those on the earth." Then I saw two trees, one looked much like the tree of life in the city. The fruit of both looked beautiful, but of one they could not eat. They had power to eat of both, but were forbidden to eat of one. Then my attending angel said to me, "None in this place have tasted of the forbidden tree; but if they should eat, they would fall."

Then I was taken to a world which had seven moons. There I saw good old Enoch, who had been translated. . . . I asked him if this was the place he was taken to from the earth. He said, "It is not; the city is my home, and I have come to visit this place." He moved about the place as if perfectly at home.

I begged of my attending angel to let me remain in that place. I could not bear the thought of coming back to this dark world again. Then the angel said, "You must go back, and if you are faithful, you, with the 144,000, shall have the privilege of visiting all the worlds and viewing the handiwork of God."[77]

SPECULATIONS CONCERNING THE NEW EARTH

When they shall rise from the dead, they neither marry, nor are given in marriage; but are as the angels which are in heaven. Mark 12:25.

There are men today who express their belief that there will be marriages and births in the new earth, but those who believe the Scriptures cannot accept such doctrines. The doctrine that children will be born in the new earth is not a part of the "sure word of prophecy." The words of Christ are too plain to be misunderstood. They should forever settle the question of marriages and births in the new earth. Neither those who shall be raised from the dead, nor those who shall be translated without seeing death, will marry or be given in marriage. They will be as the angels of God, members of the royal family.

I would say to those who hold views contrary to this plain declaration of Christ: Upon such matters silence is eloquence. It is presumption to indulge in suppositions and theories regarding matters that God has not made known to us in His word. We need not enter into speculation regarding our future state. . . .

"Preach the word; be instant in season, out of season." Do not bring to the foundation wood, and hay, and stubble—your own surmisings and speculations, which can benefit no one.

Christ withheld no truths essential to our salvation. Those things that are revealed are for us and our children, but we are not to allow our imagination to frame doctrines concerning things not revealed.[78]

It is presented to me that spiritual fables are taking many captive. . . . To all who are indulging these unholy fancies I would say, Stop; for Christ's sake, stop right where you are. You are on forbidden ground.[79]

The Lord has made every provision for our happiness in the future life. But He has made no revelations regarding these plans, and we are not to speculate concerning them. Neither are we to measure the conditions of the future life by the conditions of this life.[80]

CHRIST'S KINGDOM OF LOVE

The kingdom and dominion, and the greatness of the kingdom under the whole heaven, shall be given to the people of the saints of the most High. Dan. 7:27.

The government of the kingdom of Christ is like no earthly government. It is a representation of the characters of those who compose the kingdom. . . . His court is one where holy love presides and whose offices and appointments are graced by the exercise of charity. He charges His servants to bring pity and loving-kindness, His own attributes, into all their office work. . . .

The power of Christ alone can work the transformation in heart and mind that all must experience who would partake with Him of the new life in the kingdom of God. . . . In order to serve Him aright, we must be born of the divine Spirit. This will purify the heart and renew the mind and give us a new capacity for knowing and loving God. It will give us willing obedience to all His requirements. This is true worship.[81]

"Thine eyes shall see Jerusalem a quiet habitation, a tabernacle that shall not be taken down; not one of the stakes thereof shall ever be removed, neither shall any of the cords thereof be broken. But there the glorious Lord will be unto us a place of broad rivers and streams. . . . For the Lord is our judge, the Lord is our lawgiver, the Lord is our king; he will save us. . . . And the inhabitant shall not say, I am sick: the people that dwell therein shall be forgiven their iniquity" (Isa. 33:20-24).

"Be ye glad and rejoice for ever in that which I create," the Lord exhorts; "for, behold, I create Jerusalem a rejoicing, and her people a joy. And I will rejoice in Jerusalem, and joy in my people: and the voice of weeping shall be no more heard in her, nor the voice of crying. . . . And they shall build houses, and inhabit them; and they shall plant vineyards, and eat the fruit of them. They shall not build, and another inhabit; they shall not plant, and another eat: for as the days of a tree are the days of my people, and mine elect shall long enjoy the work of their hands. . . . They shall not hurt nor destroy in all my holy mountain, saith the Lord" (Isa. 65:18-25).[82]

THE SABBATH IN THE HEREAFTER

For as the new heavens and the new earth, which I will make, shall remain before me, saith the Lord, so shall your seed and your name remain. And it shall come to pass, that from one new moon to another, and from one sabbath to another, shall all flesh come to worship before me, saith the Lord. Isa. 66: 22, 23.

In the beginning the Father and the Son had rested upon the Sabbath after Their work of creation. When "the heavens and the earth were finished, and all the host of them" (Gen. 2:1), the Creator and all heavenly beings rejoiced in contemplation of the glorious scene. "The morning stars sang together, and all the sons of God shouted for joy." Job 38:7.... When there shall be a "restitution of all things, which God hath spoken by the mouth of all his holy prophets since the world began" (Acts 3:21), the creation Sabbath, the day on which Jesus lay at rest in Joseph's tomb, will still be a day of rest and rejoicing. Heaven and earth will unite in praise, as "from one sabbath to another" (Isa. 66:23) the nations of the saved shall bow in joyful worship to God and the Lamb.[83]

The nations of the saved will know no other law than the law of heaven. All will be a happy, united family, clothed with the garments of praise and thanksgiving. Over the scene the morning stars will sing together, and the sons of God will shout for joy. . . .

"And it shall come to pass, that from one new moon to another, and from one sabbath to another, shall all flesh come to worship before me, saith the Lord." The glory of the Lord shall be revealed, and all flesh shall see it together." "The Lord God will cause righteousness and praise to spring forth before all the nations." "In that day shall the Lord of hosts be for a crown of glory, and for a diadem of beauty, unto the residue of his people."[84]

So long as the heavens and the earth endure, the Sabbath will continue as a sign of the Creator's power. And when Eden shall bloom on earth again, God's holy rest day will be honored by all beneath the sun. "From one sabbath to another" the inhabitants of the glorified new earth shall go up "to worship before me, saith the Lord." Isa. 66:23.[85]

ETERNAL SECURITY

The Lord shall be king over all the earth: in that day shall there be one Lord, and his name one. Zech. 14:9.

The great plan of redemption results in fully bringing back the world into God's favor. All that was lost by sin is restored. Not only man but the earth is redeemed, to be the eternal abode of the obedient. For six thousand years Satan has struggled to maintain possession of the earth. Now God's original purpose in its creation is accomplished. "The saints of the most High shall take the kingdom, and possess the kingdom for ever, even for ever and ever" (Dan. 7:18).

"From the rising of the sun unto the going down of the same the Lord's name is to be praised" (Ps. 113:3). "In that day shall there be one Lord, and his name one." "And the Lord shall be king over all the earth" (Zech. 14:9). . . . "All His commandments are sure. They stand fast for ever and ever" (Ps. 111:7, 8). The sacred statutes which Satan has hated and sought to destroy, will be honored throughout a sinless universe.[86]

Through Christ's redeeming work the government of God stands justified. The Omnipotent One is made known as the God of love. Satan's charges are refuted, and his character unveiled. Rebellion can never again arise. Sin can never again enter the universe. Through eternal ages all are secure from apostasy. By love's self-sacrifice, the inhabitants of earth and heaven are bound to their Creator in bonds of indissoluble union. . . .

In the place where sin abounded, God's grace much more abounds. The earth itself, the very field that Satan claims as his, is to be not only ransomed but exalted. Our little world, under the curse of sin the one dark blot in His glorious creation, will be honored above all other worlds in the universe of God. Here, where the Son of God tabernacled in humanity; where the King of glory lived and suffered and died—here, when He shall make all things new, the tabernacle of God shall be with men, "and he will dwell with them, and they shall be his people, and God himself shall be with them, and be their God." And through endless ages as the redeemed walk in the light of the Lord, they will praise Him for His unspeakable Gift— *Immanuel, "God with us."*[87]

WHAT ETERNITY HOLDS FOR THE REDEEMED

With long life will I satisfy him, and shew him my salvation. Ps. 91:16.

All the treasures of the universe will be open to the study of God's redeemed. Unfettered by mortality, they wing their tireless flight to worlds afar—worlds that thrilled with sorrow at the spectacle of human woe and rang with songs of gladness at the tidings of a ransomed soul. With unutterable delight the children of earth enter into the joy and the wisdom of unfallen beings. They share the treasures of knowledge and understanding gained through ages upon ages in contemplation of God's handiwork. With undimmed vision they gaze upon the glory of creation—suns and stars and systems, all in their appointed order circling the throne of Deity. Upon all things, from the least to the greatest, the Creator's name is written, and in all are the riches of His power displayed.

And the years of eternity, as they roll, will bring richer and still more glorious revelations of God and of Christ. As knowledge is progressive, so will love, reverence, and happiness increase. The more men learn of God, the greater will be their admiration of His character. As Jesus opens before them the riches of redemption and the amazing achievements in the great controversy with Satan, the hearts of the ransomed thrill with more fervent devotion, and with more rapturous joy they sweep the harps of gold; and ten thousand times ten thousand and thousands of thousands of voices unite to swell the mighty chorus of praise.

"And every creature which is in heaven, and on the earth, and under the earth, and such as are in the sea, and all that are in them, heard I saying, Blessing, and honour, and glory, and power, be unto him that sitteth upon the throne, and unto the Lamb for ever and ever." Revelation 5:13.

The great controversy is ended. Sin and sinners are no more. The entire universe is clean. One pulse of harmony and gladness beats through the vast creation. From Him who created all, flow life and light and gladness, throughout the realms of illimitable space. From the minutest atom to the greatest world, all things, animate and inanimate, in their unshadowed beauty and perfect joy, declare that God is love.[88]

Key to Abbreviations

AA—*Acts of the Apostles, The*
AH—*Adventist Home, The*
1BC—Ellen G. White Comments in *SDA Bible Commentary, The,* vol. 1 (2BC, etc., for vols. 2-7)
CD—*Counsels on Diet and Foods*
CG—*Child Guidance*
CH—*Counsels on Health*
COL—*Christ's Object Lessons*
Country Living
CS—*Counsels on Stewardship*
CSW—*Counsels on Sabbath School Work*
CT—*Counsels to Parents, Teachers, and Students*
CTBH—*Christian Temperance and Bible Hygiene*
CW—*Counsels to Writers and Editors*
DA—*Desire of Ages, The*
Ed—*Education*
Ev—*Evangelism*
EW—*Early Writings*
FE—*Fundamentals of Christian Education*
FLB—*Faith I Live By, The*
GC—*Great Controversy, The*
GCB—*GC Bulletin*
GW—*Gospel Workers*
HC—*Our High Calling*
HS—*Historical Sketches*
IHP—*In Heavenly Places*
KH—*That I May Know Him*
Letter—Ellen G. White Letter

LS—*Life Sketches*
MB—*Thoughts From the Mount of Blessing*
MH—*Ministry of Healing, The*
MLT—*My Life Today*
MS—Ellen G. White Manuscript
MYP—*Messages to Young People*
PK—*Prophets and Kings*
PP—*Patriarchs and Prophets*
RB—*Revival and Beyond*
RH—*Review and Herald*
SC—*Steps to Christ*
SD—*Sons and Daughters of God*
1SG—*Spiritual Gifts,* vol. 1 (2SG, etc., for vols. 2-4)
SL—*Sanctified Life, The*
1SM—*Selected Messages,* book 1 (2SM for book 2)
1SP—*Spirit of Prophecy, The,* vol. 1 (2 SP etc., for vols. 2-4)
SR—*Story of Redemption, The*
ST—*Signs of the Times*
Sufferings—*Sufferings of Christ, The*
SW—*Southern Watchman*
1T—*Testimonies for the Church,* vol. 1 (2T, etc., for vols. 2-9)
Te—*Temperance*
TM—*Testimonies to Ministers and Gospel Workers*
WM—*Welfare Ministry*
YI—*Youth's Instructor, The*

Source References

JANUARY

1. DA 31, 32, 37, 38
2. GC 313-315
3. RH Dec. 24, 1872
4. GC 302, 303
5. GC 302
6. GC 299
7. 2T 88
8. GC 303, 304
9. Ev 220
10. Ev 218-220
11. GC 345, 351, 352, 354
12. GC 312
13. 2SM 107, 108
14. DA 633, 634
15. Ev 696
16. GC 611, 612
17. GC 300, 301
18. 3T 62
19. SW March 21, 1905
20. 3T 62
21. 4BC 1184
22. TM 118, 119
23. LS 208-210
24. WM 136, 137
25. Ev 27
26. AH 329
27. Ev 569
28. AH 328, 329
29. Ev 692-694
30. 2SM 368, 369
31. 6T 22
32. FLB 370
33. TM 117
34. TM 116, 117
35. GC 610, 611
36. FLB 289
37. 7BC 911
38. FLB 280
39. GC 464, 465
40. DA 635
41. 9T 11
42. DA 636
43. DA 634
44. MYP 88-90
45. MS 32, 1893
46. 7T 22
47. Letter 42a, 1893
48. RH Nov. 24, 1904

FEBRUARY

1. PP 339-341
2. EW 71
3. 5T 200
4. 1T 124-126
5. 1T 186-189
6. 5T 263-267
7. 5T 707, 708
8. CSW 40, 41
9. 2T 266, 267
10. 2T 265, 266
11. 6T 146-148
12. 2SM 317, 318
13. MYP 83, 84
14. TM 441-443
15. TM 440, 441
16. 5T 9-14

17. 1T 429-432
18. 2T 453
19. 2T 266
20. 2T 453, 454
21. RH Oct. 31, 1899
22. RH Oct. 31, 1899
23. RH Oct. 31, 1899
24. RH March 27, 1894
25. 2T 192-194
26. 1T 263
27. 5T 409
28. 2T 81
29. 8T 200
30. 1T 704, 705
31. 8T 292-294
32. 5T 291-294
33. 1SM 67-69
34. CTBH 54
35. CH 575
36. CH 574
37. CH 450
38. RH Nov. 27, 1900
39. 5T 294-297
40. 2T 121, 122
41. 8T 331
42. PK 386-388
43. PK 275-278

MARCH

1. PK 536, 537
2. PK 536
3. PK 626
4. 1T 158-160
5. DA 172, 173
6. 1T 502, 503
7. FE 484
8. COL 115-117
9. 5T 218-220
10. 5T 221-223
11. 8T 321
12. 5T 266
13. 5T 264-267
14. RH Feb. 3, 1903
15. KH 9
16. RH Feb. 3, 1903
17. 5T 739, 740
18. 5T 738, 739
19. 4T 374
20. COL 310-312
21. 5T 220, 221
22. MB 109
23. 2T 354-356
24. CTBH 54
25. CH 67
26. CD 167
27. 4T 622, 623
28. 5T 426
29. 5T 53
30. 3T 472
31. 5T 42, 43
32. 5T 43
33. 6T 147
34. 7BC 943
35. MYP 46
36. RH Oct. 30, 1900
37. 5T 161, 162
38. Ed 259

39. COL 149
40. Ed 257-261
41. MB 24-27
42. KH 250
43. 1T 338-340
44. 8T 99, 100
45. 6T 407
46. 2T 111
47. MH 428
48. 8T 312
49. 1SM 224
50. DA 466
51. 3T 472
52. 4T 306, 307
53. 1SM 125
54. GC 483, 489, 490
55. GC 483
56. GC 593-602
57. RH Nov. 19, 1908
58. 6T 404, 405
59. 6T 404
60. 1T 123-125
61. 1T 125
62. GCB April 6, 1903
63. EW 66, 67
64. COL 420, 421
65. IHP 227

APRIL

1. Ed 264
2. RH March 10, 1904
3. RH Nov. 22, 1892
4. 6BC 1113
5. 8T 22, 23
6. 7T 9-12, 16
7. COL 384-389
8. 6T 429
9. MH 375, 376
10. CT 169
11. 6T 429, 430
12. AA 109
13. MH 143, 144
14. MH 159
15. 9T 127-130
16. 9T 129
17. Ev 468
18. 6T 66, 67
19. RH July 14, 1903
20. FE 201
21. RH Oct. 9, 1894
22. RH Oct. 9, 1894
23. RH Nov. 27, 1900
24. 2T 132, 133
25. 6T 439
26. RH Dec. 4, 1900
27. 6T 436-438
28. CT 322-324
29. CT 321, 322
30. 6T 43, 44
31. 6T 440, 443, 444
32. SC 119
33. 8T 331-333
34. 8T 333, 334
35. 3T 61-63
36. CH 23
37. CH 20-22
38. RH May 30, 1907

39. IHP 230
40. 5T 87, 88
41. 5T 401
42. 5T 87
43. YI March 3, 1908
44. 4T 624
45. Ed 271
46. AA 109-111
47. 5T 736
48. 9T 255
49. 9T 54, 55
50. 9T 157, 158
51. 9T 254, 255
52. MH 512
53. MH 58
54. Ed 260, 261
55. 2T 232, 233
56. 2T 232
57. 4T 594-597
58. AA 599, 600

MAY

1. FLB 282
2. GC 517, 518
3. 5T 711-713
4. GC 520-522
5. Ev 601, 602
6. Ev 600, 601
7. GC 522, 523
8. Ev 221
9. EW 75
10. 8T 49-53
11. 8T 27-29
12. Te 273, 274
13. FLB 322
14. TM 117, 118
15. 7T 87
16. 7T 84
17. 8T 101
18. LS 409
19. 7T 84
20. 7T 83
21. 9T 209
22. Letter 105, 1904
23. 9T 207, 208
24. 2T 410, 411
25. FLB 342
26. AH 406-409
27. Ed 227-229
28. Ev 213
29. Ev 212, 213
30. Ev 362
31. RB 48, 49
32. GC 304, 305
33. PK 277
34. GC 306-308
35. GC 333, 334
36. FLB 344
37. Ed 178
38. GC 334, 335
39. IHP 197
40. IHP 196
41. 1T 411-415
42. 2SM 75-79
43. RB 47, 48
44. 4SG 158-160
45. 2SM 78, 79

46. 2SM 399-402

JUNE

1. GC 594
2. COL 133
3. 8T 302
4. GC 625
5. CG 555
6. GC 622, 623
7. GC 582
8. HC 340
9. 7T 14
10. PK 183, 184
11. GC 605
12. TM 472, 473
13. Letter 11, 1890
14. 5T 572
15. GC 443, 444
16. PK 717
17. GC 553
18. GC 603, 604
19. 1T 344
20. GC 561, 562
21. GC 590, 591
22. GC 559, 560
23. RH Aug. 5, 1909
24. PP 686
25. GC 464
26. 2SM 59
27. GC 443, 445, 449, 450
28. EW 33
29. EW 85, 86
30. ST May 5, 1887
31. GC 389
32. GC 604
33. 7BC 985
34. GC 605-607
35. GC 311
36. LS 429
37. 7BC 985
38. GC 390
39. WM 136
40. RH Nov. 17, 1910
41. RH Oct. 19, 1897
42. RH June 7, 1887
43. ST Oct. 9, 1901
44. RH July 16, 1901
45. Ev 27
46. MS 173, 1902
47. MS 85, 1899
48. RH April 6, 1911
49. 9T 232, 233, 235
50. CT 322
51. RH Dec. 18, 1888
52. ST June 12, 1893
53. 5T 464, 465
54. 7T 84
55. 2SM 142
56. Country Living 20, 21
57. To Those Who Are Receiving the Seal of the Living God (Broadside), Jan. 31, 1849.
58. EW 56, 57
59. DA 121, 122
60. Country Living 10
61. MS 145, 1902

62. Country Living 10-12
63. Country Living 12
64. CW 113
65. 5T 152
66. DA 121, 122
67. 9T 229
68. Historical Sketches 292
69. Country Living 31
70. Country Living 30
71. Ev 78
72. 1BC 1087, 1088
73. CH 504-506
74. CH 540, 541
75. MM 246
76. GC 607-609
77. 7T 182
78. 7BC 983
79. 7BC 983
80. GC 588
81. ST Feb. 15, 1910
82. 4SP 444, 445
83. 7BC 949
84. GC 450
85. RH Dec. 6, 1892
86. RH Dec. 13, 1892
87. ST June 12, 1893

JULY

1. 5T 451
2. GC 588, 589
3. 5T 712
4. Letter 28, 1900
5. ST May 28, 1894
6. 7BC 985
7. Ev 224
8. 2SM 98
9. 7BC 907
10. GC 440
11. 4SP 277
12. MS 17, 1906
13. Ev 236
14. 7BC 977
15. RH April 29, 1890
16. MS 30, 1889
17. TM 206
18. GC 445
19. 2SM 367-370
20. 7BC 977
21. ST May 26, 1898
22. GC 602
23. GC 608
24. PK 512
25. PK 188, 189
26. RH June 8, 1897
27. RH Dec. 20, 1898
28. MS 21, 1889
29. Letter 30a, 1892
30. RH Nov. 19, 1908
31. 5T 450, 451
32. IHP 48
33. MS 6, 1889
34. 5T 451
35. 7BC 968
36. RH Dec. 7, 1897
37. 4BC 1161
38. 5T 80, 81
39. MS 97, 1898

40. EW 269-271
41. 6T 400, 401
42. 7T 17
43. 1T 203, 204
44. 7BC 911
45. 2SM 68, 69
46. GCB May 27, 1913, 165
47. 2SM 390
48. TM 20
49. RH Nov. 8, 1892
50. TM 62
51. FE 471, 472
52. MS 153, 1902
53. 9T 16
54. MYP 51, 52
55. 6 BC 1105, 1106
56. 7A BC 911
57. 6BC 1106
58. 2 SM 96
59. 5T 698
60. RH Dec. 18, 1888
61. GC 560
62. TM 472
63. RH Nov. 17, 1885
64. MM 87, 88
65. 2 SM 51
66. 1T 302
67. 2SM 53
68. Letter 6, 1884
69. 2SM 55
70. TM 117, 118
71. GC 36
72. GC 29
73. Ev 29
74. GC 624
75. 1SM 66
76. 8T 117
77. 7BC 977
78. Ev 234, 235
79. Ev 235
80. RH May 28, 1889
81. 1SM 111
82. IHP 338
83. RH Jan 9, 1908
84. 7BC 976
85. 6T 18
86. 6T 395
87. 2SM 380
88. PK 512, 513
89. GC 604-606
90. RH May 2, 1893
91. 5T 451
92. GC 589, 590
93. RH July 16, 1901
94. 5T 546
95. TM 37
96. Ev 69
97. RH April 29, 1884
98. RH Oct. 13, 1904
99. RH July 5, 1906
100. RH EXTRA Dec. 23, 1890
101. TM 507
102. HC 346
103. HC 346

AUGUST

1. 2T 355, 356

2. 5T 310, 311
3. CG 161, 162
4. 1SM 279, 280
5. DA 331
6. ST July 23, 1902
7. FLB 113
8. 1SM 82
9. ST April 15, 1913
10. HC 19
11. 7BC 943
12. 4T 567, 568
13. MM 112, 113
14. 1SM 336, 337
15. 4T 607, 608
16. IHP 195
17. 7BC 909
18. RB 13, 14
19. RB 15-17
20. RB 52-54
21. MH 127
22. RB 55
23. RB 50-52
24. RB 14, 15
25. RB 42, 43
26. 6BC 1101
27. IHP 350
28. ST March 31, 1898
29. 2SM 369, 370
30. 3T 267
31. 5T 211, 213-216
32. 7BC 970
33. EW 58
34. EW 279
35. EW 71
36. EW 48
37. 7BC 968
38. 7BC 968
39. FLB 336
40. 7BC 968
41. 7BC 968
42. FLB 336
43. FLB 33
44. Letter 3, 1851
45. EW 32, 33
46. 7BC 968, 969
47. 7BC 969
48. FLB 208
49. FLB 207
50. FLB 209
51. Letter 37, 1887
52. FLB 209
53. FLB 211
54. FLB 213

SEPTEMBER

1. Ev 65
2. RH Dec. 18, 1888
3. Ev 69
4. MS 53, 1905
5. RH April 26, 1892
6. RH April 26, 1892
7. FE 217
8. EW 71
9. GC 425
10. EW 71
11. EW 71
12. CSW 40, 41

13. RH April 26, 1892
14. RH May 3, 1892
15. AA 54, 55
16. GC 611, 612
17. 7BC 983
18. 7BC 967
19. 7BC 982
20. EW 36, 37
21. GC 594
22. EW 85, 86
23. 1T 268
24. Ev 704
25. GC 588, 589
26. PP 104
27. PP 167
28. GW 27
29. CT 532
30. 6T 24
31. GW 470
32. COL 412
33. 5T 524
34. RH April 23, 1901
35. RH Nov. 9, 1905
36. GC 338, 339
37. GC 594
38. RH Nov. 9, 1905
39. ST Dec. 8, 1909
40. MS 1, 1857
41. Letter 58, 1887
42. GC 613, 614
43. EW 58
44. 7BC 967
45. TM 444
46. RH Nov. 23, 1905
47. GC 627-629
48. TM 182
49. 1T 204
50. EW 36, 37
51. EW 282, 283
52. GC 631
53. GC 630, 631
54. PK 605
55. GC 635
56. 1T 353, 354
57. 5T 213
58. EW 283
59. HS 158
60. EW 282
61. MS 153, 1905
62. PP 256
63. PK 513
64. EW 281
65. ST Feb. 15, 1883
66. EW 281, 282
67. 3BC 1150
68. EW 36; 37
69. GC 618, 619
70. GC 619, 620
71. RH Aug. 12, 1884
72. GC 620, 621
73. 4SP 440, 441
74. PK 513
75. 5BC 1105, 1106
76. GC 623-625
77. GC 629, 630, 634
78. GC 635, 636
79. PK 720
80. 5T 714

81. GC 636
82. EW 41
83. MS 81, 1886
84. EW 37
85. GC 654
86. PK 727
87. 7BC 983
88. GC 636, 637
89. EW 285
90. IHP 353

OCTOBER

1. GC 637
2. DA 706-708
3. COL 294
4. ST Jan. 17, 1900
5. 3SG 82, 83
6. 5BC 1110
7. MS 24, 1891
8. 4T 49
9. Letter 258, 1907
10. RH Oct. 19, 1897
11. MS 59, 1895
12. GC 637-639
13. GC 639
14. 7BC 972
15. 7BC 972
16. GC 639, 640
17. GC 640
18. EW 285, 286
19. EW 15
20. GC 640
21. EW 35
22. EW 272, 273
23. To the Little Remnant Scattered Abroad (Broadside), April 6, 1846
24. PK 720
25. GC 640, 641
26. HC 367
27. EW 15, 16
28. EW 286
29. EW 16
30. EW 286, 287
31. Letter 86, 1900
32. DA 832
33. IHP 358
34. HC 367
35. EW 110
36. SD 361
37. RH Sept. 5, 1899
38. ST Jan. 28, 1903
39. RH Sept. 5, 1899
40. GC 654-656
41. GC 642, 644
42. GC 656, 657
43. PP 509
44. RH Oct. 19, 1897
45. 7BC 983
46. 7BC 982
47. 7BC 982
48. DA 780
49. IHP 356
50. GC 641, 642, 644, 645
51. 2SM 260
52. GC 645

53. SD 359
54. SD 359
55. SD 359
56. SD 359
57. 6BC 1093
58. RH June 18, 1901
59. ST Sept. 26, 1878
60. RH Oct. 1, 1901
61. ST April 8, 1897
62. ST June 17, 1897
63. DA 388
64. DA 804
65. MLT 353
66. IHP 352
67. EW 35
68. EW 16, 17
69. CS 350
70. GC 657, 658
71. GC 658, 659
72. DA 632
73. ST Oct. 11, 1910
74. ST July 1, 1886
75. GC 645
76. COL 421
77. 5T 96
78. SD 362
79. RH Aug. 17, 1869
80. SD 362
81. SR 413, 414
82. 8T 252-254
83. 1T 381
84. 2T 160
85. 2T 520
86. 9T 105-108

NOVEMBER

1. EW 290
2. GC 660
3. Ed 304, 305
4. Ed 127
5. GC 647, 648
6. MH 504
7. 8T 267, 268
8. MLT 364
9. RH Oct. 10, 1907
10. RH Aug. 8, 1907
11. KH 371
12. SC 86, 87
13. SC 125, 126
14. EW 288, 289
15. COL 71, 72
16. 5BC 1124
17. DA 749, 750
18. 5BC 1125
19. DA 638
20. MH 473, 474
21. 6BC 1091
22. 9T 286
23. IHP 368
24. IHP 368
25. 9T 285
26. 9T 285, 286

27. 9T 285
28. IHP 367
29. CT 55
30. 8T 288
31. MLT 355
32. 1BC 1086
33. GC 645
34. RH Dec. 13, 1892
35. IHP 365
36. CT 208, 209
37. 8T 253
38. GC 648, 649
39. IHP 371
40. IHP 364
41. 5T 620, 621
42. FE 199
43. IHP 370
44. IHP 370
45. IHP 366
46. AA 601, 602
47. IHP 369
48. GC 660, 661
49. GC 662, 663
50. GC 661
51. GC 663
52. GC 664
53. GC 665, 666
54. RH Nov. 4, 1884
55. RH Feb. 2, 1886
56. RH Jan. 1, 1884
57. RH Jan. 13, 1891
58. RH March 27, 1888
59. RH Nov. 4, 1884
60. RH Nov. 22, 1898
61. RH July 3, 1894

DECEMBER

1. GC 666, 667
2. GC 667, 668
3. EW 293
4. GC 668
5. GC 668-670
6. GC 670, 671
7. GC 671, 672
8. GC 673
9. DA 763
10. SR 429
11. GC 674
12. RH June 10, 1884
13. 4T 357
14. 9T 285
15. CG 354
16. PP 50
17. RH May 17, 1898
18. CT 280
19. EW 52
20. EW 54
21. GC 674
22. 7BC 988
23. RH July 11, 1882
24. FLB 371
25. 9T 286-288

26. GC 675, 676
27. Ed 304
28. GC 676
29. Ed 303, 304
30. PP 62
31. GC 648
32. GC 645
33. FLB 364
34. YI Oct. 1852
35. MLT 175
36. SC 86
37. SR 430, 431
38. GC 676, 677
39. Ed 306
40. FE 234. 235
41. MH 504-507
42. 6T 305
43. 6T 310
44. DA 563
45. 6T 310
46. RH May 17, 1898
47. PK 730, 731
48. EW 18
49. GC 677
50. Ed 307
51. 1T 146
52. 7BC 982
53. EW 289
54. GC 674
55. GC 651, 652
56. Ed 301, 302
57. MH 466
58. CT 208, 209
59. Ed 304
60. GC 677
61. Ed 302
62. CT 162
63. MLT 361
64. Ed 304
65. Ed 307
66. MLT 361
67. MLT 360
68. ST April 25, 1906
69. GC 651, 652
70. 3SP 261
71. 4T 581
72. Ed 303
73. 7BC 990
74. Ed 307
75. 7BC 990
76. RH Sept. 25, 1900
77. EW 39, 40
78. MM 99, 100
79. MM 101
80. MM 100
81. IHP 372
82. IHP 372
83. DA 769, 770
84. PK 732, 733
85. DA 283
86. PP 342
87. DA 26
88. GC 677, 678